Annual Volunteer Recognition Event

Featuring distinguished speaker
and author, Skirball Professor
of Modern Jewish History,
New York University, Dr. Marion Kaplan

12.08.20

MUSEUM OF JEWISH HERITAGE

D1565352

Hitler's Jewish Refugees

Hitler's Jewish Refugees

Hope and Anxiety in Portugal

Marion Kaplan

Yale

UNIVERSITY PRESS

NEW HAVEN AND LONDON

Yale University Press books may be purchased in quantity for educational, business, or promotional use. For
information, please e-mail sales.press@yale.edu (U.S. office) or sales@yaleup.co.uk (U.K. office).

Set in Fournier MT type by IDS Infotech Ltd., Chandigarh, India.
Printed in the United States of America.

ISBN 978-0-300-24425-0 (hardcover : alk. paper)
Library of Congress Control Number: 2019939710
A catalogue record for this book is available from the British Library.

This paper meets the requirements of ANSI/NISO Z39.48-1992 (Permanence of Paper).

10 9 8 7 6 5 4 3 2 1

To Samuel Jacob and Sara Greta,
I hope you grow up in a kinder world,
one that extends warm welcomes to strangers

Contents

Preface
A Personal Word

When two archivists at the Museum of Jewish Heritage in New York contacted me to ask whether I might be interested in some unopened letters sent to Jewish refugees in Lisbon, I rushed to the building at the tip of Manhattan. There I discovered a trove of lost messages: 207 letters and 76 postcards. The writers had addressed most of them to relatives and friends in Lisbon, sent in care of an aid organization, the American Jewish Joint Distribution Committee (JDC). Written to loved ones in late 1941 and early 1942, the mail came from war-torn Europe and from safe lands like the United States. But the letters had never reached the intended recipients. There I sat, cautiously opening the envelopes with a single-edge razor blade.

The letters spoke of the hopes of Jewish refugees who had made it to safety far from Europe and the terrors of Jews still in harm's way. Those abroad did their best to assuage the worries of refugees in Portugal and to explain their own complicated journeys. In mail they knew would be censored, writers from Germany, Austria, and Nazi-occupied Europe begged for food—even a can of sardines—hinting at dire circumstances. These writers faced forced labor, hunger, ghettoization, and internment camps; their messages hinted at the deportations that had just commenced in the West, and the organized killings that had escalated to outright genocide in the East. Nearly all of them felt trapped. They cried out in pain, dread, and loneliness. Many feared the worst. Their letters contained final words to loved ones.

And the addressees of these letters? Most had already left Portugal after racing to provide the proper papers to authorities and to purchase ship tickets. The letters, never claimed, remained in the JDC office for years and then found their way to the museum. Most of these correspondents had permanently lost touch with one another, but more than seventy years later these unopened letters speak to us. Like literature, they convey personal trauma in a way that conventional historical writing does not. They share immediacy and anguish. This cache supplemented many other letters and cards that lay in museums and archives or that came to me once people heard of my project. Highlighting an emotional dialogue between people, they offer layered perspectives—from external predicaments to internal reactions—that expand the historical record, helping us explore the feelings behind individual, familial, and collective actions.

I have worked in archives for years, enjoying the touch and smell of old papers, the whir of microfilm machines, and the peaceful atmosphere. Sometimes this detective work proved absorbing, sometimes tedious. But nothing in my research endeavors had prepared me for these lost letters, the most moving discovery of my career. As I cautiously opened them, voices from Europe cried out. Somehow, I had to convey not only the senders' messages but also their feelings. Yet I had been trained to keep a scholarly distance from my subjects, even if I tended to choose questions or topics that engaged me. Using the tools of women's and gender history, social history, and the history of daily life, what German scholars call *Alltagsgeschichte*, I had analyzed Jewish life at the grassroots. In *The Making of the Jewish Middle Class: Women, Family, and Identity in Imperial Germany, 1870–1918*, I described nineteenth-century Jews caught between the desire to acculturate and the wish to preserve their unique identities. These efforts certainly aroused anxiety on the part of Jews and non-Jews, although their emotions, assumed but unexplored, served as a backdrop. Turning to Hitler's Germany, I recognized Jews' anguish as the government stripped them of their place in society and ultimately of their lives. The book that resulted, *Between Dignity and Despair: Jewish Life in Nazi Germany*, highlighted their dilemma. But that study also centered on their daily experiences and actions. In retrospect, it was only a matter of time, I think, before my next interest, the travails of refugees escaping Nazi Europe, would draw attention not only to the social and physical upheavals of refugee existence, but also to the emotional costs of fleeing one's home and history while begging strangers for kindness.

Social scientists and historians increasingly understand that researchers are not blank slates of detachment, but bring their feelings to their scholarship. Scholars can engage in rigorous, dispassionate analyses and still be emotionally affected by their discoveries. Indeed, the sentiments expressed in these letters forced me to contend with my family history. Only a few years before these letters arrived in Lisbon, my parents had fled Hitler's

Germany, having made quick decisions and met with good fortune. I heard some of their stories, but they always left much unsaid, causing me to wonder about their lives during their escape. I knew that the Nazis had murdered their beloved relatives and friends. Reading the grief in these letters from Europe and knowing that the Nazis had murdered most of the authors brought the subjects—and my extended family—very close. In addition, I wrote this book while tens of millions of refugees were fleeing recent and ongoing wars, terrorism, and economic catastrophes. Most of them face closed doors in Western countries today, as refugees did then. As a citizen of the United States and a daughter of refugees, I am painfully aware of both my country's efforts to keep refugees out in the 1930s and 1940s and its vigorous attempts to do the same at present.

Refugees in Portugal in the 1940s made up only a small part of a vast flood of humanity that has fled political and economic disasters since early in the twentieth century. By writing this history, I hope not only to convey certain physical and emotional reactions of Jewish refugees, but also to foreground some of the feelings that many refugees may share, no matter how widely divergent their original circumstances. Readers may want to note that the epigraphs at the head of each chapter are the words of today's refugees; they closely echo the observations and feelings of Jewish refugees on the run in the 1940s. Despite vast differences in time, place, religion, and ethnicity, the groups share similarities, not least being forced to flee homes and loved ones and hoping for a safe place while waiting in limbo. Paying careful attention to the words of refugees in Portugal may help us understand Jewish heartbreak and perseverance in the 1940s and also listen compassionately to refugees' stories in our own time.

Acknowledgments

It is with enormous gratitude and happiness that I write these acknowledgments. They signal, as always, the end of a long writing process. But they mean much more to me. The people I thank provided support and friendship. They gave me the stamina to persist, and their critiques forced me to clarify my writing and my thinking. First, I would like to thank my friends who read the whole manuscript from cover to cover: Renate Bridenthal, a sister historian and sister in so many ways, whose marginalia reminded me of her own refugee experiences as a child; Hasia Diner, a good friend and special colleague at NYU, whose hard questions made me rethink and revise and whose energy and wisdom I deeply admire; Ute Frevert, whose enthusiasm for and pathbreaking scholarship in the history of emotions sparked my interest not only in the importance of emotions to individuals and groups of refugees, but also in the history of emotions more generally; Rose Kavo, who became a close friend as we sat at the sandbox and watched our two sons play and whose questions as a psychologist helped me add complexity and contradictions to refugee experiences; and Rita Schwarzer, always curious and interested, whose journalistic expertise and instincts made me explain and research even more and who later even reread chapters to help me trim them.

At this stage in my career, I have received a delightful gift. Several of my students as well as some younger scholars agreed to read all or a significant part of the manuscript. Natalia Aleksiun, whose dissertation committee I joined some years ago, generously offered her expertise as an Eastern Europeanist and Holocaust scholar during our many walks in Riverside Park. Kim Cheng, my newest graduate student, shares an interest in the lives of refugees and asked important questions about their reactions and their interactions with local residents. To Daniella Doron, my first doctoral student at NYU and long since a special friend, I now have the pleasure of returning a thank you. A historian of postwar French Jewry, she discussed each chapter with me on Skype from Australia and kept me on track when I wandered off. Elizabeth Marcus, a generous friend and French and comparative literature scholar, applied her interests in cultural history to her careful textual criticism of my manuscript. I have also benefited from teaming up with a German historian and friend, Philipp Nielsen, who reviewed and gently critiqued my chapters, and I did the same for his book. There is something inspiring about sharing work with young friends and learning from them.

Other friends graciously read some chapters and offered sage counsel. Warm thanks go to Volker Berghahn, someone with whom I can always share ideas; Page Delano, a poet and writer obsessed with World War II and women resisters, who urged me to visit the Camp des Milles; Jack Jacobs, who shared his archive with me; Anna Koch, a former student and now a colleague and friend, who offered valuable comments and questions informed by her own research; Claudia Koonz, who encouraged me to think more deeply about the drama of this topic and to liven up my language to fit it; Jasna Perucic, whose questions as a literary scholar sharpened my introduction; Monika Richarz, from whom I have learned so much over many years of friendship; and Leo Spitzer, whose *Hotel Bolivia* and sensitive questions about refugees' memories influenced my thinking. And to Leith Mullings, thank you for the conversations during our walks, which prompted me to ask new questions and turned me into a "wannabe" anthropologist.

This book would not be the same without the careful, intelligent, and challenging comments of my German history study group. Women scholars from the Greater New York area, we have met monthly for more than thirty-five years, managing to share our work and our professional insights. This group has been one of the highlights of my professional life, a lively complement to an otherwise solitary career of research and writing. Thanks go to Dolores Augustine, Rebecca Boehling, Renate Bridenthal, Atina Grossmann, Amy Hackett, Maria Hoehn, Young-Sun Hong, Molly O'Donnell, Jan Lambertz, Molly Nolan, Kathy Pence, and Julia Sneeringer.

Several institutions helped make this book possible. First, I would like to thank the Department of Hebrew and Judaic Studies at NYU and its former chair, David Engel, for granting me the leaves to accept the fellowships that helped me write this book. Also at NYU, I received a Humanities Initiative Research Fellowship during fall 2011 and spring 2012. The following year, the Tikvah Center for Law and Jewish Civilization at NYU appointed me as a fellow, giving me more time for research and writing. In

2014, the United States Holocaust Memorial Museum (USHMM) invited me to become the J. B. and Maurice C. Shapiro Senior Scholar-in-Residence at its Jack, Joseph and Morton Mandel Center for Advanced Holocaust Studies. I thought I would finish my writing that semester. Instead, I found mountains of new and fascinating materials. Moreover, presenting pieces of my work to fellows at the Mandel Center enabled me to learn from doctoral and postdoctoral scholars.

The USHMM is a good place to begin thanking archivists and librarians. Ron Coleman shared a passion for the story of Jewish refugees in Portugal and made invaluable suggestions about which USHMM collections I had to see. He was a constant font of knowledge and enthusiasm for my project. Thank you as well to Vincent Slatt and Megan Lewis, both of whom helped me with my research, and to the archivist and curator Dr. Rebecca Erbelding for the information she shared about the War Refugee Board. The archivist Misha Mitsel, of the American Jewish Joint Distribution Committee (New York City), facilitated access to materials and speedily answered email queries. Also Hadassah Assouline, retired director of the Central Archives of the History of the Jewish People, digitized and mailed me crucial files. And special thanks to Esther Brumberg, senior curator of collections, and Bonnie Gurewitsch, archivist and curator at the Museum of Jewish Heritage (New York City), without whom I would never have come across the letters to Lisbon that I highlight in chapter 6. Indeed, my appreciation extends to all the archivists in the archives I used, even if I did not learn their names or simply had email exchanges with them. Their hidden work makes scholarship possible.

Children and grandchildren of refugees provided me with letters, photos, and documents from their families for which I am grateful; I thank them in the endnotes. More remarkably, several refugees who were children, teens, or young adults at the time, such as Gabrielle Greenberg, Ruth Hellmann, Margit Meissner, Irene Shomberg, and the late Anita Walker, shared their time and interest in this subject with me. I hope I have done their experiences justice.

Most scholarship builds on previous research, and this book is no different. I would like to thank the scholars who came before me and who inspired me to pursue this project: Avraham Milgram, Irene Pimentel, Patrik von zur Mühlen, and Douglas Wheeler. Editors, too, deserve my appreciation. Heather Gold, at Yale University Press, showed enthusiasm for the project and welcomed it to her list. Louisa McMurray worked meticulously and promptly on my manuscript, bibliography, and endnotes. Thank you also to Bill Nelson for his careful work on the two maps, to Kip Keller for his scrupulous copyediting, to Phillip King, who saw the book through its final stages, and to the Center for the Humanities at NYU for generously providing a Book Publication Subvention Grant.

Finally, a special word of thanks and love to my family. Douglas Morris, my husband, heard about the refugee crisis of the 1940s more times than either of us can count. A historian of Germany—and a Federal Defender by day—he provided enthusiasm for this project and steadfast encouragement that gave me confidence. And we share more than a historical interest in refugees: we share a passionate belief that our country, a nation of immigrants, should welcome refugees today and treat them with respect and generosity. I want to thank my children too, for their love and support. Joshua Morris: you succeeded in distracting me and keeping me abreast of what goes on in popular culture, not to mention insisting that I finally get an iPhone and then teaching me how to use it. Ruth Kaplan: you have been painstakingly editing my books since high school! A scholar in your own right, you have regularly challenged and expanded my thinking. I deeply appreciate your hard work on my manuscript, your stern but loving critiques, and your affectionate support in the midst of your own demanding career. Finally, to Ruth and her husband, Ira Fay: it has been a sheer delight to watch your family grow and to be part of it. My visits to babysit were the high points of every week as I watched your two amazing children develop into curious and warmhearted people. I dedicate this book to them.

Hitler's Jewish Refugees

The escape routes of Margit Meissner (from Prague), Kurt Israel (Hannover, Germany), and Carla Pekelis (Florence, Italy) as they headed to Lisbon.

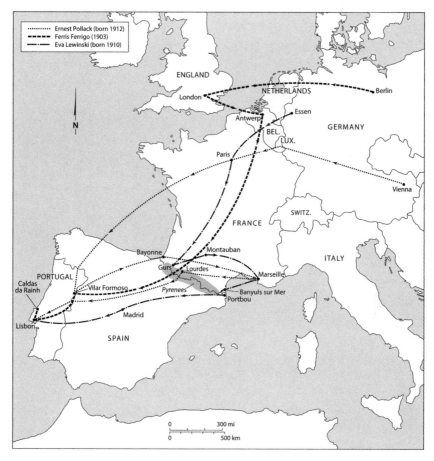

The escape routes of Ernest Pollack (Vienna), Ferris Ferrigo (Berlin), and Eva Lewinski (Essen, Germany) to Lisbon.

Introduction

In the opening scene of the classic American film *Casablanca* from 1942, the camera zooms in on a map of Morocco and Portugal. The narrator reports that refugees fleeing "imprisoned Europe . . . wait and wait and wait and wait" in this North African port city for visas to Lisbon, "the great embarkation point" for the "freedom of the Americas." The film, centered on a love triangle, depicts the travails of European refugees. As most of them while away their time in this pro-Nazi French protectorate, a handful support the anti-Nazi Free French. At the end of the film, the heroic couple flies off to Lisbon. We are left to wonder, why Lisbon? What had happened to these refugees before arriving in Lisbon and what happened to them once they got there? And how did they react, both practically and emotionally, to their plight?

As the Nazis launched the murderous project we have come to know as the Holocaust, Lisbon emerged as the best way station for Jews to escape Europe for North and South America. Jewish refugees had begun fleeing the continent in the mid-1930s from ports closer to home. But after Germany defeated Belgium, the Netherlands, Luxembourg, and France, and Italy joined the war, all in the spring of 1940, Lisbon became *the* port of departure from Europe. Jewish refugees from western and eastern Europe aimed for Portugal. Most chose overland routes, hoping to make it to the Iberian Peninsula, still unconquered by Hitler.[1] But Spain's dictator, General Francisco Franco, would not harbor them, allowing refugees to cross Spain only if they had visas to enter Portugal. In contrast, Portugal's dictator, António de Oliveira Salazar, admitted the largest number of Jews fleeing westward, between 40,000 and

100,000 people, some 90 percent of all refugees in Portugal.[2] Even so, he demanded that these refugees move on quickly, setting his secret police to harass them when they lingered through no fault of their own.

Holocaust historians have traced how Jews escaped Nazi Europe, but few have examined how spaces of flight and survival affected refugees emotionally.[3] This book, in contrast, asks how refugees experienced the sites that punctuated their odyssey, starting with their exodus through France and focusing on their interlude in Portugal. It probes how specific locations touched refugees' inner lives. Geographers refer to these spaces as "geographies of emotional life."[4] These include, for example, the borders refugees nervously crossed, the consulate lines they fretfully waited on, the smoky cafés they uneasily inhabited, and the overcrowded transatlantic ships that signaled their liberation.[5] These sites induced feelings of frustration or relief—often both.

As an emotional history of fleeing, this book offers a glimpse into Jewish refugees' angst and expectations as they encountered the overall volatility of the 1930s and the radical contingencies of World War II. Before the war, Portugal had accepted several hundred refugees.[6] Some settled there, making new lives for themselves. When Germany invaded westward, however, a second flow of refugees, many of them stateless, faced dangerous treks to Portugal amid war-torn landscapes. More dishearteningly for this new wave of refugees, Portugal offered them only thirty-day transit visas, adding one more link to the chain of dehumanization they endured. Luckily, the vast majority left in good time, heading across the English Channel or the Atlantic. But thousands of Jewish refugees lacking proper documents and ship tickets, as many as 14,000 at one point, remained in Portugal, often for months and sometimes for years.[7] And even as their numbers declined significantly, a third stream of refugees arrived in late 1942, when the Germans marched into southern France. In fact, refugees continued to slip in, often illegally, until the end of the war.

Previously, refugees who had fled to neighboring countries either hoped to settle there or anticipated returning home, if or when the Nazis were overthrown. By the time they reached Portugal in 1940, however, most understood they would not return home. They needed to cross the ocean, far from German troops. I focus on these refugees, stranded in Portugal, as well as on their fears and their struggles to leave Europe. In so doing, I highlight a transitional time, the 1940s, and a provisional space, Portugal, underlining a key moment in the refugee experience—living in limbo.

This is a multilayered story. As it examines a government increasingly impatient with refugees, it also portrays Portuguese citizens from all walks of life who greeted the newcomers with sympathy, offering them food and shelter and leaving warm, lasting impressions. Local and international aid agencies, too, came to the rescue. The small Jewish community of Lisbon worked tirelessly, stretching its own resources even when international Jewish organizations, particularly the American Jewish Joint Distribution Committee, joined in. And non-Jewish organizations, especially the Quakers and the Unitarians, greatly assisted refugees. Finally, the global war erupting around this small haven ravaged nations, affected Portuguese refugee policies, and sent regular shock waves through the refugees in Portugal.

This context offers an important backdrop, but my attention centers primarily on refugees' terrifying flights and their strategies for physical and emotional survival. In a world gone awry, short-term safety and assistance notwithstanding, refugees confronted extreme situations. Having once felt entitled to a secure middle-class life, many suddenly faced poverty as well as statelessness. They had lost control over their lives. Much like the 65.3 million currently displaced people who have fled their homes and who long for safe countries to accept them, they felt stuck between home and nowhere. And as often happens today, governments, whether for economic, racist, or religious reasons, erected "paper walls"—bureaucratic requirements in addition to quotas—against immigrants, thereby only heightening their insecurity.[8]

Refugees' Relief and Dread

This focus on spaces that refugees traversed or waited in and the feelings that they triggered can enhance our understanding of refugees more generally, but can also expand our knowledge of the Holocaust. Vast in scope, the Nazis' Final Solution radically disrupted the lives of even the lucky ones in Portugal, far from the deportations and murders in the rest of Europe. Drawing attention to the periphery does not detract from the genocide, but in fact highlights the range and reach of the Holocaust and its impact even on those who got away. We learn about the reactions of Jews driven from Europe and living in transitional spaces: How did they react to abrupt mass flight and major loss? How did they feel as they begged for mercy on foreign soil? How did they respond to Portuguese citizens' kindheartedness while agonizing about family left behind and risks ahead? And how did they describe their states of mind during an anxious hiatus in an oddly peaceful purgatory?[9]

Studies of refugees emerged belatedly in Holocaust scholarship. In part, scholars had to wait until the sources came to light. Whereas concentration camp survivors began to share their accounts of the Holocaust in the early postwar era, refugees who traveled through Portugal, and this may hold true for other refugees as well, rarely recorded their journeys immediately upon arrival in safe lands. Many who escaped even hesitated to refer to themselves as "refugees," preferring "newcomers" or "immigrants."[10] Their experiences paled in comparison with those of concentration camp survivors, and they saw themselves as "all right," simply because they had escaped the worst. The guilt and sadness of surviving when many loved ones had perished may have inhibited many refugees from dwelling on or even admitting their anguish. And the need to tell contended, perhaps, with the struggle to forget.[11] These memories would have remained lost to historians if archivists had not sought out refugees as well as camp survivors, if libraries had not also gathered less dramatic stories and those that took place far from the killing fields and camps. Even when former refugees reflected in memoirs and interviews or discovered their old letters and diaries, they emphasized their distress in their homelands as antisemitic persecution grew or their difficulties at their final destinations. They either skipped Portugal or gave it second or third place in their narratives.

Yet relief had vied with dread in Portugal. On one hand, the country provided a safe haven, but on the other, refugees could not remain there. And the German Army might have invaded at any moment. Homeless and uprooted, refugees had entered liminal spaces that dissolved familiar, comfortable social hierarchies, rendered prized customs obsolete, and cast futures, once blithely taken for granted, into doubt.[12] They demonstrated both fragility and resilience as they ran from death, searching for strategies to move on. This book paints a picture of the feelings provoked by these "in between" weeks, months, or, in some cases, years of waiting in Portugal.

As sources appeared, the field of Holocaust history began to incorporate refugees, along with those who survived in hiding or with fake identities, as well as postwar displaced persons.[13] Museums, too, expanded their interests. In other words, the core of Holocaust studies is expanding. Nevertheless, even when scholars turned toward Jews who hid or escaped, they generally focused on trauma or on what psychologists now refer to as posttraumatic stress, at the expense of a wider palette of other strong feelings. In contrast, I intend to stress the varieties of individual responses in the 1940s, writing an emotional history "not just from the bottom up but from the inside out." And since individuals' emotions can have a collective effect, the stories gathered here also describe an emotional terrain endured by Jewish refugees—and maybe most refugees.[14]

The feelings of Jews on the run or waiting for resettlement connects them with "Holocaust landscapes" and "emotional geographies," sites of fear and of uncertain relief. Whereas traditional historians of the Holocaust have focused on institutions and political actors, historians interested in geographies uncover environments that victims endured, passed through, died in, or created. Depicting the genocide of the Jews as "a profoundly geographical phenomenon," they stress that the Holocaust changed the "meaning as well as the materiality of every place and space it touched."[15]

The project of Holocaust geography is especially revealing when analyzing refugees' frightening journeys and nervous waiting.[16] Because this book shows that space affected human emotions, it is organized according to shifting sites of anxiety and hope. Certain locations turned into barriers for refugees; for example, the homelands that persecuted them, the harrowing paths and borders over the Pyrenees, or the lines and waiting rooms at consulates. These spaces—and more obviously, the guards, the police, the consular officials executing decisions of governments far away, or other refugees at those locations—could evoke the terror of rejection or the relief of acceptance. Understandably, refugees reacted to the decisions made by people in these offices, not just to the site per se, yet refugees refer to fears of these places as well as of the people there, often blending the two.

Other sites meant safety or further insecurity, depending on the decisions of strangers. In ordinary times, the same travelers might have taken borders, consulates, or tiny villages for granted as they planned a business trip or a pleasant vacation. But these were not ordinary times. Even seemingly safe spaces, such as Portugal, removed from the centers of conflict, grew more unpredictable over time, requiring snap decisions and intensifying refugees' feelings of vulnerability. Even less frightening locations, such as social welfare offices, cafés, or epistolary spaces and post offices, nevertheless stirred conflicting feelings in refugees. Emotions were intertwined inextricably with spaces.

Holocaust geographers explore the scale of these spaces, "from the scale of the body to the scale of the continent." This book, too, shifts from one country, Portugal, and one city, Lisbon, to smaller clusters of people in cafés, to correspondents sharing love, and finally to a border crossing where a single woman waits in fear. Additionally, geographers observe that "genocide was on the move" and consider (among other sites), countries, cities, concentration camps, and even railroad cars.[17] Jewish escape routes, also "on the move," generally followed the geography and chronology of Nazi aggression: the subjects of this book passed over intermediate national borders—frequently as many as five or six—and waited in offices, cafés, and sometimes in jails. They also relied on linkages and connections in nations across the Atlantic.

Geography intersected with time. The later that refugees fled toward Portugal, the fewer the options that remained open to them, and the more harrowing their escapes. Leaving Germany in 1935, for example, meant being able to choose among more countries of potential refuge than was the case five years later. By 1940, most European safe havens had ceased to exist: first they rejected refugees, and then the war and the German occupation engulfed them. Further, those who had been on the run since 1933 had fewer resources, especially psychological energy, upon arrival in Portugal than those who fled in 1939 or 1940. Finally, refugees felt greater impatience in Portugal if they had to wait a year than if they left in a month, especially before the war turned against Germany. Similarly, they worried more about a German invasion in 1940 than in 1944. In all cases, time was of the essence.

Still, even temporary sanctuary prompted gratitude. Refugees felt deeply thankful to Portugal as their short-term safe haven. For that matter, they showed appreciation toward other nations that accepted them, even for a short time. *Casablanca* depicts this symbolically through its "battle of the anthems" at Rick's Café. As German army officers sing the patriotic "Watch on the Rhein" ("Die Wacht am Rhein"), the refugees there drown them out with "La Marseillaise," the French national anthem that extols the fight against tyranny. These refugees, at least momentarily, experienced feelings of loyalty toward a Free France that fought the Nazis, even if most hoped to leave this French colony. Identification with and allegiance to geographic sites or countries that provided havens fluctuated, depending on erratic feelings of security in wartime.

Refugees not only reacted to geographical locations that signified liberation or terror. They also imbued these places with their own feelings. Scholars remind us that "emotions are not just done to but also done by a person."[18] People's feelings could shape their experiences in these settings. Celebrating a Jewish holiday among friends in a café, for example, could turn that mundane space into a momentary sanctuary. At other spots, apprehension could drive someone either to persist or to give up. After an exhausting escape over the Pyrenees, the German-Jewish philosopher and literary critic Walter Benjamin faced Spanish guards who would not let him or his travel companions through. They had to sleep in Portbou at the French-Spanish border. For Benjamin, it was the final straw; tragically, he committed suicide that night. His fellow travelers held steady and received permission to continue toward Portugal the next morning.

We often notice a disjuncture or a dissonance between the external and internal experience of many refugees. From the outside, their lives in Portugal looked safe, even comfortable. They did not learn crucial details about friends or relatives who suffered German occupation, even if they grieved for those left behind: "As lovely as the beach was, as gorgeous as the ocean, one had little desire to enjoy [them] and thought of other things: . . . the liberating oversea visa . . . the relatives and friends who did not have the luck to get out . . . in time."[19] They may have felt guilt as well, although they could not imagine the genocide taking place; they resided in a peaceful land while the rest of European Jewry increasingly faced annihilation. Still, many did not feel either sheltered or safe as they did their utmost to leave Portugal.

Refugees also feared arrest, jail, and possible deportation back to France or Germany. As the historian Frank Caestecker has shown, several neutral states started rigorously "protecting" their borders against refugees in the 1930s and also sent refugees back to Germany before 1940. Indeed, some, such as Luxembourg, deported those with legal papers.[20] That this rarely happened in Portugal did not lessen refugees' distress. No longer in flight, they had traveled as far as they could. Now, they felt backed against a wall—in this case, the Atlantic Ocean—and at the mercy of the Portuguese government. And the possibility of an encroaching war frightened them even more. We know that they were safe, would eventually emigrate, and fared far better than others trapped in Nazi Europe. But they did not know that.

Nor were their anxieties groundless, exaggerated, or self-inflicted. Nazi Germany had created the terror that surrounded Jews. As refugee and trauma studies scholars have shown, becoming a refugee "is not a psychological phenomenon per se; rather, it is exclusively a socio-political and legal one." But these scholars underline that being a refugee can lead to "psychological implications."²¹ How did some of those "psychological implications" permeate Holocaust refugees' daily lives during their hiatus in Portugal?

Since feelings are key to individual lived experiences, it is surprising that a focus on emotions is a relatively recent contribution to historical studies. Unlike anthropologists, sociologists, psychologists, gender studies scholars, or philosophers, historians have focused on political, economic, and social history, and more recently on the history of daily life. They have associated feelings with private lives, as if private lives did not constitute "history." Academic gender politics also contributed to the shunning of emotions, since historians, most of them men, consigned the history of emotions to studies of premodern, female, and nonwhite groups. Their analyses further defined modern bourgeois masculinity as the ability to regulate feelings.²² A writer such as E. L. Doctorow could therefore contend, "The historian will tell you what happened. The novelist will tell you what it felt like."²³ An emotional history of fleeing, I hope, challenges this assertion.

The pathbreaking work of Peter and Carol Stearns and Peter Gay in the 1980s and 1990s insisted that historians take people's feelings as well as their emotional contexts into consideration. More recently, a burgeoning field led by, among others, Ute Frevert and Jan Plamper has analyzed the place of emotions in societies and asks whether emotions have a history. Historians of emotions have also asked how social class, gender, and nation helped form individuals' emotions.²⁴ This book does not contribute to the project of rethinking emotion historically; it focuses instead on the experience and expression of refugees' feelings. I use the terms that refugees employed repeatedly, particularly "feelings."²⁵ And I focus specifically on how sites—whether barriers such as borders or neutral spaces such as cafés—affected refugees' emotions, as well as on how refugees' emotions influenced their perceptions and behaviors at these sites.

Jewish History and the Topic of Emotions

Research on the emotions of Jews in wartime can contribute to an understanding of emotions more generally, just as studying feelings can augment Jewish history. To the first point: as a religious and ethnic minority, Jews encountered aggression and murder for millennia as well as limited acceptance and integration. In moments of political or economic persecution, they calculated whether to stay or to go based on both rational and emotional judgments. Jewish experiences provide a unique perspective on diaspora histories and refugee studies. More speculatively, some behavioral scientists suggest that groups historically subjected to persecution or war may pass on high rates of stress and anxiety, not only culturally but even biologically, to future generations. This surely is not a problem that historians can answer, yet it raises questions: Did traditions of trauma and escape affect Jews transgenerationally, priming them for flight in the 1930s? And do other, very different groups, like descendants of enslaved people, share some of these characteristics?[26]

As for how studying emotions enhances Jewish history, I underline that feelings matter. First, feelings have always prompted or "co-determined" decision making and actions. They may have been influenced by history, culture, and class, and they may have been idiosyncratic, but as psychologists have documented, feelings can drive decision making.[27] For example, Jewish refugees' feelings influenced whether to go or to stay once Germany invaded France. Second, certain emotions buttressed coping strategies; most of the time, hope trumped despair. Third, and crucially, Jews grasped the link between their emotional stress and their physical health. Once in Lisbon, some took pills to calm their nerves, a few gambled or had affairs to forget their losses, and many constructed "Jewish spaces" in the nearest café, encouraging each other to pound the pavement for visas and rallying hope.[28]

Certainly, not everyone felt the same emotions. Cultures and historical epochs deal with feelings in their own way.[29] Additionally, people have individual temperaments, and each person manages her or his own personal emotional landscape. Further, although most Jewish refugees in Portugal came from similar urban, middle-class, central European cultures—about half to two-thirds came from Germany[30]—they had absorbed class and regional variations. Age made a striking difference: children and young people could treat crossing borders or staying for a long time in Portugal as an adventure even as their elders considered such dislocations nightmares. Gender, too, produced varied reactions. Although men and women faced similar insecurities and material losses, men had lost more status in the public sphere and perceived their losses as greater.

Finally, although we cannot notice significant changes over time in what some historians call "emotional regimes"—modes of emotional expression dominant in particular eras or cultural contexts—we can see a time- and space-specific Jewish response. Those Jewish refugees who made their way to

Portugal and then sat in cafés understood themselves to be part of a "community of fate," or *Schicksalsgemeinschaft*.[31] We also observe a short but fraught interim when refugees reacted to sites of frustration with resilience and a steadfast determination to get out. Yet once they left Europe and settled elsewhere, we cannot know whether their agitation subsided or they remained on heightened alert for a long time, perhaps forever.[32]

1930s and 1940s Refugee Crises: Non-Jewish and Jewish

To appreciate the situation in which Jewish refugees to Portugal found themselves, we turn to the generally unwelcoming circumstances that faced them. In the last quarter of the nineteenth century, European and American nationalism, racism, economic depression (1873–96), and protectionism led governments to implement tighter immigration policies against "undesirable" immigrants. The United States (in 1882) and Canada (in 1885) limited Chinese immigration in North America, and in the United Kingdom, the Aliens Act of 1905 targeted Jews, other Europeans, and the Chinese. Michael Marrus's *The Unwanted* details the flight from persecution and poverty starting in the late nineteenth century. He points to well over ten million refugees—"too many to count precisely," in the words of a more recent observer[33]—trying to escape World War I and the collapse of the Russian, Ottoman, and Austrian Empires. In addition, survivors of Turkey's Armenian genocide searched for refuge, and by 1917 opponents of Bolshevik Russia were fleeing its territories.

The Flood of Refugees

With the Nazi accession to power in January 1933, the refugee crisis erupted again.[34] The political enemies of fascism, particularly communists and socialists, including some Jews, fled Germany. By the spring of 1933, the Nazis had turned on Germany's 525,000 Jews, less than 1 percent of the population, purging them from careers, cultural life, schools, and universities. Economic boycotts, racist laws, occasional violence, and the fear of more violence motivated some to flee. By 1937, Jewish refugees outnumbered political refugees. Jews who could leave did so from German harbors like Hamburg or from ports in nearby Holland or France. The November Pogrom (also known as *Kristallnacht*) of 1938, when the Nazis incited assaults on Jews, their homes, shops, and synagogues and incarcerated 30,000 Jewish men in concentration camps, caused over 125,000 Jews to line up at American consulates in Germany and in German-annexed Austria.[35] Jews needed to get out.

Even before the November Pogrom, the Nazi government had driven Jews to leave Germany. And they did. Mass emigration occurred in three stages. As the Nazis extended their control in 1933 and 1934, about 60,000 Jews left, although some hoped to, and did, return.[36] In the fall of 1935, the Law for the Protection of German Blood and Honor, one of the three Nuremberg Laws, defined Jews as a race and created a new category, Reich Citizenship, which excluded Jews. These laws prohibited future intermarriages and extramarital sexual relations between Jews and those whom the Nazis called "Aryans" or "pure-blooded" Germans. As a result, a second wave saw 48,000 refugees flee in 1936 and again in 1937, and another 40,000 in 1938. The November Pogrom and Germany's increasingly onerous anti-Jewish measures spurred the third and most massive flight: 78,000 in 1939.

In 1939, the Nazi regime exerted huge emigration pressure on the Jewish leadership, the Reichsvereinigung der Juden in Deutschland (Central Association of Jews in Germany). And after initial wartime victories, the Gestapo (the Nazis' secret state police) demanded "mass emigration of *all Jews in Europe*" (emphasis in the original). Yet the Nazis enacted wildly contradictory policies. By levying punitive taxes on émigrés and prohibiting asset transfers to other countries, the regime filled its coffers but turned émigrés into paupers, impeding emigration.[37] Emigrating Jews lost 30 to 50 percent of their capital in the years 1933 to 1937, and 60 to 100 percent between 1937 and 1939. New laws and decrees pushed Jews out but robbed them of the means to emigrate.

Jewish leaders had already made a public appeal emphasizing that "orderly emigration" could proceed only if Jews had enough money to leave, since safe countries would not accept impoverished Jews. But Nazi authorities remained stubbornly inconsistent. These contradictions reached their high point from June through October 1941, when Nazi Germany simultaneously pushed emigration in the western part of its territories while murdering Jews in the newly conquered eastern lands. Germany finally banned emigration on October 23, 1941. Ultimately, about three-fifths of German Jewry emigrated, although not all to safe countries.[38] About 83 percent of Jews under the age of twenty-four fled, and couples and families with children also emigrated. They left behind mostly women, of whom two-thirds were over the age of forty-five.[39] Among the 160,000 German Jews murdered, this combination of gender and age proved lethal.

German-Jewish flight coincided with other streams of refugees. Between 1936 and 1939, the Spanish Civil War drove 500,000 antifascist combatants and civilians over the Pyrenees to France, where they endured filth and hunger in internment camps. Jews in Poland, Hungary, and Romania faced radicalizing, ultranationalist, and antisemitic regimes, and thousands attempted to flee westward. With Germany's annexation of Austria on March 12, 1938, Austrian Jews joined the refugee tide. Of about 186,000 Jews living in Austria in 1938, approximately 125,490 managed to escape; the Nazis murdered 50,000 of those remaining. Some Czechoslovakian Jews, seeing an imminent German takeover, began emigrating after the Munich Agreement of September 29, 1938, in which France, Britain, and Italy allowed Germany to take over parts of Czechoslovakia along its borders. With the German conquest and breakup of Czechoslovakia in March 1939, Jews as well as political opponents of fascism fled, generally westward. While some Jews could still escape, the Nazis murdered about 78,000 Czechoslovakian Jews.[40]

Once Germany triggered World War II by attacking Poland in September 1939, many Jews fled east and others fled west. And when Germany invaded the Netherlands, Belgium, and Luxembourg in May 1940, additional refugee streams flooded into an unprepared Paris. Soon thereafter, one-fifth of the French population—Parisians and the French population from the northern and eastern parts of the country, Jews and non-Jews—escaped south to avoid the German invasion. By July 1940, about 8 million refugees, including 6.2 million French, had taken part in that exodus. Yet by the end of summer and into the fall, about 3 million French refugees returned home.[41] The Dutch government even sent buses from Amsterdam to Marseille for some of its citizens. Not so for Germany's "enemies," such as Jews, foreigners, political undesirables, and the stateless, all of whom the expanded German Reich barred from repatriation.[42]

Jewish refugees faced increasingly harsh and arbitrary laws in countries they had earlier deemed "safe." And as German conquests spread, Nazis and their collaborators deported many refugees from these lands. Despite their generally comfortable lives before the Nazi onslaught, and despite the help they received from aid organizations or from relatives abroad, the Jewish refugees of the 1930s and especially of the 1940s began to take on a politically imposed identity, appearing increasingly as "refugees" not only to onlookers but also to themselves. They could not remain, but had nowhere to go. They found themselves in emotional torment, "jittery with fear at the idea of staying and paralyzed with fear at the idea of leaving."[43]

While biding their time in Portugal, Jewish refugees shared a certain legal status—or lack of one.[44] Hannah Arendt, still reeling from her own experience as a Jew who fled Germany via France and Portugal, reflected upon refugees like herself. In *The Origins of Totalitarianism* (1951), she observed that no state and no law protected the displaced: "The calamity of the rightless is not that they are deprived of life, liberty and the pursuit of happiness, but that they no longer belong to any community whatsoever." Physically and emotionally, many were transformed into impoverished, undocumented people, without citizenship and therefore without, as Arendt concluded, "the right to have rights." Young Werner Goldberg, who waited in Lisbon for five months, drew the same conclusion: as "stateless" persons, "we do not have any protection."[45]

Yet Jewish refugees also differed significantly from others fleeing fascism and war. On one hand, Nazi Germany had targeted them specifically since 1933. On the other hand, local and international Jewish philanthropies as well as non-Jewish American aid organizations had sprung into action to help them. By the time most Jewish refugees arrived in Portugal, they found philanthropies that addressed some of their needs. Refugees may have been hungry, but they did not starve. They may have had no change of clothing, but they had access to the bare necessities. Alarmed about arrest, they looked to aid organizations to intercede with Portuguese police. Finally, their middle-class backgrounds meant they had education, language skills, and experience in dealing with governments and bureaucracies. Many wrote letters to friends and strangers asking for affidavits that would vouch for them, petitioned the Portuguese and other foreign governments for visas, and importuned aid agencies for financial assistance.

Despite these relative advantages, they experienced increasing vulnerability. The middle-class structures of their former lives had provided continuity, optimism, a sense of entitlement, and socioeconomic privilege. Most had imagined a positive trajectory. Threadbare clothing, homelessness, and hunger indicated a painful deterioration in their social status and expectations.[46] These Jewish refugees thus exemplified middle-class refugees more specifically, people who had not only lost their nations, their homes, and their sense of belonging, but also their always-gendered class status. Uprooted from a familiar life with clear goals, middle-class refugees had watched the economic and political structures in which they had prospered turn against them. Conventional perceptions and practices frequently failed them; they had lost their sense of how to act in new and unexpected situations. These Jewish wanderers barely recognized themselves.

Countries of Immigration

Countries of immigration treated political and Jewish refugees differently. The former received privileges, such as longer-term residence status, explained in part "by the fact that political fugitives corresponded more closely to the traditional image of a refugee; of people who, because of their political ideas and deeds, had suddenly to flee their country to save their life or freedom." With the intensification of antisemitic persecutions in central and eastern Europe, western European "safe" states could no longer deny the political roots of Jewish persecution. Still, they controlled the flow with strict visa policies, although "no two countries enforced the same set of policies." Further, as the number of refugees multiplied, "the aversion to refugees [became] an international problem, and the treatment of refugees remains one of the darkest chapters of the war."[47]

Despite this "aversion," at first some countries did take in refugees, however grudgingly. The experience of German Jews can serve as an example of early admittances but also of changes in refugees' destinations. France, Holland, and Czechoslovakia took in over one-third of Jews fleeing Germany in the first years of the Nazi regime.[48] British Mandatory Palestine accepted another 37 percent of German Jews, and about a quarter aimed for lands overseas. In the years following, Europe appeared less attractive and overseas countries safer, so that by 1937, 60 percent of German Jews were fleeing overseas.[49] When the war started, most refugees considered the United States their primary choice. And as ports such as Genoa or Marseille first limited and then stopped passenger shipping, Lisbon developed into Jewish refugees' port of last resort.

Because a majority of Lisbon's refugees hoped to enter the United States, it plays a special role in this story. World War I saw a "spy" hysteria, which translated into increased anti-foreigner sentiment in the United States, leading to further immigration restrictions. The Immigration Act of 1924 set exclusionary quotas establishing an immigration policy, but not a refugee policy.[50] The Hoover administration stiffened a "likely to become a public charge" provision enabling consuls abroad to reject applicants based on their impression of an applicant's ability to earn a living in the United States. By the early 1930s, these quotas, restrictions, and the Great Depression had increased opposition in countries of refuge to those fleeing political persecution or violently exclusionary ethnic states. In addition, throughout North and South America, immigration policies reflected racial prejudice, and antisemites used coded phrases such as "desirable human seed-stock" or "race and inborn quality" to limit immigration.[51]

Although Americans strongly opposed the taking in of refugees, President Franklin Roosevelt called for a conference on the refugee crisis in July 1938, inviting thirty-two countries to meet in France at the resort Évian-les-Bains on Lake Geneva.[52] Before Évian, the United States had promised that no country would be asked to raise its immigration quotas. The organizers had not bothered to invite Portugal, although they would later consider Mozambique and Angola, Portugal's African colonies, sites for refugee settlement. Encouraged to join the Intergovernmental Committee on Refugees set up after Évian, Portugal declined the invitation.[53]

That fall, even after the cruelty of the November Pogrom and despite public opinion being "solidly against the Nazis' treatment of Jews," only 23 percent of Americans surveyed would have allowed more refugees into the country.[54] To make matters worse, until 1937 the United States had admitted only between 5 percent and 24 percent of its yearly quotas of people from Germany and Austria, and these immigrants included non-refugee Germans and non-Jewish refugees.[55] As Jews realized that the countries they had aimed for were refusing them asylum and that they could not use the new languages they had studied, gallows humor made the rounds of a small German town: "'What language are you learning?' 'The wrong one, of course.'" More sadly, one refugee summed up the situation this way: "Every door and portal is firmly locked and bolted—and so is every heart."[56]

By the end of the war, the United States, Palestine, and Great Britain had taken the most Jewish refugees who fled westward or south. The United States admitted 35 percent of the refugees, and the rest of the world 65 percent.[57] Totals included United States, 200,000; Palestine, 138,000; Latin America, 85,000; and Great Britain, 70,000.[58] Fleeing eastward between 1939 and 1941, about 200,000–300,000 Polish-Jewish refugees crossed into the new Soviet occupation zone after the outbreak of war and, later, into the Soviet Union. The Soviets forcibly transferred many to remote areas, including Siberia and Central Asia. Still, most survived. Since the Final

Solution destroyed the lives of six million European Jews, these several hundred thousand refugees scattered around the globe were lucky to escape. But refugees in Lisbon did not share our hindsight. Smarting from the wounds caused by massive personal losses, untiring efforts, and rejection on numerous fronts, some refugees unburdened themselves in letters, diaries, and memoirs. We turn to these documents now.

"You Hear Me Speak. Can You Also Hear What I Feel?":
Ego-Documents as Sources

Like other historians, I have used archival materials, museum collections, and newspaper reports, along with journalists' observations, to help provide overviews of the refugee dilemma. But refugees experienced their plight as individuals. Personal details mattered; they exposed deep-seated feelings, allowing us to see the trees, not just the forest. Contemplating his own death, Montaigne wrote, "Wholesale, I could master it: retail it savaged me."[59] Adding individual perspectives to the general story, combining "wholesale" and "retail," evokes a wrenching image of what mass flight meant to the woman and man on the ground.

To consider individuals' feelings, I read sources that belong to the "more or less private" category of "ego-documents," or "life writings," consisting of memoirs, diaries, and letters, and I viewed videotaped interviews. The use of refugees' voices from and about Portugal allows them to shape their own stories and reveal their emotions. Even if these feelings and their expression were culturally molded by refugees' backgrounds and times, these intimate documents present crucial quotidian experiences as well as individuals' anxieties and values. They offer grassroots views of what historians read in newspapers, government statements, and social workers' reports. They illustrate private journeys but also personal perspectives on the historical moment, bringing an indispensable qualitative sentiment to public records.[60] Writing and speaking of memories was and is a highly emotional process.[61]

Personal testimonies provide voice and depth while also describing the actions and feelings of the writers or interviewees.[62] In the 1970s, when historians began to write working-class and women's history, many turned toward oral histories as well as life writings to uncover the history of nonelites and the worlds they created. Similarly, for Jews in Portugal, memoirs and oral histories put refugees' behaviors and subjectivities at the center of the story. They bring the agency of ordinary people to light. I have also interwoven observations from a few non-Jewish refugees fleeing the Nazis and waiting in Lisbon. Sometimes their perspectives fill gaps, at other times they confirm the reactions of Jews, and at still other times they provide contrasts to Jewish refugees' feelings or expectations. There is no way to know how random or how typical these sources are. But they add important details, along with additional information. Indeed, they may not be representative, "but they are telling."[63]

Like all sources, ego-documents have limitations. Since "memory is the raw material" for this project, we need to concede that memory can play tricks, can be selective and episodic. A memoir or interview is one person's sometimes-skewed perspective, reworked by time and forgetfulness; "memory is notoriously fallible . . . [and] there is such a thing as honest (and healthy) forgetting." Memory may also minimize or exaggerate emotions, since memory is the distance between "the experience of an emotion and the memory of an emotion."[64] Further, writers or interviewees had readers or viewers in mind. In representing themselves to this imagined audience in the best light, sometimes called "self-fashioning," they may have emphasized or omitted portions of their narratives. Nancy Miller addressed this conundrum: "I could write down what I remembered; or I could craft a memoir. One *might* be the truth; the other, a good story."[65] Moreover, in 1930s and 1940s Europe, letter writers could not safely tell the truth, because of censorship and the desire to minimize the worries of the recipients. And class can skew the story: the memoirs and interviews available to us tend to come from the educated middle classes, mourning their losses, as well as from their children, who were less aware, more adventurous, and more optimistic.

Like poetry, personal documents allow us to read the expression of feelings, but we can only guess the actual state of refugees' feelings.[66] The German-Jewish poet Gertrud Kolmar, later murdered in Auschwitz, cautioned her readers: "You hear me speak. Can you also hear what I feel?" Fear serves as an example. Can historians recognize "everyday manifestations of fright in the past?" Can we tell the difference between fear, anger, or even hatred when a refugee approached a consul who had withheld a visa? And can we distinguish between fear—often mentioned in personal writings—and anxiety, even if psychologists may do so? Indeed, "what is fear for one individual or group may be an anxiety for another."[67] German-language sources confuse the issue even more, since *Angst* means both, immediate fear as well as more general anxiety. Furthermore, fear can coexist with hope; even if refugees focused on fear in the present, they often acted with hope for the future.

We also miss gestures, facial expressions, or intonation in memoirs, diaries, and letters, losing physical signs and speech volume that communicate moods and meanings at the very heart of language.[68] Nor can we determine when writers of ego-documents chose to privilege their feelings over their actions during a crisis. Finally, we can discover the connections between subjective suffering and bodily reactions only if the writers tell us so, although scientists have studied these links. Still, written expressions and physical states need not be binaries. How refugees wrote about their bodies— "My heart was pounding and my mouth was very dry"—alerts readers to their emotional state. These problems notwithstanding, I attempt to use letters, memoirs, and interviews to understand what individual Jewish refugees felt. As John Demos wrote: "We can only speculate—only imagine— but that much, at least, we must try."[69]

Ego-documents conceal, but they also reveal. Whereas they may suppress some personal details, they also uncover the world beyond the individual. They often include the mentalities of companions and highlight an ephemeral refugee culture. Their observations help us visit the material culture that surrounded refugees: the taste of strong Portuguese coffee, the smell of frying fish, the sounds of noisy streets. These memoirs, diaries, and letters alert us to the arbitrary nature of refugees' lives and to their reactions to chance encounters, setbacks, and support. They form a collage of displacement and frantic activity during escapes and of self-control, frustration, and resilience while waiting in Portugal. We can use refugees' voices, as Saul Friedlander vividly did, as "lightning flashes that illuminate parts of a landscape."[70]

Gender and Memory

This landscape was gendered. In 1933, Nazi propaganda, boycotts, decrees, and violence targeted Jewish men. As businesses owned by German-Jewish men declined, others lost their jobs in the predominantly male civil service, the judiciary, the national health insurance program, and the legal profession, as well as in the arts and culture. During the annexation of Austria in 1938, Jews faced more violence and even swifter downward mobility than in Germany. These unemployed, harassed, and frightened men could no longer find "traction in the ways of being that had provided continuity and optimism." One man stopped eating, explaining that "no one had the right to eat when he did not work."[71] Women, for whom Austrian universities opened in 1895 and most German universities in 1908, had only begun to enter the professions. Middle-class women generally focused on their households and children. While many men suffered deep humiliation, most women attempted to salvage what they had—their families. They took on previously "male" behaviors, scrutinized the political and social environment, and strategized ways of responding. Determination rather than shame dominated their responses.

As conditions worsened, many German and Austrian middle-class Jewish women expanded their roles further. Jewish women experimented with new behaviors rarely before attempted by any middle-class German woman. Publicly, they interceded for their men with the authorities, and privately they demanded that their families emigrate. After the November Pogrom, the Nazis released only those men incarcerated in concentration camps who could prove they would emigrate quickly. Women strained every muscle and nerve to free them, often staying behind to pack after sending husbands and brothers on their way. Women also sent children off on *Kindertransports,* sold their homes on their own, and decided on countries of refuge by themselves.[72]

The outbreak of war spurred mass flight. During this exodus, women who had taken on "male" responsibilities at home could share new tasks more equally with men. Both genders approached consulates and police; both sought shelter and food.[73] Certainly, biological and gender differences remained: physical differences, motherhood, even the ability of a young woman to use charm to gain safety. Men and women confronted police authorities with different apprehensions, vulnerabilities, skills, and talents. At border crossings or police stations, some women dreaded sexual assault. In Spanish jails, both men and women needed cups and spoons, but young Margit Meissner felt deep embarrassment at requesting pads for her monthly cycle.[74] Women sometimes recalled moments when their bodies created danger or opportunity.

Women and men also expressed themselves differently: women revealed more emotions in their writings and interviews, while men tended to be more descriptive. Women "live with more feeling" and report this when interviewed, according to the Nobel laureate Svetlana Alexievich, whose own work interlaces women's observations of war with their emotions. She argues that men "are more impressed with action" and report on the sequence of events.[75] I have found gendered memories in which women not only evoke private thoughts and feelings more readily than men, but also include details of daily life as well as observations about families and friends. Men tend to focus on their experiences, particularly those "worthy of public notice."[76]

These discrepancies notwithstanding, in moments of flight and in locations of limbo like Portugal, events and reactions appear less gendered, more shared. In Portugal, for example, poverty equalized men and women. Men had lost their place as breadwinners. Previous positions in the increasingly distant past counted for little, and men no longer possessed the social or actual capital that had once elevated their status above that of women. The duration of their stay further leveled their standing; both men and women asked for the support of aid associations or pleaded with consuls. So it may not be surprising that gender differences do not stand out in these refugee narratives, since gender roles while fleeing or waiting lost some rigidity, and the memory of trauma is usually only as gendered as the trauma itself.

We need more research as we begin to analyze gender dynamics during the refugee crisis. Did women and men face equal danger while fleeing? Did border guards, consulate officials, or aid workers treat men and women differently? Who took children on dangerous treks? We have learned about men who braved the mountains while escaping from France, but we need to find out more about women like Lea Lazego, who crossed those same mountains with her two children and an infant. Some of these questions will be answered here as we note the gender lens both blurring and, only occasionally, coming sharply into focus.

༺✦༻

This book is structured chronologically and geographically, along the trajectory of Jewish refugees' journeys. The first three chapters set the context, starting with the arrival of refugees in Portugal before World War II and then after the fall of France. Refugees' voices describe sites such as borders and landscapes such as the Pyrenees that caused them emotional turmoil while on the run. They also depict their hopes and fears once inside Portugal. In the last four chapters, refugees' experiences at specific locations push the narrative forward. These chapters tell us how particular places at particular times affected refugees viscerally.

Chapter 1 details how early refugees, those who fled increasing persecutions in Germany and German-annexed Austria, came to Portugal between 1933 and 1939. Some settled there; others moved to distant destinations. This situation changed dramatically with the outbreak of war, particularly when Germany invaded France. Struggling to reach safety, refugees crowded roads and waited at borders. With or without proper visas, many aimed for Portugal. Chapter 2 traces initial experiences in Lisbon. The westernmost part of Europe, sun-drenched Portugal offered an ambivalent respite. Refugees arrived in a dictatorship that required them to move on quickly. Trying to find visas and ships that would take them out of Europe, they faced delays and dreaded arrest. The welcoming generosity of many Portuguese people provided the only bright spot. In chapter 3, we see that while the vast majority of refugees left Portugal in a few weeks or months, many remained longer, some for years. Local and American Jewish organizations as well as nonsectarian American aid organizations provided shelter and food to a growing group of impoverished refugees and also intervened for them with the increasingly impatient Portuguese government. Refugees as well as aid groups worried about an expanding war, terrified that German armies, poised at Spain's borders, might attack Portugal. Chapter 4 considers refugees' responses to life in Portugal. Adults felt intense dismay as they lingered between a destroyed past and an uncertain future. Many mourned their loss of home and homeland, amounting to a loss of self. But young people often experienced excitement and adventure, and looked forward to the future. Women and men also reacted differently to their losses and helplessness, even if gendered behavior flattened a bit.

Chapter 5 follows refugees as they participated in a demoralizing and constant routine of waiting while applying for visas and begging for ship tickets, all as time-sensitive documents threatened to run out. They stood on lines at consulates, post offices, and aid and shipping bureaus. And when they came back empty-handed and full of angst, the Portuguese government remanded hundreds to what it called "fixed residences," small villages that they could not leave, even though they needed to get to Lisbon to pursue their visas. Chapter 6 looks at how refugees found support while waiting. Regular visits to cafés allowed them to reach out to one another to share moods and create caring communities. Letters to and from loved ones also ensured that bonds of family and friendship continued despite distances. But café friendships proved transitory, and epistolary spaces could cause grief, especially when refugees in Portugal learned of the dangers and hunger facing Jews in Nazi-occupied Europe. The last chapter is about departures. With the crucial visas in hand, refugees jammed shipping agencies to buy tickets. Then they crowded the docks. What had they learned about the genocide occurring in eastern Europe during their stay in Lisbon, and how did they feel as they watched Europe, the site of many pleasures and yet much terror, fade into the horizon?

Focusing on how geography intersected with emotions, this book homes in on Jewish refugees' confrontations with daunting obstacles and on the physical and emotional toll their efforts took. Taking my cue from the pointillists, who painted images with tiny dots, I use many individuals' stories to create a large portrait of the daily lives and feelings of Jewish refugees caught between a lost past and an unpredictable future.[77]

1. Escaping Terror and the Terror of Escaping

Before and After the War Turned West

The young people told us to walk the next 1 km to the
border in complete silence. I asked why, we have young children.
They told me that all along the top of the mountains are government
soldiers. If they hear anything, they shoot immediately.

Refugees reached Portugal in three waves. The first group, mostly of central European Jews, arrived sporadically between 1933 and 1939. These several hundred refugees generally turned up with proper documents and faced few obstacles. Some even started businesses and settled there comfortably. But the second, much larger influx of central and eastern European Jews came via harrowing journeys after the fall of France in June 1940. They numbered as many as 70,000, probably more, and many had fled without having all the necessary papers just at the moment when Portugal resisted taking them in.[1] A third group of about 10,000 appeared during the summer and fall of 1942 when France began deporting Jews and Germany occupied all of France. Most did not have the necessary visas. Still others in smaller numbers continued to arrive until war's end.

Whereas the first wave usually came directly from home, fleeing increasing persecution and occasional violence, those in the last two waves had often escaped interim safe havens such as Holland, Belgium, or France. These fleeing Jews confronted bewildering and frightening sites of anxiety. Roads through France and consulate lines there caused relentlessly mounting fear. Border crossings, too, evoked intense anguish because they exposed refugees to terrible danger if guards turned them back. Still, after mid-1940, refugees needed to push on toward Portugal, the major transit point for Jewish refugees heading toward the Americas.

Before the War: Arriving in Portugal Between 1933 and 1939

About one-third of German and Austrian Jews had fled their homelands before the war, although few headed for Portugal. Most had never traveled to the Iberian Peninsula and did not consider Portugal, a poor agricultural country under a dictatorship, an option. They thought of Portugal as an interim stop before moving on to North or South America. Indeed, many did move on. Those who settled early had left well before German bombers and hostile border guards could stymie or terrify them. Less traumatized than those who came later, during the war, they still faced the tribulations of all newcomers: learning a foreign language, finding jobs or setting up businesses, worrying about their children's educations, and looking for community. Their flight from their homelands could cause sadness, even nostalgia, and their new efforts could cause concern, but they focused on making new lives for themselves.

Despite estimates that Portugal could only accommodate about sixty or seventy refugee families, several hundred arrived between 1933 and the fall of France.[2] The Davidsohn family, for example, searching for a safe haven in 1935, headed for Portugal after they heard that in "Portugal there were no antisemitic feelings." When Ruth Arons's family drove from Berlin to Portugal, they knew only about "Port wine, cork and sardines."[3] Both families settled there. Most Jewish refugees chose Lisbon, the capital, a port city of about 600,000. The majority of Portuguese Jews, some 400 families, or between 1,000 and 2,000 people, lived in Lisbon.[4] Other Portuguese Jews could be found in cities such as Porto, in northwestern Portugal, in middle-class occupations.

Portuguese Jews had a long history to look back on, having lived in the area during the Roman era, before the nation of Portugal came into being. Jews had lived in relative peace under Muslim rule beginning in 711 CE and under Christian rule as Christians gained back territory starting in the early twelfth century. Jewish religious life and communal structures prospered, as did individual Jewish scholars, traders, and artisans. They also developed a Jewish language known as Ladino, a combination of fourteenth- and fifteenth-century Spanish mixed with Hebrew and other languages. But the tolerance they had enjoyed ended in 1497 when King Manuel I of Portugal demanded that all Jews convert to Christianity. Many converted, but others fled. The Portuguese massacred some 2,000 Jews in Lisbon in 1506. Twenty years later, the newly established Portuguese Inquisition attempted to root out new converts who secretly practiced Judaism (labeled conversos, and later, crypto-Jews), and Portuguese cities publicly burned more than a thousand suspected converts at the stake between 1540 and 1794. Jews who originated on the Iberian Peninsula, self-identified as Sephardim, scattered to exile in France, Turkey, Italy, North Africa, the Middle East, the Caribbean, Holland, and England, and to cities such as Hamburg.

This Jewish escape from the Inquisition continued into the modern era. But in the nineteenth century, small groups of Sephardic Jews from North Africa, especially Gibraltar and Morocco, moved to Portugal, forming a community in Lisbon that had grown to about 300–400 members by midcentury. With the downfall of the monarchy and the ascendance of the anticlerical First Republic in 1910, observers noted that Jews enjoyed a significant measure of tolerance even before their full legal emancipation in 1912. Numbering about 1,000, they ran small businesses, prepared their sons for professions, and served the state. By then, Lisbon housed three small synagogues. The community continued to grow: by 1939, about 3,000 Jews lived in Portugal and made up 0.04 percent of a population of over 7 million.[5]

The story of Jewish refugees from Nazi Germany in Portugal in the prewar years is one of calm before the storm. The Lisbon Jewish community responded quickly once refugees began to arrive. Dr. Augusto d'Esaguy, a renowned dermatologist and active leader of the Jewish community, claimed that the community attended to most refugee Jews "as best as we could." The Lisbon Jewish community "immediately . . . formed a committee for the care of refugees," known as COMASSIS (Comissão Portuguesa de Assistência aos Judeus Refugiados, the Portuguese Commission to Assist Jewish Refugees), chaired by d'Esaguy. Despite coming from different cultures—the Portuguese from a Sephardic background and the others from Ashkenazic (central and eastern European) roots—the Sephardim treated the Ashkenazi refugees generously. Jewish observers counted about 650 Ashkenazic Jews from Poland and Germany in the Lisbon Jewish community during the interwar years.[6]

Directly after 1933, the several hundred Jews who settled in Portugal had some financial means, since the Portuguese government allowed in only refugees with the capital or skills to live there. Jewish newspapers abroad remarked that the country welcomed Jews who could open small businesses, in particular (and in this order) women's tailors, men's tailors, knitters, watchmakers, jewelers, furriers, and shoemakers. In addition, Jews could work at a firm if employers showed proof that Portuguese nationals could not fill the position.[7] Those with money founded businesses in Lisbon and Porto as importers, manufacturers, doctors, engineers, and merchants. Others found jobs as representatives of German or American companies.[8] A lawyer opened the first laundry in Porto, and a publishing executive started a business importing printing equipment.[9]

The combination of wealth and luck simplified a move. When fifty-eight-year-old Gustav Blum, the former owner of a large lumber business, returned from three weeks of detention in the Buchenwald concentration camp after the November Pogrom, his four-person family experienced a sudden stroke of good fortune. An unknown and distant cousin, an attorney born and living in Portugal, contacted them. This man helped them acquire an entry permit for Portugal in January 1939 as well as permission for a thirty-day stay. He also found a place for them in the village of Estoril, where they could "recuperate a little in this sunny, friendly country." An aunt in New York lent the family $1,000. In addition, rent from three small apartment houses that they owned in Rotterdam provided a comfortable though modest existence in a furnished apartment. Within a short time, Gustav Blum took out mortgages on the Rotterdam houses and invested, with five partners, in a tin mine in Portugal. The government, nevertheless, sent the family an expulsion order, which it simply disregarded, as it did a similar order that followed six months later. This time the secret police arrested Gustav Blum and took him to Aljube prison in 1940. There he could pay for adequate accommodations and meals from nearby restaurants. After partners at the tin mine filed a petition with the Ministry of Interior and another colleague spoke directly to Salazar, the government released Blum and extended his visas automatically. Having established a new business, rented a finer apartment, and found schools for the children, the family planned to stay in Portugal, although ultimately, fearing the spread of war, they left.[10]

As with the Blum family, relatives in Portugal facilitated immigration and adjustment in the years before 1939, easing refugees' transitions financially, emotionally, and even legally. In late 1938, Friedrich Westheimer managed to get his sister into Portugal on the very day that the government required visas that neither she nor her family had. Westheimer succeeded in stretching the rules for her. He then rented a large apartment for his sister's family in Lisbon. That way she could sublet rooms and offer meals to boarders, ensuring her family's subsistence.[11]

Jewish networks, familial and communal, served to buffer newcomers, offering material help and community. For example, the Sephardic Jewish Cassuto family of Hamburg had once supported the building of the Porto synagogue. They fled Hamburg for Amsterdam in April 1933; while there, they received a letter from the leader of the Porto synagogue, offering their son, Alfonso Cassuto, the directorship of a Jewish school in Porto. They subsequently moved to Porto. Similarly, when Dr. Rudolf Hirsch had to flee Hamburg, the Cassuto family, by then settled in Portugal, facilitated his first job there as a mohel, performing ritual circumcisions. In the same way, other Jewish familial networks aided new refugees. Ironically, the history of Jewish persecution in Portugal allowed some Jews to acquire legal entry into Portugal. When individuals from the Hamburg Sephardic community made their way to Portugal, they attained special status as families whose ancestors had fled the Inquisition. They received Portuguese passports and could even return to Germany to claim their property.[12]

Capital and connections proved valuable, but not essential. Some refugees started tiny businesses. A young Jewish refugee in Lisbon, seeking to support herself, sold baked goods such as the Berlin donut. The German donuts grew popular in cafés in Estoril and Lisbon, renamed *bolas de Berlim*. (Today, Portuguese bakeries offer *bolas* as standard fare.) Hungarian pastries baked by refugees appeared in Lisbon cafés around the same time. The Davidsohns from Berlin lived precariously in the town of Cascais. Home-baked goods, peddled by the children, and the occasional sale of their belongings kept them afloat. Later, Mr. Davidsohn supported his family from a small shop he set up in Lisbon.[13]

Ingenuity also helped some earn their living. Arriving in Coimbra in 1933 from Poland, Glikla Wakman joined her husband, who had already set up a tiny watch repair shop in a space under a stairway. She made ice cream and hired a boy to sell it on her three-wheel bicycle. She saved enough money to pay for her husband's first trip to Switzerland, where he contacted Swiss watch designers and became their representative in Lisbon. When Ursel and Herbert August fled Hamburg, arriving in Portugal in 1936, Ursel earned a minimal income as a dressmaker until wealthy Portuguese families hired her as a nanny. Herbert tried to make money several ways, including by establishing a room rental service and becoming a door-to-door salesman. He set up a toy workshop in his basement once they moved out of Lisbon. They earned enough to bring Ursel's parents to Lisbon in 1939. Miriam Brodheim, born in Poland, reached Portugal with her mother in 1937 at the age of sixteen and taught ballet and piano to children. As her interest in teaching grew, she took correspondence courses in the Montessori teaching method, raised money, and set up the first Montessori school in Portugal with a friend. She was eighteen.[14]

Interim jobs and language tutoring helped some refugees stay afloat. The author Ilse Losa arrived in 1934 and worked as a governess, later teaching private German lessons before embarking on her writing career. A few people managed to find short-term positions in the emerging film industry. The 1934 film *Gado Bravo* (Wild Cattle), one of the first Portuguese sound films, included many German refugees in its cast and crew. Still others found work in the import-export trade. Curt Schwerin, arriving in 1936 with a doctorate from the University of Heidelberg in economics, chose Portugal because he did not need an immigration visa at that time. Until the war, he worked as a commercial agent for Czech, Austrian, French, and British firms and later, until Pearl Harbor, for American firms. After the entry of the United States into the war, business collapsed and he needed help from social welfare organizations.[15] Efforts to find temporary jobs show that adapting required resourcefulness and flexibility but that the context—dictatorship and war—imposed the final results.

Refugees lacking wealth, family ties, or luck could turn to the small Portuguese Jewish community for economic and moral support. Between 1933 and 1940, the Lisbon community found jobs for several doctors and professors, enabled some lawyers to enroll in university courses, and obtained residence and work permits for other (most likely, male) refugees "to incorporate them into and make them useful elements of the Portuguese community." By 1941, d'Esaguy concluded: "Many of these refugees and especially the doctors, engineers and small industrialists live today happily in my country and have managed to get their family and friends to join them." Furthermore, individual Portuguese Jewish families invited refugees to their homes for the Sabbath meal. Miriam Brodheim met her future husband at just such an event. They remained in Portugal.[16]

Finally, the erratic flexibility of the Portuguese government helped, too. The Gelehrter family had no difficulty immigrating in 1936. The Portuguese consul even gave permission for Dr. Gelehrter to import his dental equipment and a piano, toll free, to his new home in Porto. However, the government did not recognize his German degree, circumventing economic competition with Portuguese dentists. Instead, it allowed him to open a practice with a Portuguese dentist, producing a successful collaboration.[17]

Such help notwithstanding, a growing trickle of refugees from central Europe alarmed the Portuguese government. Between 1926 and late October 1938, German citizens could enter Portugal freely, that is, without a visa. They could even, until 1936, obtain Portuguese nationality through marriage or substantial assets. By that time, the Portuguese secret police had counted about 600 refugees from Germany. A few Sephardic Jews from Hamburg and some Polish Jews had also fled their homelands.[18] In 1936, the police worried that "strangers of suspect origin in Portugal" might be engaged in "espionage or international agitation." The police focused on those with "visas made for Russians, Poles, *heimatlos* (stateless), individuals whose nationalities differ from the country documented."[19] They did not single out Jews, although "Russians, Poles, and *heimatlos*" surely included Jews. In 1938, a Portuguese envoy in Berlin notified his government that Germany had issued new passports to Jews after they promised never to return. Once these Jews left Germany, they automatically became stateless people. Nervous about a "mass immigration of German Jews," the envoy recommended requiring visas for those going to Portugal. Other government representatives expressed inconsistent attitudes when it came to Jews. In November 1938, officials on the island of Madeira, a Portuguese colony in the North Atlantic, shared the envoy's misgivings that too many European Jews might "ruin tourism," but welcomed Jews from "US, England, France, etc. etc."[20]

Portugal grew stricter on October 28, 1938, less than two weeks before the November Pogrom. Its Circular #10 decree awarded thirty-day tourist visas only to persons who could demonstrate the ability to pay expenses in Portugal and who held visas to overseas destinations plus ship tickets. It also barred "aliens and Jews" from settling in Portugal. Furthermore, as more refugees came and as their stays lengthened, the police could reduce the thirty-day visa to twenty or even ten days. Having to regularly face the police escalated refugees' anxiety. Still, they came.[21]

Jewish refugees cooperated fully and fearfully with harsh governmental agencies, but often benefited from the goodwill of Portuguese non-Jewish neighbors. Noemi Gelehrter emphasized that "the people were so good to us." When the customs collector charged her father for importing his own furniture, he could not pay. The collector paid the sum on his own, remarking, "One day, when you have the money, you will pay me back." Shortly thereafter, Noemi succumbed to a strange condition that paralyzed her for months, and the Portuguese doctor treated her "without demanding a penny." Having adjusted to hateful daily interactions with non-Jews in Germany, Gelehrter reacted with grateful surprise to the kindness of Portuguese neighbors and officials.[22]

Casual acquaintances, too, helped out. Having missed the relative who had promised to meet them in Lisbon, one family of four "stood abandoned on the pier with hand luggage and 10 Reichsmark" (at that time the equivalent of $4.00 or 100 Portuguese escudos). A Portuguese stranger they had met on board, with whom they could speak only in broken French, "saw us lost . . . [and] took us under his wing and brought us to his home." Refugees benefited from anonymous help too. As early as the spring of 1933, when the first refugees appeared, the Jewish community made a local appeal for support. Non-Jews responded generously, and the pastor of a Protestant church in Lisbon made the first public collection and conducted prayers for Jews in Germany.[23]

This type of generosity is particularly noteworthy from a population that had very little experience with foreigners. Before the war, Portugal attracted mostly Spaniards, who visited the small beach retreats. And by the 1930s, wealthy Europeans, including European royalty, were patronizing a few luxury hotels and casinos in Estoril or Cascais, near Lisbon. Most Portuguese therefore had little to no experience with immigration or with refugees except at the Spanish-Portuguese border. There they helped some Spaniards escaping the civil war, although a half-million Spaniards fled toward France, not toward Salazar, Franco's ally.[24]

Salazar's government, committed to Catholicism and anticommunism, arrested thousands of Republican refugees and returned many of them to Spain, into fascist custody. In August 1936, the *Chicago Tribune* described the murder of socialists and communists in Spain, and added: "Blackest of all: the Portuguese . . . are turning back . . . hundreds of republican refugees to certain death by rebel firing squads." The reporter added that a "talkative frontier policeman said, 'Of course we are handing them back. We can't have

Reds in Portugal.'" The Portuguese swept up some Jewish refugees in these roundups as well, although the government "stressed . . . that these deportations were not caused by anti-Semitic motives."[25] Although the police tried to return suspected "Reds" to Spain, Portuguese citizens aided them with food and kindness, in much the same way that they helped Jews.

Heading Toward Portugal After the Fall of France

Before World War II, the hundreds of refugees who settled in Portugal faced the customary challenges of newcomers: adjusting to their new circumstances, securing permission to remain, finding jobs, and learning a new language. They started to build new lives slowly. Though they missed friends and loved ones, they remained hopeful about the future. Their later memoirs and interviews describe positive experiences with and feelings about their new homes and neighbors.

The situation in Portugal changed drastically, however, for the tens of thousands of desperate refugees who arrived there after the fall of France. The German offensive triggered a stampede of millions: Jews, political refugees, and escaped Allied prisoners of war headed for Spain, Portugal, and North Africa. A small but significant group of affluent and well-known people, Jews and non-Jews, also fled toward Portugal: Peggy Guggenheim, the Jewish heiress and art collector; Calouste Gulbenkian, the Armenian oil magnate; the Duke and Duchess of Windsor, in a four-car convoy; and King Carol II of Rumania. Jewish artists such as Marc Chagall and writers such as Anna Seghers and Arthur Koestler also headed south, as did Margret and H. A. Rey, carrying the manuscript of *Curious George* on their bikes with them. The American Emergency Rescue Committee, set up by Varian Fry in Marseille, saved some of these intellectuals and political leaders trapped in southern France. Their escapes appear to have been relatively benign compared with those of other refugees. Yet some of them, too, feared for their lives. The Jewish writer Alfred Döblin had fled Germany in 1933 and spent the next seven years in France. With the Nazi victory over France, he headed southward, dreading that he might be "rushing into the jaws of the enemy." He and other refugees made contingency plans: "I was prepared for this, as were others I had spoken to in Paris and during the journey. Some of them carried a revolver with them to put an end to it if they fell into the hands of the Nazis. . . . Death towered over me and behind me."[26]

Sites of Anxiety: Roads to and Lines in Marseille

Experiences of fleeing after June 1940 differed from those of earlier years as refugees traversed landscapes now threatened by German armies. Geographers refer to these sites as "geographies of emotional life" or "emotional geographies"[27] and examine the interplay between emotions and place, for example, the way a home can feel safe but suddenly turn frightening when a stranger breaks down the door and enters. In pre-Nazi times, traffic jams or lines at a consulate could imply an upcoming family reunion. Now travelers no longer progressed toward a happily anticipated goal. Crowded roads or long lines at consulates could stymie an escape and endanger a life. These sites had turned ominous.

For German Jews, exasperation with lines had begun much earlier, in 1933. As Nazi persecution grew, they stood for hours while seeking financial and emigration assistance from Jewish organizations. Lines grew longer, patience shorter: "Counsellors and suppliants alike, caught in the same vise, grew more and more irritable. . . . The entire community was on edge, rubbed raw by . . . oppression." In German-annexed Austria, too, Jews waited on long lines at embassies, shipping companies, and government offices, "desperate for papers: exit visas, transit visas, receipts for tax payments, clearance forms, ship tickets, train tickets." Some young people made extra money by lining up early and saving a space for adults.[28] Overwrought, some Jews blamed the local Jewish agencies and governmental bureaucracies for callousness as they waited and waited.

With German victory in France, Jews, political refugees, and French people fled the German occupation, "crawl[ing] along roads by day and night, bombers overhead, accidents by the way." German planes strafed the fleeing masses, and the desperate dove for shelter alongside the roads. An English refugee, Ronald Bodley, escaping the Germans by car, noticed "the vanguard of refugees in cars, rapidly succeeded by the advance guard in carts, and the main body on foot." Thirteen-year-old Rudolf Graf, one of those on foot, just "wanted to be safe" as his family fled southward. They "didn't know where [they] were," had no map, and used the sun to guide them.[29]

Few have left memories of what they saw on these roads, but the writer George Rony did. Going no faster than ten miles an hour in his overloaded car, he had time to observe his "crazed fellow travelers" but also the "abandoned houses: . . . In some of them radios continued to blare. . . . Howling dogs and cats scratched at locked doors. . . . Lights still burned in some of the windows and through many an open doorway we caught sight of . . . a table still heaped with a half-finished meal." He had witnessed "a cataclysm": "Human beings trapped in the midst of the homely tasks, the coziness and the joys of everyday life—trapped and overwhelmed in one . . . moment."[30]

Many paused in the Pays Basque, the borderland near Spain, in cities like Bayonne, or in the South, in the major port of Marseille. At these locations, tensions escalated to near intolerable levels as refugees faced unpredictable and confusing options. They heard that most French prefects were withholding the required exit visas, and the Spanish refused to let them cross without Portuguese visas. Further, they learned that the Portuguese objected to accepting any more refugees. When Bodley arrived in Bayonne, the German invasion had already passed Bordeaux, 115 miles to the north, and the land route over Hendaye, the most southwesterly town in France, "was . . . out of the question." The sea route held little hope, since ships leaving from Bayonne could hold only about fifty passengers at best. In addition, the local French authorities refused to allow refugees to leave on these boats without orders from the central government: "As no one knew where the French Government was, or if there was a French Government, this was tantamount to saying that we could not have the ships."[31]

Refugees flooded small French towns, sites they might have enjoyed in better times. Now these towns offered little relief: the city of Cahors (about 185 miles from the Spanish border), where about 13,000 people lived, suddenly faced an influx of 75,000 people and began running out of food. Bordeaux, a city of about 300,000, strained to accommodate close to 1,000,000: "One spent hours trying to find a place to eat." Franz Werfel, the Austrian-Jewish author of *The Forty Days of Musa Dagh*, set during the Armenian genocide, escaped through France with his wife. He observed millions of refugees clogging the small towns of France, including people from France, Belgium, Holland, Poland, Czechoslovakia, and Austria as well as German refugees and soldiers of the defeated armies: "One could only quiet one's hunger in makeshift ways. There was no shelter to be found."[32]

While the German occupation oppressed Jews in the north of France, the government of Marshal Philippe Pétain actively collaborated with and often preempted Germany in pursuing Jews in the South. His Vichy regime treated them, in Varian Fry's words, with "a combination of muddle and brutality." The Vichy police caught two leaders of the German Social Democratic Party, Rudolf Breitscheid and Rudolf Hilferding, in Marseille, and handed them directly to the Gestapo. Breitscheid later died in Buchenwald, and Hilferding died in a prison in Paris after being tortured. Refugees could not rest. They faced arbitrary mass roundups, or *rafles,* in Marseille: "One or two paddy wagons would roll up to the sidewalk in front of some café frequented by foreigners. The police jumped out and rounded up any number of men in the café or on the street who looked 'suspicious.' They pursued Jews or foreigners whose papers were not quite in order." To complicate the situation further, the Gestapo, which had an office in Marseille, lurked among the refugees, and no one knew when the Germans might continue southward and occupy the city.[33]

The menace to all refugees—but to German Jews and German dissidents most ominously—intensified as a result of the armistice on June 22, 1940. Defeated France agreed to "surrender on demand all Germans named by the German Government in France." This included those whom the Nazis considered enemies, whether political opponents, cultural leaders, or Jews.[34] Even before the war, the French government had interned some foreign Jews in camps, including German Jews often alleged to be "fifth columnists," or enemies in disguise. These camps entrapped Jews without the proper papers or with the wrong citizenship.

The hapless victims of this armistice clause wound up in French jails or internment camps, some of which later served as assembly camps for deportations to the East, such as Gurs, Rivesaltes, Le Vernet, or Les Milles. By September 1940, thirty-one detention camps held prisoners in the southern zone of France. Conditions worsened over time. The Quakers (the American Friends Service Committee, or AFSC) in July 1942 reported "crowded squalor, disease and a high death rate" in these camps, along with rampant typhus and tuberculosis. The standard fare included watery soup, ersatz coffee, and stale bread.[35] Later, in the summer of 1942, even before the Germans invaded the south of France, Vichy rounded up more than 2,000 Jewish refugees in Marseille and its environs, held them at the camp Les Milles, and then shipped them to Drancy, near Paris, and onward to Auschwitz. Vichy also deported inmates of the Gurs camp to their deaths that summer. These mass roundups prompted a renewed wave of refugees fleeing toward Portugal.

Lion and Marta Feuchtwanger, fifty-six and forty-nine years old, spent two months in great agitation, uncertain of each other's condition, he in the camps Les Milles and Nîmes, she in Gurs. There they faced starvation and disease. Feuchtwanger, a renowned German-Jewish novelist and playwright as well as a fierce opponent of Nazism, escaped the camp with the help of an

American vice-consul. He later wrote about his reunion with his wife near Marseille: "We were walking toward each other, alive and well. . . . My wife, Marta, is a good-looking woman of the athletic type. . . . Her hair had turned strikingly grey. My heart went out to her. Marta did not complain much. . . . But her looks and her nervous incoherence did not bear out [her] optimism." In addition, "she threw herself upon any food that was set before her." He added that she "was greatly shocked by my appearance." Many years later, she recalled how terribly sick he had looked, having suffered from dysentery.[36] After reaching Marseille, they could not rest, but instead had to steel themselves to get out of France.

Getting out meant standing on never-ending lines at the right consulates. These sites demanded perseverance and resilience from battered people. In Marseille, summer temperatures reached the mid-eighties, and central European refugees, dressed in the suits and jackets with which they had escaped, baked in the sun as they waited on line at numerous consulates. Fifty-one-year-old author Franz Werfel and his wife stood on two consecutive lines to attain transit visas for Spain and Portugal. Alma Mahler-Werfel's diary entry describes the scene: "The refugees stood in line before the consulates from sunrise until closing time, if they did not faint in the glistening heat or leave, to keep from fainting. A man with Werfel's heart could die on the spot." The Werfels possessed an American visa, which made the process a bit easier at the Spanish consulate as long as they bribed the doorman. Next, they sweltered in a line extending from the Portuguese consulate: "We went to the end of the line. It inched forward with maddening slowness. At high noon, the pavement seemed to melt under our feet. Werfel kept mopping his brow. His eyes burned in his dripping face; he suddenly looked ashen."[37]

The scholar Alfred Kantorowicz, doubly endangered as a Jew and a communist, contended with the same lines as the Werfels. In anguish, he considered Marseille the "waiting room to hell" and felt that the Americans there treated him as a potential robber and murderer. Hugo Marx, a former district court judge, had fled Nazism as early as 1933, spending some years in France acquiring a new law degree. In Marseille, Marx and his wife waited in front of different consulates. Marx recalled: "Often enough I felt like a wasp that keeps hitting its head against a closed window and that can only escape if someone opens the window. Looking back, I wonder how we managed." Sometimes those on lines "whil[ed] away the hours sociably."[38] But at other times, they grew impatient with one another. Waitstill Sharp, of the Unitarian

Universalist Service Committee (USC) in Marseille, observed people in long lines "when it's 90° in the shade and fifty clients [are] scrambling for each official, and tempers are short and injustices are done."[39]

For refugees, these lines, usually the second or third set they had stood in since leaving their homelands, represented a foreign state, potential rescue, and a new world. Yet the applicants had no rights. The front of the line came up against an arbitrary bureaucrat, with whom refugees pleaded. Nor did these lines disappear after the consulates closed, since desperate people persevered through the night in order to gain entry the next morning. Some let themselves be locked in the consulates, refusing to leave in the evening when the consuls left work. Others clambered over roofs to avoid the long lines. One could not avoid lines in other cities either. A Belgian-Jewish family stood on a line in Bayonne: "We would take turns guarding our place. It rained. We spent at least one night in that line. I remember being cold and hungry and scared (the Germans were presumably on their way.)."[40]

Once they reached the front of the line, many could not pay for visas or ship tickets. Raised to value financial independence, they felt embarrassed to ask for financial help from friends, family, or aid workers. Indeed, some refugees overcame these emotional obstacles by resorting to the black market, another site of anxiety. It took a toll on them, as previously respectable and generally law-abiding citizens, to break the law in order to survive. In addition, taught to be thrifty, many felt disoriented when dealing with the outrageous prices on the black market. And going to the black market increased their vulnerability to arrest, since "everyone knew the addresses of the black market-eers," the former judge Hugo Marx noted.[41] While those with some resources could avoid the black market, they feared they could not avoid the Germans.

Aside from the dangers of waiting in Marseille and reckoning with possible arrest by the French police collaborating with Germany, refugees discovered that French ships, although cheaper than those out of Lisbon, no longer provided reliable options. Ships sailed erratically from Marseille, often only to North Africa or Martinique. In March 1941, the release of prisoners from Les Milles camp depended on finding ships to take them abroad. Since these ships proved unobtainable, many of those remaining in the camp later faced deportation to Auschwitz. Refugees also learned that some French ships had been stopped at sea and that some never arrived at their destinations. Hans Sahl, a journalist, noted the mood of others like him, their "hopelessness, the waiting for ghost ships that would never embark, for visas, that would never arrive—the thought of being locked up, doomed here at the edge of Europe." They had to find a way out of Marseille and also avoid the Mediterranean and the British-controlled Straits of Gibraltar.[42] Other ports too became inaccessible to refugees seeking Allied havens. Italy joined the war on Germany's side in June 1940, so two more ports, Trieste, annexed by Italy in 1921, and Genoa closed to refugees. Irregular ships from Barcelona or Bilbao, illegal immigration to Palestine,[43] or the long journeys east through the USSR, Japan, or Shanghai in order to reach the United States or other countries in the West provided scarce opportunities.

The French Resistance activist Lisa Fittko wrote, "In the apocalyptic atmosphere of 1940 Marseille, there were new stories every day about absurd escape attempts; plans involving fantasy boats and fictitious captains, visas for countries not found on any map, and passports issued by nations that no longer existed."[44] By mid-1940, most ships leaving for the United States or Latin America left from Lisbon. Options had narrowed. To get to Lisbon, Jews would have to contend with additional sites: treacherous borders between France and Spain.

Sites of Anxiety: Borders

Fleeing the Nazi occupation of France meant traversing four borders, each with its own lines and difficulties. First refugees waited on the French side of the border, then on the Spanish side; once the refugees had crossed Spain, they had to wait on the Spanish side of the border with Portugal and, finally, on the Portuguese side, where a ten-hour wait at the passport office at Vilar Formoso no longer shocked anyone.[45] A best-case scenario at these emotionally painful frontiers meant enduring long hours in cold or heat while suffering angst about getting in, being heard, and receiving the desperately desired permission to stay or the crushing order to leave. Crossing borders no longer meant routinely heading from one place to another. Borders, but even more so the guards at the borders, signified life and death. Guards required multiple visas, stamps, signatures, and seals, which had the power to transform a refugee's identity from a potential victim to a free person.

Focusing in this section on the French-Spanish border, with its two sets of guards, and only briefly on the Spanish-Portuguese border, with its two sets, illustrates the terrors refugees faced at all these crossings. Today, we know the border between Spain and Portugal permitted easier passage and held fewer deadly consequences than the French-Spanish border. At the time, however, refugees could not know which location might be easier and assumed the possibility of rejection at any of the four. Moreover, all the borders required refugees to exhibit composure and rational behavior, despite their mounting fears and rage. Refugees had to force themselves to act patiently and politely, to rein in their fight-or-flight responses, that is, their normal, human reactions to fear. They had to suppress their acute stress in order to escape the Nazis. Everything depended on acting properly and calmly. Wait-still Sharp assessed the situation pessimistically in the summer of 1940: "You simply cannot realize the difficulties blocking emigration from France. The Nazis have ordered the French government to prevent the exit of every able-bodied male of any nationality, except American. . . . And so it becomes meaningless to cable us to give our time to emigration work. There is no hope of its success in *darkest France*" (emphasis in the original).[46]

Border crossings represented not only a "traumatic parting" from one's homeland but also one of the "central emotional experiences" of flight. They stirred ambivalence, a "mosaic" of border experiences. The Hilberg family felt relief, but realized they "were free and—to be precise about our new status—refugees." Bitterness merged with apprehension at these sites. Max Eschelbacher remembered: "We had been told that whoever crosses the border initially feels only a sense of unutterable relief. We did not feel that way. We could not sense anything but the certainty of having lost our home and everything that we had loved, that there was no return and nothing in front of us but a dark future."[47]

To traverse borders, Jewish refugees could turn for help to several aid organizations with offices in Marseille. Varian Fry dealt with famous writers, artists, and anti-Nazi political figures, but also hired several refugees to work in his office. Private donors as well as HIAS (Hebrew Immigrant Aid Society) and HICEM (a merger of three Jewish groups) aided the needy, arranged for necessary papers, and expedited transportation possibilities out of France.[48] The JDC (American Jewish Joint Distribution Committee, or Joint), founded to alleviate Jewish suffering during World War I, offered financial support. HICEM also cooperated with the Quakers and Fry's office to forward packages to internment camps and arranged guarantors for those without relatives or friends in the United States willing to vouch for them. All immigrants needed American "affidavits"—sworn testimonies of a sponsor's intention and financial ability to care for a refugee. HICEM furthermore paid or lent the cost of ship passage from Lisbon to New York. In addition, HICEM worked in several internment camps in France to alleviate conditions there and to intervene with French authorities.

Leaving Nazi-Controlled Europe Legally and Illegally

Refugees undertook these border crossings in at least three ways: as individuals with legal papers; as groups in "sealed" or collective transports (*geschlossene Transporte* or *Sammeltransporte*, respectively) sent by Jewish organizations with Nazi approval; or as people with fake documents or none at all. Yet all approached the French-Spanish and Spanish-Portuguese borders with great alarm, never sure what unforeseen event might stymie them or whether they had all the necessary money or papers.

Starting off legally, for example, meant gathering dozens of documents for the German government while seeking visas and transportation. When Regina Spindel, a woman of some means, fled Berlin in 1941, she took a plane, thereby avoiding four borders, but not the necessity of having the required documents. She gave the emigration office of the Reichsvereinigung der Juden in Deutschland about 340 Reichsmarks (RM) for one plane seat and RM 64 for luggage weighing about sixty-five pounds. (In this era, an average worker in Germany earned less than RM 3,000 per year.)[49] An elderly woman hoping to join her son in America, Spindel had to gather at least twenty-five official documents over an eighteen-month period—not including her passport, visas, or tickets. She wrote a governmental agency and "politely" pleaded that some of the money from her confiscated property, "in use for the benefit of the German Reich," be expended to pay her flight from Berlin, her subsistence, and the cost of visas and fees. Her son would pay for the ship tickets to the United States.[50]

A letter from the American consulate in Berlin invited her to an interview on January 27, 1941, in order to see whether her papers and her formal visa application complied "with the immigration laws of the United States." The consulate letter cautioned: "It is in your interest not to take any definitive preparation to dissolve your household until you possess the immigration visa."[51] These applications, consisting of many sheets, demanded details of one's life going back decades. Form B, which needed to be filled out on both sides, ran to the equivalent of six pages. Luckily for Spindel, she escaped. Other fortunate plane passengers also managed to land in Portugal, but not without insult. To get to their ships on time, some Jews had paid for costly flights, including meals, on Lufthansa. Upon arrival, Jewish passengers looked "tired and harassed." The crew had refused to serve them any food.[52]

Whether flying or facing more arduous border crossings, all refugees had to scale legal and bureaucratic hurdles. Most importantly, they first needed a passport from their country of origin. Governments began issuing passports in early modern Europe, though travelers rarely used them. The first modern passports, established during the French Revolution, sought to regulate migrants and may have impeded travel between states during the early nineteenth century, but passport rules loosened considerably after 1860, especially for middle-class travelers. Still, European states sought to monitor migrants even as they allowed a free flow across their borders. Governments reintroduced passport constraints throughout Europe during World War I. Concerns about enemy aliens caused tightened restrictions on foreigners, but governments also attempted to stem the emigration of young male citizens whom they needed for their armies. These requirements stiffened in the interwar era as the passport came to symbolize the "enormous increase in modern states' control over individual existence."[53] Still, hundreds of thousands of refugees, stateless people, and those deprived of their national passports possessed no official papers. Starting in 1922, the League of Nations offered "Nansen passports," identity certificates (or substitute international passports) to stateless people. These papers first aided Russians and Armenians in the 1920s, and refugees from Germany, Austria, and the Sudetenland received them in the 1930s. Although many nations accepted these documents, Portugal greeted them with suspicion.

Lion Feuchtwanger wrote: "Without papers it was simply impossible to move from a hostile France across a hostile Spain and a not exactly sympathetic Portugal and [then] reach an overseas country that was itself fussily bureaucratic." Refugees understood and despised this sign of their new, diminished human status. The dramatist Bertolt Brecht noted bitterly that the little booklet had acquired much more importance than the human being who possessed it: "The passport is . . . accepted when it is good, whereas a human being can be ever so good and still not be accepted." The author Stefan Zweig likewise wondered about the preeminent status of passports: "Formerly man had only a body and soul. Now he needs a passport as well, for without it he will not be treated like a human being."[54]

Even with passport in hand, refugees had to obtain a slew of other papers—in reverse order. This proved hard enough in peacetime, but heartbreaking and terrifying during the war. Persons fleeing from France via Portugal to the Dominican Republic, for example, needed a Dominican visa first. Once they had this, they could ask for transit visas from the United States (since they had to travel via Ellis Island), and then from Portugal. Obtaining a Portuguese transit visa depended on possession of the previous two documents plus a paid ship passage. Only then could the refugee acquire the Spanish transit visa and then the French exit visa. And if all of this did not fall into place within the required deadlines, the Portuguese visa could be renewed only once, and the ship tickets might have expired. Despite assurances from a variety of Jewish and non-Jewish rescue groups,[55] no country gave refugees permission to pass through its borders until they showed proof that another country had allowed them entry. Lisa Fittko concluded: "Every country was afraid that the émigrés would settle in with them like bedbugs."[56]

Even with legal passports and visas, refugees faced French intransigence. France created a huge stumbling block by refusing to grant exit visas, or *visas de sortie*. The Nazis had initiated incoherent policies when they forced France to sign the armistice. On one hand, the Nazis wanted Jews out of Europe. On the other hand, they made France agree to refuse exit visas to refugees from Greater Germany (Germany, Austria, and parts of Czechoslovakia). In addition, Vichy declared men of military age, between seventeen and forty-eight, ineligible for exit visas. So just as the refugee crisis in southern France intensified, the French increasingly refused to grant exit visas. By mid-1941, the French had discontinued providing exit visas in almost all cases, and canceled them altogether when Germany occupied Vichy in late 1942.[57]

On the ground, changing rules triggered confusion. Some refugees received two letters on the same day, one threatening jail if they did not leave the country immediately, the other threatening jail if they tried to leave the country without an exit visa. If one appealed these decisions and had the immense good fortune to obtain a precious French exit visa, its expiration date could still run out before one had acquired all the other necessary papers. At times, a thoroughly maddening dilemma ensued: the U.S. consulate would not give an entry visa until the refugee produced an exit visa, and the French would not issue an exit visa until they saw an entry visa to the United States.[58]

Refugees fled France for Spain on their own and with families, some by car or train with the proper papers, others on foot, usually missing some or all of the necessary papers. They used two major routes over the Pyrenees, one by way of the Basque country (Bordeaux, Bayonne, Irun) and the other via Catalonia (Marseille, Perpignan, Portbou). Even those with official documents did not have an easy time of it. The lines of people and cars waiting at the Hendaye border, south of Bordeaux, appeared endless to the Russian-born writer George Rony, escaping from Paris with his wife and ten-month-old son. They saw "at least two miles . . . covered by waiting cars," mostly owned or rented by people who had fled southward from Paris. The Czech author Jan Lustig noted in his diary: "Thousands and thousands of cars, in an unceasing chain stood at the border post. . . . Cars are abandoned on the sides of the roads: one has a better chance to get over the border on foot. Thousands of people have been waiting here for 36 hours, having spent two nights in the car." Lustig met a friend plagued by persistent anxiety who "was wiping cold sweat from his brow," worried that "at any minute, the border could shut." But walking did not really speed up the process: Ronald Bodley, who had known "the Franco-Spanish bridge since childhood [and] had crossed it many times . . . had never imagined that [he] would ever have to spend an entire day between its iron railings." He felt a "nervous restlessness set in": "Was it not possible for German planes to appear and bomb the . . . ranks of cars? They had done that . . . to refugees in the north!"[59]

Train travel could prove easier, but not always more secure. Subject to capricious shifts of governmental policies, the whims of local administrators, or even the moods of the border patrols, train passengers with proper papers (or mostly proper papers) had to prepare for and tolerate any contingency. The American reporter Wes Gallagher described refugees—"not all Jews"—in a dusty train in August 1941 who exuded "the crushing, invisible net of fear." As they reached the border, "papers—those scores of papers that refugees must carry—are nervously checked for the one hundredth time to make certain everything is there." Then the police collected the passports, required passengers to leave the train to answer questions and have suitcases inspected, and took those without a perfect set of papers into custody. Felix Oppenheim experienced this paper drama: the German guards on the French side of the French-Spanish border at Hendaye examined his papers, which included a "false visa, of course," and let him pass. Arriving at the Spanish side, the guards told him that his Portuguese visa had expired and ordered him to go back: "Back I went over the bridge. But the Germans . . . said 'you have left; you cannot return!' I do not remember how long I stood in the middle of the bridge . . . trapped, like a mouse, between the two barriers."[60]

Many refugees faced harsh scrutiny by German border patrols at the French borders, including being forced to strip completely. Some endured internal bodily examinations as well, both women and men. At each crossing, anxieties skyrocketed: "Borders meant danger ... something could go wrong, perhaps one didn't have all the papers." The novelist Erich Maria Remarque captured this moment: "No residence permit, but no exit permit either. They won't let you stay and they won't let you leave."[61]

The Nazi regime allowed, indeed encouraged, refugees to take trains out of the Reich. In April 1940, for example, the Austrian SS captain Alois Brunner, head of the Office for Jewish Emigration in Vienna and Adolf Eichmann's assistant, commanded the Viennese Jewish leadership to prepare an essay on emigration for its newsletter, urging Jews to contact relatives abroad to help them acquire entry permits and ship tickets. Brunner warned the Jewish leaders that they should completely fill trains with émigrés heading toward Italy and that most would have to travel third class. Only people with special needs could book second-class wagons. The Nazis insisted that Jews quickly leave Europe, but at their own expense and as uncomfortably as possible. In January 1941, the German authorities authorized the visit of Dr. Josef Löwenherz, director of the Viennese Jewish Community, to Lisbon to negotiate emigration to Portugal and to ask the World Jewish Congress for assistance.[62] In addition, the Nazis allowed the Reichsvereinigung in Berlin to hire an official German travel agency to send Jews with proper documents—as many as 15,000 in 1940 and 6,000 in 1941[63]—in sealed transports out of the Third Reich. The JDC and HIAS/HICEM subsidized these trains. For one year, starting on November 27, 1940, the Reichsvereinigung booked twenty-five such "transports" to Spain and Portugal. Trains with only one passenger car designated for Jewish émigrés could accommodate up to sixty-three people, and trains with the largest number—eleven cars—held 777 Jewish passengers. These travelers came mostly from Germany (4,808), but also from annexed Austria (981), and the Czech lands of Bohemia and Moravia (156). After Jews entered the trains, "the Germans sealed the doors." The passengers understood "sealed" trains to mean "like a prisoners' train," and the New York–based German-Jewish paper *Aufbau* called them "Gestapo forced transports."[64]

Having overcome numerous hurdles to escape the Nazis, Martha and Richard Lenk received permission to embark on just such a sealed train in February 1941. Before they could leave Berlin, however, they had to follow instructions on a six-page document from the Reichsvereinigung detailing multiple steps. Travel preparations included the costs of the train ride from their home in Stuttgart to Berlin, an exit visa from Germany (RM 8); an entry visa into Spain (RM 1); a Spanish transit visa (RM 1.65); three photos; and an entry visa to Portugal, which the Reichsvereinigung would acquire. For that, the traveler needed to hand in a passport; a passport photo; a copy of the ship ticket; and confirmation from the travel agency that the ticket had been paid. The journey from Berlin to Lisbon came to RM 225 per person, paid to the Reichsvereinigung. An additional $42, provided by foreign relatives or friends, went to the JDC in New York. And the Reichsvereinigung required an "emigrant levy" to subsidize emigration for those too poor to pay.[65] The traveler could take only RM 10 out of the country and needed to exchange this amount for French francs and American dollars in order to pay for small expenses while traveling through France and Spain.

The Reichsvereinigung recommended that everyone also take 150-gram bread coupons, two thermoses of drinks, a blanket, and a pillow. In addition, the government stipulated that travelers could bring only two suitcases that together could not exceed 110 pounds, and they had to carry their own luggage. They also had to fill out packing lists. Individuals needed to keep these, along with rail and ship tickets, passports, identification cards, exit permits, and foreign exchange, in a special envelope so that the documents would be easily accessible at border crossings and during inspections. The trip took twenty-seven hours from Berlin to Paris and another fourteen hours to the Spanish border.[66] Some travelers then headed toward other Spanish destinations (Bilbao, Cadiz, Madrid, Vigo, Barcelona) where they could still embark by ship. Most continued on another sixteen and a half hours to Lisbon. For those able to support themselves with help from family or friends abroad, the Reichs-vereinigung recommended several hotels as well as two kosher boardinghouses in Lisbon. Refugees with no means had to depend on an aid committee.

Lest one get the impression from these requirements that Nazi procedures appeared clear or predictable, they were anything but. In June 1941, the Quakers in Vienna deplored the situation: "We try all sorts of means to help the people with their emigration but when you think you have found a way today—everything is turned over tomorrow."[67] Seeking a clear path amidst changing rules meant to harass caused delays and deep distress for refugees and their helpers. Ultimately, however, clarity meant disaster: in October 1941, Germany forbade all further emigration, commencing the deportations of Jews eastward to their deaths.

Whereas most of those who approached border crossings early or in group transports had proper papers, many refugees—at times as many as half—faced the terror of being arrested or turned back, since they possessed "quasi-legal" visas, often bought or forged. The Portuguese Ministry of Foreign Affairs found that refugees could buy fake Portuguese passports at the Portuguese consulates in Vienna, Prague, Toulouse, Berlin, Hamburg, and Athens. Even Cook, the staid English travel agency, sold false transatlantic tickets, which were needed to prove that one could embark from Lisbon. Indeed, forged passports and papers "were the currency of survival during the war."[68] In the chapter "Forgery Is a Fine Art," from his book *Surrender on Demand*, Varian Fry described how he put refugees in touch with excellent forgers. The refugee author Karl Frucht, aided by Fry, expounded upon his "work" in France: "I prepared false receipts from fictitious shipping companies for ostensibly paid voyages to the USA. With these, some of us could acquire visas for China and transit visas through Spain and Portugal. . . . Of course, these papers . . . needed false dates and stamps." Writing to Thomas Mann in early 1941, the author Hans Sahl described Fry as having established a "corporation to save endangered people" by hiding behind a "legal façade. . . . a masterstroke!" Hired by Fry, Sahl crossed the border not only with his "brand new Danish passport," made by "one of the best craftsmen in this field," but also with secret information hidden in toothpaste tubes and shoe polish containers.[69]

Fry had little compunction about supporting these activities and harbored deep anger that the United States was accepting refugees too slowly. In 1944, he responded to his editor, who had cut comments critical of the United States from Fry's memoir: "[It] MUST BE SAID, namely that at a time when the Jewish refugees in France were being treated like cattle, the United States did virtually nothing. It doesn't matter a damn that there is now a War Refugee Board: there was nothing then, when something could have been done." Some enterprising persons, whether to participate in rescue operations or for private gain, also forged papers. In September 1940, Klaus Mann wrote his mother that an acquaintance had bought a "very nice Polish passport for 200 Francs (= two dollars)" as a matter of necessity: "It [that is, emigration] just didn't work legally anymore." Fry, who hired smugglers, forgers, and black marketeers to arrange illegal escapes, thought of "illegal emigration as the normal, if not the only way to go."[70]

For many Jews, breaking the law became a means of survival but also symbolized a heartbreaking social descent. The evasion of Nazi directives started in Germany when some Jewish women, almost always in charge of packing, smuggled valuables out of the country. What they managed to salvage could not compare to what the Nazis stole from them, but it helped them subsist for a short while. One woman recalled smuggling jewelry for a relative: "Naturally one did many forbidden things, but because, in fact, everything was forbidden to us Jews, one had absolutely no choice." Jews had to learn to defy the law. This did not come easily to law-abiding middle-class and middle-aged Jews who, not long before, had staunchly supported German laws and the German *Rechtsstaat* (a state run by the rule of law) that had emancipated them. They lost and mourned their identities as upstanding individuals. Echoing the sad bewilderment of many Jews, the famous non-Jewish anti-Nazi author Heinrich Mann "looked as solemn as a condemned man about to die" when he received his false papers. At the age of seventy, he lamented, "We are obliged to act like real criminals!"[71]

Refugees with inadequate papers climbed the Pyrenees in order to avoid official checkpoints as they fled France. Many braved such nerve-racking and complicated escapes that the memories plagued them years later. They had to bypass French patrols and border guards in the mountains. They usually clambered over the lower ridges, using a safer but more strenuous route via Cerbère, located on the French-Spanish border, or another one from the seaside village of Banyuls, about eight miles from the Spanish border. From Cerbère, some refugees used a small map that Varian Fry gave them; it showed a route running along a cemetery wall, over the hills, and down to a Spanish sentry post, which allowed them to avoid the French checkpoint. The mayor of Banyuls advised and supported guides like Lisa and Hans Fittko, suggesting the best routes and the best times to start out, well before sunrise. The climb could take between three and ten hours up the mountain and two hours back down. Most took at least four to five hours to reach the lowest point of the mountain range, often in burning sun. Luckily for some, in mid-1940 Vichy checkpoint guards often allowed refugees with overseas visas to pass into Spain without the precious French exit visa. Some French soldiers even directed refugees toward Spain. However, the French government quickly hardened its stance. Thereafter, its patrols in the Pyrenees aimed to shoot trespassers.[72]

As the danger from Vichy intensified, more refugees resorted to these precarious routes. Alma Mahler-Werfel recorded in late 1940: "The French had promised us exit visas, but when time passed we did not get them, any more than others did, we began to think [about] leaving without them. Crazy escape plans were hatched. One—to travel to a small border village, spend the night there, sneak up to a cemetery at 5 a.m. and meet someone who would be waiting behind a shack and would smuggle us through the cemetery and across the border—was rejected as too vague." The Werfels ultimately agreed to this plan, since it seemed to be their only option. She described the perilous journey: "[A] steep, stony trail that soon vanished altogether. It was sheer slippery terrain that we crawled up, bounded by precipices. . . . If you skidded, there was nothing but thistles to hold on to."[73]

A French guide took Eva Lewinski, a member of the ISK (Internationaler Sozialistischer Kampfbund, or International Socialist Combat League), a socialist organization active in the Resistance, and three other refugees over the mountains. She held proper papers for the United States, Portugal and Spain, but could not acquire a French exit visa. Yet her Jewish and socialist background put her in grave danger if she stayed in France. She recorded what happened after the French guide left: "We got lost . . . when the fog rolled in . . . we had no idea in which direction was Spain. Strange feeling of blindness, of helplessness, nobody to turn to. And then, like a miracle, we hear a train whistle in the fog. Since we knew that the railroad went along the coast, we suddenly knew where we were. . . . When after another climb, an old peasant woman with a donkey crossed our path, and we said 'Buenas Tardes' to each other, and she smiled—we knew we had made it." The Emergency Rescue Committee as well as other groups kept changing the routes over the mountains for security reasons.[74]

The need for these treacherous escapes did not cease after 1940–41. Indeed, in the summer and fall of 1942, the danger for Jewish refugees in France increased radically. In July, the French rounded up foreign and "stateless" Jews in Paris and delivered them to the Germans; in November, Germany invaded all of France. Thereafter, the Germans used specially trained dogs and alpine soldiers in addition to French guards to keep refugees from fleeing France. Still, a third wave of about 10,000 refugees headed for Spain and Portugal.[75] Among these, the French Jewish resister and (later) poet Claude Vigée attempted to escape France with his mother in October 1942 after learning of his imminent arrest. Facing "uprooting, uncertainty, exile, and loneliness," the twenty-one-year-old feared that their false papers would not fool the French passport control. Recognizing that "it was a situation of life and death," they headed toward Canfranc, on the snowy border in the Pyrenees. Luckily—"and at the crucial turning points in human life, everything is luck and coincidence"—the

French customs official glanced at his passport and recognized his family name (then Strauss). That man's father had worked for Vigée's great-uncle for almost fifty years. With that, the official waved mother and son through without examining the passport closely. He even helped them move their "miserable refugee baggage, tied together with string and wire," to the Spanish side of the train station. Writing in 1970, Vigée relived his sheer terror and his relief at this site. He had learned that a few days later the Gestapo arrived at Canfranc and that "the waiting room turned into a mouse trap."[76]

One small group epitomizes the mix of refugees who fled across the treacherous mountains that cold autumn. On November 14, 1942, nine people who paid $1,000 ($15,442 in 2019) to their guide made it to Spain over snow-capped mountains "almost perpendicular in spots." They included an American married to a French prisoner of war in Germany and her four-year-old daughter; a widowed Polish doctor; three German Jews; and three Belgian Jews. In January 1943, the Quakers in Lisbon estimated that 80–100 people crossed the Pyrenees illegally every day, and the JDC suggested that the figure was closer to 150–200. By then, civilians needed special travel permits issued by the Germans for the French border regions. Forgers carefully duplicated German certificates.[77] But some refugees made the desperate decision to flee France without any papers at all. Lea Lazego, with two children and a three-month old infant, climbed the Pyrenees on foot in 1943. Her odyssey had taken her from Poland to Belgium to France, where her husband languished in Les Milles camp and later joined the French Resistance. She arrived in Lisbon in time to have the children sent to relatives in the United States, although she could not acquire a visa for herself until 1944. The Germans and the French militia managed to catch some would-be escapees, yet the flow continued into 1944, when the Germans could no longer spare enough soldiers to patrol the huge mountainous territory. In the spring of 1944, small groups took two to five days to cross. Helped by what some described as the "Jewish underground," they succeeded in avoiding German guards.[78]

Smugglers and local residents who knew the rocky terrain played a crucial role in these escapes. The Jewish Labor Committee, founded in New York in 1934 in response to Nazism, paid guides to bring Jewish cultural and political leaders as well as Jewish and non-Jewish labor and socialist politicians who did not have all of the proper papers over the Pyrenees in 1940–41. Karl Frucht led refugees over the Pyrenees, worrying that they might all land in Spanish jails. The Maquis, guerrilla fighters in the French Resistance, who facilitated the escape of British soldiers and pilots, also helped some refugees. Without their guidance, the Karp family of three would not have escaped from France, having failed several times. George Karp, a Jewish doctor who had a degree from the University of Vienna and had served a stint in the French Foreign Legion, his wife, and five-year-old daughter spent three days and nights in cold, rainy November 1942 following a smuggler hired by the Maquis. They had packed a "small suitcase with seemingly important items," but later abandoned it due to the steep climb. Giselle Karp learned "that you can get along with practically nothing, except maybe for a toothbrush." They avoided normal routes and climbed over rocks and stones at night, hiding in caves during the day and plagued by hunger. They had to grab onto thorny branches and rocks to prevent falls, and his wife's hands bled from the sharp spurs.[79]

To survive the arduous journey, refugees needed extra assistance, and some gratefully recalled the help of local peasants and smugglers. Eva Lewinski, safe in the United States in late 1940, praised the people who facilitated her escape over the mountains:

> We all . . . who came out of France, have we not, despite much degradation, repeatedly felt humanity? . . . The wine grower in the south of France, who left his vineyard and led us on our walk through the Pyrénées . . . who declined our modest offer of money; the women farmers in Spain with their donkeys, who did not understand our language, and yet spoke the liberating words: "There lies Portbou and that is the Spanish border"; . . . the stranger in Madrid who drove us through the city . . . because he knows: here are comrades. Because he himself is a French metal worker, who himself escaped from France over the Pyrénées—they are all proof of the living humanity, that no fascism can extinguish, that no bombs can completely destroy.[80]

These individuals had reaffirmed her faith in others.

Fleeing through the area, alert only to danger and obstruction, few refugees reported on the physical splendor around them. Dreading the border guards, none left records of the stunning French landscape, dotted with castles and covered with vineyards overlooking the azure Mediterranean. Their silence regarding the beauty of southwestern France illustrates their frame of mind during their escape. Hungry and terrified of being caught, of falling, or of freezing, they experienced the landscape as a series of pitfalls, and they had little emotional energy to appreciate its famed beauty. Visiting the grave of her good friend Walter Benjamin in Portbou in late 1940, Hannah Arendt exclaimed, "It is by far one of the most fantastic and most beautiful spots I have ever seen in my life." Yet she did not admire the landscape during her own—legal—flight. Such omissions are understandable from an emotional and a practical perspective. Even if they had noticed the beauty around them, refugees focused on border guards and expunged these landscapes of trauma from their memories. In addition, on a commemorative trek across the Pyrenees years later, a writer observed, "A really tough walk is an absolutely rotten way to enjoy a landscape; you tend to keep your head down and your eyes on the boots in front, concentrating on each step."[81]

Arriving at the Spanish Border

Having made it across the French border, the next hurdle loomed: the Spanish border, where unpredictability reigned. Franco's insistence on Spain's nonbelligerence during the war resulted in his police and intelligence services cooperating with the Gestapo and his wavering about border crossings. At first, it appeared that the Spanish would let in people without French exit visas as long as they held proper transit visas. In addition, refugees had to show that they had enough money to travel to Portugal.[82] Sometimes, showing leniency, Spain's border guards accepted either a Portuguese transit visa, proof of ship tickets, or a visa for a third country, but at other times they sent refugees back to France into the hands of Vichy and the Germans.

Later on, many refugees dealt with border guards who enforced or ignored rules randomly. The harried travelers could not see the whole picture—the guards' behavior often depended on decisions made in Madrid or on the course of the war, and those contingencies could vary the severity of treatment at the borders. Varian Fry saw the toll this unpredictability took on refugees. He wrote that the Spaniards "opened and closed the frontier again and again," making it "hard to imagine a crueler way of torturing human beings."[83]

Even those with legal papers faced scrutiny and arbitrariness. Guards asked for papers and then searched luggage. An American reporter observed that "the Spanish went through the luggage which the French and Germans had just inspected." One refugee couple, delayed six hours under a "blazing sun . . . no shade; there was a scorching hot wind, and smoke from occasional trains," watched as the "Spaniards turned every car inside out, ransacked every piece of baggage, and searched all occupants." The man concluded, "The real explanation of what was going on was . . . psychopathological, a kind of politically tinged sadism," even if the officials managed "to combine a devilish malice with smooth courtesy."[84]

Did border guards treat women differently from men? And if so, could this disparity work in their favor or endanger them? Two incidents offer some insight into gendered experiences. Marta Feuchtwanger, lacking a French exit visa, climbed the Pyrenees with a backpack full of cigarettes. In Marseille, the U.S. vice-consul, Hiram Bingham, had told her that one "could get a lot done in Spain with Camel cigarettes." She arrived at the Spanish customshouse, "tossed handfuls of packs onto the table," and asked with feigned naiveté whether it made sense to bring them over the border, given the customs fees. The border guards "jumped on the cigarettes and didn't even look at me." Twenty-five-year-old Miriam Stanton, on the other hand, feared that a guard had taken a sexual interest in her. As she waited for a Spanish border guard to examine her legal papers in the spring of 1941, she saw him return all the passports to people on her train. But he kept hers: "I had hardly started on my journey and now, was it over? . . . Nothing of me could move. . . . My heart was pounding and my mouth was very dry. I could hardly stand because my knees . . . were too weak to hold me up anymore."[85] The Spanish guard kept her waiting in order to ask her for a date and then wondered, "Did I frighten you?" By promising to meet up with him in Barcelona—which she reneged on—she managed to get her passport back and reboard her train. These anecdotes suggest that women may have had gendered experiences at the border. What we do know is that border guards wielded enormous power and that *all* refugees felt at their mercy.

If refugees with legal papers faced frightening borders, those with forged papers had even more to dread. At Portbou, the authors Franz Werfel and Heinrich Mann and their wives confronted this predicament after having avoided the French patrols while climbing the Pyrenees. Alma Mahler-Werfel recalled: "Like poor sinners we sat in a row on a narrow bench while our papers were checked against a card index. . . . Heinrich Mann was traveling with false papers. . . . After an agonizing wait we all got our papers back." The situation could get worse for young men. Two brothers, Jews born in Germany but with freshly minted Romanian letters "in lieu of passports," arrived at Portbou and showed their papers with "a collection of stamps, visas, and permits . . . a visa for the Republic of Panama, a Spanish and Portuguese transit visa." Their parents had paid handsomely for these documents. Both waited in terror as Spanish guards examined their documents. The Spanish government would have sent such men of military age back to Germany if it had known their true origins. Karl Paetel, a political refugee, had to rely on the momentary mood of Spanish guards after he had clambered around in the Pyrenees for thirty-four hours with his false passport. He feared he would not survive when Spanish border guards unexpectedly approached him: " 'Hands up!'—Strange, how one understands this order in every language, when a revolver underscores the . . . exclamation." Luckily, the guards let him pass. Friends of his had ended up in a Spanish prison camp.[86]

Those with some means but without the proper papers could try bribes. Aid workers and some refugees knew that many Spanish border guards took bribes or sold entry permits. Thousands of Jews, few of whom held Spanish transit visas, made it past Spain's borders, meaning that those with their own money or funds from aid groups had a better chance of passing than those without it. Willem Friedman, born in 1919 in The Hague, headed toward Portugal to meet his family. They had arrived there with visas provided by Portugal's consul in Bordeaux, Aristides de Sousa Mendes. First, Friedman had to get out of the German-occupied part of France into the Vichy zone. He managed to smuggle himself in a funeral cortege that crossed into Vichy. Without a French exit visa, he tried crossing into Spain. The Spanish police arrested him, but he successfully bribed the border patrol with money.[87]

When refugees did not have cigarettes or other valuables to use as bribes—and most did not—the unpredictability of border guards could prove lethal, as the fate of Walter Benjamin confirms. Having fled Germany in 1933 for exile in Paris, he headed southward as the German army invaded France. In Marseille, he received a U.S. entry visa and transit visas for Spain and Portugal. The French, however, refused him an exit visa. So in September 1940, led by the Resistance smuggler Lisa Fittko and accompanied by several others, he crossed the mountains, bypassed the French border, and arrived in Spain illegally. At Portbou, guards—possibly under Gestapo surveillance— refused to let him pass, since he could not produce a French exit visa. He took his life that night. The next day, his companions made their way to Spain. His friend, Hannah Arendt, wrote of his "uncommon stroke of bad luck."[88] A day earlier or a day later, he could have passed through. Precisely this kind of happenstance, depending on timing and luck, plagued refugees.

The next month, Anna Geyer and her child tried to cross the mountains several times. Their first attempt ended in failure: the French caught them and forced her to undergo a "terribly embarrassing" physical exam. Released the next morning, they tried again that same day, but got lost on a cold night high up in the mountains. Then they reached Spain, only to be sent back to France by the "abusive and mocking" Spanish patrols. By that time, they had not eaten in forty-eight hours, but managed to find soup in a border village. Six weeks later, they tried again—and finally succeeded— making it through a "breach in Hitler's invisible barrier." Similarly, another refugee tried to climb the mountains four times that November, facing an "icy wind" and storms that "knocked us over many times."[89]

Franco's stance on refugees crossing into Spain had grown increasingly opportunistic and unreliable by mid-1942 and early 1943. In early winter of 1943, young Frenchmen evading conscription into the German labor force fled to Spain. And Gestapo pressure at the border increased. Still, Spain occasionally cooperated with Jewish organizations. In 1943, for example, Joel Sequerra, stationed in Barcelona as a Portuguese representative of the JDC, received several hundred Jewish children sent by the French-Jewish Resistance: "We were constantly in contact with the Spanish border and when a group of Jews . . . had crossed the French-Spanish border illegally, we were notified. . . . After the Jewish refugees were kept there a few days to check their papers, they were freed and we took them to Barcelona." This desperate flow of refugees persisted through 1944, even after the Iberian countries had secured their borders more energetically. Small groups continued clambering over the "thorny and rocky" Pyrenees. Those who made it could breathe a sigh of relief; Paul K. recalled that all cheered when they crossed the Spanish border. But those sent back to France "felt hopeless, their money used up," and at the end of their rope: "Desperation. Suicidal feelings among many."[90]

Without the required papers or money, some refugees walked through Spain. In 1942, it took eleven-year-old Annette Finger and her parents three months. Fifty years later, she evoked the feelings of "having to walk at night in fear." One night as they tried to sleep in yet another barn, warmed by the breath of cows, she realized it was December and began to cry. Tired of running—"no home, no food, no clothes, no safety"—she declared, "It must be Hanukkah and we have no menorah." This moment turned into a lasting memory when her father responded: "What do you mean, we don't have a menorah, we have the most beautiful menorah in the world." Opening the barn door a crack, he said: "Pick out the shiniest star . . . That will be the shamas [the candle that lit the others] . . . Now find the other candles." And

Annette did so: "I found four on each side and we lit a menorah in the sky." This may have been the one bright spot in her wanderings, for she also recalled the sound of a dog barking as "one of the most painful sounds . . . the sound of domesticity, of normal life going on, and of thinking of children being tucked into bed, in real beds with a real blanket, having had a real supper." And she remembered thinking, "They just don't know how lucky they are." Arriving in "sunny" Portugal, she finally felt secure: "Nothing felt as good as the feeling that we were safe. We were now alive and were going to stay alive."[91]

Some, however, not lucky enough to make it to Portugal, faced incarceration in Spanish prisons, released only when a Jewish organization furnished the documents or paid to support their travel out of the country. The prisons provided the barest minimum of subsistence, but the rest of Spain faced starvation as well. One mother, Schendel Margosis, and her three teenagers endured such prisons. They had hired smugglers to take them over the Pyrenees soon after the Germans occupied southern France in 1942. Her forged safe-conduct papers got them as far as Barcelona. There the Civil Guard discovered them, confiscated their valuables, and imprisoned them. With his mother and sister in one prison, the fourteen-year-old boy waited in an orphanage until the JDC freed them about a week later. The older boy, remanded to Miranda de Ebro concentration camp, had to wait several weeks to join his family in Barcelona. In 1943, the youngest received a place on a children's transport out of Lisbon to the United States. The older teenagers joined Youth Aliyah and made it to Palestine, and the mother managed to get smuggled from Spain into Portugal in 1944. Other refugees learned that the Miranda camp meant brutality. Spanish guards arrested twenty-year-old Egon Bamberger from Germany for lack of proper papers. At Miranda, he endured regular beatings, had to sleep on the ground, and received inedible food. Luckily for him, his father paid a Portuguese diplomat $300 to bribe Spanish officials, who then released Egon from his six-week detention.[92]

Jews did not point to Spanish antisemitism as the source of their troubles. Indeed, the Nazi regime's consulate complained in 1941 and in 1943 of the weak development of antisemitism in Spain. But the Falangist press and individual party members did propagate antisemitism, and local antisemites harassed Jews. Further, on several occasions Franco denounced the "Jewish spirit" or the "Judeo-Masonic conspiracy."[93] He and his allies, moreover, targeted the "Left" and "Freemasonry" as enemies, and European antisemites had historically used both terms to mean "Jews." In general, Spain's regime sought to keep the number of its Jewish citizens—about 6,000—down and to move refugees through the country quickly. In addition, it sent about 500 refugees (not specifically Jews) without papers back across the border, to their possible doom.[94] Some historians argue that Spain could have saved more lives had it acted sooner, but it did let the vast majority of Jews transit. Between 35,000 and 80,000 refugees crossed Spain (scholars still debate how many) without being turned back, but of course refugees did not know the numbers as they grimly set out for the border.[95]

Jewish volunteers and the JDC in Barcelona and Madrid helped send needy refugees on their way. Many refugees traveled through Spain third class for two days in compartments on wooden benches facing each other. One such passenger reported "not very clean and terribly overcrowded" situations. He added: "What we did not realize was there were three more [Spanish] passengers hiding under the seats . . . and many police inspections." One refugee reported that Spain, too, used sealed trains, and that at every station stop Spanish soldiers lined up to make sure that refugees who stepped off the train to buy food did not leave the station. Refugees noticed suffering and destruction as they traveled on the trains. They expressed shock at the starvation and "indescribable poverty" they witnessed in the Spanish countryside, even as they rationed their own sparse provisions and bought some cheese and crackers that tasted like soap, but "no bread which could have stilled our hunger."[96] A sixteen-year-old at the time recalled: "Everyone would cry for bread." Spanish guards stopped a train traveling from Berlin to Portugal and demanded that all the passengers give up their bread before allowing the train to proceed.[97]

Observing the destruction in Madrid in March 1941, two brothers saw "bombed out and collapsed buildings one next to the other, not yet touched [since] the Civil War." Eugene Bagger traveled through "some of the more hopeless stretches of Dante's Inferno." And Alma Mahler-Werfel thought Spain looked like "one bleeding wound." The town of Irún, bombed and burned during the civil war, endured as a "ghastly heap of rubble, a city of inconsolable misery. And so is the whole country."[98] Driving through Spain, George Rony described "Franco's paradise": "Hollow shells of churches, roofless houses, scorched black earth plowed up by explosives." This "long wail of grief" ended at the border with Portugal. When Karl Paetel had to wait six hours in Badajoz for the train to Portugal, he asked another traveler whether he should see the sights. The man responded, "'Sights?' Poor people's housing and—ruins from the Civil War—that's it,'" adding that the Falange had shot all the men in town and that "Badajoz has remained . . . a city without men."[99]

Leaving Spain, few remarked on the bleak, dry landscape between Madrid and the Portuguese border, known as Extremadura. Once again, even those with adequate visas faced long waits: "The Spanish customs-house officers seemed to be of the opinion that the refugees needed just that little extra touch to make them never wish to see Spain again, and took a sadistic pleasure in their examination of the cars passing into Portugal." Moreover, the officials interspersed car searches with inspections of passenger trains. Those who came by car or on foot could walk around while waiting, but the train travelers "were locked up in their carriages, many of them with nothing to eat or drink, and kept there for hours." Elisabeth Bab made it past the Spanish guards, but those same Spanish guards sent back an unlucky passenger whose visa had just expired. Moreover, those who had arrived illegally needed to avoid the customs areas entirely or else try to bribe the guards. Cigarettes did the job once again. An official at the British Embassy in Madrid gave a Jewish refugee some escudos and "several packages of good English cigarettes," which he might need to "bribe [his] way across the [Spanish-Portuguese] frontier."[100]

Entering Portugal

Having successfully traversed Spain by showing proper papers, climbing the Pyrenees, begging for mercy, or bribing guards, refugees met more obstacles at Portugal's border. Neither legal papers nor a train ride guaranteed entry, since guards vacillated in accordance with their government's changing policies. On June 24, 1940, after a thirty-six-hour trip, Jan Lustig's train came to a complete halt at the Portuguese border town of Vilar Formoso. Police locked the doors: "The Portuguese don't seem certain as to what to do with us." Rumors flew: "We would have to stay in the train a few days, we would be sent back to France, or we would be locked up in a concentration camp." They had no light in the train, no food, and nothing to drink. About fifteen hours later, the Portuguese freed them but soon informed them that they could not enter Lisbon. Instead, after another long delay, the officials sent them to small villages, and the Lustigs wound up in Figueira da Foz, arriving at two in the morning. Fear, thirst, and hunger notwithstanding, they had achieved their goal. The author Marguerite Douhaerdt summed up these escapes in a letter to a friend: "I could write a novel about the situation and the dangers of the past five months."[101]

More ominously, a train with 290 Jews expelled from Luxembourg made it to Vilar Formoso in November 1940. There the Portuguese police held the train for eight days. These refugees coped with "impossible sanitary conditions" and, no doubt, increasing dread.[102] Then the police forced the train to return to Bayonne, France. There, the German military took charge of the terrified refugees. The commander requisitioned an old factory and cots for the Jews, who remained there for many weeks in the cold. According to Ernest P. from Vienna, it felt "kind of like a camp." The French authorities had provided them with "what we call food," mostly beets, that refugees prepared in garbage cans. Relatively "lucky" with their German commander, they appreciated that he let them buy food on the black market. They hung their provisions on lines from the ceiling, but "the black river rats had a picnic with us" and got the food anyway. Sardonically, Mr. P. referred to them as "house pets." From the vantage point of 1988, when he gave his interview, the experience sounded like—and maybe felt like—a misadventure with unpleasant side effects. But a letter of January 1941 from Albert Nussbaum, who had headed the Jewish community of Luxembourg and then directed the Transmigration Bureau of the JDC in Lisbon, referred to the "desperation" of these refugees in Bayonne. Although the Gestapo pushed for their imprisonment in the Gurs internment camp, Jewish organizations managed to bring most of them to Marseille. There, Ernest P. and his wife could not find a room and finally took a spot between two staircases, "happy to stay there." They suffered from hunger: "Sometimes we got horse meat, which was a holiday!" but only "very seldom."[103] Finally, Jewish organizations helped them get to Portugal again.

Sometimes frustration and fear at the border turned into rage and imagined violence. One family had left Berlin on a train with all the appropriate papers. With very little money, they rode third class in unheated wagons and were ravenous as they arrived at the Portuguese border. Even though they had legitimate, carefully gathered, and expensive documents, the Portuguese patrols turned them back. Faced with a border official "cold as a dog's snout," the infuriated father fantasized: "Should I punch this official in the face so that blood spurts from his nose and mouth? Had I been alone, I would have done that without thinking of the consequences. I might still be sitting in jail now and the official might still be in the hospital." Finally, after almost a month spent mostly in Spanish jails, the family could make its way to Portugal in January 1942.[104] Revenge remained a fantasy.

Forged documents could lead to serious problems. Portuguese border guards frequently arrested suspect persons and sometimes sent them back to Spain. Felix Oppenheim, the refugee who had been trapped on the bridge between France and Spain, tried to avoid the Spanish-Portuguese border by taking a flight from Madrid to Lisbon. His very first—and very expensive—flight failed. The Portuguese passport control agent announced, "That visa is a fake," and remanded him to an airport jail, a cell "without window or bed." He had to take the next plane back to Madrid at "my own, and high, expense." A few other refugees, too, faced expulsion on Portuguese runways, since that simply meant putting them on the next return flight. This could mean capture upon landing. Still, refugees with false or inadequate papers did get through. When thirteen-year-old Rudolf Graf and his Viennese family arrived on the Portuguese side of the border, the Portuguese guards claimed they had improper visas and refused to let his family in. He got very sick at the border, and the "Portuguese took pity" on him and allowed him to pass.[105]

Those with inadequate papers had to make quick decisions. Nadia Gould's family hired smugglers: "Our guides . . . were real smugglers who only occasionally took people like us across the river into Portugal. They preferred to smuggle merchandise which was a more lucrative and less risky venture." The smugglers "were annoyed with my father who had conveniently forgotten to tell them there would be children in our group." Extra money calmed the situation. The smugglers knew the routines of the border police but nervously eyed the two-year-old and fed her caramels so that she would remain silent. The family had to bend low as the smugglers paddled them down the river: "We could hear each other['s] heartbeats." Finally reaching Portugal, they came to a house, where the smugglers fed them sardines and dry bread. In Lisbon, they "met other refugees like us"—from "all over Europe" and without papers.[106] Ultimately, the Quakers sent Nadia to the United States with a children's transport. Illegal papers and smugglers saved many lives like Nadia's.

Children Arriving on Their Own

Unlike Nadia, some Jewish children undertook hazardous escapes alone or in groups. They came from Germany or from Western nations under German occupation and had grown up under terrifying conditions. Even little ones had sensed the danger around them, although they did not always understand it. In France, frightened children heard or saw Jews being arrested, they listened to forbidden radio broadcasts quietly, and one woman recalled that her "parents whispered to each other about the horrible rumors and what happened to people: one jumped from the window, the other was arrested, etc." Contemplating her childhood in Vienna decades later, Ruth Kluger began her memoir with the revelation, "Their secret was death, not sex. That's what the grown-ups were talking about, sitting up late around the table."[107]

Many children dreaded uncertain and threatening situations. Luckily, some headed for safety after the November Pogrom. About 8,000–10,000 Jewish children from Germany, Austria, Czechoslovakia, and the Polish borderlands near Germany managed to escape via the *Kindertransports* (children's transports), which started in December 1938. These unaccompanied children from major cities in central Europe took group trains to ports in Holland and Belgium, after which they sailed to England. The last *Kindertransport* from Germany ended with the outbreak of war, and the last one from Holland left on May 14, 1940, when the Dutch army surrendered to Germany.

Jews in France had no access to *Kindertransports*. But thousands of Jewish refugee families there sent their children to orphanages or to the Resistance. Initially, the French-Jewish OSE (Oeuvre de Secours aux Enfants, or Organization to Save the Children) gathered many of the children, including some from the Gurs internment camp, and cared for them.[108] And in June 1940 when Clarence Pickett of the Quakers established a nonsectarian committee to save refugee children—mostly Jewish—from Europe and bring them to the United States, the OSE safely transferred those children to the Quakers. Supported by Eleanor Roosevelt and the JDC, USCOM (United States Committee for the Care of European Children) functioned in Vichy France until America entered the war. It saved close to 800 Jewish children, bringing them to Spain and Portugal before they proceeded to the United States.

One example illustrates the arduous process that the children endured. In June 1941, USCOM helped 101 unaccompanied children escape from southern France to the United States via Lisbon. The Quakers selected the children in France, choosing between the neediest and those who might make a better impression in America. One social worker later compared the process to interviews for a Rhodes Scholarship, terrifying the applicants. The Quakers provided the children with clothes, vaccination certificates, and collective passports and found them ship passage. The trip took days in a dirty train in which the social workers had to tie the doors closed and keep the children away from broken windows. Then they endured long waits at the Spanish border. Many children got sick, skin infections flared because of a lack of washing facilities, and one child developed acute appendicitis. Arriving in a small Portuguese border town, the children had "the first excellent meal . . . and it greatly impressed all the children. . . . The children did not believe such food existed."[109] Many had suffered separation from their families and deprivation in the camps. Morris C. Troper, chair of the European Executive Committee of the JDC noted: "As they arrived, they looked like tired, wan, broken, little old men and women. None dared to laugh aloud and few smiled. . . . Their clothes were in tatters." Philip Conard of the Quakers in Lisbon agonized: "Of course the whole thing is a heart-breaking tragedy, as each of the youngsters represents the salvage of a horrible experience."[110]

During their one-week stay in a children's camp sponsored by the newspaper *O Século,* the adults who accompanied them praised the "generosity, kindness and comprehension" that the Portuguese and, especially, the editor of the newspaper showed the children. He and his family came by every day, visited the kitchens and dormitories, and asked whether the children needed anything.[111] Yet the children, without their parents or old friends, remained anxious. American social workers remarked: "After their experiences of the last few years, they simply didn't know how to relax. They played grimly as though expecting that at any moment the sun, the beach, the food and this new unaccustomed liberty would be snatched from them and they would be thrown back into the misery and distress from which they have escaped." The aid workers predicted: "They will arrive in New York a bit bronzed and looking fit," even though it would take much longer to "erase the imprints of their bitter experiences." Two additional groups of children arrived in Lisbon in the summer of 1941 and sailed to the United States in September.[112]

The Quakers in Portugal looked back on their days of helping the USCOM children with mixed feelings. Although happy to have helped, they nonetheless reflected, "It was one hell of a rat race!!! Our office was like the hallway around the Campo Pequeno on bullfight day! With typewriters going in three rooms, interviewing buzzing along in various corners, interviewers running frantically to and fro looking for interviewees, for pencils, for blanks . . . Children were bewildered by it all." Overwhelmed by the problems they had managed to tackle, Conard concluded: "When one remembers all the difficulties in the way of success for this audacious venture in child saving, it seems that nothing but a series of miracles can have made it possible."[113]

The rescue of children continued well into the war. In 1941 and 1942, the Quakers chose Jewish children from children's homes and refugee camps in southern France for USCOM to send to the United States. Underground groups continued sporadically to help them escape. As late as June 1944, one guide led a group of five children and teens over the Pyrenees. One of them, Gisela Edel, born in Stettin, Germany, and on her own for four years since the age of twelve, had hidden in children's homes in France and in a convent-run old-age home. Elisabeth Hirsch, an OSE operative, escorted a different group over the Pyrenees to Spain in August 1944. The icy mountain temperatures tormented the twelve children, ages eight to fourteen, as well as the five adults and the six guides. They lost their way, but finally reached Spain. The Spanish guards interrogated them, and the JDC facilitated their further escape to Lisbon in October.[114]

Also in 1944, Isaac Weissmann of the World Jewish Congress (in Lisbon) organized the smuggling of children, ranging in age from five to fourteen, from France into Portugal. His use of clandestine political contacts and illegal methods, including forged identification cards and birth certificates, alarmed the more legally-minded JDC and the local Jewish community in Lisbon. Weissmann's planning brought in small groups of children led by professional smugglers. The children's clothing and shoes did not protect them adequately from the mountain cold, but they arrived safely. Most had lost contact with their parents and siblings. Weissmann had received permission to have three hundred children pass through Portugal at a time, meaning that the first group had to transmigrate before the second group could enter the country. Hundreds of these children headed to Palestine, the destination that Weissmann had hoped for, and dozens traveled to relatives in the United States.[115]

Two Ominous Odysseys

The perilous journeys of two Jewish refugees best capture the panic, privation, and sheer unpredictability of these escapes. Despite their differences in age, gender, nationality, and politics, these individuals highlight landscapes and sites that evoked fear or relief as they struggled to move westward. Emil Gumbel, born in 1891, fled Germany and then France with his wife and child;

Margit Meissner, born in 1922, left Prague and later joined the exodus from Paris with her mother.

Gumbel, a Jewish pacifist, socialist, arch-opponent of the Nazis, and formerly a professor of mathematics at the University of Heidelberg, had opposed Hitler for years before the Nazis came to power.[116] The Nazis, in turn, despised Gumbel for having chronicled political murders by right-wing fanatics and for identifying the judges who acquitted them during the Weimar Republic. When Hitler took power, Gumbel happened to be out of Germany. As a Jew, but even more so as an early anti-Nazi, he could not return. He received asylum and later citizenship in France, teaching in Paris and Lyon. But when the Germans invaded, Gumbel fled again. As the "noise of the [German] guns became always louder," he, his wife, and her small son "over-loaded" their car and drove until dark, when they paid a peasant to let them rest on some straw. Two nerve-racking weeks passed. They slept on floors, gas grew scarcer, the car broke down, and the German army kept getting closer. Finally, they arrived in Marseille. There Gumbel faced typical bureau-cratic hurdles: he spent five or six hours a day on line at consulates, "in order to state my case to the officials in one or two minutes, and then get no answer." This was maddening: "This waiting was much worse for the nerves than the bombing or fleeing had been." Rumors tormented him, too: "The Germans will enter Marseille; the Germans have occupied the Spanish border." More-over, he assumed that the Nazis had a special enemies list that included his name, and he knew that Gestapo agents had fanned out into France. He grew a beard to disguise himself—"my fear of death actually grew that beard."

In August, the American Federation of Labor provided him with a temporary U.S. visa—but that meant separating from his family, since he faced immediate peril. He confronted the difficult choice of leaving his wife and child in order to ensure his own safety. (His wife, the daughter of a German general, and her son from a first marriage, hence both "Aryans," did not face arrest, and they followed the next year.) He needed a steamship ticket, a Portuguese transit visa, a Spanish transit visa, and permission to leave France. He spent weeks securing these permissions; just as he left France, the Spanish border closed. The next day, after a full body search at the border, he journeyed on to Barcelona and then Madrid. He avoided staying in hotels, afraid of having his name reported to the authorities, and he ate sparsely because of the scarcity of food. At the Portuguese border, he had to give up his passport. For six hours, he suppressed mounting panic, terrified that the border guards had telephoned the Gestapo. Entering Portugal, he heard rumors of Nazis crossing into Spain, but "slept twelve hours and ate three times as much as [he] could stand."[117]

Margit Meissner left Prague for Paris in 1938 at the age of sixteen. Fearing Nazi aggression, her mother had resolved to send her daughter to safer grounds. She also insisted that Margit learn dressmaking, more useful in most lands than her ability to speak Czech, French, English, and German. Her three brothers had also scattered around the world. In May 1940, her mother joined her, but the French police ordered the older woman to turn herself in at an assembly point in the South. A month later Germany invaded France, and the now eighteen-year-old fled Paris on her bicycle. Learning that the French had imprisoned her mother at Gurs, she went to a town near the camp. During the confusion of these months, some internees managed to escape Gurs, and she and her mother found each other.

The two women entered "the chaos that was Marseille." In a run-down area near the Old Port, they rented a room with a shared toilet in a bordello.[118] Using her housekeeping skills resourcefully, her mother turned their little balcony into "an outdoor kitchen" with a tiny stove. She sold these meals to other refugees. But this woman from a wealthy bourgeois background "became totally paralyzed" when she learned that she might have to bribe or lie to get a visa. The mother's passivity launched a difficult role reversal for mother and daughter. Margit alone approached every consulate, finally winding up with a visa to the Belgian Congo. In addition, she applied to the Czech consulate for papers in her "flawless" Czech, even though she and her mother had been born in Austria. With these papers, she received Spanish and Portuguese transit visas, but the French refused to issue the crucial exit visas.

Having spent all their money, they borrowed some from Varian Fry in Marseille. Still they grew increasingly desperate as the expiration dates of their Spanish and Portuguese visas loomed. They decided to cross the border illegally at Cerbère and took a train: "Close to the border the police checks became more frequent. At one point a severe-looking gendarme . . . was almost at our seats; just then the train entered the station. . . . We darted out of the train and quickly hopped back on at the rear. . . . Another time we hid in the toilet." When they reached the border, the French guards asked for their exit visas: "We told him that yesterday the border police had let Czech women cross . . . without exit permits. He said 'that was yesterday; today is today.'" Watching their train depart without them, the two women stood "alone and despondent." Here, again, Margit's mother appeared totally "passive and uninvolved." Margit was forced to find a solution: "The absent, expressionless look on Mother's face made me realize that I was now truly responsible for both of us. She who had always been a pillar of strength now relied on me entirely." Perhaps sympathizing with the two women, a young man suggested that they find a particular person in Cerbère who might help them. The latter gave them directions for climbing the Pyrenees toward Portbou, which they succeeded in doing. But since they had crossed illegally, despite their transit visas, the Spanish border guards refused to let them pass. Terrified, they knew they faced deportation back to France. However, the Spanish police, possibly taking pity on the women, decided to imprison them instead.

In Gerona, one of the major Catalan cities, both Meissner women shared a prison cell with dozens of women sleeping two to a cot. The latrines, "mere holes in the ground," caused a terrible stench. At five in the morning, the guards forced them to rise and sing the fascist anthem. Those with cups received ersatz coffee, but the two Jewish women had none. Later two "simply dressed country women" gave them "a life-saving cup and spoon" for the thin soup ladled out at lunch. Most of the women in the prison had opposed Franco or worked as prostitutes. The latter helped Meissner out of another quandary. They gave her washable sanitary napkins: "What a precious gift! They had saved me from a terrible predicament. But how ironic that I, who never expected to meet or talk to a prostitute anywhere, found myself eternally grateful to these two women and in awe of their generosity." After about a week, friends managed to free them from jail and extend their legal stay in Spain and Portugal. Their odyssey took about four months from Paris to Lisbon. "Multiple exiles," both Gumbel and Meissner fled first to Paris, hoping to stay, and then to Portugal. Yet even when they reached physical safety, their emotional turmoil continued as they sought to reestablish their lives.[119]

In their memoirs and diaries, refugees voice one consistent, powerful, and enduring feeling about the physical, logistical, and emotional sites along their journey: anxiety. Roads, lines, and borders—Holocaust landscapes—frightened and hindered them. Many experienced the unceasing tension between the desperate need to flee and the endless agony of waiting. They had stood on lines to leave their homelands, and those lines grew even longer as the war went on. Human vulnerability came up against unfeeling bureaucracies and all-powerful border guards. Ultimately, some of those who reached Portugal did so with the help of forged documents, smugglers, or their own daring. Still, their terrifying escapes from occupied Europe haunted them, and Portugal refused them indefinite sanctuary. These refugees could not rest. They needed to get out of Europe.

2. The Exasperations and Consolations of Refugee Life After 1940

Fear of Portugal's Regime and Appreciation of Its People

> Given the war we have come from . . . she found it in herself to
> [share her house with five refugees]. . . . It has given us an amazing
> impression of people. It has lifted our spirits, given us hope.

Portugal, an interim site between danger and safety, evoked feelings of relief and frustration among refugees. Although the police harassed them, the Portuguese people showed remarkable hospitality. The wary refugees stood at a point where Salazar's grudging minions and generous peasants and towns-people intersected. Mixed messages abounded. The refugees had arrived at an ambivalent respite that left them bewildered. And these refugees stood at another intersection as well. Portugal served as "a playground for every possible intelligence service," an intense and nervous site where the Gestapo and British military intelligence roamed the streets.[1] Having reached ostensible, but temporary, safety, harried refugees endured an incomprehensible, unpredictable haven that heightened their anxieties but also their hopes.

Portugal, a Peaceful Purgatory

During World War II, 40,000–100,000 refugees—of whom 90 percent were Jewish by religion or "race"—migrated through Portugal to the Western Hemisphere, Africa, Great Britain, and Palestine. With the onset of the war, the Portuguese government provided a reluctant sanctuary. Its dictator,

António de Oliveira Salazar, had never planned to offer even momentary shelter to refugees, but they came anyway. The Portuguese government pushed refugees to leave, but allowed the small Jewish community in Lisbon and international groups to assist the newcomers. Most arrived from Europe, but others left France by boat to Oran in Algeria and made their way to Casablanca in Morocco, always, like the characters in *Casablanca*, hoping to get to Lisbon. Thousands with the skimpiest documentation, including visas to China, the Belgian Congo, and Siam, found temporary safety in Portugal.[2]

Portugal initially demonstrated generosity toward those entering its borders. Proclaiming formal neutrality on September 2, 1939, one day after Hitler attacked Poland, the small country first "reap[ed] a refugee harvest" of North and South Americans escaping Europe. These sudden guests spent money in Lisbon during their short stays and gained quick access to ships headed toward home. Portugal's tourist trade boomed. Its hotels, casinos, beaches, and cafés entertained "wealthy but homeless people" from all parts of Europe and from both warring sides, some of whom remained for the duration of the war.[3] Jewish refugees, however, including rather well-known central European authors and scholars such as Franz Werfel, Arthur Koestler, and Hannah Arendt, had to produce transit visas to show that they would move on.

Then, on November 11, 1939, Portugal publicized Circular #14, a decree stating that applications for transit visas would be decided in Lisbon, not in more lenient Portuguese consulates abroad. Even more stringent than the earlier Circular #10, the new regulations barred certain foreigners, described as being "of undefined, contested or disputed nationality, stateless persons, bearers of Nansen passports," and Russians, as well as "Jews expelled from the country of their nationality or from those they come from." Whereas immigration circulars had previously mentioned nationalities, Circulars #10 and #14 specified Jews for the first time. Attempting to stem the tide, the secret police, or PVDE (Polícia de Vigilância e Defesa do Estado, Police of Vigilance and State Defense), had already, in May 1940, blocked some who held valid visas.[4] Thereafter, consulates could issue transit visas only to people who had visas and ship or plane tickets to a third country. As Germany occupied part of France in June 1940, the Portuguese regime decreed that its consuls abroad could no longer provide visas and promulgated Circular #23, harsher yet than the earlier ones. Only the PVDE, rather than the Ministry of Foreign Affairs, could now review applications for visas. Salazar did not want Portugal to become a "dumping ground" for refugees. Yet in October 1940, the German consul in Lisbon wrote

Berlin that any foreigner could start a business in Portugal; although the Portuguese police considered Jews "undesirable," they could still open shops.[5]

The government also sporadically closed its borders to train traffic. In August and October 1940, two large groups of Jews expelled from Luxembourg faced barriers at the border until Augusto d'Esaguy, of the Lisbon Jewish community, intervened for them. And as we have seen, in November the Portuguese frontier guards trapped a group of close to 300 Luxembourger Jews on their train, eventually forcing them back to Bayonne, France, from where some managed to sneak into Portugal.[6] By December, the PVDE was reviewing all transit visas.[7] In late 1940, Spain began refusing to take refugees back, and Portugal changed its policy and stopped rejecting Jews at the border.

Time and the war made a difference. In April 1941, Portugal announced it would not issue transit visas to those heading to the Americas, but then lifted that ban in May. With America's entry into the war, the Portuguese government, assuming that refugees would not be able to find safe passage across the Atlantic, again suspended transit visas temporarily. Once the war turned decisively against Germany at Stalingrad (in the winter of 1942–43), Portugal relented again, allowing refugees in and opening its borders at irregular intervals. Indeed, by December 1942 the *Christian Science Monitor* reported that the "sympathetic and understanding Portuguese authorities" would give "all clandestine refugees . . . either in hiding or in prison" full legal status as transit travelers. The decision affected hundreds of people of different nationalities and religions who had escaped from occupied Europe. This solution reportedly had the support of Salazar. Those who came illegally and had the misfortune of being arrested might nevertheless occasionally benefit from Portuguese consideration: in 1943, a New Year's directive pardoned refugees in prison, granting them a thirty-day transit visa and releasing them to the village of Ericeira under the care of the JDC (American Jewish Joint Distribution Committee). Despite these contradictory policies, refugees continued to arrive.[8] They had no choice.

The Portuguese government held firm with regard to one situation: it refused to allow refugees into its colonies. Leaders as prominent as Franklin Roosevelt discussed proposals to settle refugee Jews in the Portuguese colonies of Angola and Mozambique. But those leaders did not consult Portugal, just as they had not invited Portugal to the Évian conference in 1938. Salazar's government opposed British and American interests in populating its colonies. Salazar's stance stood in marked contrast to that of Portugal's First Republic, which he had toppled and which had shown interest in populating Angola with white settlers—in that case, Jews. Salazar saw the colonies as central to Portuguese collective identity.[9] Hoping to spread Catholicism, opposing miscegenation, and intending to "civilize" the colonies, his regime had no intention of settling Jews there. Further, instability in the colonies caused concern, and the Portuguese leadership concentrated on containing those areas, not on adding new immigrants.[10] With the outbreak of World War II, the Portuguese regime resisted not only settlement in, but even passage through, its colonies. Portugal under Salazar showed greater antipathy toward refugees entering its colonies than to those coming to Portugal itself.

Because of Portugal's contradictory but relatively liberal practices, by mid-1940 it had transformed itself into the "fire escape of Europe." That October, the American journalist William Shirer logged in his diary that Lisbon served as "the one remaining port on the Continent from which you can get a boat or a plane to New York."[11] Floods of harried refugees arrived; they "shot out of the ground like mushrooms after the rain," and the "town had become an enormous rooming house." The next month an English visitor could find only a cellar room in "jammed" Lisbon. The journalist Eugen Tillinger conveyed his findings in the *Aufbau*. Addressing his mostly middle-class readership, he evoked better times as he compared Lisbon to high season at the Salzburg Festival, when, overflowing with music and drama lovers, hotels rented out bathrooms and laid mattresses in hallways. More darkly, Arthur Koestler, who tried to get to England in the fall of 1940, referred to Lisbon as the "last open gate of a concentration camp."[12]

While tens of thousands soon continued their exodus by boat or plane, Lisbon housed 8,000–10,000 refugees in December 1940, many of whom held useless visas. Refugee numbers ebbed and flowed with the tides of the war. In early June 1941, about 14,000 Jewish refugees required shelter, and the Lisbon Jewish community increased its expenditures for refugees from $400 to $10,000 in just four weeks. At that moment, the Nazis directly or indirectly controlled most of Europe with the exception of Sweden, Switzerland, Spain, and Portugal. In the West, Britain stood alone in the battle against Hitler's armies.[13] A few weeks later, 3.9 million Nazi troops invaded the Soviet Union. By early 1942, only about 800 refugees remained in Lisbon, most having found the visas and ships to leave, but that figure rose again to 10,000 with the German invasion of southern France that fall. Overall, the fluctuation in the number of those unable to leave Portugal was as follows:

December 1940, 8,000–10,000
June 1941, 14,000
Early 1942, 800
Late 1942, 10,000
Mid-1945, 1,000[14]

Salazar and Neutrality

Salazar, formerly a university professor of economic policy, ruled his authoritarian "New State" (Estado Novo) from 1932 until 1968. He also assumed
the role of foreign minister and minister of war between 1936 and 1945,
stressing Portugal's neutrality. His government's shifts in refugee policy
formed one part of its delicate balancing act of maintaining wartime
neutrality. He and his minions believed that the country's stability and
precarious economic situation could seriously deteriorate if it entered the
war. Observers at the U.S. mission concluded that "Portugal transformed
from a fairly stable and well settled authoritarian regime exercising little, if
any, influence in world affairs, into a country throbbing with the stresses and
strains placed upon its neutrality by the belligerent powers."[15]

Salazar had led a very insular life. As a young man, he left Portugal only
once—to attend a Catholic Congress in Belgium—and as Portugal's leader he
left his country one more time, to meet Franco at the Portuguese-Spanish frontier. He carefully monitored international politics and the ideological debates
of his times, upholding "God, Fatherland, Family and Work" and opposing the
infiltration of modern, secular, and democratic ideas. Fearing and despising
communism and leftist parties in general, he subjected them to severe repression. He also harbored suspicions of all aliens, Jewish and non-Jewish, as
possible liberals and leftists who might destabilize his regime. In February 1938,
a pamphlet announcing a competition for the "most Portuguese village in
Portugal" began with its mission: "to combat, using all available means, the
entry into our country of any worrisome ideas that might fragment national
unity." The government intended to idealize rural life and the virtues of the
peasantry, "who have not suffered harmful foreign influences."[16]

Although he mistrusted foreigners, Salazar himself did not express
antisemitism. His regime made distinctions based on perceived notions of
race in its colonial empire, but at home Salazar did not subscribe to the raciali-
zation of religion. Citizenship meant political and legal status. Salazar even

critiqued the Nazis' Nuremberg race laws of 1935 in his book of essays, *Como se Levanta um Estado* (*How to Raise a State*, 1937). These laws defined any German with three Jewish grandparents as a Jew and created an inferior form of citizenship for Jews, making them "subjects" of the state. The laws further prohibited "racially" mixed sexual relationships. In his book, Salazar lamented that German nationalism highlighted racial characteristics and warned that making a distinction between citizen and subject would have dangerous consequences. Following this line of thought, the Portuguese government treated Jewish refugees originally of Portuguese nationality differently from Jews of other nationalities, constricting the actions only of the latter.[17]

Similarly, Salazar sent a telegram to Portugal's envoy in Berlin in July 1938 in an attempt to protect Portuguese Jews in the Reich after the government had demanded lists of their possessions. He asked that the envoy alert the German authorities "that in our constitution there is no difference between citizens of the Jewish race (*Rasse*) and others," so that the Portuguese government felt as duty-bound to protect Jews as it did any other of its citizens. And when Brazil refused visas to Portuguese Jews, Salazar's government protested, arguing that Portuguese Jews "enjoy equal rights" and that discrimination against them meant discrimination against all Portuguese. Salazar also privately told an Italian minister that if the Nazis won, "Hitler, drunk with victory, would Germanise Europe," adding that Hitler's soldiers "carry a neo-paganism of mystic and racist origin that is contrary to our Roman and Catholic traditions."[18]

In Salazar's political rise, he did not scapegoat Jews. He came to power in 1932, at a time of virulent antisemitism in Europe, without endorsing it. Although he ruthlessly suppressed communists and regularly opposed "liberals" and "republicans"—terms that could have been interpreted as code words for "Jews"—he did not use expressions like "Judeo-Bolshevik" or "world Jewry," as did many European fascists. Even Portuguese fascist groups like the Blue Shirts shunned the antisemitism rampant in northern Europe. They admired Hitler, yet did not oppose Jews entering Portugal to escape his violence. Indeed, Salazar's government not only rejected modern racial antisemitism but also accepted Judaism. The few dozen Portuguese Jews in Porto, Portugal's second-largest city, officially established a Jewish community there in 1923. As refugees came to Porto, its Jewish leaders rented space for another synagogue in 1938. The Porto synagogue held Sephardic services, and the refugee synagogue followed Ashkenazi rituals. The following year, when Samuel Schwarz, a Jewish author and mining engineer, restored the fifteenth-century synagogue of Tomar and donated it to the Portuguese state, the government agreed to support it as a museum.[19] Then, in the 1940s, the Shaaré Tikvah (Gates of Hope) synagogue in Lisbon, consecrated in 1904, underwent major restoration. Had Salazar, Jesuit-trained and deeply religious, objected to these synagogues, the Jewish community could not have restored or established them.[20]

Salazar never married and had a minuscule circle of friends and advisers. But he had a close Jewish colleague, Moses Amzalak, who may have influenced him. A prominent economist from a well-known Jewish family, Amzalak served as vice-rector and, later, provost of the Technical University of Lisbon, president of the Academy of Science, and a leader of the Jewish community for fifty-two years, until his death in 1978. Amzalak typified the community's religious identity. Its members insisted on their religious distinctiveness while underlining their Portuguese culture and nationality. Walking a tightrope, Amzalak willingly assisted refugees already in Portugal but did not attempt to rescue Jews facing danger abroad. Additionally, like his powerful friend, he detested communism and saw the Nazis as defending Europe from it. In the mid-1930s, at a time when he must have known about Hitler's antisemitic screeds and decrees, he even accepted a medal of excellence from the German Red Cross.[21]

By 1938, Amzalak understood the danger of Nazism. Very likely, his institutional role, friendship with Salazar, and personal antipathies influenced his changing opinions. At all times, however, he offered major assistance to Jews and Jewish aid organizations in Portugal. And the paper he co-owned, O Século, one of Portugal's major daily papers, published sympathetic photos of refugee orphan children enjoying their time at an O Século children's camp in Portugal. Indeed, although Salazar was alarmed that newspapers would bring attention to the refugees, and censors tried to limit news about refugees, O Século printed some stories. Rumors within the Portuguese Jewish community suggested that the Portuguese police often closed their eyes to false visas because Amzalak and Salazar had agreed on a strategy. The police would arrest refugees with false or no papers, but would not deport them. Instead, the police freed some refugees after a few days or weeks and sent them to fixed residences—small fishing villages used like holding pens—that they could not leave.[22] In other words, Salazar, full of contradictions, did not harm Jewish refugees, but also did not want them.

Even if Salazar was not concerned about Jewishness, his regime evinced anxiety about immigration. Geography played a role here. One could not simply pass through Portugal; it lay at the very edge of Europe. As one refugee put it, "We had two alternatives, either to go back eastwards or into the deep blue sea." The economy mattered as well. The small Portuguese middle class worried about business competition from Jewish refugees. Leaders wondered whether Portugal, historically a nation of emigrants, could absorb huge numbers of refugees. Between the mid-nineteenth and the mid-twentieth centuries, nearly two million Portuguese emigrated to the United States and Brazil in search of economic opportunity. By 1940, this outflow had left a population of about 7,722,000.[23]

At first the Portuguese economy benefited from the influx of refugees and foreign currency. Additionally, collection of a Portuguese embarkation tax helped fill state coffers.[24] But by the 1940s, prices had begun to rise as demand exceeded supply. In 1942, Britain's precautionary purchases of sardines, tungsten, animal hides, and wool products, as well as its naval blockade limiting goods into Nazi-controlled Europe, caused inflation. By 1943, the cost of Portugal's main staples such as sardines and *bacalhau* (salted dried cod) had doubled; by 1944, sardine prices had tripled. That year an American reporter noticed that some foods had become scarce and that "there is a black market for everything." By midyear the government had begun rationing staples.[25]

Salazar's interest in stabilizing the domestic economy worked in tandem with his desire to stay out of war. Six months before the war, Portugal had minimized the peninsula's vulnerability by signing the "Iberian Pact," a Treaty of Friendship and Non-Aggression with Spain. Salazar and Franco agreed to respect each other's borders and to refuse assistance to any nation that attacked either of them. His neutrality as a "self-interested noncombatant" paid "handsome dividends," boosting the Portuguese economy despite inflation. Further, Portugal had political and economic ties to England. An alliance dating back to the fourteenth century (1373, 1386) had been renewed in 1899. Britain and Portugal also maintained a centuries-old commercial relationship, valuable to each side (though less so for Portugal).[26] Portugal also depended on American oil, iron, and steel, among other supplies. Both warring sides relied on Portuguese tungsten, used to harden steel for armaments and machine tools. In 1942, Portugal supplied more tungsten than any other European nation.[27] Germany paid with looted gold and used bribes and smugglers, but, in the end, received less tonnage than the Allies. Portugal ranked second to Switzerland in the amount of looted gold it received from the Nazi government.[28]

The warring countries had more at stake than tungsten. Covert Allied and Axis schemes in Portugal could have made material for a spy thriller. An American reporter in Lisbon regarded the Aviz hotel as an American haunt and the Palacio Hotel in Estoril as accommodating "Gestapo men, all in civilian clothes but painfully German in their movements." Refugees, too, warned each other that the Gestapo roamed Lisbon. Walter Schellenberg, who later in the war headed the German Foreign Intelligence Service (of the Reichssicherheitshauptamt, or RSHA, the Reich Main Security Office and a division of the SS), came to Lisbon to inspect a villa that sent secret information to Berlin. He also took photos of the harbor while having other spies pose as tourists.[29] Dubbing Lisbon a "seething cauldron of espionage and counter-espionage," George Kennan, counselor to the American diplomatic mission (legation) in mid-1942, coordinated American intelligence activities there. The African-American dancer and actress Josephine Baker came to Lisbon twice from Paris to hand over information from the French Resistance to the Allies, for which she later received the French Medal of the Resistance.[30]

Ian Fleming based his novel *Casino Royale* and his main character, James Bond, on a trip that he took to Portugal in May 1941 as a Royal Navy intelligence officer. He lived in Estoril, where the wealthiest refugees stayed. In fact, so many former kings, ex-regents, and aristocrats assembled there that *Life* magazine claimed "their presence has given the town a nickname: the 'royal morgue of Europe.'" Many gambled at the casino in Estoril, aware that spies of both warring sides played there as well, surely a mélange of mistrust. Looking back at his stay in Lisbon, the American journalist Eric Sevareid saw Lisbon as a "nervous place" where "British planes bound for London, German planes bound for Berlin, passed each other in the sky over the city." In fact, British and German planes stood side by side in the Lisbon airport, where the pilots and passengers ate in the same small restaurant. One plane would fly to Berlin, the other to London, and "passengers appear more than ordinarily anxious to make sure they are on the right plane!"[31]

The Portuguese secret police (PVDE), too, played both sides of the conflict. Its men routinely tortured perceived enemies in the 1930s, particularly liberals and communists. The Portuguese novelist Miguel Torga described the political atmosphere of the era as "suffocating," one in which those who refused to succumb to the "Catholic-cum-military dictatorship" choked in the "lurking and nightmarish presence of the secret police." A German spy observed "a contest between us and the British to gain the greater influence

with the Portuguese police." The British secret service, MI5 (domestic counterintelligence) and MI6 (foreign intelligence), had, in fact, infiltrated the
PVDE, and the Germans established several German-paid and Portuguese-
staffed spy networks. Further, several cases in which Germans bribed lower-
level officials resulted in the arrests of refugees, including Jews.[32]

The PVDE was divided at the top, too: British observers thought that
its director, Agostinho Lourenço, the recipient of the Royal Victorian Order
(CVO) in 1921, leaned toward England. But two of its other leaders, Paolo
Cumano, known unofficially as SS leader Heinrich Himmler's "satellite in
the police," and José Catela, leaned toward Berlin. Trained by the Gestapo in
Berlin, both agreed to have Italian and German advisers instruct the Portuguese secret police. The Nazis' Reich Main Security Office continued to
influence the PVDE and Cumano, meaning that the PVDE watched German
Jews in particular. The RSHA and the PVDE exchanged information and
technical assistance through 1942.[33]

Catela, as early as 1934, supported the restriction of visas to Jews still
living in Germany, particularly Polish Jews. Catela's argument, rife with antisemitic tropes, claimed that Polish "undesirable elements," mostly Jews who had
emigrated from Germany, trafficked in rum, drugs, and espionage. The
Ministry of Foreign Affairs (Ministério dos Negócios Estrangeiros, MNE)
seemed to agree that "certain foreigners" should not enter Portugal because of
the danger that they might be Russian or Polish spies. Two years later, Catela
insisted again that foreigners could enter only with PVDE authorization. This
time, Lourenço and the MNE agreed that foreigners wanted to settle as peddlers
and prostitutes. Yet the police and the National Assembly also created obstacles
for refugees with excellent skills, for example, doctors. In 1939, Lourenço
demanded that border patrols control the influx of "revolutionaries and undesirables."[34] He saw refugees as "people without a clear conscience" claiming to
have escaped persecution. Overall, "bribery or outright German pay" provided
leverage on the police. The PVDE showed less enthusiasm for the Allies at
the time than did the general population, which was "carefully following the
progress of the war and revering Salazar."[35]

Many refugees, too, understood Portugal's attempt to placate both
the Allies and the Axis. They observed secret agents stalking their foes in the
cafés. Gisela W. reported, "My mother was very nervous about staying in
Portugal because of all the Nazi infiltrators . . . We were constantly worried."
On occasion, a spy might attempt to lure a refugee into service. When a

German-Jewish refugee received a phone call from an unknown woman, inviting him—in German—to her hotel room, he hung up: "I could not take any chances. The Germans are supposed to have an efficient staff of agents in this town, and regarding sex, I usually like to make my own arrangements."[36]

The regime's rigid neutrality alarmed refugees. They had free rein in Lisbon, but German influences were ubiquitous. Kiosks sold newspapers from both sides of the war: "The English and German papers hang next to each other and always in equal numbers." Ads for shortwave broadcasts from America, London, and Berlin appeared in rectangles of identical size as well. One refugee "noticed a very strange sight": "A German propaganda office with big swastikas and a little further the American office with the American flag. All major countries were represented. They all were trying to convince the public of their good intentions." Portugal also allowed ships from warring sides to dock in Lisbon. A Portuguese newsreel of the early 1940s depicted a stopover by a German battleship and two submarines to Lisbon harbor as a "kind act," symbolic of the two countries' "friendship." Another newsreel similarly portrayed a visit by the British home fleet as "peaceful and friendly." Both of these censored news reports claimed that masses of Portuguese came to see the ships, emphasizing Portugal's neutrality.[37] Although refugees did not comment on these events, seeing Germany's battleship and submarines at close hand would certainly have heightened their fears.

At points, an American observer like Varian Fry of the Emergency Rescue Committee thought that Portugal supported the Axis. In September 1941, he believed that "Portugal . . . is more and more under German influence." The Portuguese historian Irene Pimentel agrees. But after 1943, with Germany clearly losing the war, the Portuguese regime favored a "neutral collaboration" with the Allies, and the PVDE tilted toward the presumed winners.[38] Similarly, by later in 1943, Portugal had leased naval and air bases in the Azores (in the North Atlantic) to the British. By then, Germany had suffered a major defeat at Stalingrad, the Allies had already landed in Sicily, and Mussolini had been deposed. Ultimately, but quite late, Portugal tipped toward the Allies.[39]

The International Context of Portugal's Response to Refugees

The international context, particularly the policies of the United States, played a role in Salazar's reluctance to accept refugees. Since Portugal officially allowed people in transit, it would likely have provided more temporary visas if the United States and other countries had accepted refugees expeditiously. After all, refugees in transit brought money and left quickly. But Salazar knew that the United States, the hoped-for destination of most refugees, had slowed its acceptances and soon blocked them.

During the war, Americans continued to voice anti-immigrant and antisemitic sentiments, and their leaders fretted about spies or "fifth columnists," supposed Nazi agents who might sneak into the country in the guise of or among refugees. In his fifteenth Fireside Chat, delivered on May 26, 1940, as Germany was invading the nations to its west, President Roosevelt worried about "the Fifth Column that betrays a nation . . . [made up of] spies, saboteurs." And Assistant Secretary of State Breckinridge Long, a "nativist and restrictionist," believed that the German government allowed only German "agents" to come to the United States. This "spy hysteria" led to severe entrance limitations.[40] On June 15, 1940, the United States changed its policy of admitting unobjectionable aliens to allowing only those to enter whose admission "affirmatively appear[ed]" in "the American interest." Then, on June 26, Long sent a memo to State Department officials, stating: "We can delay and effectively stop . . . immigrants . . . by simply advising our consuls, to put every obstacle in the way . . ., which would postpone and postpone and postpone the granting of the visas."[41] In effect, this suggestion became policy and blocked the issuance of most new visas.

Long's attitudes reverberated at U.S. diplomatic missions. That summer, Varian Fry observed prejudice in favor of the wealthy and against Jews at the U.S. Legation and Consulate General in Lisbon.[42] He complained that the famous fashion designer Elsa Schiaparelli, a non-Jewish French citizen, had no trouble at the American mission. When another woman asked why she had to wait and Schiaparelli did not, the consul responded that the designer "will make millions in the United States." U.S. application processing slowed to a crawl, taking over six months for authorities to come to a decision, if at all. The applications required long forms, six copies of which had to go to Washington. Even then, the consul in Europe could refuse to grant a visa. The Reverend Charles Joy of the Unitarian Service Committee in Lisbon wrote: "The whole attitude of America seems so selfish and cruel. It would be so easy to open our homes to every one of the endangered ones, with no hardship to anyone anywhere. But we will not."[43]

By 1941, in response to continued nativist pressure, the United States began requiring statements from U.S. citizens attesting to an immigrant's upright character, known colloquially as the "moral affidavit." Americans "of responsible standing" who knew the alien personally had to attest that this applicant had a praiseworthy character and would not become an agent of foreign powers. In addition, the signer had to promise to observe the alien's actions once in the country. A moral affidavit written by a Quaker in Philadelphia for a refugee in Lisbon, for example, stated the following in rather formulaic and somewhat evasive prose (since she did not know him personally): "That . . . is a man of high moral character, a fact known to mutual friends and myself, that he entertains no views or intentions that are subversive of the best interests and welfare of the United States. That he has at no time been associated with any political party or any movement that is or was inimical to the Government of the USA . . . that he deserves to become a citizen of the USA and that his admission will be an advantage to that country."[44]

To make matters more complicated, in the spring of 1941 the State Department centralized visa permissions in Washington, which meant that local consuls like Hiram Bingham in Marseille, known to have helped some refugees, lost power. Other bureaucrats assumed that refugees might undermine the United States because the Nazis could use their relatives in Europe as hostages. That June, Congress passed the Bloom–Van Nuys bill, which imposed the "close family" rule, decreeing that the U.S. would reject refugees with relatives in occupied territories. And in July, the United States required even more onerous procedures and new forms. Its new "Manual on Immigration" filled eight and a half single-spaced pages. Finally, on July 1, 1941, the United States closed all consulates in Germany, Italy, and Nazi-occupied lands, meaning all cases had to wait to be determined in Washington, at a "time when an expired visa could . . . spell tragedy."[45]

In October 1941, Germany stopped the legal emigration of Jews. About 800 people in possession of all necessary papers for the United States remained trapped. Had their papers arrived sooner, they might have reached safety. That same month, as Quakers in Lisbon complained to one another that U.S. policies caused refugees in Portugal "to get more entangled in the new regulations," Varian Fry concluded, "People in Washington sit in great offices dealing with papers . . . It may be boring . . . but it doesn't tear their hearts out. It doesn't take their souls and twist them like towels until they can hear the fibres crack."[46]

Concerns about fifth columnists affected U.S. domestic policy as well as its refugee policy. In 1942, after the bombing of Pearl Harbor, the American government forcibly relocated more than 100,000 Japanese Americans, the majority of whom held U.S. citizenship, from the West Coast to internment camps in the interior. The government also sent about 2,000 Italian nationals resident in the United States to internment camps and detained about 11,000 mostly German nationals (Jews among them), although not in internment camps. American concerns about the alleged disloyalty of those associated with the Axis powers caused great pain to its domestic victims and meant certain death for Jews stranded in Europe. Although the United States ultimately had taken in approximately 200,000 Jews by 1945, attempts to persuade its government to allow the entrance of more refugees "ran into the stone wall of antisemitism . . . and Depression-induced fear of future job competition," just when Jews needed open doors.[47]

Salazar and the Consuls

More willing to open their doors than the Americans and not always in step with Salazar's twists and turns of policy, several Portuguese consuls aided refugees, against the orders of superiors. This disobedience reflected a generally neutral attitude toward Jews among Portugal's elites. When the German Foreign Office requested information about anti-Jewish laws in Portugal in September 1941, for example, the Portuguese legation in Berlin responded that the government had not passed such decrees. Similarly, in February 1944, when Germany asked its consuls in Lisbon to describe the effects of German anti-Jewish activities in Portugal, they responded that the Jewish "problem" did not exist there.[48]

Portugal's consul general in Bordeaux, an exceptional man in an extraordinary moment, stands out from other consuls, but illustrates the attitudes of some important elites. From June 16 to 19, 1940, as millions fled German armies streaming into France, Aristides de Sousa Mendes issued thousands of visas for refugees from every part of Europe. He worked for three days and three nights, helping mostly Jews, but also opponents of fascism and prominent politicians from Belgium and Luxembourg. After the Germans bombed Bordeaux during the night of June 19–20, he also aided Jews in Bayonne and Hendaye. Despite instructions to get the approval of the MNE, and knowing that his government had rejected refugees' requests for visas, Sousa Mendes felt compelled to act as he did: "I cannot let these people die. Many of them are Jews and our constitution states that religion and political views shall not constitute grounds for . . . being refused asylum in

Portugal. . . . Even if I am dismissed from my post I cannot act but as a Christian, faithful to the dictates of my conscience." Rabbi Chaim Krüger, fleeing Belgium with his wife and five children, had befriended Sousa Mendes in Bordeaux. While assisting the consul with paperwork, Krüger reported that Sousa Mendes mentioned hoping to make up in some way for the crimes of the Inquisition.[49]

Sousa Mendes was not alone in remembering the Inquisition of the late fifteenth century. Portuguese Jews like Augusto d'Esaguy did as well, confirming this in a speech entitled "Repaying a Debt Four Centuries Old." Harking back to the Inquisition, he asserted that Nazi persecution had "made it possible for the people of Portugal to make amends for the persecution of the Jews by their forebears." He claimed to have heard this "remarkable attitude voiced by many" Portuguese.[50] This statement may be impossible to verify, but certainly Sousa Mendes exceeded the limits of generosity.

Continuing to stamp more visas until June 23, Sousa Mendes angered Salazar further. On June 25, the government declared the Portuguese visas granted at Bordeaux invalid, but by then, many had found safety in Portugal, and its government relented toward others. Sousa Mendes saved about 10,000 Jews (and this number continues to grow as more people discover relatives whom he helped).[51] In 1966, some twelve years after his death, Israel awarded him the honorary title "Righteous Among the Nations" for saving Jewish lives. Few consuls from other nations did as much.[52]

Sousa Mendes faced severe discipline, possibly because of the timing of his actions. His insubordination took place as German tanks headed toward the Pyrenees. Personal reasons may have played a role as well. The aristocratic Sousa Mendes family had lived in the same region as Salazar's far more modest family. The government recalled him, stripping him of his job and forbidding him from earning a living with his law degree. It also blacklisted his fifteen children, preventing them from attending university or finding professional employment.[53] With a large family and a small income, he appeared at the Jewish soup kitchen with some of his children. Isaac Bitton, born in Lisbon, reported that one day a large family walked in speaking fluent Portuguese. They wore good clothing, "not dressed like a refugee . . . not with crumbling clothing." Bitton, who volunteered in the soup kitchen, spoke Portuguese to the man, explaining, "This is for refugees." Sousa Mendes responded in Portuguese: "We too are refugees," and visited the kitchen several times. The Jewish community paid his medical bills, and later, HIAS (Hebrew Immigrant Aid

Society) helped some of his children emigrate to the United States.[54] All his children but one left Portugal.

A few other Portuguese diplomats, too, intervened to save Jews, although not in such numbers. Many consulates issued visas despite instructions from Lisbon and ignored the traffic in bogus entry permits, especially for South America, presented by refugees. Those with false permits had been duped by corrupt officials, paying for documents that later proved inadequate. These consuls saved thousands of people. Giuseppe Agenore Magno, the Portuguese consul in Milan, gave out visas with the knowledge, but disapproval, of his government. In fact, Magno gave Saul Steinberg, a Romanian-Jewish refugee and later a renowned American artist, a visa to enter Portugal from Milan in the spring of 1940, against the Portuguese government's wishes.[55] For helping Steinberg, the government removed Magno from his position, but he continued working for the consulate.

In late 1941, a month after Germany forbade Jewish emigration and began shipping Jews eastward to their deaths, the Portuguese consul in Genoa, Alfred Casanova, defended Magno in a letter to Salazar. Salazar had Casanova demoted, transferring him to Marseille. By 1944, Salazar no longer objected to the pro-refugee acts of his envoys. Carlos Sampaio Garrido, Portugal's ambassador in Budapest, and Carlos de Liz-Teixeira Branquinho, chargé d'affaires at the Portuguese Embassy in Budapest, saved as many as a thousand Jews. Salazar's decision occurred just when other countries agreed to do the same thing.[56] Additionally, these consuls issued safe conduct passes to anyone with relatives in Brazil, Portugal, or its colonies as long as they used Portugal as a transit—not a permanent—destination.

Just as Portugal severely penalized Sousa Mendes and mildly punished other diplomats, contradictions abounded and changed over time. Those refugees who came with transit visas, many signed by Sousa Mendes, not only gained entry to Portugal, but also found housing that the Portuguese government permitted and camps that it established at the border in Vilar Formoso for temporary shelter (and as a place to check identities). Nor did the government stop several English businessmen from Porto who sought to help out in the frenzied late weeks of June 1940. They drove to Vilar Formoso, where they served refugees two thousand kilograms of bread, five thousand eggs, and two steers' worth of roast-beef sandwiches, as well as canned milk for babies. They financed most of the costs themselves, with a small subsidy from the British consul in Porto.[57]

Portugal and Antisemitism

Vacillation by the Portuguese government contrasted with the helpfulness of some consuls and, as will be seen, with the generous acceptance of refugees by innumerable Portuguese individuals. This raises the question, to what extent did antisemitism motivate any part of the population? Historians have found a small circle of radical elites who advocated "racial nationalism" and antisemitism well before and after Salazar came to power. Traces of these conservatives, radical monarchists, and small circles of conservative Catholics supported by the Church can be read in the books they published. In the 1920s, Portugal saw the appearance of three intensely antisemitic books, including a 1923 translation of the *Protocols of the Elders of Zion,* a Russian fabrication first published in 1903 alleging that Jews planned to take over the world. In addition, *The Masonic Age,* published in 1943 by Father Amadeu de Vasconcelos, proclaimed that the "strongest force the world had ever known" consisted of the "Trinity": British imperialism, Masonry, and Judaism. These books gained little traction with the public, Portuguese intellectuals, or Salazar.[58] They certainly did not frame refugees' experiences.

Besides these books, evidence of antisemitism remains sparse, which is why an antisemitic series in the conservative newspaper *A Voz* (The Voice) stands out. The author of the articles, which appeared in March 1938, worried about a worldwide "Masonic-Jewish conspiracy" with "revolutionary" and "Bolshevist" elements that intended to convert crypto-Jews into practicing Jews. This distrust of crypto-Jews harked back to the Inquisition. But the more recent activism of Artur Barros Basto, a military hero, also alarmed the Church. Barros Basto, a crypto-Jew who had formally converted to Judaism, established the Porto Jewish community in 1923 as well as a yeshiva in 1929. He founded the Jewish magazine *Há-Lapid,* which he published from 1927 to 1958, and he proselytized crypto-Jews in the 1930s.[59]

The articles in *A Voz* raised additional concerns that refugees, including "German" doctors, journalists, businessmen, and representatives of the Comintern (the Communist International), might "infect the environment." The writer staunchly opposed allowing refugees to settle in Portugal because of the "well-known errors of the Jewish race (*raça*)." Yet even as *A Voz* targeted Jews, it praised Jews from Lisbon and Jews in general, stating that the paper harbored no hostility toward Portuguese Jews but toward "undesirable foreign elements."[60] The paper furthermore printed a sharp rejoinder by Samuel Schwarz, an author and self-identified Jew.

Why this seeming contradiction? With the exception of praising Lisbon Jews, *A Voz* advanced almost every antisemitic stereotype in a censored press—hence, the articles had the approval of higher-ups. Still, the censors and the press would have taken Salazar's opinions into consideration and likely knew of his distaste for anti-Jewish racism and his friendship with Moses Amzalak. In addition, they realized that a Portuguese Jewish elite, made up of successful businessmen, also served the state.[61] Praise of the Lisbon Jewish community could have softened the articles' antisemitism enough to make them acceptable to the censors.

Native Portuguese Jews countered this type of antisemitism earlier than the *A Voz* articles. Adolfo Benarús, a philologist and communal leader, wrote a 300-page book in 1937 underscoring the absence of antisemitism in Portugal. Later, Jewish leaders hand-delivered a letter to Salazar about the articles in *A Voz*. Alerting him to an antisemitic movement "in our country," they asserted that Portuguese Jews felt "profound wellbeing, while assuring Portugal of their absolute dedication."[62]

Other newspapers followed the plight of Jews with compassion. Two in particular inclined toward positive assessments of Jews: *O Século,* co-owned by Moses Amzalak, and the *Diário de Notícias,* run by Augusto de Castro, a non-Jewish member of the Portuguese intellectual and political elite. During the November Pogrom, *Diário de Notícias* and *República* (claiming to be the "afternoon newspaper with the largest circulation in the whole country") headlined the event by describing "antisemitic" and "religious" persecution. The papers reported reactions abroad, including demonstrations in New York and Washington. At the end of that month, *República,* referred to "the difficult situation of German Jews." Even *A Voz* featured the November Pogrom on its front page. And *Novidades,* a Catholic journal, condemned Nazi paganism while fretting about religious persecution, particularly against the Church. In December 1938, *República* referred to the "human problem" of the "wandering Jews," and during the following years, one could occasionally find articles about "homeless people" and refugees—mostly children. *Diário* also reported on refugees leaving for Palestine. One such article described the happiness of the departing Jews, their gratefulness toward the "good Portuguese people" for their "kindness and sympathy," and, tipping its hat toward the censors, their thankfulness for the head of the secret police.[63] Refugees would have concurred with regard to ordinary citizens, but they surely would have omitted appreciation of the police.

Because most central and eastern European refugees could not read Portuguese, they missed isolated antisemitic discourses as well as the more compassionate news items about themselves. Daily interactions mattered more. Jewish observers inside and outside Portugal reported that Portugal did not have a "Jewish question." Its government treated its own Jews equally, and its citizens either accepted Jewish newcomers or did not inquire about their religion.[64] In addition, one refugee concluded in late 1940 that "the people seemed . . . to side with the Allies, to judge by the number of RAF (British Royal Air Force) pins in their button holes."[65]

Jewish and American journalists and aid workers agreed. The German-Jewish press in Vienna remarked on the pleasantness of many Portuguese to foreigners, noting they behaved honestly and courteously. One could get along with them if one mixed a bit of French, "broken" Italian, or Spanish into the conversation, or, according to the observer, if one also spoke with one's hands. The *New York Times* reporter James Reston marveled at the kindness of impoverished Portuguese. On December 15, 1940, he wrote: "The Portuguese people have . . . taken [the refugees] into their homes and given them clothes, for many arrived with nothing but what they wore at the time, and the government has consistently extended their visas to allow them to remain here until new homes can be found. Salazar has even cooperated in establishing schools for refugee children." A Portuguese-Jewish man who lived in Lisbon during the war and helped refugees, insisted he had never felt antisemitism there.[66]

The Catholic Church, in this overwhelmingly Catholic country, may also have played a positive role, not by denouncing antisemitism, but by criticizing Nazism. Cardinal Cerejeira, who had founded Catholic Action in 1932, a movement loyal to Salazar, accused Nazis of trying to destroy the Catholic faith by persecuting Catholic organizations. Even though the Church approved of the Nazis' anticommunism, the cardinal condemned the German regime in a Catholic journal, *Lumen*, as a "pagan" and "violent" cult that believed a state could be based on "race." Further, the Portuguese Catholic Church looked askance at Nazi eugenics and German attacks on the physically and mentally disabled.[67]

Besides disapproving of Nazi racism, the Church had every reason to support Salazar's authoritarian, pro-Catholic government. This included Salazar's generally benign attitude toward Jewish refugees. Pietro Ciriaci, the papal nuncio in Portugal since 1934, signed a concordat between Portugal and the Catholic Church on May 7, 1940, three days before Germany invaded the Low Countries and France. The agreement allowed Catholic religious instruction in all public schools, enabled the Church to incorporate and hold property, and gave tax exemptions to the Church and its seminaries, among other benefits. The pope issued an encyclical celebrating the 800th anniversary of the Portuguese Reconquista, its establishment as an independent kingdom after having vanquished Moorish conquerors. Thus the Church and Portugal's "New State" cooperated closely in this "clerical-conservative" state, unconvinced by Nazi racial ideology.[68]

Local priests, on the other hand, imbued with anti-Judaism, could have spread negative attitudes, even if they did not promote racial antisemitism. The wider public attended church and confession regularly, and may have heard anti-Jewish sermons. Evidence is sparse, but one Portuguese woman, hired by a Jewish family that arrived in 1933, worked for them for five years. When her priest told her that Jews were bad people and when she realized the family was Jewish, she burned their curtains and left their employ. The maid of another Jewish family that had lived in Portugal since the 1920s cried one day, telling her employers that at confession her priest had enjoined her not to work for Jews. But she had stood up to the priest, responding, "They let me go to church," and remained with them. That Jewish family made a church wedding for the young woman when she married.[69]

This is not to argue that racism did not exist in Portugal. For example, the Portuguese ambassador to Germany used the term "racial" in a letter to Salazar when referring to some Jews, but thought rich Jews could be useful. But Salazar's circles did not trade in overt racism. In contrast, the Portuguese government and its functionaries exhibited no compunction about using racism and the language of color as a near synonym for "race" in the Portuguese colonies. Some Portuguese anthropologists, too, used a racial approach when studying colonial subalterns. They intended to underline the "racial unity" of the (white) Portuguese and also to define them against colonial people of color. And in 1934, the chair of the Department of Anthropology at the University of Coimbra argued against racial mixing. Yet even as 1930s Portugal saw some confusion between terms like "nationality" and "race," the term "race"—at least in Portugal itself—generally referred to a historical, national, cultural community, not a biological or ethnic one. Jews did not face expulsion from the Portuguese national community for reasons of race or religion.[70] In January 1944, Isaac Weissmann of the World Jewish Congress could write to a colleague, "Anti-semitism as we know it does not exist in Portugal."[71]

Salazar and the Holocaust

An absence of overt antisemitism did not ensure that Salazar would welcome refugees, even when international organizations paid their way. What did he understand about the situation of Jews? Did he know of their annihilation and still resist helping them? Starting in the fall of 1941, Salazar could have obtained information from Portugal's approximately twenty consuls in Germany, who had either observed deportations firsthand or received reports about them. By that time, he had learned of mass executions in Poland and atrocities in the Soviet Union. In May 1942, the Polish government-in-exile informed the MNE of "German savagery," including massacres and slave labor, in concentration (not extermination) camps. In September, the Portuguese government could have heard of the mass murders of Jews from Nobel Prize winner Thomas Mann's broadcasts on the BBC. That December, the British foreign secretary, Anthony Eden, gave a speech to the House of Commons condemning Germany in the name of eleven Allied governments for the "cold-blooded extermination" of the Jews, and Allied newspapers carried the speech.[72]

With this horrific information at hand, the Portuguese leadership faced an unusual demand from the Germans. At the beginning of 1943, the German Foreign Office, intent on maintaining trade with neutral nations as part of its war effort, issued a "repatriation ultimatum" (*Heimschaffungsaktion*), allowing neutral nations to take back their Jewish citizens living under German control. If they did not, the Jews would "be subject to general Jewish measures." The Germans thereby hoped to avoid offending neutral countries, by allowing them to repatriate "their" Jews. Until then, the Germans would not force these Jews to wear the yellow star and would not deport them. Germany sent this ultimatum on February 20, 1943, with a deadline of March 31, urging the Portuguese "to avoid delays" by sending individual names upon learning of them, rather than creating a list.[73]

This ultimatum presented several nations with an opportunity to save more Jews, even though many of them had never lived in or spoken the languages of the countries whose passports they held. Salazar, however, hesitated to allow Jews who claimed citizenship to return. He tolerated the transit of tens of thousands of Jews without any claim to citizenship, but dithered when it came to Jews claiming citizenship from the fifteenth- and sixteenth-century expulsions or from documents they had received during Portugal's First Republic (1910–26). He did not want Jews to settle in Portugal, and he rejected decisions made by the government he had overthrown. In the end,

Portugal, like many other neutral nations, played for time, stalling until May 1943, even as more information about the genocide continued to reach it.[74]

The German ultimatum concerned about 1,000 Jews of Portuguese extraction, people with Portuguese citizenship or of Sephardic heritage, living in France, Belgium, and Greece. Ultimately, Portugal accepted about 227 Jews from France and Belgium who had some—but not all—necessary documents. After the intervention of the United States, Portugal accepted 19 out of 25 Portuguese Jews in Greece, but too late to bring them to Portugal. However, Portugal treated Dutch Jews of Portuguese extraction, numbering over 4,300, much more cruelly. The government insisted on official documentation, which they did not have, at a time when the number of transiting refugees in Portugal had declined significantly. Fewer than 500 survived. Some historians have argued that neither Portugal nor Spain "made serious efforts to repatriate Jewish nationals from danger areas."[75]

Yet other historians comparing Spanish, Portuguese, and Turkish responses to the repatriation ultimatum contend that Portugal was less restrictive than Turkey or Spain, both of which demanded that refugees have all documents, and that of the three countries, Portugal acknowledged the highest percentage of its Jews as citizens. Studying Turkey, Corry Guttstadt found comparatively few interventions to save Jews of Turkish nationality living under Nazi domination.[76] Spain showed an unwillingness to take in Sephardic Jews even with proper Spanish identification papers and insisted that some Jews move on before allowing others to enter.[77]

News about annihilations continued to arrive in Portugal's high government circles, where it remained. Nor did Salazar's censored press comment on the genocide. When *A Voz* attempted, in 1942, to publish information about Germany's terrible cruelties against children, censors cut the information, arguing that the stories could not be true. Additionally, the Portuguese press had received reports about Auschwitz by January 1943. In sum, as the mass murder of Jews increased and continued until the very end of the war, neither Salazar nor his press made a statement about the genocide, although according to his biographer, news about the Final Solution "must have been accessible to him."[78] Nor did the PVDE receive orders to liberalize its stance toward Jewish refugees. Salazar chose to look the other way.

This raises the more general question of how people involved with refugee rescue on the ground and historians much later have assessed Salazar's and Portugal's policies toward Jews. In *Portugal, Salazar, and the Jews,*

Avraham Milgram considers Portugal's record disappointing, arguing that Portugal did not live up to its potential to help. Even as Germany began to lose the war, around the time of Stalingrad (1943), Portugal did not open its borders to Jews, and when Portugal permitted their entry, it did so late. Milgram claims that other neutral countries did more. Similarly, the historian Jorge Martins argues that Salazar pursued an "ostrich policy," preferring not to rescue people whose fate he knew: Portugal "could have done a lot more if Salazar had wanted to, but he did not want to."[79]

In contrast, aid organizations on the ground held more positive opinions. In late 1941, an internal Quaker memo from Lisbon reported that "Portugal has succeeded in a remarkable way in keeping her doors open and in maintaining her reputation for fair dealing." In early 1943, the JDC expressed satisfaction that it had established offices in Portugal rather than Spain. Police pressure in Spain appeared "much more pervasive than in Portugal; one is watched much more carefully and one's movements and activities considerably interfered with." JDC officials deemed the Portuguese government "generous" toward refugees as well as "cooperative" with American aid groups. At the beginning of 1944, the JDC observed: "There have been no instances in which the Portuguese authorities have turned back people at the border," and the Quakers corroborated this finding at the end of that year.[80] And as late as 1944, as we have seen, the Portuguese police gave the World Jewish Congress entry permission for three hundred refugee children who had fled over the Pyrenees. After the war, the government agreed to let "a few hundred" children liberated from concentration camps recuperate in Portugal before continuing on.[81]

Portuguese Citizens Respond

Warm Welcomes

Whereas refugees worried about the Portuguese government, they felt relief when they met individual Portuguese citizens. The contrast between the government, which grudgingly accepted refugees, and those Portuguese people who welcomed them could not have been greater. Like refugees who came in the 1930s, those of the 1940s appreciated the compassion of many "warm, friendly and hospitable" Portuguese people.[82] These newcomers contrasted Portuguese kindheartedness with the increased animosity they had experienced at home, the overall brutality of wartime Europe, and relentless Nazi aggression. In comparison with the social death and violence they had endured, the personal goodwill of the Portuguese raised their spirits. Maybe not all Portuguese greeted them with open arms, but when Jewish refugees recalled their time in Portugal, both immediately and years later, they repeated the same leitmotifs: kindness, helpfulness, and generosity offered by poor people to formerly middle-class refugees.

Refugees encountered courtesy at the border, the first time since their mad dash through France and the overwhelmed towns there. In June 1940, George Rony, forced to sleep in his car, described the Portuguese customs official who "politely told everyone the cause of the delay": "today by train and automobile such floods of refugees had arrived at the border that it was impossible to take care of them all." The six-member Pekelis family began its escape from Italy in late August 1940, heading to Lisbon via Nice, Paris, Tours, Haut Bagnac, Marseille, Perpignan (near the French border with Spain), Barcelona, Madrid, and Badajoz (near the Spanish border with Portugal). Even with legal papers and some money, the family endured an arduous trip, its two elderly grandmothers arriving exhausted. When they reached the Portuguese border at the end of 1940, a uniformed official directed them to a shady tree and brought them cold water—"cooler and more refreshing than any I had ever drunk," according to Carla Pekelis—while they waited for passport inspection.[83]

Border residents offered even more. As refugees inundating the border town of Vilar Formoso sought a room for the night or slept in their cars or in nearby fields, townspeople brought soup, bread, and fruit to the hapless crowds. One Portuguese witness recalled how rural families opened their homes to shelter refugees and how his aunt and other women distributed the contents of huge pots of soup that they had cooked. A Czech-Jewish family on the run happened upon "smiling villagers . . . distributing their gifts of food."[84]

Refugees also met with friendliness more generally, not just at the border. Lisbon and Porto, as port cities, had some experience with foreign businesses, especially English, Italian, and German ones, and appeared open to strangers. The sixty-five-year-old Austrian-Jewish writer Leopold von Andrian, grandson of the German-Jewish composer Giacomo Meyerbeer, wrote a friend from his bed in Lisbon, detailing his utter exhaustion, both physical and emotional. But he recognized the Portuguese as very genial and easy to get along with. Another refugee described them as "very nice in every respect." If it had not been for the war, she would have had a good time.[85]

That refugees often could not pay for this help did not deter the Portuguese. After the fall of France, many refugees "had to swallow the bitter pill of the exchange rate," since the franc's value had plummeted—"no longer worth anything." Most arrived "flat broke." One woman, on a train heading to Lisbon and obviously starving, eyed a boy eating a roll. The conductor, observing her glance, gave her a loaf of bread and a place to lie down in a first-class compartment. In another incident, Portuguese passengers on a train from the Spanish border to Lisbon noticed that the author Alfred Döblin's child needed to sleep: "In a crowded compartment. . . . They cleared off a whole bench for him to lie down on. Those who had been seated there stood at the window or corridor." A stranger with whom they spoke French on another train to Lisbon stepped out of the train at a rest stop and booked lodgings for Döblin's family in an "affordable *pension* that he knew." He continued to visit them until they left for the United States.[86]

Courtesy was also extended to foreigners on the street. One refugee remarked, "No Portuguese takes advantage of the stupidity of the foreigners (or so it must sometimes seem to them). If we asked the way to the post office, for instance, two or three people would show us the way in the politest manner." Heading toward Lisbon, the Shadur family "had completely run out of money" and stopped in Alcobaça, about sixty miles north of the capital. On a cold December night, the five of them slept "in our cramped positions" in their car. But two young Portuguese men stopped and asked whether they could be of assistance: "They went off, only to return soon after to tell us that the citizens of Alcobaça would not countenance strangers spending Christmas on the street in their town, and that the mayor invited us all to stay in a hotel and to a Christmas dinner." These young men continued to assist the family until it sailed to the United States. Miriam Stanton's spirits rose because of similar street friendliness: "The Portuguese people were so good to refugees. They would even go up to someone in the street . . . and ask if any help was needed." "People in all walks of life—doctors, business people, laborers, etc." gave their names and addresses to refugees and told them "to call if there was anything they could do." In Coimbra, one of the oldest university towns in Europe, Lucie Matuzewitz asked a student the address of police headquarters. He not only accompanied her to the station, but also paid her fare. Another student told her, "We know you are Jewish, we also were Jews here, but that was a long time ago."[87] Perhaps these students realized that Coimbra,

A group of Jewish refugees just arrived at Lisbon's Santa Apolónia train station, September 1941. (U.S. Holocaust Memorial Museum, #59588, courtesy of Milton Koch).

one of the seats of the Inquisition, had an ancient Jewish quarter that dated back to the twelfth century.

Other Portuguese, too, provided goods and services for free, their empathy aroused by the emotional and physical distress they witnessed. In Lisbon, a refugee woman asked a shop owner the price of a hat that she liked, but then realized it cost too much. As she walked away, the shop owner came after her and gave it to her as a gift. Also in Lisbon, Margit Meissner had been eager to learn the language, but could not pay for lessons. A man taught her Portuguese without charging her. In small towns like Figueira da Foz, too, doctors aided refugees for free "because they didn't have money." And in the village of Goveia, when the Rony family stopped to feed their baby with the only provisions they had, a banana, villagers showed up with bread, eggs, butter, cheese, and milk. When George Rony took out some Portuguese money, "they would have none of it." In another village, a man introduced himself as a veteran of World War I and invited the family to sleep in his house overnight, insisting that they take the master bedroom and providing them with dinner. Later, he "gravely waved aside" Rony's attempt to pay. An assistant at the Lisbon Jewish community concluded that the Portuguese "were very generous—peasants and rich people."[88]

Refugees often wondered, in retrospect, why very poor people offered a helping hand. The fact that the government forbade refugees from working in Portugal and competing with its citizens may have created a situation in which positive feelings about refugees could develop. Yet it would be wrong to insist on an economic interpretation alone. Meissner surmised about her teacher: "I think he just wanted to help the refugees." Grete Friman, who remained in Portugal for the rest of her life, noted that the Portuguese not only aided Jewish refugees like her but also sheltered postwar Germans (probably fleeing Nazis). She concluded that they simply took care of people they presumed to be in need.[89] In fact, villagers along the 750-mile border between Spain and Portugal had assisted refugee Spaniards just a few years earlier, during the Spanish Civil War. They had hidden them from Portuguese border guards without asking about their political affiliations. Some villagers may have simply responded to the plight of victims of war.[90]

Poverty, counterintuitively, also encouraged generosity. When George Rony's host rejected any payment, he explained: "The people of Portugal are poor—very poor. But they have a deep understanding and compassion for those who are more miserable than they. Always will we share bread with strangers who need it." Anthropologists suggest that "walking in the other person's shoes" can create empathy. Social psychologists, too, show that lower-class subjects evince greater empathy toward the suffering of others.[91] Indeed, many Portuguese had experienced economic and political troubles and may have felt vulnerable to unforeseen events that could plunge them, just like these newcomers, into destitution. Nor did they seem to care about the refugees' religious or ethnic backgrounds. Isaac Weissmann observed that the Portuguese showed "indifference" about whether a "foreigner is or [is] not a Jew."[92]

Some hotels and rooming houses also assisted needy Jews. Alma Mahler-Werfel described trying to pay her Portuguese hotel bill: "[The clerk] seemed to sense that it would leave me short of cash. 'Never mind paying the bill,' he said. . . . 'You can send me the money from New York.'" In Curia, a landlady who had carefully negotiated the price of her rental with a refugee family refused to take their money when they left. In Coimbra, the pension manager where Sergio DeBenedetti, an Italian-Jewish physicist, had lodged insisted on accepting "only a tiny sum—much lower than the price we had originally agreed upon."[93] Portuguese landlords also helped refugees by demonstrating discretion: "You will find a pleasant society. [The landlord] will want to meet you, but will not ask you anything," wrote Leopold von Andrian in 1940.

Wondering about the affability of the Portuguese, Döblin wrote, "It seemed almost impossible . . . that someone would take such an interest in us for no practical reason. But that was the case. There was nothing behind it other than philanthropy and goodwill." He added: "Having experienced the war and the chaos of retreat and escape, we were to learn that all of that was only one side of humanity."[94] In Portugal, refugees encountered the first widespread acts of sympathy since beginning their devastating journeys.

While appreciating the hospitality of most Portuguese, refugees dreaded the Portuguese police intensely. In their remarks and memories, refugees generally separated their positive impressions of the kind "Portuguese" or "Portugal" from their fear of the Portuguese governmental authorities and police. The Hungarian-born refugee Eugene Bagger recorded his loathing of the police. Along with a "tidal wave of homeless and frightened men and women and children," he and his wife had landed in Portugal. The couple had fallen "in love" at first sight with Portugal, but the police had "poisoned" their brief eighteen days there."[95] Most refugees who reported generosity from ordinary Portuguese seemed to draw a line between the government and the police, the authorities that harassed them, and the rest of the population. They did not acknowledge that those who frightened them were also Portuguese.

Gendered Irritations

Clashing gender cultures caused mutual misunderstandings. When Portuguese people voiced any annoyance toward refugees, they did not focus on the influx of foreigners but on the unusual public appearance of refugee women, especially in cafés. Portuguese middle-class and working-class men went to cafés, not women. While refugee men fit into the café scene more easily, refugee women presented a stark contrast to the gendered practices of Portuguese women. The café offered refugee women a small public space to feel at home while chatting, writing letters, or smoking, but much of Portuguese society neither understood nor approved of this behavior. According to Noemi Gelehrter, who later made her life in Portugal, "Until the refugees came, a Portuguese woman rarely sat in a café; then the refugee women came and sat there the whole day, some even alone. . . . It was almost a scandal."[96]

Portugal had urbanized more slowly than northern European countries, so activities considered the norm in cities farther north could surprise many Portuguese. In 1930, Portugal was half as urban as the rest of Europe (excluding Russia), with most of its urban population, about 60 percent, concentrated in Lisbon and Porto. Yet even in cities, most Portuguese women and men lived in a traditional society that accepted domestic and subservient gender roles for women. Salazar's government promoted the "Portuguese home" and "the sacred Portuguese family." In a 1933 speech, Salazar underlined his values: "Women's work outside the family sphere disintegrates home life, separates its different members, and makes them strangers to each other." He maintained that men should work and support the family and that "the married woman . . . and similarly . . . the spinster who is a member of the family" should remain within the home. He added, "There never was a good housekeeper who did not find plenty to do."[97] Salazar's Constitution of 1933 declared equality for all before the law "except as regards women, the differences resulting from their nature and from the interest of the family." A year later, a decree forbade hiring women or children where men still faced unemployment. The government also set minimum wages lower for women. Although women could enter the legal profession as of 1918, during the secular republic, under Salazar the few professionals among women had to submit to government-imposed gender restrictions. For example, female teachers had to refrain from wearing makeup and to ask the Ministry of Education for permission to marry.[98]

In 1937, Salazar established the organization Work of Mothers for National Education (Obra das Mães para a Educação Nacional). It encouraged every young woman "to be a wife, to be instructed in matters pertaining to the home, family, and the spirit . . . [and] to raise and educate the future men of Portugal." Women also lagged behind men in literacy: in 1930, about 70 percent of women remained illiterate, in contrast to 53 percent of males. And the women's organization, closely linked with Salazar, urged girls' education to focus on God, homeland, and family.[99] Voting also put Portuguese women at a disadvantage. Only widows, divorcées, and women whose husbands lived abroad could vote, and then only if they had a secondary school degree or a university education.

Geography and class influenced women's roles. In 1940, 52 percent of Portugal's population still worked in agriculture. Peasant women toiled outdoors in the fields. Poor urban women served as breadwinners, much like their husbands, but strict gender conventions limited them to markets and groceries. In 1940, women constituted about 30 percent of the workforce in Lisbon and 40 percent in Porto. They made up 45 percent of the workforce in the whole country, although this is probably an underestimate.[100] In the cities, refugee women noticed barefoot Portuguese women with flat baskets on their heads selling fruit. One woman "gasped at the way women [carried] heavy loads of fruit and fish." This seems to have been a common practice: in 1941, *National Geographic* displayed a photo of Lisbon women chatting with one another while balancing large baskets of produce on their heads.[101]

For Portuguese higher up on the social ladder, this Catholic patriarchal society expected women to remain secluded, especially in the cities. There, leaders of the New State assumed that men would take on occupations in industry and commerce, but that "ladies" would leave home only accompanied by their husbands or parents. An Englishman observed, "There are no tea shops where girls, unaccompanied by male escorts, meet as in London or Paris." A guidebook from the U.S. Office of Strategic Services (OSS) in 1943 warned that the cafés on the Rossio in Lisbon were "not frequented by unaccompanied ladies and never by ladies of the better class." At age seventeen, Denise Hahn reported that when she sat in a park with her older and younger sisters in Porto, with "no man to watch over" them, they "quickly understood that this was unacceptable behavior for proper folks." They "sometimes took the tramway to the shore," away from disapproving gazes.[102]

Cafés in particular served as male spaces: "The year over, [women] struggle to keep by their side husbands who prefer to talk with other men in the noisy cafés of the Rossio." The refugee writer Ilse Losa added that women who went out alone after dinner could be taken for prostitutes. One Lisbon café refused to seat unescorted women at night, and some male refugees believed that "young girls" in a particular café who wore jackets with "1/4 length sleeves" earned their living as "street walkers."[103] More generally, refugee women such as Peggy Guggenheim found the public invisibility of Portuguese village women, apart from peasant women carrying fish from the beach to the marketplace "and a few whores," shocking. In the fishing village of Cascais, the homes seemed "hermetically sealed, their walls closing up the lives of all the women, who were not allowed on the streets." Portuguese middle-class men in cities also watched their female relatives carefully: "Even the most liberal father is likely to forbid his daughter to have a date alone with a boy." Young people did go out in groups. But according to the OSS, parents kept "an eagle eye on their daughters and no eye at all on their sons." It therefore warned its agents of prostitution and venereal disease, since "chastity is not expected of the Portuguese male, despite the purity demanded of the women."[104] In villages, too, parents watched carefully. Heinz Wisla joined "a few young refugees and some dashing Portuguese guitar players in the market square to sing ... under the balconies of ... young ladies. ... Always with [the] mother as chaperone nearby."[105]

Most refugee women chose not to abide by local norms, ignoring male monopolies in cafés or on sidewalks. In addition, because of their enforced idleness, tight living quarters, and appreciation of the sunny climate, many refugee women spent their days at outdoor cafés, enjoying public spaces. As a result of refugee women's public visibility, Portuguese cafés underwent a radical transformation from male spaces to international sites in which the sexes mixed and families, including children, found seats. Customs slowly began to change. In the more traditionally gendered town of Porto, Portuguese men allowed Ilse Losa to enter into "typically male" conversations as long as her brother accompanied her to the café. They stepped outside their gender order because they found foreign women, "in any case, odd." More astounding, sometimes refugee women asked men to dance in cafés, something the village of "Ericeira had never seen the likes of!"[106]

Intersections between age and gender norms meant that young northern European women's dress habits "shocked some Portuguese." While refugee men wore clothing similar to that of Portuguese men, refugee women's dress habits differed significantly from those of Portuguese women. Women from poorer families who had recently migrated from the provinces covered their hair, and middle-class urban women dressed in black with hats and gloves, even in the heat of summer. In contrast, many bare-legged refugee women wore colorful short-sleeved summer garments, and most young refugee women walked about in public without hats, something only prostitutes did in Lisbon. Jews already established in Portugal warned newly arriving refugee women to dress modestly. The aunt of a young refugee in Porto urged her to wear a hat and something "decent" over her short-sleeved blouses.[107] Pants, too, caused unwanted attention. Police arrested two refugee women in the small town of Figueira for wearing pants. Refugee women slowly grew aware of the difference in clothing; one young woman recalled her embarrassment when a Portuguese friend asked her critically whether the woman she had seen without a hat and gloves was her mother.[108] Still, these northerners had neither the desire to buy clothing appropriate to Portuguese norms nor the money.

Social and police norms dictated the types of beach attire that women wore. The two-piece bathing suit caused consternation. A Portuguese girls' magazine, for example, warned girls not to follow refugee bathing-suit styles.

A disgruntled English observer commented, "During the summer . . . a kind of panic seized the government over the possibility of these nomads from the north contaminating Portuguese moral standards." In the middle of the season, the authorities condemned what they called "nudism." Women wearing two-piece bathing dresses and men in trunks without tops could be arrested and punished, although most seem to have been fined. A surveillance force "of tactless police" implemented these strict norms. Unaware of or uninterested in Portuguese norms, Marta Feuchtwanger, walking to Estoril, stopped at a beach to take a swim because she had not had the opportunity to take a bath in a long time. Already wearing her two-piece bathing suit, she simply took off her dress, a custom common on northern European beaches. Spotting a man approaching her, she thought he might be interested in her—"that would have been much easier." Instead, he identified himself as a police officer, told her that wearing her two-piece bathing suit constituted a "crime" against morality, and fined her for it. Peggy Guggenheim voiced annoyance with these strictures in her autobiography: "We were always being taken up by the police for wearing what they considered indecent bathing-suits. As they could not speak French or English they used to measure the outstanding parts of our bodies, make scenes, and then proceed to fine us. We protested violently and went back to the shops. . . . They exchanged them for others, but the police were never satisfied." In her case, the police also harassed her partner, Max Ernst, requiring him to wear a shirt on the beach.[109]

Ruth Arons, who remained in Portugal, offered a more nuanced view. She recalled that Portuguese observers, depending on age, class, and sometimes gender, found refugee women's behaviors either outrageous or fascinating: "Lisbon was like a village and then suddenly all these refugees came, sat on the esplanade with coffee and cream cakes, women went to cafés alone and smoked. It was all an unusual sight for the natives." Wittingly or unwittingly, central European women broke taboos and challenged the double standard of gendered behavior in Portugal. Yet strict cultural codes notwithstanding, some middle-class Portuguese women appreciated this new behavior, made friends with refugee women, and went to cafés as well. A Jewish male refugee who stayed in Portugal for years observed Portuguese reactions and concluded sanguinely: "One not only got used to this . . . but realized that the world did not go under when people wore lighter and brighter clothing in summer, and [Portuguese women] began to do the same."[110]

A few liberal male Portuguese writers seemed to agree, suggesting that the newcomers had influenced young Portuguese women positively. They noted that some Portuguese had freed up their own lifestyles, at least along the coast, where young middle-class women began to dress more casually, do without stockings and gloves, talk with their hands, smoke in public, go to the movies or the theater together, and wear new hairstyles "*à refugiada*." The writer Luis Cajão, born in Figueira in 1920, described not only the women, but also the futility of Portuguese male strutting: "Blonde women wearing short skirts . . . with handkerchiefs tied round their necks . . . smoking outdoors, exuberant and indiscreet, indifferent to the gazes and comments from the Adonises who passed them on their way to the beach." The journalist and author Alexandre Babo focused on the Suíça (Swiss) café in central Lisbon, an important site in the Portuguese imagination about refugees. Before the arrival of refugee women, this café did not serve single women. He commented that women sitting openly and freely in the cafés, smoking and showing their legs, caused a "blow to national provincialism."[111]

These gendered perceptions of refugee conduct resulted from a craving that most refugees felt. They saw going to the café as essential to their peace of mind. As one café regular explained, refugees "would rather forego a hot meal or a night in a hotel than miss seeing their comrades who shared an identical fate (*Schicksalsgenossen*) and whom they would surely encounter here."[112]

Limited Integration

Aside from concern over refugee women's dress and behavior, Portuguese in cities and small towns took most refugee behavior in stride. Open conflicts between refugees and residents occurred—if at all—rarely enough that refugees and aid organizations did not mention them. Surely, the government's lack of overt antisemitism smoothed the way, as did the fact that refugees could not compete for employment with Portuguese. Refugees came and left in waves and did not appear to be a stagnant mass of needy people, which might have triggered annoyance or anger. Nor did refugees appear destitute, since the Jewish community and aid groups assisted them, even if minimally. And refugees brought business to cafés, boardinghouses, and groceries. Finally, they did not intervene in Portuguese politics or culture. Aside from their mere presence and unusual gender mores, they remained friendly but remote, focusing on their own problems. The few documented cases of tension ensued when several refugees ignored restrictions forbidding them to peddle or to work.[113]

Nazi agents nevertheless tried to create dissension between Portuguese citizens and Jewish refugees. In 1941, for example, the *American Jewish Yearbook* of the AJC reported that Nazis tried to undermine "the morale of this hospitable people" by spreading rumors that the Gestapo had lists of Jews and non-Jews who would later be treated as anti-Nazis. Even then, this major American Jewish organization, like many others, recognized the amiability of the Portuguese people and the cooperation of the Salazar government. As late as 1944, the non-Jewish author Suzanne Chantal, a keen observer of Portugal, penned a few suspicions about "embryonic" antisemitism in her novel *God Doesn't Sleep* (*Deus não dorme*). That same year, the German Embassy, probably to its consternation, noted the absence of antisemitism in Portugal.[114]

Since most refugees saw Portugal as an interlude, lasting friendships among Portuguese and Jewish refugees rarely occurred. Yet a variety of relationships emerged. The German-Jewish refugee Heinz Wisla, confined by the police to a fishing village, learned basic Portuguese quickly and conversed with fishermen as they repaired heavy nets: "They are wise men despite their lack of education." A Belgian-Jewish teenager recalled warmly that "when we left Lisbon, there were about a dozen Portuguese friends of various ages on the pier waving goodbye."[115] The several hundred German Jews who had come before the refugee tide, many intending to settle in Portugal, made more friendships than those who arrived later. Some of these earlier immigrants, mostly women, married Portuguese men and remained in Portugal the rest of their lives.[116]

Smaller cities and towns may have offered more opportunities to meet local residents. Renée Liberman married the Portuguese doctor who cared for refugees in the village of Caldas da Rainha. Ilse Losa appreciated the welcome she received from the surrounding population in Porto. She met her husband and had her children there. Her Portuguese neighbors' cordiality gave her a sense of belonging. One of the characters in her novel begins to feel that he fits into society in Porto upon befriending a Portuguese, and another concludes that "friends make up our riches, not the lovely cities, one survives because of one's friends." Losa liked Portugal's slower, more casual life, compared with Germany's; a "tempo" that proclaimed, "If I don't come today, I'll come tomorrow."[117]

Schools provided an opportunity to reach out to Portuguese children. One Jewish student noticed that in contrast to her dread of Nazi persecution and the expanding war, her classmates "were children without worries." A few Jewish children made friends for life. For example, having attended a girls' school as two of seven Jews among one thousand Catholics, the two Westheimer sisters remained in touch with their Portuguese friends, and when one sister died, decades later, a Portuguese friend had a Mass said for her. This same Portuguese friend still went to church every day, she wrote the other sister, fifty years later, but "every once in a while, I go to your synagogue to feel close to you."[118]

The few refugees—about fifty—who remained in Portugal seem to have integrated into middle-class Portuguese society, although some also maintained their own refugee cultures and circles. Ruth Arons exemplified the first group. She arrived at age thirteen in 1935, attended university in Lisbon, and married there. When the dictatorship ended, she served as the first elected mayor of a district of Lisbon. Interviewed in 2012, she stated: "My country is Portugal now. I love Lisbon. . . . I know all the people on this street where I've lived for 50 years." Ilse Losa maintained both cultures. She wrote prize-winning novels and children's books in Portuguese, cultivated her German language, and published in German for an adult audience. Daniel Blaufuks depicted his grandmother's weekly canasta group of "refugee ladies" in a film. They mixed both cultures. Several of these women had married Portuguese men, learned the language, and integrated into Portuguese daily life. Blaufuks's grandmother brought up a "Portuguese daughter and two Portuguese grandchildren." Still, they spoke German with one another and ate homemade German apple pie: "That canasta table was a country . . . [where] they found a part of themselves again," their German-Jewish culture. Yet this same family celebrated victory over Germany with its Portuguese neighbors. On the street, they "could hear good wishes and shouts such as 'Long live the Jews.'"[119]

⚜

Portugal opened and shut its door unpredictably. Once refugees had made it past the border, the government accepted those ready to leave, remained patient toward those with proper papers awaiting their ships, and harassed or interned those whose papers had expired or who had no visas. But none of this was clear from the perspective of refugees. A good word from an aid agency or from the Jewish community or a well-placed bribe might change the picture for an individual or a family. Jewish refugees had to interpret mixed messages, confront a bewildering array of possibilities, and control their resulting hopes and fears. Most retained memories of the kindness of Portuguese people, although they had suffered from the confusing policies set by Salazar's authoritarian state. Fewer made permanent friendships with Portuguese: "It wasn't integration, but living together."[120] Most simply appreciated the peace and tranquility of this liminal space. Still, they needed to seek aid from consulates and international organizations in order to leave, while avoiding the Nazis prowling Lisbon and dodging the Portuguese police.

3. "Lisbon Is Sold Out"

Relief and Hope, Nazis and Dictatorship

I'll wait here now to see if they will give me status. . . . I want
very much to be legal. To have documents.

Having arrived in Lisbon by train, by plane, or on foot, refugees could breathe a momentary sigh of relief. Nevertheless, many had no papers, and even those with proper documents felt physically and emotionally in transit. Experiencing Lisbon as a complicated and contradictory site, they appreciated the peace and help they found there, but felt threatened by the presence of local Nazis and the German tanks that stood at the French border with Spain. And refugees' illegal or expired documents could mean jail or even prison, locations that caused great fear. Most refugees had neither the energy nor the serenity to become tourists in picturesque Lisbon, "built on seven hills with a valley running down the middle to the waterfront."[1] They could not let down their guard.

Peace

In Erich Maria Remarque's novel *The Night in Lisbon,* the city's streetlights and "carefree illumination" startled an anxious character who had just passed through darkened, occupied Europe: "In the countries I had come from, the cities at night were black as coal mines. . . . I keep thinking somebody has forgotten to turn [the lights] off and the planes will attack any minute." This "city of light" (Cidade da Luz), where the sun reflects off the Tagus River and where the whiteness of limestone buildings and sidewalks contributes to a sense of brightness, impressed newcomers, particularly if they were not refugees. An American Quaker admired Lisbon, "scattered across rolling hills," and appreciated the Avenida da Liberdade, with its lively shops, restaurants, and cafés. Looking up, he saw the "remains of a large Moorish castle dominat[ing] the highest hill." A guidebook for the American armed forces—in the event that the war required them to enter Portugal—praised "the most old-fashioned capital in Europe," pointing out "vista on vista of azure walls, white arched windows and wrought-iron balconies." The author admired the "brightly lighted open-air cafes, often with bands," and Praça do Comércio, "one of the most beautiful squares in the world." The colors, too, elicited admiration. The French writer Suzanne Chantal acclaimed Lisbon as a "city of a thousand colours . . . the finest shades of green, yellow and above all pink, stressed here and there by the varnished blue of the *azulejos* (painted tiles) as the city spreads out over the hills bathed in limpid light."[2]

The noises of Lisbon startled newcomers. The Unitarian worker Martha Sharp registered her surprise, labeling the Rossio, Lisbon's main and oldest plaza, "the noisiest square in Europe." She saw beggars hawking and "loudspeakers outside the movie houses . . . advertising the latest American thrillers . . . [and] careening cars speeding by on two wheels. All was color and excitement." The Rossio reminded Charles Joy, also of the Unitarians, of New York's Times Square. Others witnessed taxi drivers "blowing their horns joyously and continuously."[3] Refugees, too, reacted to the clamor of Lisbon's streets. The novelist Alfred Döblin described trams clanging, cars honking, and people singing: "Day after day we encountered merry musicians and singers of both sexes. . . . And if you haven't experienced the shouting of the newsboys here at seven in the morning, you don't know what the human voice is capable of." Yet as Jewish refugees tried to make sense of this new "hot, bright, southern, peaceful world," their observations of the city often differed from those of aid workers or writers. They did not comment on the bullfights, parades, or fiestas or, perhaps, even notice the wide panoramas over the sea, the brilliantly tiled and painted walls of recently restored buildings and monuments, or the black-and-white mosaic patterns that decorated the main plazas.[4] Colorful vistas could not erase their forebodings.

A refugee in Anna Seghers's semiautobiographical novel *Transit* described her feelings as she fled through Europe: "I'm sure that I haven't seen most of the really important things that happen in this city. . . . Cities shroud themselves from those who are just passing through." Others compared Lisbon to the traumatic scenes they had just witnessed. Although Döblin acknowledged Lisbon's "light, music, and laughter," the city gave him a "jolt": "Not far from here France was in agony. . . . People were suffering and hungry. . . . Millions lived in terror. . . . We couldn't enjoy it. We could only think of what we had left behind." Refugees' letters and memoirs rarely detailed their brief stays. A few weeks after leaving the city, one person rather typically wrote, "Lisbon is a very beautiful and busy place, but I . . . rather write to you about our . . . trip from Lisbon to New York." One letter, from 1951, mentioned that the writer had "locked Lisbon in [his] heart" and would surely visit it again, but most refugees' memories jumped from the trek to Lisbon to the difficulties of moving on.[5]

Perhaps some purposely kept from exploring the city, trying to conserve their savings and their strength for the paper chase they were engaged in. Others probably feared the police. A character in Remarque's novel knew only the churches and museums, because in front of the statues and artworks, one was still a person, "not an individual with dubious papers." Not even Lisbon's Exposition of the Portuguese World, which opened in the fateful month of June 1940 on the double anniversaries of Portugal's founding in 1140 and its independence from Spain in 1640, attracted the notice of refugees enough to enter their later reflections. From June 2 until December 3, 1940—exactly when refugees were flooding into Portugal—more than three million Portuguese visited this extravagant historical and political fair. The exhibition, looking back to Portugal's "golden era," consisted of huge pavilions, water displays, tropical gardens, imposing statues, and an amusement park. This spectacle, along with parades, festivities, and the opening of the restored Lisbon Opera House in December, celebrated Portugal's history and Salazar's achievements. In fact, buses to take huge crowds of visitors to the exposition lined up on the Rossio, where so many refugees gathered daily.[6]

In normal times, many of these newcomers would have watched parades, visited museums, and enjoyed the opera. Not now. Heinrich Mann explained his indifference, echoing other refugees' feelings: "A remarkable colonial exhibition had been set up," but he did not bother to visit it. Alluding to his recent escape from Germany, he recorded: "This is what parting does, one feels it internally and is very pre-occupied [by it]. What might have otherwise captivated is overlooked." Even when he passed the replica of the sailing vessel of Vasco da Gama, the renowned Portuguese explorer, he remained unmoved: "The famous traveler could have stood there and waved his hat: my approaching journey belittled his. Didn't he return?"[7]

Nor did refugees engage with the three Fs that many Portuguese believed summed up their nation: fado, football, and Fátima. Fado, a melancholy and mournful genre of Portuguese music, often expressed feelings of loss. It evoked the liminal space in which refugees found themselves: "We hardly needed this type of music because our own circumstances created enough natural sadness. While the coffee houses appeared packed every day, the refugees rarely visited the fado clubs." Football (soccer) did not attract their interest either. The sport had grown popular in Portugal and Germany in the early twentieth century, with enthusiasts following local and national teams. If the teenage Peter Gay's devotion to Hertha, his favorite Berlin team, is any indication of German-Jewish youngsters' passion for soccer, then most refugees had lost or suspended interest in their previous sports clubs or had too little energy to learn about Portuguese teams.[8]

The village of Fátima, about seventy-five miles from Lisbon, also escaped their attention. According to Catholic belief, an apparition of the Virgin Mary appeared to three children there in 1917. One of the most important Catholic shrines in the world, even today about five million people a year visit it. Popular religiosity helped conservative forces claim Our Lady of Fátima as the guardian of Portugal, and in 1938, Pope Pius XII thanked the Virgin for saving Portugal from communism. Salazar's connection to Fátima legitimized his own political position as well as that of the Catholic Church.[9] Jewish refugees, however, did not appear to reflect upon the politics surrounding Catholicism.

A few refugees did notice that Lisbon showed signs of stark class inequality and highly visible, "indescribable poverty." Men, women, and children begged in the streets. The non-Jewish political journalist Karl Paetel thought Lisbon "was gorgeous—if one stayed on the main avenue and refrained from wandering left or right into the darker streets where men and women prepared their meager meals on log fires in front of their squalid houses: Slums." And directly after the war, when Simone de Beauvoir visited Lisbon, a male character in her novel *The Mandarins* found squalor: "Barefooted women—everyone here went barefooted. . . . In cellar apartments opening onto the street, not a bed, not a piece of furniture, not a picture; nothing but straw mats, children covered with rashes, and from time to time a goat." An elderly anti-fascist in the novel commented, "Lisbon, a beautiful façade, isn't it?" Then they toured the "starving villages surrounding Lisbon."[10] Most Jewish refugees in transit in Portugal, however, preoccupied by their own problems, rarely mentioned the stark gap between rich and poor. On a personal level, such poverty may have frightened them, reminding them that they depended on charities and that their own savings had shrunk or hit rock bottom.

Instead, refugees focused their psychic energy on "freedom and peace": "The 'new world' seemed to begin here. Only one more step and Europe with its oppression and hatred lay behind us." They no longer had to worry about bombing raids, blackouts, or Nazi troops directly behind them. New arrivals began to sleep better. Fred Mann, a teenager from Leipzig, reflected on why sleep came more easily: "Our minds weren't clouded with fear. For the last six months we had lived with the dread of facing the Nazis at any moment."[11] Sometimes the ocean provided time off from the daily grind: a mother recalled that her children did not leave the water when they went to the beach and that she, too, found swimming to be her "only pleasure." As he entered Lisbon, Felix Bauer, freed from a Swiss internment camp, felt "an aura of peace": "After all the strain of the past, it was hard to comprehend all this." His memoir, written shortly after his stay, described Lisbon as the "first place that was normal . . . in two years. . . . a place with civilization," adding, "We were in seventh heaven there." Another refugee's letter (from 1941) referred to Lisbon simply as "paradise."[12]

But they needed money to live in this paradise. Those whose money had run out while awaiting postponed departures met with agencies that doled out limited funds: "relief funds: . . . were meant to keep people from starving, not in luxury." Morris Troper of the American Jewish Joint Distribution Committee (JDC) in Lisbon "spent [the] entire day listening [to] pitiful pleas [of] refugee groups asking us not [to] reduce already meagre allowances." By late 1940, the JDC was providing refugees with rent and six meals plus 23 escudos per week (the equivalent of 90 cents, but also 3 escudos more than the weekly income of a skilled male worker). Troper continued, "A great many complaints are heard on all sides, but some of these, as we all know, are more or less to be expected in this type of work." Yet he asked the JDC in New York for more money, since refugees occasionally needed some clothing and medicine, and at least one other meal a day, plus two meals on Saturdays: "You can see that this basis is really lower than the most elementary form of human treatment demands."[13]

People and Places Offering Help

The Portuguese regime allowed local and international organizations, especially Jewish ones, to help out. These latter groups depended on the advice
and support of the tiny Portuguese-Jewish community of Lisbon, which
distributed aid through COMASSIS (Comissão Portuguesa de Assistência aos
Judeus Refugiados, the Portuguese Commission to Assist Jewish Refugees).[14]
Its chair, Augusto d'Esaguy, at first allowed the refugee committee to operate
out of his office. He saw "unexpected scenes of inexpressible joy" when families who had lost track of one another were reunited by coincidence while
sitting in his waiting room, after having "feared the worst." COMASSIS paid
for medical help at the Israelite Hospital (Hospital Israelita). And its Lisbon
cemetery offered a few refugees a last respite from, as d'Esaguy put it, "the
effects of the hardships they had suffered before they reached us."[15]

COMASSIS sent representatives to the Spanish-Portuguese border to
help people arriving by train or by foot. Ernst Levy, an earlier refugee and
barely twenty years old, served as one such local go-between. He explained
the Portuguese situation to Jews who had just set foot in the country. Despite
his own discomfort—he slept in the cold attic of the local train station—he
understood from experience that these refugees had "suffered a major
emotional blow." In Lisbon, another community aid worker, Yvette Davidofe,
wrote: "Many problems were so huge that we could not solve them. During
the first few weeks, I cried at home every night." Lucy Frucht, an Estonian
Jew who had fled to Portugal, worked for d'Esaguy and the refugee committee
for two years. She took names and reported the needs of refugees: "What did
they need? Money? Papers? A place to stay?" Before international aid groups
appeared, the small Jewish community "did it all by themselves," and she
added that Portuguese Jews "were very, very generous."[16]

The Portuguese-Jewish community used its political influence to protect
refugees and obtain permission for them to reside temporarily in Portugal.[17] In
early 1943, for example, Elias Baruel, vice president of the Jewish community,
and the secret police's Lourenço had a tense exchange. The police complained
that the Jewish community supported undocumented refugees, and that it
made no sense that "a Portuguese institution" would assist people who flouted
Portuguese law. Baruel quoted Salazar, who had stated that Portugal "is among
all the nations the one that shows itself to be the most liberal and generous
towards foreigners, in its legislation, tradition, and care." Baruel wrote that
he understood that the police required people who entered Portugal illegally

to come to their offices, where they would be assigned a fixed residence from which they needed special permission to leave. Refugees also preferred to regularize their status in this way. But recently, he noted, rumors had scared some refugees into believing that they would wind up in jail if they went to the police. They hid in Lisbon instead.[18] Politely, Baruel suggested that refugees would cooperate with the police if they did not fear prison. In fact, most refugees, including those entering illegally, did not end up in prison. But all dreaded the possibility of arrest or worse, deportation, by the Portuguese secret police. Baruel and the Lisbon Jewish community assisted refugees, mediating between them and the police into the 1950s, well after other aid organizations had left.[19]

Augmenting this modest but energetic local help, international organizations, offering humanitarian assistance, worked tirelessly. These groups, mostly American, gathered money in the United States or lobbied Congress and the White House. Others provided care on the ground, including help with visas. Still others supported political opponents of Nazism and fascism, artists and intellectuals, and Christians of Jewish ancestry. The JDC, the International Red Cross, the Portuguese Red Cross, the World Council of Churches, Catholic Relief Services, the American Friends Service Committee (AFSC, or Quakers), the Unitarian Service Committee (USC), and, much later (1944), the War Refugee Board, among other groups, opened offices in Lisbon. In addition, certain national committees, like those of the Poles and Czechs exiled in London, assisted their citizens.[20] Aside from the national committees, made up of opponents of Nazism, the American groups consisted of many Protestant and Quaker social workers. The Jewish groups included American Jews, but in Lisbon, refugees with better language skills than the Americans worked for the Jewish committees as well.

The Unitarians set up the Unitarian Service Committee at the beginning of the war to help refugees. With close ties to Czech Unitarians, the USC first carried out rescue and relief operations from Prague, attempting to aid intellectuals, students, and anti-Nazis. In 1940, it established offices in Marseille, Geneva, Paris, and Lisbon. The USC made contact with Varian Fry's American Emergency Rescue Committee in the hope of facilitating the emigration of refugees from France. Like the Quakers, the USC originally focused on non-Jews, but they advanced the cases of many Jews as well as "non-Aryans" who had converted to some form of Christianity. In Marseille, 90 percent of the USC's efforts centered on Jews or former Jews, and in

Refugees in a Lisbon soup kitchen supported by the JDC, 1940s. (Photograph by Roger Kahan, NY_06714, Courtesy of JDC Archives, New York).

Lisbon, the USC staff maintained warm relationships with the Lisbon Jewish community. As the war progressed, several of the USC leaders in Lisbon spied for the OSS. Moreover, one of the USC's mainstays, Martha Sharp, founded Children to Palestine, to assist children hiding in France to get to Portugal and then travel to Mandatory Palestine.[21]

The Quakers, too, mobilized to aid refugee children in camps under the Vichy regime and grew into the main support for the Foundation for Refugee Children (1940), which helped Jewish children settle in the United States. In February 1941, Marjorie ("Marnie") Schauffler opened the Quaker office in Lisbon. It supported refugees for a few days to many months, intervening with the police, prison authorities, and consulates. Philip Conard of the Quakers, working long hours and weekends, wrote: "You have heard of the 'wandering Jew.' Here you have him in person!" The Quakers worked with people of all religions. They also cared for converts to Christianity, stateless people "of Jewish ancestry" who did not identify as Jews, and partners in Jewish-Christian mixed marriages. In the first half of 1942, for example, the Quakers aided 55 Jews out of 152 people listed as Christians and "Unknowns." When the Glauber couple, a Jewish husband and Catholic wife, faced internment in

Caldas da Rainha, they appealed to the Quakers. Glauber maintained that the Jewish community would not support his wife.[22] The JDC often paid the way for Jewish converts and Jews in intermarriages whom the Quakers or USC helped, but JDC leaders believed that since their funds came from "Jews by faith," they needed to focus on Jews by faith.[23]

Jewish organizations, by far the most active in Lisbon, concentrated on Jews defined by religion. Starting in the summer of 1940, the Jewish associations—the JDC, HIAS (Hebrew Immigrant Aid Society), HICEM, the World Jewish Congress (WJC), the Jewish Agency for Palestine (Jewish Agency), and the Portuguese-Jewish relief committees—supported refugees in order to offer solidarity to Jews in trouble but also to prevent them from burdening the Portuguese state and thereby generating governmental hostility. A telegram of August 1940 from the JDC in Lisbon to its New York office went straight to the point, namely, the "importance [of] not endangering present hospitable attitude." In mid-1941, the JDC, "anxious to avoid difficulties," reminded Portugal's minister in Washington that "thus far no refugee has become a charge on the public purse nor is any refugee likely to become one so long as American philanthropic agencies are in a position to render their services."[24]

HIAS, founded in 1881, merged with HICEM when it was established in 1927, consolidating three organizations. HIAS had served as the largest Jewish aid group in France before Vichy disbanded it and it moved to Lisbon. HICEM also moved to Lisbon. A grateful Hans Sahl described what HICEM meant on the ground: "HICEM paid the hotel and the hair cutter, HICEM paid for the cake that one devoured, the fruit, the chocolate, everything edible. . . . HICEM paid for the doctor and the drug store . . . the American visa," even the ship ticket that he bought in a café once his visa arrived.[25]

The JDC, with offices in more than forty countries to assist refugees, moved its headquarters from Paris to Lisbon in 1940 "a few steps ahead of the Germans." Under the leadership of Joseph Schwartz in Lisbon and his assistant, Herbert Katzki, the JDC offered sustenance and shelter, although many refugees who stayed only a short time managed to support themselves or had relatives abroad subsidizing them.[26] Of 8,000 refugees still in Portugal at the end of 1940, the JDC supported 1,500. The JDC also contributed the main support to the Lisbon Jewish community. Whereas HIAS-HICEM aided individuals, the JDC attended to "the wholesale business," paying for train transports from Germany, booking ship passages for trainloads of refugees, and even chartering boats. The JDC also helped Jews who had been smuggled into Portugal apply for American "Affidavits in Lieu of Passport." By October 1941, the deluge of refugees and their needs had overwhelmed the office. Anticipating winter, an aid worker saw the need for shoes and clothing, "as the reserves of the refugees are almost exhausted."[27]

Seeking funds to meet the overwhelming demands on its budget, the JDC established a Transmigration Bureau in New York in 1940. It accepted deposits from friends or family in the United States toward the travel costs of Jews emigrating from Europe. Aside from these basics, the JDC supplied religious necessities to Jews, such as matzot on Passover.[28] It sent fifteen thousand pounds of matzot to Lisbon in 1943, paying the Horowitz Bros. & Margareten Company $1,350. Between 1936 and 1944, the JDC allocated over $1,130,000 (the equivalent of $20,667,700 in 2019) to refugee aid in Portugal.[29]

Social workers in Lisbon experienced intense and conflicting feelings, ranging from happiness to anguish. They labored long hours, interviewing refugees; intervening with government, police, consulates, and shipping agencies; finding medical care, clothing, and subsidies for the needy; writing lengthy reports and letters; and taking phone calls. While the detailed work could be tedious, Conard of the Quakers insisted that "every week is 'unusual,'" since he regularly confronted a problem or a person that "fill[ed] the time and mind and heart." Still, aid workers felt overwhelmed. One Quaker employee lamented that agencies "trying to give assistance to stranded refugees are doing their utmost, but their resources cannot provide anything beyond the most inadequate relief." At moments, clients seemed inconsolable. Other times, social workers expressed prejudices, as when one worker wrote that a client exhibited "an exaggerated feminism, but she is very capable." They occasionally had to shut down their feelings and steel themselves against applicants' requests, warned by their colleagues, "Don't let . . . a flood of tears break you down."[30]

Some, like Lawrence Parrish, a Quaker, felt troubled by their careers. Parrish, who made a weekly visit to groups of refugees, observed in his diary:

> In some ways, it is not a pleasant job. The people whom one meets are usually very nice, and it is interesting to talk to them, but they usually have such a tragic story . . . and their present and future are so dark. . . . One of the most unfortunate things, however, is the

relationship which exists between the person receiving the relief and the person representing the agency giving the relief. The poor refugee is . . . asking for and accepting money from someone else. . . . It also makes me uncomfortable to realize I hold such power over the lives of these people.

Similarly, Morris Troper of the JDC wrote, "To listen to the stories of these people and to be unable to do anything for them is one of the most harrowing experiences that one can ever live through. It is almost impossible to work in an atmosphere of this kind." Most understood that refugees needed emotional support. One appreciative refugee wrote to the aid worker who had helped him: "Refugees are grateful for a good little word and if they feel that there is someone who gives them moral help and shows understanding, they very often are happier than they would be with any amount of money." Most social workers thought that they had contributed to something important. Noel Field, devoted to helping Jewish and antifascist refugees, summed up these feelings in a letter to his mother: "Never in our lives before had we been so intensely alive and so—if I may say so—worthwhile. And I hate to think of all the things left undone, and the many hearts that must be crying for us in their still greater need."[31]

All these agencies faced issues of legality. The Jewish community, as represented by Moses Amzalak, proudly emphasized its good relations with the police and the government. Augusto d'Esaguy, head of COMASSIS, asserted that the Portuguese Ministry of Foreign Affairs dealt only with him and with the JDC regarding Jewish refugees. The JDC, cooperating closely with the Lisbon Jewish community, tried to stay within the law, helping those who had arrived illegally to acquire the necessary papers. On occasion, the JDC as well as other American agencies may have bribed the police to gain their cooperation. In at least one case, the JDC hoped to keep a situation "sweet," but lacked the necessary funds. More generally, the JDC supported relief but not rescue. Its leaders worried that clandestine rescue operations that brought Jews from Nazi-occupied Europe into Portugal would flout Portuguese laws and that the government might retaliate by refusing entry to other refugees. Letters from the JDC and HICEM regularly informed the police of problems affecting refugees.[32]

The Quakers, too, respected Portuguese law and cooperated with the JDC. In late 1941, Conard managed to obtain an appointment with "the

Chief of Police, said to stand next to the Dictator in power at least with regard to . . . dealing with us foreigners." He stated, "Our relations with the police have been good (though it requires endless patience), and I am confident that an understanding of our work and purpose on the part of the Chief, and an understanding on our part of the problems they have to deal with, will make our relations still more fruitful." Yet in 1981, Conard's daughter implied that he may have broken some rules: "Father was fully aware of how dependent the success of the AFSC work was on the sufferance of the host country. . . . He was meticulous about observing the rules and using established channels. However, on occasion a situation would arise where there was a conflict. When asked what he did under those circumstances (a case where a refugee's life depended on some 'unofficial action') he explained: 'I step out of my role as the Quaker representative, take care of the matter, then step back into my role again.' "[33]

Unlike the official Portuguese Jewish community and the Quakers, the Unitarians and the World Jewish Congress engaged in semilegal or even illegal actions, cooperating with each other, especially regarding clandestine rescues over the Portuguese border. Isaac Weissmann of the WJC used legal and illegal means, including connections with professional smugglers and with the Portuguese police, much to the consternation of the Lisbon Jewish communal leadership. Robert Dexter, who founded the Unitarian Service Committee and served as the War Refugee Board representative in Lisbon in 1944, felt the JDC did not do enough to rescue people in imminent danger of death. Years later, his wife, Elizabeth Dexter, who also worked in the USC's Lisbon office, told an interviewer:

> We rather specialized in illegals for two reasons. One was that the illegals . . . were . . . people that because of their leadership in some field or another would be in more danger . . . [and] because neither the Joint nor the Quakers who both had offices there liked to work with illegals. They did at times, but it was really against their principles, because both felt that they could help more people in the long run if they did not go counter to the laws of the country . . . I know that sometimes they helped people when they weren't supposed to, but they were very glad indeed if we would take them off their hands.

In 1944, one of the USC leaders remarked upon the close cooperation between the JDC and Quakers, likening the relationship to that between a "mother and baby kangaroo—Quakers being the baby." They all "get on all right. . . . but USC need not expect real help from either." That same year, the War Refugee Board painted a more complicated and more negative picture, concluding that the JDC seemed to think it had a "monopoly on rescue and relief operations." Yet overall, the USC and the JDC saw themselves as cooperating with each other to form a sometimes-fractious "work troika" of the JDC, Unitarians, and Quakers to support refugees.[34]

The surprise attack on Pearl Harbor, on December 7, 1941, dramatically curtailed the delivery of relief, at least for a time. Within days, the United States called back most American citizens in Europe. American-Jewish organizations could no longer function openly in a neutral nation and officially relied on the Portuguese-Jewish community to assist refugees. COMASSIS closed its offices when d'Esaguy left for the United States. But Portuguese Jews and some refugees employed in these offices provided continuity, and the JDC replenished the Jewish community's bank accounts.[35] Also, as long as the U.S. Treasury Department maintained oversight, it allowed money transfers by the JDC.[36] It does not seem, however, that the JDC, HICEM, HIAS, the Quakers, or the Unitarians withdrew completely, and by very early 1942 the JDC had apparently started working overtly again.[37]

Individuals, too, engaged in rescue efforts in Lisbon. The businessman and philanthropist Wilfred Israel, who tried to relocate refugees from Lisbon to Palestine, serves as the most prominent example. Earlier, this fifth-generation offspring of the family behind one of the largest and oldest Berlin department stores, N. Israel, had helped obtain the release and transport of thousands of Jewish men from German concentration camps to transit camps in England. Israel further supported the Youth Aliyah movement, founded by Recha Freier in 1932, which brought Jewish youngsters to Mandatory Palestine. And after the November Pogrom, he helped expedite the *Kindertransports* of ten thousand children from Germany to England. In March 1943, he undertook a mission to Portugal for the Jewish Agency. There he distributed entry certificates to Mandatory Palestine, anticipating that as Jews left Portugal, others from occupied Europe could take their places. He also studied the situation of Jewish refugees in Portugal and planned to rescue Jewish children from Vichy France. En route from Lisbon to England in June 1943, German combat aircraft shot down his plane; the other twelve passengers included the famous English actor Leslie Howard. The latter's death made this tragedy international news. Ninety-seven certificates for Palestine went down with Wilfred Israel.[38]

Nazis in Portugal

Finding some peace and help in a relatively safe location did not mean that Jewish refugees had entirely escaped Germans or Nazis. Local Germans, increasingly attracted to Nazism, disturbed the composure of Jewish refugees, especially those who had lived in Portugal since the 1930s. Many Germans in Portugal joined the Nazi Party. In addition, Gestapo, Security Service (Sicherheitsdienst), and German propaganda agents agitated for the Nazis under cover of German firms, cultural organization, and consulates. German expatriates and businesspeople in Portugal, about 2,000 in all, including 1,200 in the "German Colony" in Lisbon, had expelled German Jews from their clubs and organizations by 1937–38. The Bartholomäus Brüderschaft in Lisbon, for example, founded by merchants from the coasts of northern Europe in 1290, was one of the oldest German fraternal organizations abroad; it endorsed Nazism in 1935. It pressured its local Jewish members to withdraw, although Eduard Katzenstein, who had joined in 1907, did not resign until 1938. The German club, with about 300 members, collected money for the Nazis' Winter Help organization in Germany and arranged dinners consisting of a simple stew in order to save money for Germany. That club also published a newsletter that advertised Nazi Party meetings and Nazi organizations in Portugal, and propagandized Nazi achievements.[39] Nazi enthusiasts in Lisbon rented empty storefronts and placed placards in the windows praising the "invincible" German army and Germany's "anti-Bolshevik" crusade. In Porto, the growing antisemitism of the German community caused Jews as well as anti-Nazi Germans to spurn German activities. Jews there knew exactly where the Nazi Party held its meetings.[40] Once Germany started the war, German clubs in Lisbon and Porto no longer waved their Nazi flags in public, even though the banners still decorated their clubs' interiors.

As Germans increasingly joined Nazi groups, they dismissed their Jewish employees. When the German consul in Lisbon demanded that businesses "aryanize" by the mid-1930s, Germans complied by firing Jewish personnel. Even "half-Jews" had to go, though later. Arriving from Germany in the summer of 1938, Rosalie Anschel worked at a German firm. Because she had a Jewish father, however, she lost her job when the war broke out, even though she and her mother were Catholic. And nationalistic German housewives living in Portugal did their part, boycotting Jewish vendors who sold German foods.[41]

German schools in Portugal also turned hostile toward German-Jewish children. In Porto, for example, local Nazis barred Ilse Losa's daughters from the German kindergarten. Losa still wrote in German, and she had wanted her children to study her native language. In addition, the school library discarded books written by Jewish authors. Losa noticed that German children did not publicly dress in Hitler Youth uniforms, but wore them under their coats until they got to the school, perhaps a sign that they hoped to avoid Portuguese disapproval. The German School of Lisbon (Escola Alemã de Lisboa, or Deutsche Schule zu Lissabon) fired its Jewish teacher. The atmosphere and curriculum at the German School continued to deteriorate. From 1933 on, all the children had to sing the Nazi anthem in school. Besides creating an environment hostile to Jews, the German School began to include instruction in racial studies and to minimize French instruction. Two young Jewish girls had attended the German School for three years when, in 1934, the German students started to taunt them. The Jewish girls left that school and joined the Portuguese *liceu* (middle and high school) for girls. Rudolf Aberle, a Dutch-Jewish child whose father worked in Lisbon, attended the German School from 1926 until 1935. By then, all the Jews and "non-Aryans" had left the school. He added that he only heard the epithet "Jewish swine" in German, never in Portuguese.[42]

Nazi organizations, such as the Association of German Girls, the German Labor Front, the Hitler Youth, and the welfare organization (*Volks-wohlfahrt*) established auxiliaries in Portugal. In 1938, the Hitler Youth visited Portugal to march with the Portuguese Youth Movement and members of the Italian Fascist Youth in honor of the anniversary of Salazar's revolution. Portuguese boys between the ages of seven and fourteen had to join the Mocidade Portuguesa, the only youth organization allowed, wearing its uniform, giving the fascist salute, and practicing military maneuvers. Still, this Portuguese youth organization, very Catholic, nationalist, and Sala-zarist, also criticized German youth groups for their "virile, pagan, atheist" behavior. It leaned toward Germany until 1940, when its new leadership shifted toward England and transformed the group into one similar to the Boy Scouts. According to the historian Irene Pimentel, the German Colony in Lisbon split into three parts: a small, old elite that disliked the Nazis and greeted each other with "hello" rather than "Heil Hitler"; a middle group that gave money to German Winter Help and hoped no one saw them give the Hitler greeting; and a group of ardent enthusiasts.[43]

A Spreading War?

Local Nazis notwithstanding, most Jews focused on the war, galvanized by the latest German offensives or defeats. The fear that Hitler might invade Portugal gnawed at Jews in stages, especially between June 1940 and November 1942. They read a "vast assortment of newspapers . . . written in every language," with contradictory reports prompting long discussions. That papers often arrived overdue did not deter the readers. Those in Lisbon also watched British and American newsreels. Like many who had barely escaped the advancing Germans, Hans Sahl feared that the feeling of safety "was deceiving": "Hitler had occupied almost all of Europe. Why should he spare Portugal? . . . We had to ensure a passage before it was too late."[44] In July 1940, the Austrian dramatist Leopold von Andrian wrote a friend that he believed the war would also engulf Portugal, and a few weeks later, Kurt Israel's analysis made sense: "After all, Portugal is also Europe." That October, the author Marguerite Douhaerdt noted, "I have to get out of here, because one day the Germans will come." Even in a small seaside town outside Lisbon where the Berenholz family "went to the beach every day," they kept "maps on the wall following the armies in the war." When the author Antoine de Saint-Exupéry, who had flown for the French air force, crossed into Portugal in December 1940, Lisbon appeared a "sad" paradise; he believed "it spoke . . . of imminent invasion."[45]

Rumors spread anxiety. American aid workers believed that a German invasion of Portugal would threaten not only refugees but also Portuguese Jews. Despite their worries, most Portuguese Jews remained, but a few German-Jewish families that had settled there earlier decided to leave. The Davidsohn family, which had arrived in 1935 and planned to live there, sent their thirteen-year-old daughter to the United States, splitting the family, with all the tension that entailed. Their older teenage daughter assisted one of the refugee aid committees in Lisbon and also sent packages of food to relatives in concentration camps. The Blum family, which had settled comfortably in Portugal after the November Pogrom, fled to the United States in mid-1941. They heard "partly in jest, partly in earnest, that Germany would take Spain in a day and capture Portugal by telephone."[46]

Not only refugees were afraid—everyone was afraid. Waitstill Sharp of the Unitarians reported as fact the wildly inaccurate rumor that sixty thousand Nazi tanks stood at the Spanish border in the summer of 1940. That September, his colleague, also reacting to the "hotbed of rumor" in Lisbon, shared Unitarian concerns regarding the alleged mobilization of Portuguese troops at the Spanish border. His office planned to ship all completed cases to the United States, since it would be "very unfortunate" if the Germans invaded Portugal and found them. The American war correspondent William Shirer expressed alarm in his diary entry of October 15, 1940, in Berlin: "For some time I've been getting information from military circles that Hitler is making ready to go into Spain in order to get Gibraltar." A few months later, the American reporter Eric Sevareid, living outside Lisbon, wrote: "One morning at nine, the German passenger plane roared alarmingly low over the Palace Hotel. I asked a waiter why the pilot should go off his course . . . 'We think it's to get us used to the Swastika,' he said. 'The first time he did it, the visa line at your consulate grew much longer.' "[47]

In April 1941, JDC social workers in New York shared concerns about an invasion. One reported: "Of course, all Lisbon is full of rumors that . . . Hitler would soon come to Portugal." Philip Conard, still in Lisbon, however, remained skeptical, dismissing rumors as "recurring waves of 'jitters' " and believing them to be part of the "psychological 'war of nerves' " that Germans planted. After Pearl Harbor, all the Americans at the JDC in Lisbon, except two, left for the United States: "Everyone was so certain that when the United States came into the war . . . the Germans would take Lisbon . . . and that it would be only a matter of days or even hours." Around that time, the Quakers experienced "the worst case of nerves," assuming they would have to "be getting out, probably very soon." But they stayed, and by January 1942, Conard could report: "Things . . . calmed down to about the feeling of general insecurity that has been sensed all along."[48]

Most Jewish refugees dared to feel relief only when the Allies landed in North Africa in November 1942: "the palpable fear of a Nazi march through Spain into Portugal lifted." As a Portuguese citizen put it, "Germany no longer seemed invincible." And yet a few refugees remained on high alert as late as fall 1943. They continued to read the censored press, which reported on "occasional victories of the Allies" without realizing the significance of the Nazi defeat at Stalingrad. The Portuguese government, too, remained vigilant into 1943. As late as October of that year, the government held practice blackouts throughout the city. The Portuguese had earlier observed German submarines near the coast, and their navy intended to evacuate the government to the Azores in case Germany invaded Portugal. British leaders also believed that Hitler would not stop with Spain. When the British engaged the Axis powers in North Africa in November 1941, rumors spread that Germany might invade the Iberian Peninsula to gain access to North Africa. The British Embassy advised its subjects to prepare to leave and considered a general evacuation of Allied governmental employees from Portugal.[49]

Indeed, Nazi leaders did consider strategies that would have engulfed Portugal and other nations. After defeating the Soviet Union, they had planned to launch Operation Isabella, to secure bases in Spain and Portugal. Moreover, the minutes of the meeting to coordinate the destruction of European Jewry at the Wannsee Conference of January 20, 1942, included statistics encompassing the Jews of the United Kingdom and the neutral nations of Spain, Switzerland, Sweden, Ireland, Turkey, and Portugal. And in 2012, Jochen Thies published a book that described Hitler's intention to attack even New York City with long-range bombers. Luckily, "the demands of war forced the Germans to adopt more modest approaches."[50] Of course, no one in Lisbon knew about Wannsee or the plans more recently revealed, but they sensed the magnitude of the threat. They knew their fate hung on an Allied victory.

Portuguese Dictatorship

Despite gratefulness for even the fragile safety of Portugal, Jews had not eluded authoritarianism. Refugees had entered a single-party state employing zealous political police. Although *Life* magazine enthused about Salazar, dubbing him "by far the world's best dictator," the *Saturday Evening Post* pointed out the militarization of society: "The Portuguese love uniforms, and every officer seems to be wearing a different kind. Spurs jut out, decorations flash and sabers slap against booted calves." The government's Secretariat of National Propaganda, established in 1933, promoted nationalism and an "organic" and corporatist society. Charged with enforcing censorship, it also choreographed mass demonstrations and shaped leisure-time activities. In 1936, the state organized paramilitary groups such as the Portuguese Legion. But militia organizations did not take up as much street space with raucous rallies or parades as similar ones did in Germany or Austria, since Salazar also emphasized a conservative ideology that depended on the Church, docile state officials, and provincial elites.[51]

Jews understood that Portugal was a dictatorship. They had reached a police state run with "low-key terror." The Jewish refugee and political writer Emil Gumbel described the Salazar government as an "old-fashioned, patriarchal dictatorship aimed at Catholic ideals": "The dictator did not orchestrate the demagogy well known in the other fascist states: the dictator never appears in public, never makes speeches over the radio. There are no mass parades. Whereas Italy, Germany, and Spain display the picture of the Duce, Fuehrer, and Caudillo at any possible occasion, the picture of Salazar is shown nowhere. While the Spanish [leader] boasted about his relations to the Nazis . . . the Portuguese dictator hid (in general) these relations."[52]

The Romanian writer Valeriu Marcu felt similarly: "The Portuguese dictator is discretion itself. You can live in Lisbon for weeks and never hear his name or see his picture." The immediate terror that they had suffered during their exodus from the war zone eased up. Finally, they felt some relief, and some might even have felt admiration for Salazar. Indeed, Leopold von Andrian saw him as an unusually "skillful and talented" statesman who, "like his fellow countrymen, hoped to lead his people unscathed through this complicated period."[53] Probably these refugees did not know the worst parts of the regime, like its infamous prisons or the particularly horrid Tarrafel prison camp for political opponents on the Cape Verde Islands. Still, most Jews remained wary of the Salazar regime and its minions.

Even refugees with legal papers experienced the police as xenophobic, anti-immigrant, and antisemitic. The Mann family had to update its visitors' permit at the police every two weeks, and if it had not been for the dread that this stirred, Fred Mann noted, "we could have easily lulled ourselves into believing that this was a holiday." Refugees reported that the police seemed "impatient." Police in one town regularly taunted a couple that each residence permit would be its "very last." The wife recalled this torment more than fifty years later. Miriam Stanton, too, recorded her terror more than fifty years later. She had her passport taken away when she appeared at police headquarters. Frantic, she agonized:

> Why do these officials have to take our passports . . . This is not
> peacetime, not a normal time. To get these passports . . . we had
> spent a great amount of money and money which we could not

afford. . . . These passports mean life to us, to the refugees, and yet
. . . officials just take them away and say 'you can collect it in a few
days. . . .' How do they think that a refugee can sleep at night if that
precious passport . . . is lost? It is not only the money, it is our
lives. . . . Yet these officials do not seem to realize our worries.

Another refugee, who stayed in Portugal for the rest of her life, recalled
leaving the police office in a "cold sweat . . . it was as if I had been pulled out
of a bath."[54]

Aside from the panic they caused, police appointments made refugees
lose time spent waiting on police lines. Since they possessed time-restricted
transit visas for Portugal and time-restricted entrance visas for countries of
immigration, and also needed to line up at shipping agencies, this could mean
missing a deadline. Additionally, extensions of transit visas proved costly.
Original Portuguese transit visas issued in Marseille, for example, cost $180–
$275 in October 1942. Once in Portugal, the police demanded a $10 payment
for each visa extension, a high sum for people paying five cents (U.S.) for a
meal. For a family of three, that might mean trying to evade the police altogether. In a few cases, money helped fend off the police. In 1940, after a
harrowing escape to Portugal, Heinrich Mann and his wife, Nelly, stayed four
months, apprehensive about their fake names and papers. However, the
Emergency Rescue Committee supported them, and they did not live in
Lisbon, but in more expensive and exclusive Estoril, where the police did not
harass wealthy people.[55]

Even if the PVDE, like the regime itself, attempted to maintain neutrality,
refugees remained on guard. The most antisemitic of all Portuguese official
agencies, the PVDE took charge of all foreigners, issuing visas and residence
permits and rounding up refugees who lacked visas or were suspected of
harboring communist sympathies. In 1937, possibly as a result of a failed assas-
sination attempt on Salazar, the PVDE expelled some refugees. Thereafter,
however, under pressure from Britain and the League of Nations, the police
rarely forced refugees out of the country. In fact, in 1939 the Portuguese-Jewish
community reported that the authorities had "kindly set free" refugees retained
for "irregularities" in their papers. Nevertheless, in 1939 the PVDE threatened
the Jewish community with the "wholesale internment" of refugees.[56]

Police harassment created psychological agitation and fear. Rumors
about deportations to Germany intensified refugees' nervousness. They

heard talk of "concentration camps and getting sent back home." In the summer of 1940, the writer Lion Feuchtwanger heard stories that the Nazis planned to kidnap refugees in Lisbon. Since he had used false identification papers to get into Portugal, he fled immediately, making use of an emergency visa to the United States. And Marta Feuchtwanger, too, felt "at risk of abduction." In fact, the authorities spread some of these rumors. When the U.S. Mission turned Lily Lewis and her parents down, they applied to Cuba. Still, they had to wait eleven months before leaving, and the Portuguese government notified them that they "only had four weeks left to stay, and then they would be deported back to Germany." Although the regime did not follow up on its threat, the family nearly despaired.[57]

The police do not seem to have delivered Jewish refugees to the Germans—except in one notorious case.[58] In October 1941, the Portuguese secret police, cooperating with the Gestapo, kidnapped Berthold Jacob, a well-known German-Jewish journalist and anti-Nazi, in broad daylight in the center of Lisbon, and dragged him to Berlin. He died in 1944, the result of his incarceration. The Jacob case reverberated in the refugee rumor mill. On the whole, however, the Portuguese police did not target Jews for deportation, although they jailed about three hundred people without papers between 1937 and 1945, rounding them up by using a favorite tactic, raiding cafés.[59]

HICEM, the JDC, the Quakers, and the Lisbon Jewish community wrote reports and scores of letters to the PVDE in attempts to intercede for refugees and mollify its directors. These groups also provided lists of all their workers in their Lisbon offices, hoping to avoid any repercussions if the PVDE took umbrage at the organizations or at refugees. Like other aid workers, Howard Wriggins of the Quakers recognized the political situation: "Portugal was clearly a police state. . . . Informers were thought to be everywhere—at railroad stations, post offices, and in stores. Telephones were assumed to be bugged, travelers without proper identity cards could be arrested. . . . Like everyone else, we too felt that we were being watched." Fearful refugees trying to avoid incarceration pleaded for help from the aid agencies: "We came to Portugal with transit visas and the police is not willing to grant us permission to stay here longer than another fortnight or a month. So, instead of the land of liberty, a prison is awaiting us. Some of us are already in prison."[60]

Refugees who arrived illegally—sometimes as many as half of those who came after the summer of 1940—had more to worry about. Prison terms could be lengthy. Ernst Lieblich, who did not get his U.S. visa in good time, spent fifteen months in Aljube prison in Lisbon. At some prisons, money could improve conditions. At Aljube, for instance, extra money would allow refugee inmates to leave for doctor visits and visa appointments, escorted by the police. The Quakers concluded: "Treatment friendly and polite." In the fall of 1942, Heinz Wisla, a German-Jewish refugee with fake papers, spent ten days in jail near the Portuguese border, where he and a friend had slipped past guards. Although locked up at night, they could wander the village during the day, accompanied by two wardens. He concluded that the "atmosphere [was] very friendly" and the officials "cordial." When the police released them, after the intercession of the British Embassy, they drank "several glasses of dark Port wine" with the wardens.[61] Not all arrests worked out so well.

Indeed, still without papers, Wisla wound up at the infamous Caxias prison for men. After posing for a mug shot, getting fingerprinted, and being searched, he entered Caxias, an "old, old fortress, it still had a rampart," where soldiers stood guard with rifles. It felt like having "stepped back to the 13th . . . century." Social workers who saw these conditions described the cells in Caxias as overcrowded cages intended for ten men but holding thirty. Wisla described a three-tiered system: third class housed twenty to thirty men, who slept on straw on the ground in cellars made up of "cave-like halls and cells." Second-class prisoners, whose families paid a small amount, lived on the second floor, in cells with wooden cots. He inhabited a first-class room that held two people and offered real beds and linens, financed by "several sources," most likely the JDC and the Quakers. The "frugal" meals came from a nearby restaurant. It took thirteen days to set him free.[62]

Others stayed longer. Another Caxias inmate, Kurt Lenkway, remained there because his transit visa had expired. His cell, crammed with "an awful lot of people," had a hole in the floor on one side and a faucet on the other. Marched to the dining hall, the Caxias prisoners remained standing until ordered to sit. Then they trooped back to their cells. Prisoners sometimes peeled potatoes and also washed corridors and toilets. His parents, awaiting their American visa in Lisbon, eventually arranged for the prison administration to transfer him to what seems to have been a "second-class" cell, for which they paid extra. There, eight men of different nationalities lived in cramped conditions, together with a "full complement of bedbugs and fleas." At one point in 1944, the government had imprisoned twenty-six male refugees. The largest group, fifteen, remained in Caxias. In a 1944 letter to the

American legation in Lisbon, Elizabeth Dexter suggested that the U.S. government could protest against "brutality in the treatment of imprisoned refugees."[63]

A few young Jewish women reported short stays in prison and gave positive accounts of their confinement. Arriving without papers in 1943, one woman tried to hide for a month but eventually had to go to prison. The government released her after four days, but transferred her to a fixed residence in a small town. The police arrested a couple for not having visas the day after they showed up in Lisbon. Interviewed decades later, the woman may have repressed the stress she felt during her incarceration, reporting that "the jail was very nice." But she contracted typhus there. When she recovered and her husband got out of prison, the government required that they remain in a fixed residence until they left. Another woman who spent time in a prison found the situation tolerable. She thought the system strange because men and women could mingle during the day. Also, she believed that "the guards in the prison did not discriminate against Jews, because Jews and Portuguese look alike, and also because Portuguese people are nice and help out."[64] Her perceptions fit with general refugee assertions that the Portuguese people did not differentiate between Jews and others.

Jewish organizations helped the prisoners. When Heinz Wolfsohn finally got to Lisbon after several failed attempts, the police caught him and started to deport him. One of the Jewish organizations sent a plea to the head of the PVDE, Agostinho Lourenço, asking for a reprieve and promising to acquire a visa for Wolfsohn so that he could leave Portugal. The police allowed him to stay, but kept him in prison for two months. When Jewish groups refused to assist a particular prisoner because of religious conversion, as in the case of Kurt Winter, a convert to Protestantism, the wounded German World War I veteran appealed to the Unitarians and the Quakers. He began a hunger strike in prison when they moved too slowly for him. He had attempted to get visas, but his "unsuccessful attempts everywhere" had landed him in Caxias. He underlined the terrible state of his health, both "in the moral or physical condition." If he remained in prison, death seemed certain: "Without any fault of my own I seem to be condemned to perish miserably."[65]

Imprisonment could result in great distress for the prisoners and for their families. Isaac and Sara Glozer did not have proper papers, and so, along with their four children, they went to prison for a short time. After the mother and children gained their freedom, they moved into two windowless rooms in Lisbon with the help of HICEM. Sara Glozer needed to bring food to her husband because of his "delicate" health, and she had no one to watch the children, the youngest of whom was four months old. One can only imagine the children's anxiety when she left them alone daily to travel ten miles by slow rail or bus to Caxias prison. HICEM later found a babysitter and also provided a layette for the infant. Social workers worried that Sara Glozer seemed "desperate and quite subdued by unhappiness." When prisoners finally got interviews at consulates, prison guards accompanied them to make sure they would return.[66] Still, appearing at a consulate with a Portuguese prison guard could hardly make a good impression on the consular staff.

Few refugees have left positive impressions of the Portuguese police, and these concern only individual officers. The government had forbidden refugees to work, and the police enforced these orders, with rare exceptions. In the town of Figueira da Foz, for example, one teenage refugee enhanced his meager subsidy by tutoring the local librarian in French three times a week. The librarian practiced his French by complaining about the Portuguese regime, but sometimes the chief of police also stopped by for these lessons. Then the three concentrated on grammar, and the police officer "seemed to want to be nice, even protective with me." In Lisbon, Miriam Stanton also had an unusual experience. Returning to police headquarters to reclaim her passport, she reported, "[My] heart must have stopped for a minute and I must have looked to the young man in front of me as if I were going to faint." Taking pity on her, he led her to the police chief's office: "I thought at any minute . . . I would have chains dangling round me." Instead, the police chief offered her a cigarette, "and after a few puffs I started to feel human again." Conversing with her in French, he offered to help her. He also invited her to his family home the following Sunday for lunch. Their association continued after she left Portugal: "This friendship lasted for the rest of his life. He died in the mid 1950s."[67]

Some Portuguese observed arrests from afar and sympathized with the foreigners. A deferential but irate letter to Salazar of August 12, 1940, for example, accused the Portuguese bureaucracy of taking advantage of Jews "whose only fault" seemed to be that "some of them are rich and all of them are Jews." The letter writer accused the Portuguese bureaucracy of being corrupt "vultures," imprisoning Jews at Caxias and only freeing those who could pay. He added that the Jews "were not criminals or enemies of the order nor the society but on the contrary the majority are people who had a high social position in the countries they had to leave." He suggested that the president sweep this bureaucratic "pack of wolves" out of the country in order to save Portugal's reputation.[68]

⁌⁊

As a site of refuge, Lisbon meant the end of blackouts, bombings, and starvation. The colorful lights and the serenity of the sea calmed some people, and many refugees came to appreciate the kindness of ordinary Portuguese people. Also, the Portuguese-Jewish community and aid organizations assisted where they could. But refugees' ordeals continued. They could not fail to notice the Nazi presence in Portugal, feared a possible German invasion, and faced police harassment and, sometimes, prison. Refugees thus experienced Portugal as a nerve-racking site, one where their emotions seesawed between comfort and distress.

Most refugees hoped to leave Europe entirely. Waiting in Portugal without a definite plan to move on gave them time—too much time—to plan. On the one hand, they had time to calculate and recalculate their strategies for escaping to distant lands, which raised both hope and anxiety; on the other hand, they had time to confront losses: their past homes and homelands and also their previous places in the world. As adults tried to understand their options without knowing where they might end up, fearing the unknown and unknowable, children and young people looked forward to new lives in new worlds.

4. Emotional Dissonance

Adults Mourn Losses, Their Children Look Forward

Refugees do not only have to cope with finding safe shelter, paying for food and medication. A lot of them also have experienced violence themselves and are now living under very stressful conditions.

Portugal offered adult refugees the space and time to look back with sadness. In a relatively safe location, rather than on the run, older refugees mourned their homes and their places in the world while agonizing about impending hardships. Ordeals under fascism, harrowing escapes, and the escalating desperation of family and friends left behind haunted them. Hannah Arendt, who had endured four weeks in the internment camp at Gurs, grieved over the fate of friends who remained trapped in concentration camps living "in unimaginable circumstances."[1] In contrast, while their elders had lost their past and present, as well as the futures they had counted on, children and teenagers took the opportunity to explore new spaces and to imagine prospects yet to come.

Loss of a Past and Fears for the Future: Adult Grief

Loss of Homes and Homelands
Despite Portugal's sunny and peaceful setting, older refugees continued to feel intense dislocation, identity crises, and drastic downward mobility. Most of them had lived relatively organized and recognizable middle-class lives. Their homes had offered familiar sounds and smells, and delivered a sense of

safety and comfort. When refugees fled, they "were cut from the security of bourgeois life," losing homes as well as hopes, fantasies, and self-representations.[2] In addition, they also left personal and familial histories behind.

"Place can acquire deep meaning for the adult through the steady accretion of sentiment over the years," the geographer Yi-Fu Tuan reminds us. Every corner holds a memory or "tells a story." Some of these stories included the several generations who had lived and died within the same walls. And physical spaces also helped form and re-form individual identities; not simply dwellings, rooms became a "mirror of self," providing the setting in which one grew up or watched one's children flourish. Martin Feuchtwanger lamented "leaving everything behind, my house, portraits of my ancestors."[3] These physical spaces incorporated memories of holidays or life-cycle celebrations, signifying social and familial relations.[4]

Psychologists have observed that "a sense of spatial identity is fundamental to human functioning" and that relocation can cause a kind of grief that is "strikingly similar to mourning for a lost person." Historians concur, emphasizing "the innate human desire to be connected to a place."[5] Further, the power of the home as a respite, according to a neuroanthropologist, "is not just in what we accomplish when we have it, but in what goes wrong when we do not." Insecure homes or homelessness is "more than an economic tragedy: [it is] a developmental and psychological disaster."[6] The loss of homes also meant the obliteration of physical boundaries that enclosed comfortable familiarity in private spaces and provided walls against outsiders and the outside world. Instead, refugees dwelled in shabby rooms and spent most of their days in public. Finally, their loss of home meant more than leaving a specific place. It signified disempowerment, choicelessness. They had not chosen to relocate. They had lost all agency.

Besides losing their physical homes, Jewish adults had also lost their legal homes. They found themselves doubly homeless.[7] Like the early twentieth-century central Europeans in Robert Musil's novel *The Man Without Qualities,* Jews had lived within "laws, regulations, and historical traditions," assuming that there would always be "a proper framework of law and order." An allegiance to the law affected Jews in particular, since they had benefited from liberal constitutional governments in Europe, whether in France during the revolution, in Austria in 1849, or in the German states incrementally—and later, at the inception of the German Empire in 1871. Western European Jews felt strong attachment to the lands that had emancipated them, most displaying nationalistic pride. But with the rise and expansion of Nazism, their parliaments and the *Rechtsstaat*—the rule of law—turned on them, leaving them bereft of any trace of security. They felt profoundly disoriented when laws that had served them well boomeranged to hurt them. Arendt later argued that depriving Jews of their legal rights, that is, "putting certain categories of people outside the protection of the law," even though all people need a state to safeguard them, led to the subsequent violation of their human rights.[8]

Portugal's refusal after October 1938 to give refugees legal or political standing beyond the thirty days covered by a transit visa heightened Jews' sense of abandonment. And if trust in modern society "was linked to ideas of mutuality and reciprocity, of openness and transparency," then refugees could not trust Portuguese institutions or laws, since they were relying on complete strangers in inscrutable institutions and in foreign languages.[9] Losing equal citizenship (as German Jews had in 1935) or the claim to citizenship altogether (as when Nazi Germany revoked it from Jews living outside Germany in November 1941) tore at them. Hans Reichmann lamented, "We lost our footing . . . with . . . no home. . . . Every day tugged at my roots, until they finally tore loose." Emerging from a train in Lisbon, a Jewish couple grasped the devastating impact of their situation: "stateless . . . dispossessed, uprooted."[10]

Having fled her Paris home for London, the Jewish refugee and philosopher Simone Weil pondered this need for roots. She took for granted that human beings required physical supports, such as food and housing. But she emphasized that they also needed conditions "necessary to the life of the soul," including roots, nourished by "collectives" ranging from small groups to one's nation. Collectives and the foundations they fostered provided "food for the souls of those who form part of it." Eric Hobsbawm, exiled from the Austria of his childhood, also pointed to the collective: "It cannot belong to us as individuals. We belong to it, because we don't want to be alone." He lamented that homelessness and exile "are among the worst of conditions, alienation and estrangement, the feelings of greatest despair."[11] Jewish refugees, especially the adults, had fled previous collectives that had viciously betrayed them, whether nations, regions, neighborhoods, or social networks.

Jews, like other western Europeans, had assumed their national belonging, their "emotional citizenship," in the lands they had willingly supported. They understood home as a political space as well as a domestic one. As patriots, most Jews had earnestly believed that they belonged to their homelands. But in only a few disastrous years, those lands had turned on them, and many wondered whether their countries had ever truly been theirs, whether their loving relationship to their homelands had been an illusion.[12] Before the war, German Jews had six years to come to terms with and act on this disappointment, Austrians had almost two years, and French Jews only a few months. In Portugal, they stood unprotected by the rights of citizenship and also bereft of psychological connections with their nations of origin. Polish Jewish refugees in Portugal, by contrast, had a different experience with homelessness. Their relationship to Poland, always fraught in reaction to antisemitism, ended quickly for those who could escape the German assault. Despite increasing antisemitism in 1930s Poland, they fled from Nazi armies, not from the nation of Poland. Western Jews, particularly Germans and Austrians, fled homelands they thought had been theirs.

Bertolt Brecht spoke for all refugees: "We didn't emigrate from free choice, . . . we fled. We've been expelled, we are banished." This rupture may have devastated World War I veterans in particular. German-Jewish veterans believed that their World War I decorations and the "gratitude of the fatherland" (*Dank des Vaterlands*) for their service would shield them from persecution. Veterans could keep their jobs, but only until President Hindenburg, the famed World War I army general, died in August 1934. Austrian Jews had given their property and blood (*Gut und Blut*) for Habsburg Austria during World War I.[13] Jewish women had knitted for their nations, sent packages to the front, and lost husbands and sons in the war. The French-Jewish leader Raymond-Raul Lambert had received the Legion of Honor for his service in World War I. Vichy racism devastated him. He exclaimed after the first Jewish Statute (Statut des Juifs, 1940), which defined Jews by race: "Racism has become the law of the new state. What boundless disgrace! Yesterday evening I wept, like a man who is suddenly abandoned by a woman who is the only love of his life."[14]

German-Jewish refugees, especially adults, endured still another loss, that of their homeland, or *Heimat,* an emotional attachment that tied one's personal identity to a national consciousness. This concept bound Germans, including German Jews, by birth and personal histories, by physical land and patriotically construed nation, to "an ideally shared communal memory." The idea of *Heimat* connected adults not only with particular spaces, smells, sounds—even the wind—but also to the "wistful, thoroughly romanticized . . . longing for the past that has been lost or perhaps never quite was." For those brought up in nationalistic Germany, the term *Heimat* evoked a particularly strong reaction, connecting them with their physical environment.[15] A sentimentally charged, personal sense of belonging, predicated on early childhood emotional experiences, including school and family outings to German lakes, mountains, and forests, reverberated later in life. Forests, in particular, formed the basis of German mythology and childhood fairy tales. Indeed, this German national myth grounded and authenticated itself in part by using the ancient Roman historian Tacitus's *Germania*, in which he described Germanic tribes emerging from and bonding with deep, primeval woodlands. Additionally, a German literary tradition going back at least as far as the Romantics, coupled with an artistic outpouring by nineteenth-century painters like Caspar David Friedrich, united place and people. This connection to landscapes of memory continued to resonate. Peter Gay's family even "took a quick holiday trip through Germany . . . a kind of tacit farewell tour" in 1936, posing for a photo with a backdrop of the Rhine River and its forest-covered hills.[16]

The simultaneous loss of home and *Heimat* magnified refugees' distress. German-Jewish adults in England and the United States, during and after the war, experienced a loss of place, whether the physical countryside or their city of birth. Basking on the sunny coast of Portugal, refugees felt dislocated, coming from a northern society that lauded and idealized hikers, mountains, and forests. For them, "mobility and dislocation increase[d] the currency of *Heimat*."[17] The refugee author Ilse Losa exemplified this. Arriving in 1934, she fashioned a full career and family life for herself in Portugal. But her three major novels, written in Portuguese, dwelled on the loss of a homeland. The beauty of the southern seaside could not replace her loss of the German forest. Indeed, *Heimat* meant as much to non-Jewish Germans like Heinrich Mann, painfully torn from his history and culture, as it did to Jewish ones.[18] Jewish refugees did not dwell on the trope or history of the "wandering Jew," nor refer to themselves as part of an ongoing diaspora from a biblical home, but saw themselves as deeply rooted members of a community and nation— a home—that had newly cast them out.

Despite their selectively imagined, verdant *Heimat*, most Jewish refugees had fled from cities. Yet they had arrived in urban centers relatively recently. By the end of the nineteenth century, for example, most Viennese Jews had come from elsewhere in the Habsburg Empire, such as Bohemia and Moravia or Hungary, and finally, Galicia. When they fled in the 1930s, many Viennese Jews were part of the first generation born there. In Germany,

Jews had migrated to cities in the later nineteenth century in order to improve their living and business potentials. They took pride in their new, mobile identities.[19] But as they fled Nazism, their mobility no longer carried an aura of brighter prospects, but of a displaced, disorienting present.

Sometimes, refugee Jews did not even know how to identify themselves. Like other groups in Europe, "a continent of regional identities," Jews saw themselves as hailing from local or national identifications. Among other Europeans, for example, German Jews acknowledged their Germanness. But with other German Jews, they conveyed their regional or urban diversity, for example, as Bavarians or Berliners. None of these identities, however, helped them in Portugal. They felt more and more homeless as time went on. "We were *heimatlos*" meant much more than losing their native soil or mountains.[20] Their *Heimat* had formed them.

Some middle-aged refugees, especially those from Vienna and Prague, even carried their sentimental memories across the Atlantic, at a safe distance from a harrowing reality. Austrian Jews had danced to Viennese waltzes, sipped wine in the Grinzing district, and relished café culture. Jews from Prague still loved their city. Prague, as Kafka knew, "doesn't let go": "This little mother has claws."[21] Some Czech and Austrian Jews turned New York City into "a place of remembering," creating nostalgic musical evenings at cafés where the food evoked the tastes and smells they had loved. With names like "Old Vienna" (Alt Wien) or "Café Grinzing," participants revived an idealized "world of yesterday"—not surprisingly, also the title of a book written in exile by Stefan Zweig, a Viennese Jew.[22]

The Austrian-Jewish cabaret star Hermann Leopoldi, only a few years after his release from the Dachau and Buchenwald concentration camps and safely in the United States, composed and performed songs dedicated to Vienna and Prague. The lyrics of one song (1941) described a fictitious family, the "Novaks from Prague." While Leo dreamt of Montevideo, Anna of Havana, and Marianka of Casablanca, in the end, they all desired Prague. The Austrian-Jewish refugee Ernst Lothar concluded: "Homesickness is an overlooked disease." Thomas Mann echoed this sentiment; he, too, suffered from the "heart asthma of exile." Yet this was a Janus-faced nostalgia, combining an "imagined community" and past memories with the "bitterness of rejection and expulsion."[23]

German-Jewish adults, in contrast to Jewish refugees from Vienna and Prague or to a few Germans like Mann, did not yearn publicly for their

Heimat. The critic Julius Bab, for example, wrote: "I long for Europe (Paris! Perhaps also Zurich), not for Germany. That nerve has become dead." German Jews still extolled Germany's physical beauty and its high culture, but their shame that Nazism had begun in Germany and their fury at the German people tamped down public yearning for Germany or its capital, Berlin. Those who did recall Berlin pointed to a Berlin personality, sharp witted with quick rejoinders, rather than to the city as such.[24]

Refugees also longed for their language. The mother tongues in which they expressed quotidian needs, good manners, and their deepest feelings no longer served them. They needed Portuguese for daily interactions and English for the aid organizations and consulates. Although Theodor Adorno, one of the exiled few who could still make a living by writing in German, concluded that "for a man without a homeland, writing becomes a place to live," most refugees had to adjust to new languages and new ways of speaking. Hannah Arendt explained, "We lost our language, which means the naturalness of reactions, the simplicity of gestures, the unaffected expression of our feelings." Many years later, Arendt reflected, "I write in English, but I have never lost a feeling of distance from it. There is a tremendous difference between your mother tongue and another language." The lawyer Hans Reichmann added that language had never simply served as a means of being understood: "It was part of our very being" (*ein Teil unseres Wesens*). Older refugees did not lose their native languages, and even some younger ones retained their first languages. Fritz Stern, for example, only twelve when he fled Germany, declared almost seventy years later, "I am a citizen of one country, but my love belongs to two languages."[25]

As the war turned in favor of the Allies, some Jewish adults considered going back to Czechoslovakia, Holland, Belgium, Italy, or France. Observers noticed that refugee morale improved in Portugal with the Allied landing in North Africa in November 1942 and with the Soviet army's success at Stalingrad: "Some of the more optimistic believe they will be able to leave Portugal for their old home towns by next autumn."[26] For the most part, however, the longer that refugees stayed in Portugal and the more they learned, the more they realized that they could never go back.

In stark contrast to the vast majority of Jewish refugees, forced to confront an unknown future, some non-Jewish political refugees contemplated a return. Saint-Exupéry, for example, biding his time in Lisbon as an exile from France, consoled himself with thoughts of his eventual homecoming: "The essential is that somewhere there remains the relics of one's existence. Traditions. Family gatherings. The house of memories. The essential is to live for the return."[27]

Loss of Mementos, Loss of Status, Loss of Self

Loss of home and homeland meant the loss of most possessions, sold or abandoned as Jews scrambled to flee increasing persecution. One woman recalled that one could "only set one's heart on as many things as fit into one suitcase." Like other middle-class adults, Jews had participated in a consumer culture, buying furniture and objects that helped them display their identities. In Berlin and Paris of the 1920s and 1930s, for example, Jews used home furnishings not only to feel "at home" but also to express similarities and differences with non-Jews of their class and region as well as with other Jews. On the run, Jews abandoned furniture, dishes, cutlery, and other items that consumers tend to choose to "convey to others the person they think they are (or hope to be)."[28] Moreover, objects have a chronology. They may not have started off as emotionally meaningful—a few books one bought on a whim, for example— but could evolve into stand-ins for losses of home and family, as mementos that evoked nostalgia for a former, happier life. Hans Reichmann sadly wrote of "taking leave" of his books—"who knows how—if we will see them again." His furniture would "wander to strange owners" as he and his wife "also wandered" away. Perhaps Primo Levi, stripped of every belonging as he suffered the torture of Auschwitz, best expressed this kind of loss: "Consider what value, what meaning is enclosed . . . in the hundred possessions which even the poorest beggar owns; a handkerchief, an old letter, the photo of a cherished person. These things are part of us, almost like limbs of our body." The loss of home and possessions meant a partial loss of heritage and of self.[29]

Souvenirs from previous lives served as a link with memories, since possessions, too, have "biographies," connections with when and why they were acquired, and who bought them. These materials influenced their owners, evoking memories. For some, they recalled better times. For others, they provided a "tangible reminder of family," helping them grapple with upheaval. Having carefully saved a towel given to him by his mother in 1939, a man donated it to a museum in 2001 so that it would be an "eternal" reminder of her. The loss of these keepsakes endangered memory itself. Even minor losses hurt. Objects held symbolic meaning; they represented "memories of one's personhood and cultural background": "each knickknack, every book, carries the trace of a particular where and when and with whom," and when we lose or give up that object, "part of who we are goes with it." One father, grateful to receive his daughter's luggage from Lisbon, left behind when his family departed without it, wrote from the United States: "Even . . . with Doris' shoes and dresses far too small, we are glad just the same. . . . I guess you know how one feels about little things regardless of their money value. One got used to love them . . . with all the big things gone."[30]

Few adults who made it to Lisbon had managed to hang on to a beloved item. In contrast, Pola Zandmer insisted on keeping a black hat with two white ribbons circling the broad brim, bought in Monaco when she and her husband escaped from Belgium to Portugal. She often told her grand-daughter about that "beautiful" hat. In late 1942, pregnant and with her hat in a paper bag, she crossed the Pyrenees in the middle of the night while hiding from Spanish, French, and German patrols. Was this a frivolous gesture? In the 1940s, many saw hats as morale boosters in difficult times, and in France some thought of them as "pièces de résistance," or "resistance pieces," against the Nazi occupation. For Pola Zandmer, her granddaughter believes, it represented a remnant from her old life, with its comfort and elegance, when others had treated her as a human being. She could not let it go. Perhaps it also served her need to maintain appearances and dignity. She made sure to wear that hat for photos taken in Portugal. While a few had arrived in Lisbon on trains with "leather baggage, in impeccable style," many reached safety on foot, "poorly dressed," and with only backpacks. Some lost everything. When a mother managed to get her son from Belgium to Lisbon with the help of smugglers, her husband embraced her at the train station and then asked about her luggage. She rested her hand on the head of her ten-year-old and answered, "This is it. This is all I bring you."[31]

For many adults, lost objects signified their lives "before." But they had lost more than objects: they had to adjust to the expectations of stran-gers, whether police, consular officials, or social workers. Most had grown up with schedules in mind, from the ordinary way to spend a day to the time-table for building families. Bourgeois men in particular had once charted their futures in order to achieve success in businesses or in the professions. Women, although brought up to marry, had increasingly attended business schools, and some had entered the professions. Men and women had expected to plan and to steer their lives. Suddenly, all bets were off, and all ached to "finally lead a normal life."[32]

Pola Zandmer-Katzengold with her husband, Henri Katzengold, in Lisbon. (Courtesy of Pola Zandmer and Flora Cassen, photo album, 1942–43).

Used to fast-paced environments, refugees encountered different attitudes to time and had to adapt to Portugal's rhythms, including *paciência* (patience) and the "slower pace of a warm climate." For those hoping to start new lives abroad, this caused frustration. But one German-Jewish refugee who remained there for the rest of his life saw it differently. He appreciated the slower pace: "You do not check your watch to be on time, but to see how late you are." Even as they began to notice the new conventions, they carried their physical and emotional habits and former "memory spaces" with them. More disorientingly, many refugees confronted customs of public behavior foreign to them. As members of the middle classes, they had used soft voices and genteel demeanors when going about their business.[33] Now they faced situations in consulates and shipping agencies that required them to be pushy and never take no for an answer. Old norms and intuitions no longer applied.

Moreover, many fell into poverty. Some, like Siegfried Kracauer, could ask family or friends in safe lands to mail money or to send partial support. He explained to a friend in New York that it cost at least two dollars a day to survive in Lisbon: "Compared to France, life in Lisbon was extremely expensive." Others immediately sold everything they had carried with them. Advertisements in Lisbon newspapers offered jewelry, cars, and fur coats for sale in English, French, Spanish, and Portuguese. "After that they had no possessions, just sadness," wrote a Portuguese author. A handful of people thought ahead and hid their money in Switzerland before emigrating. Stephanie Wieser's mother, who had arranged the entire family's paperwork in Berlin, smuggled out money and jewelry to Switzerland: "[It was] dangerous, very dangerous, but she did it. And that was the money we had when we left." Nevertheless, their money ran out in Lisbon. Rent and food costs grew, but mostly, she noted, "we had to bribe our way to stay longer each month."[34]

Finding themselves paperless and penniless, middle-aged refugees appealed for charity. A polite letter from Mr. and Mrs. Werner Goldberg asked a social worker "whether [she] would have the amiability to grant . . . an appointment," adding, although "[we are] absolutely unknown to you, I dare to hope that the following account would find your human comprehension." He and his wife had fled Germany in 1937, resided in France for three years until the French interned them, and had lived in Portugal for six months. They needed advice badly and ended with the request "please have the great kindness to receive us." Having lost the basic minimum, Irma Bernhard, whose visa had run out, asked an aid group for shoes, soap, toothpaste, shoe cream, and "some other smaller daily necessities."[35]

Since refugees needing documents or tickets did not know how long they would be in Lisbon, they tried to conserve their money. Alfred Döblin's small family "spent a lot of time in our hot, crowded, noisy pension." The need for frugality was paramount: "Our son's shoes were coming apart, but we didn't dare pay to have them resoled. We had no clothes." In Lisbon's subtropical climate, they, like many others, still wore the heavy wool garments in which they had escaped and which had turned grimy and threadbare. Others, with lighter clothing, pleaded with aid groups for warmer garments as winter approached. Even if winters averaged around 57–61 degrees Fahrenheit, summer clothing would not suffice. A lawyer from Vienna, Heinz Paul, needed a winter sweater. He reminded the Quakers that he had been a refugee for nine years, whereas others had fled more recently, hence, "their clothes are . . . still alright." He requested a sweater in October and again in November, and his letter of December 16, 1942, noted that he had not received it. The organization required a doctor's note that the man needed a warm sweater, which, according to Paul, the doctor refused to write, "thinking it incompatible with his profession to give a certificate for the only reason that the patient has not the money to buy all necessary things himself." These words surely articulated his own humiliation and frustration, whether or not the doctor had uttered them. Walking a fine line between request and complaint, Paul continued: "The clothes . . . protect us from cold and preserve our health. They were not meant for luxury. All my shirts are torn and mended."[36]

On the streets of Lisbon, some refugees' "bewildered looks and the condition of their clothes" announced their plight. The escape had taken its toll even on those with means. Alma Mahler-Werfel, fleeing through France, commented on her and Franz Werfel's clothing. A salonnière known for her attractiveness and several marriages, she had begun neglecting her appearance: "After weeks in the same clothes, unable to wash properly, much less to bathe, we buried our vanity and lapsed into general indifference." New clothing, therefore, not only protected refugees' bodies but also lifted their spirits. One social worker explained, "We all believe that dressing the ragged people decently does more for their morale than anything else. I wish you could have seen the change in one woman . . . who came in looking worse than a . . . beggar. Yesterday she came back beaming . . . in a . . . neat black suit." Hannah Arendt observed that many of these refugees had "felt entitled from their earliest childhood" to the accoutrements of middle-class status: "They are failures in their own eyes if this standard cannot be kept any longer. . . . They constantly struggle with despair of themselves."[37]

A few lucky ones could eke out a living even though Portugal forbade refugees from working. Margit Meissner, for example, earned "enough money to live on" by dressmaking; her mother helped sew buttons and hems. Sometimes she also worked for another Czech refugee, Nelly de Grab, who used native Portuguese fabrics to make pleated skirts and later became a well-known fashion designer. Another woman, who spent eight months in Portugal, cooked kosher meals for several other refugees, supporting her family. The *Saturday Evening Post* photographed a Czech cartoonist seated at a café, sketching its patrons for small fees. Most refugees, however, lacked these kinds of skills. One woman wrote to the editor of the *Aufbau*, "I am without money or any possibility to work."[38]

As they transformed into supplicants, most refugees lost their self-assurance. That erosion had started earlier, when governments persecuted and interned them. A former political prisoner explained the difference between Jews and political prisoners in camps: "[Politicals] know why they have been interned. They played a game, knew the consequences if they lost, but played anyway. Those who were Jews played no game, they had no choice anywhere along the line which made them liable to such a fate or which would liberate them from such a fate. It just happened to them without their being in any way responsible." The betrayal by countries they had loved eroded their self-assurance. Hannah Arendt explained: "We lost our home, which means the familiarity of daily life. We lost our occupation, which means the confidence that we are of some use in the world."[39]

Even more than the loss of trust in themselves, Jewish refugees had lost a sense of self. They longed for their old selves. A social worker in Lisbon sympathized with them: "It is pitiful to see people who once were upstanding citizens of consequence, and most of these are in that category, now rushing about frantically and helplessly from pillar to post in their desire to get to a place where at least they can feel they are out of the net." Arendt captured this moment: "Once we were somebodies about whom people cared, we were loved by friends, and even known by landlords as paying our rent regularly." But as refugees, these "somebodies" had become Arendt's "new kind of human beings—the kind that are put in concentration camps by their foes and in internment camps by their friends."[40]

Arendt saw "parables of increasing self-loss" and described a frustrated middle-aged man who had appeared before countless aid committees "in order to be saved." At one aid organization, his emotions triggered an exasperated exclamation, "Nobody here knows who I am!" Nobody knew who he had been, or the kind of people he had come from, or the heights from which he had dropped. In despair, he realized that he could not overcome the gap between how others saw him and how he wished to be seen. Similarly, a character in Ilse Losa's novel *Unter fremden Himmeln* (*Under Strange Skies*) expresses rage at his status in an aid office: "Demoralization and fear, alarm at his social decline appeared in his light blue eyes. 'Damned bunch.' He continued. 'As if they were better than one of us!' "[41]

Arendt's middle-aged man, Losa's fictional man, and others like them had already endured the contempt of their nations. Beneficiaries of what Peter Gay dubbed "the bourgeois experience" in the nineteenth century, many, especially those who left memoirs, had lived successful middle-class lives. Many Jewish men had also survived the November Pogrom, a "public degradation ritual," and tens of thousands had suffered violence in concentration camps. Now they demonstrated a combination of pride at what they had once achieved, disbelief regarding their current condition, shame at their role as supplicants, and impotent anger that bureaucrats and strangers did not adequately respect them. Reflecting on the embarrassment of receiving aid, Arendt wrote, "If we are saved we feel humiliated, and if we are helped we feel degraded."[42]

Gender expectations surely influenced the depth of men's anger and frustration, their insistence on "who I am." European gender behaviors had changed over time. Whereas an eighteenth-century European gentleman could weep, the nineteenth-century bourgeoisie expected more self-control from white male elites. This meant controlling their drives, gestures, senses, and feelings to achieve a balancing act between outright expression and constraint, even when facing danger. These men believed that restraint gave them the aptitude to lead, and construed the people they governed—minorities, working classes, and women—as childish and emotional.[43] German-Jewish men in particular adapted to such nineteenth-century bourgeois standards, and not just privately. Since German governments had demanded "self-improvement" before granting civil equality to Jewish men, these behaviors also served performative purposes. Jewish men therefore believed they had proved their entitlement to citizenship. As refugees, their self-control no longer garnered the results they expected.

More generally, most western European Jewish men had attained middle-class status in the business and professional worlds as well as through their engagement in civic or political life. They felt pride in the multiple activities that made up who they were. Work, for example, did not mean simply making a living, but had special class, political, and gender relevance to German-Jewish men, who made up the majority of male refugees in Portugal. While hard work brought middle-class men success in the nineteenth century, Jewish men went a step further. They underlined their occupations and financial accomplishments not only in order to become middle class, but also in order to achieve political equality. Given the energy that Jewish men devoted to their jobs or businesses and the relationships they encountered there, work acquired emotional importance, earning them public respect as shopkeepers or businessmen, and professional and civic respect as members of business or municipal organizations. Work could become as significant as private life. Indeed, as breadwinners, they put in long hours in their businesses or shops to ensure upward mobility for their families and also to earn respect from wives and children. Men thus valued their work as part of their self-expression, usefulness, and self-worth. Indeed, one man vowed to travel to any country that would let him work. By the end of the nineteenth century—when many of the refugees in Portugal were born—Jewish men of all classes had absorbed the bourgeois motto "If you are standing still, you are moving backwards."[44] Forced idleness in Lisbon surely made some feel they were moving backward, losing status and honor.

Western European men had absorbed cultures of honor, especially those who had grown up before or served during World War I. Wartime governments, for example, produced images of honorable men protecting families, and soldiers believed they fought for the sake of women and children. In addition, honor mediated between an individual and a group: it provided individual respect and well-being within a society. Jewish men, like their countrymen, had adhered to this culture, forming university dueling fraternities in late nineteenth-century Germany and Austria to defend their contested honor. After the war, Jewish veterans, countering antisemitic charges that Jews had shirked their duty, mobilized to protect the honor of Jews who had fought courageously.[45] In the 1930s, Jewish men attempted to maintain their individual, family, and community honor against Nazi slander. By the 1940s, they had lost that struggle, but they still clung to a diminished individual status. In Portugal, they lost that battle, too. "Nobody" knew who they were.

Without work, without institutional and familial acknowledgment, without treasured possessions, men experienced a humbled, emasculated self. Morris Troper, with the Lisbon JDC, reflected to his wife in November 1940: "The pity of it all is not the physical aspect . . . but honest, decent-looking men come to me in tears and in quivering voices lament the fact that they are losing the respect of their little children! Think of it—they are sorry they ever escaped. . . . [What] we need is a bridge . . . like a rainbow . . . from despair to hope or even to despair with dignity."[46]

Other social workers noticed that wives often helped their families adjust: "Loyal and enterprising wives . . . are a big factor—perhaps the biggest in solving such cases." Generally, only young women born around the time of World War I expected to enter—or had just joined—the job force. Most others had derived their status from their fathers or husbands.

Not used to being in control, they may have felt a class status decline, but they did not take this as personally as men. Nor did they dwell on this loss in their writings or interviews. Having been the ones early on to urge emigration from Germany on reluctant male family members, they may have felt relief more consciously than status anxiety. Nevertheless, those refugee women who had accepted homemaking as uniquely women's duty had lost one of their main jobs, namely, running a household. Their homes had offered husbands and children a "haven in a heartless world" and had represented husbands' achievements. Homes also reflected the assiduous diligence of housewives. The efficient and talented homemaker, "an enthroned fixture," "was idealized as part of the cult of domesticity, and was accorded special social status."[47] Thus, housewives, too, lost their occupation as well as their standing. Coming from a society that valued cleanliness and orderliness to the extent that male civil servants could be fired if officials deemed their families disorderly, homemakers aspired to high standards. On the road to Portugal, however, housewives could not wash clothes, bathe children regularly, or even buy soap. Still, as women lost one mission, they took on others.

Writing about Jewish families during the Holocaust, Nechama Tec concluded, "Ironically . . . because of their consistently subordinate roles, women may have [had] an easier time adapting to traumatic changes than men." Societies that had traditionally labeled women the more emotional and more present-oriented sex and men the more rational and future-oriented one found their stereotypes upended. In Nazi Germany, for example, while Jewish men suffered in concentration camps after the November Pogrom, women tackled their families' futures.[48] Once in Portugal, although both sexes raced from office to office trying to leave Portugal, the longer men remained in a place where they could not resume their work, the greater their status loss and worries. By contrast, quietly and resolutely, women persisted.

Some adult refugees clung to their old identities, refusing to acknowledge their status loss, an overwhelmingly difficult undertaking. On the one hand, Hannah Arendt urged refugees to remain themselves and "insist upon telling the truth." She meant they ought not only to acknowledge their pariah status, but also to understand their place in history: "They know that the outlawing of the Jewish people in Europe has been followed closely by the outlawing of most European nations. Refugees driven from country to country represent the vanguard of their peoples—if they keep their identity." On the other hand, a harsh observer noted they "could not forget themselves or what they had once been," and "never missed an opportunity to tell the pension proprietors . . . how many baths there were in their homes, and the important people with whom they had been on intimate terms." Arthur Koestler, too, considered refugees who insisted on their previous identities peculiar, "not because they had been driven out of their past, but because they carried it with them." Antoine de Saint-Exupéry, a more empathetic observer, also stranded in Portugal, called the Jews "my emigrants." He affirmed their desire to cling "with all their strength to some kind of significance. 'You know, I am so and so . . . I came from such and such a place.'" He understood that their pasts felt as "warm and fresh, and living, just as recent memories of a love affair."⁴⁹ Still, hanging on to one's old self well after losing all support structures could cause grave disorientation, frustration, and sadness.

Some refugees admitted as much to social workers. They emphasized their emotionally fragile states, whether in desperation or strategically. A letter from "a group of about a hundred Jewish refugees" written to the office of the JDC in Lisbon emphasized the magnitude of their losses: "Most of us have already lost our homes . . . and went through all possible pains and hardships during our exile. We are getting poorer every day and are losing both our physical and moral power of resistance . . . We do not want to go into details but we are really not fit to stand such bitter disillusion anymore." Some noted increasing dejection. Miriam Stanton, waiting to leave for London, reported frustration, depression, and sleeplessness. Sergio DeBenedetti, despite good contacts and two letters of recommendation from Nobel laureates, still had to face incomprehensible obstacles from the local police in Coimbra and, consequently, missed his appointment with the U.S. mission. He wrote, "Difficulties excite me, stupidity depresses me. I spent the next few days in bed, waiting, unable to carry on." Refugees felt restless and despondent, forbidden to earn a living, and "supported and guided like children."⁵⁰

Some refugees experienced emotionally driven physiological symptoms, accepting "the pills for anxiety and . . . sleeplessness" that local doctors prescribed. Others needed hospitalization for breakdowns. Similar reactions occurred in other lands of refuge as well. In Palestine in 1937, the novelist and Freudian devotee Arnold Zweig gave a lecture entitled "Emigration and Neurosis." Zweig alluded not only to individual neuroses but also to those of Jews as a people, fleeing homelands since the days of Titus and reacting to cycles of expulsions. He observed that escaping and adjusting to constantly changing circumstances took enormous psychological energy. In Lisbon, those with this kind of energy pushed forward stoically, at least for a while. One woman waited until after the war before allowing "the dammed up feeling, suppressed for years," to flood to the surface. Swallowing the humiliations and strains, she had paid "the price of courage" by putting her "feelings on ice."[51]

Social workers noticed the emotional state of the refugees who came to them. As early as the summer of 1940, Varian Fry commented on the fragility of refugees who had made it to Marseille. Hungry, sleep deprived, and destitute, they had "badly frayed nerves" that gave way altogether as they succumbed to breakdowns. Unitarian aid workers understood the need for "morale boosting." They acknowledged that the refugees "often feel that they are being treated as second-class people, nowhere welcome and forever looked down upon as 'case number so-and-so.'"[52]

The Quaker Howard Wriggins agonized over the precarious psychological state of these applicants when he could no longer hold out one hope and had to "substitute another to give them enough strength to go on." The refugees' psychological state had to be considered: "And it all must be done so gently, since they are near the edge already. . . . Some do go off the handle in my office." This happened when Dr. Heinz Paul and his wife, both from Vienna, visited the Quaker office to ask for a larger subsidy in the middle of what turned into a two-year stay in Portugal. Dr. Paul "grew quite excited" when his wishes could not be met. Fearful that his rage would alienate the aid worker, "his wife tried to quiet him, by words at first, to no avail and then by tugging at his sleeve, finally by putting her hand over his mouth." The aid worker understood: "I had the impression that these things just had to come out. . . . He seemed to calm down just by releasing these thoughts."[53]

Emotional crises could develop into the kind of intense and crippling anxieties now known as post-traumatic stress disorder. The Quakers in Lisbon cared for a German-Jewish man who had served in the French Foreign Legion until the collapse of France and then endured imprisonment in a Vichy concentration camp. His brother in New York succeeded in having him released, and the man made it to Lisbon in 1941. There, he refused to leave his room, insisting, "They'll get me at my room. If not at my room, they'll get me at the port when I go on board. If they let me go on board, they'll get me in New York." The Quaker representative concluded: "He was still in the grip of the terror that so long had dogged his every step."[54]

Social workers worried particularly when their charges threatened suicide or took sleeping medications "to forget their past trials and to obviate spending the night a victim of their fears of what is to come." The rate of suicide among central European Jews rose as the early Nazi terror intensified. In Germany, for example, between 1932 and 1934, the Jewish suicide rate was 50 percent higher than that of the rest of the German population. It climbed with the annexation of Austria and, again, during the November Pogrom. In relatively safe Portugal, but still dreading arrest, deportation, or an expanding war, some succumbed to their anguish. The author Hertha Pauli recalled a young friend who killed himself in Lisbon, and Arthur Koestler, having endured several stays in jail while in transit to Lisbon, tried to commit suicide there. Another refugee heard of suicides when the American consul turned people down.[55] In December 1942, a friend described a man in hiding from the police in "a fearfully desperate situation and mood." Others fantasized about suicide: Salamon Dembitzer's autobiographical character in *Visas for America* asks, "Why didn't you commit suicide on the way," and Jan Lustig, who reported one suicide, felt that many refugees seemed "close to suicide." Hannah Arendt, having left Lisbon for New York, dwelled on suicides. She decried the many suicides "not only among the panic-stricken people in Berlin and Vienna . . . but in New York and Los Angeles, in Buenos Aires and Montevideo." She knew that refugees in Europe as well as in safety "struggled with despair." Therefore, when someone committed suicide, other refugees imagined "all the trouble he has been saved." She added, "Many of us end up wishing that we, too, could be saved some trouble, and act accordingly."[56]

These fantasized or actual suicides could occur when refugees felt overwhelmed and totally degraded. Social workers surmised this, noting that one reason why they received few letters of gratitude from refugees had to do with their mortification at having had to beg for relief. Nevertheless, social workers, overworked, under-resourced, and facing a "stream of people," admired these humiliated refugees' "guts" and held them in esteem. In 1941, Philip Conard observed: "We are helping people in general very superior in capacity, training and experience. . . . People who have the background and ability of these persons, and who have been through the tragedies they have seen and suffered, give one a new respect for human nature." Still another Quaker praised the refugees' "human greatness," which "illumines the grimness of the situation, so instead of despairing, one is truly inspired."[57]

Consular officials rarely showed similar empathy. Ronald Bodley, a privileged non-Jewish English refugee, but still a refugee, remarked upon callous officials and thousands of other refugees: "One becomes a kind of degraded outcast for whom the only sentiment is pity mingled with contempt. . . . That one is unwanted is emphasized on every possible occasion." Anna Seghers, a Jewish refugee, had the main character in her novel *Transit* refer to the bureaucrats who stamped refugees' passports as "dogcatchers," implying what they thought of refugees.[58]

Accepting New Possibilities: Young Refugees Look Forward

Whereas parents mourned their loss of home and homeland and coped with terrible worries, children and teenagers often moved into new, freer spaces. Young people had only fledgling roots in their homelands and had faced abuse by teachers. Their circles of friends had grown ever smaller as non-Jews ostracized them. And just at the age when young Jewish teenagers might have started roaming beyond their homes and neighborhoods, they confronted dangerous streets and hostile public spaces. Their world shrank, raising their insecurity and anger and confining them within their nervous families. Reports from a neurologist who studied 600–700 Jewish girls and boys in 1934, as well as observations from Jewish teachers, underscored that these children felt "at the mercy of [an] unpredictable fate." This unstable, chaotic sense of things "had as its consequence a deep-seated state of agitation, restlessness, and excitability." Many had fought with their reluctant parents, demanding to leave.[59] They looked forward to new lives.

As they fled toward Portugal, young refugees encountered exciting new languages, vistas, and customs. They could explore unlimited spaces and their own potentials. Once in Portugal, few mourned their pasts; they may have wished for a better present, but they saw an open future. Children and youth had less to lose than their parents and therefore retained some optimism and equilibrium. Additionally, children did not face immediate responsibilities. Parents dealt with paperwork, obsessed about money, and faced intimidating police and indifferent consulates. During the escape of Raul Hilberg and his family from Vienna in 1938, he recalled that "despite the advent of rootlessness and poverty," his parents still provided for him: "I was carefree." Rosy S. and her family stole into Portugal. While her parents pleaded for transit visas, she recalled, "As a teenager, I had a good time there." Fourteen-year-old Joseph Shadur waited a week in the Portuguese border town of Vilar Formoso while his father begged the authorities to allow Joseph's grandmother into the country. Joseph recalled the lovely countryside, the farm animals, and the many other Jewish children with whom he and his sister played: "We quickly made friends and were extremely happy there. I hardly remember seeing my parents. We were always out in the wild countryside." Only when he reread his father's and mother's memoirs, decades later, did he recognize his father's desperation. At the time, Joseph seemed aware only that the border guards had let his grandmother stay. When his family had to wait two months for their ship to leave Lisbon, the children amused themselves with games, drawing, stamp collecting, and walking around Lisbon, especially "the large covered market with all the good food in it."[60]

For some youths, emigration offered a first encounter with the wider world. At age twelve, Hilberg, who embarked from France before the war, recalled, "I was expanding my acquaintance with the world exponentially." For children who came to Portugal, this "world" consisted of a few Portuguese cities, especially Lisbon. The Sucher family took more than two years to travel to Portugal. In late 1940 and 1941, as his parents struggled to acquire visas to travel on, Joseph and his sister spent eight months "roaming around," playing on huge piles of cork, and acquiring free movie tickets from a local restaurant owner. Like many children, they did not attend school, which required tuition and a knowledge of Portuguese. Instead, they delighted in watching many hours of English-language films with French subtitles, like *Superman, The Adventures of Robin Hood,* or *The Adventures of Kit Carson.* Temporarily settled, some, like teenager Nadia Gould, felt safe enough to be mischievous. She and a new friend decided to pour water on women's hats as they passed beneath the window of her hotel: "We laughed so hard we could hardly straighten up again." Panic set in with the arrival of the police, but "the affair was settled somehow."[61]

Teens had time to explore. Fred Mann, arriving in 1940 at age fourteen, spent fifteen months in Lisbon, appreciating the flowers at intersections and some of the "best pastries in the world." He could wander around, flout his parents' strictures against smoking, and absorb the language. Since he worked for the Jewish community and earned a bit of money, he could also visit movie theaters. Even those whose parents remained in occupied countries or in Germany and who waited in Lisbon until social service agencies found them ship tickets seemed to enjoy their stay. When they arrived in New York, they reported that many German Jews, friends and relatives of their families, had called on them in their Lisbon boardinghouse and had taken them to cafés and movies. And the Lisbon Jewish community, too, tried to help them.

Several children reported that a Jewish community member visited them in their boardinghouse every day and invited them to her home.[62]

Synagogue communities did their best to provide some camaraderie and a sense of Jewishness to these fluid, ever-changing groups. The children of refugees who planned to remain in Portugal interacted with the visitors. Teen-agers, whether transient or residing in Portugal, could gather on Saturday afternoons in the synagogue, where Rabbi Diesendruck held Zionist youth meetings. He gave a short talk on the weekly Torah portion, after which the participants sang Hebrew songs, danced the hora, and talked. Later, the young people attended evening prayer services. One of the regular members, Irene Shomberg (née Westheimer), born in Portugal of German-Jewish parents who had emigrated there in the 1920s, recalled that recent arrivals described their escape experiences and discussed their aspirations. But she also noted "lots of silences" about the fate of parents or about the November Pogrom: "Safety was the main thing." These young people went on outings together, enjoying local parks, sports, and picnics. Permanent group members, aware of the poverty of many refugees, "always made sure to take the lunches of the refugees (bread and butter sandwiches) so that the refugees could have our sandwiches (egg, tuna, sardines). . . . Basically, we wanted [them] to have a proper meal, without appearing to give them charity." Older teens went to the beach together, or the boys played soccer while the girls watched: "They always seemed like a very jolly group, with a devil may care attitude. Today, as an adult, I wonder, were they really this jolly, or were they masking a deep hurt?" Shomberg concluded that youth groups provided a "temporary respite from sadness and insecurity about their future."[63]

Young refugees with families reached out to Portuguese youths during their hiatus in Portugal. Many learned some Portuguese. Henri Deutsch, twenty-two, relished his stay in Porto, where he met college students who took him "under their wings." In Ericeira, Albert Lichter, twenty-five, joined a Jewish soccer club and made friends with young Portuguese players. In Lisbon, Fred Mann met young Portuguese women and even asked one for a date. To his surprise, when he picked her up at home, her parents, uncle, and aunt joined them. He lamented: "This was my first exposure to Portuguese dating culture." A fifteen-year-old Belgian-Jewish boy in Figueira da Foz made "many friends," both with refugee and Portuguese youths; fell "in love" with a young Portuguese woman, with whom he conversed in "pidgin Portuguese"; spent time in cafés near the beach; and even acted in a French play at

Margit Meissner on an excursion with two Portuguese friends, 1941. (U.S. Holocaust Memorial Museum, #28936, courtesy of Margit Meissner).

the local casino. Only years later did he reflect that his family of five had lived in one room and that his parents "must have suffered terrible anxieties."[64]

Refugee girls and young women probably experienced more freedom than if they had remained in their previous staid, bourgeois surroundings. Although the 1920s had seen some urban "New Women" in paid employment and at universities, enjoying short hair, city life, and urban culture, parents tended to control girls and young women more than boys. But with parents distracted and absorbed in acquiring travel documents, young women expanded their frontiers. A fifteen-year-old enjoyed meeting teens her age in Curia during the summer of 1940: "We didn't have to go to school, we had fun . . . going to the beach, going for walks. . . . I had a great time in Portugal. It was a good life." Similarly, Margit Meissner delighted in beach outings with Portuguese friends during her nine months in Portugal. Indeed, another young woman, left to roam Lisbon with her sister, met her future Portuguese husband there.[65]

Not all teenagers felt carefree, however. Some became caregivers. At eighteen, Liny Yollick eased the financial burden on her family in Lisbon by translating at the Dutch legation. Fifteen-year-old Stephanie Wieser also found her first job in Lisbon, teaching German to a young Portuguese girl. She felt pride "earn[ing] some money" for her family. Similarly, Kurt

Lenkway acknowledged that "our little sister," at age seventeen the youngest of three, helped support her parents and siblings by finding a position as a governess in a wealthy Lisbon family. She emerged as the breadwinner.[66]

More resilient than their elders, a few young people found themselves attending to their parents, both physically and psychologically. Maria Bauer, twenty-one, noted a radical change in her relationship to her parents: "My attachment to them was no longer of a dependent child; now I was responsible for them and it was they who entirely relied on me." Margit Meissner, too, saw that her mother could not cope with increasing adversity. At eighteen, she and her mother exchanged roles. Economic independence and increased physical freedom could cause disputes between youths and their parents. Eighteen-year-old Sabine Arnholz supported her family by working as a stenotypist for the JDC. When she craved friendships with young Portuguese people, her parents objected. Her father had been a banker in Berlin, and they wanted her to keep company only with people of "her social level." Sabine, experiencing her first taste of independence, refused to comply, asserting that the family had lost its social position and that she had to live her life as best she could. The rift grew serious enough to come to the attention of social workers who assisted the family.[67]

The more positive outlook of children and teenagers stemmed from their relief at escaping hostile schools, persecution, and war. They may also have had less information about the war, more age-related joie de vivre, and a greater sense of adventure than their parents. Nevertheless, some grasped their parents' concerns and even shared them. Fourteen-year-old Joseph Shadur, once safely in Lisbon, "increasingly thought and talked of our many friends and acquaintances who did not reach Lisbon ... among them my Jewish schoolmates." Nadia Gould, another fourteen-year-old, delighted in "living in a fairytale," not attending school, and walking on the deserted beaches with her friend. Nevertheless, she worried that "we were missing important years of learning." More somberly, Edith Jayne, whose family escaped Vienna and, due to quota restrictions, remained in Lisbon from 1938 until 1941, "picked up the feelings of anxiety and fear of my parents and found the experience of emigrating ... where I did not speak the language and had difficulty understanding ... utterly bewildering." Over sixty years later, she divulged that nightmares of "racism ... homelessness and lack of material resources" continued to plague her. Similarly, fifty years after her odyssey from Paris to Lisbon, Annette Finger admitted, "I felt I was on borrowed time since I was ten."[68]

Sending Children Away from Portugal

Between 1941 and 1943, some Jewish refugee families in Portugal made the desperate decision to send their children to the United States. America had agreed to provide visas exclusively for children, and Jewish organizations had to promise they would not intercede later for the parents. This was not the first time that some European-Jewish parents had chosen the option of sending children abroad without them. After the violence of the November Pogrom, Britain had agreed to take in some ten thousand children from Germany, Austria, and the Czech lands, and grief-stricken parents made the decision to send their children ahead on what became known as the *Kindertransports*. Some of the parents in Portugal had probably heard of these transports and the programs that brought children to Palestine. Now they had to decide whether to risk a German invasion or send their children away with no guarantee they would ever see them again.

These parents faced unbearable choices. Miss Nicholson, a social worker from the Child Guidance Clinic in Philadelphia, spent six weeks in 1942 visiting refugee families restricted to small villages north of Lisbon. Upon her return, when she tried to describe to her supervisors the kind of lives the refugees led, they noticed her barely concealed distress: "[She] retained the kind of stiffness that indicates efforts at holding back tears and . . . focused her eyes on one spot somewhere, because it was so painful to her to face us. To her, who has not been close to refugee misery anywhere, the lives of the people in this—comparatively speaking the safest spot for Jews in Europe—are so full of horror, so unbearably insecure, that she could hardly bear the memory." Miss Nicholson and several colleagues met families from a "variety of nationalities," who lived "without any hope." Most children did not attend school or received only rudimentary instruction. Many of these people had come to Portugal "as the last station in a series of migrations and persecutions." They feared a Nazi invasion and "imprisonment through the Portuguese government whose policies and attitudes are not at all reassuring."[69]

Some parents listened attentively when social workers offered the possibility of helping their children emigrate. The parents did "not expect their children to be placed where they would enjoy unusual privileges." Instead, "they want them to live where they can still be protected as children should be, go to school and have certain opportunities for normal development." The social workers explained to distraught parents that they might face an indefinite separation from their children and that their agency could not expedite the parents' journeys—they would have to do that on their own: "One anguished mother burst out 'We have already lost so much! Must we now give up even our children?'" Faced with this excruciating dilemma, many parents asked the social workers, "What would you do if you were in my place?" And "quite a number decided they could not be separated from their children for an indefinite time."[70]

Parents who opted to send children between the ages of five and fifteen to the United States needed guidance. Social workers explained the American foster care system, finding that "even though the idea was new to many of them, they stated that it was good to know that another woman would take on where the mother had to leave off." Other aid workers warned Orthodox parents that their children might not be able to "live up to every letter of their former teachings" and made it clear to parents that no child should go to the United States "with the fear that God will punish their parents if they at any one time fail to observe a part of the ritual." Social workers found parents surprised by the idea that their sons might join the U.S. army a few years after their arrival. Some parents worried about that, while others "expressed satisfaction," but few apparently realized "that their children would become Americans and might move away from them in every sense." Ultimately, two hundred Jewish refugee children made their way to the United States from Portugal.[71] They stayed in orphanages, with relatives, or in foster homes. Their parents endured losing all control over their children's lives and needed to come to terms with the magnitude of the separation across the ocean and over time.

Having made this heartrending decision, parents began to pack their children's luggage. Social workers understood that the items "showed loving care and preparation, but obviously by very poor parents." They fretted that parents packed too many clothes and books, causing unwarranted expenses, given their meager resources. One social worker added, "For an American it would be very hard to identify the individual garments they had as to their uses." They emphasized that children outgrew clothing quickly and that styles differed in the United States. In addition, U.S. censors often confiscated books in foreign languages. And besides, the children did not look at them after a few weeks. Despite their frustration, the observers understood that the baggage reflected the parents' efforts to make life easier for the children. Only via the items they sent with or to their children and—more importantly, as we will see—letters to the children or to the agencies could parents attempt to intervene in their children's fates, since children did not write as often as parents hoped they would. Scholars have pointed to the suit-case as symbolic of worries about how much refugees could retain of their old lives, as well as of hopes for the future.[72] These suitcases containing mementos, books, and clothing conveyed precisely these feelings.

Portugal provided an interim space where refugees hoped, worried, and waited. Although all had lost home, homeland, and security, younger gener-ations, bolder and more curious than their elders, felt that they were on their way to something better. Older generations wondered whether they would ever feel "at home" again. One man confided: "You know I feel without a home. . . . I feel *heimatlos* . . . in Italy, in Spain, in Germany, in Portugal. I wonder if I shall feel really at home in England or the United States."[73]

As time went on, refugees confronted more lines at consulates and police stations, their visas ran out, and many faced quasi incarceration in small villages, locations that the Portuguese government called "fixed resi-dences." Howard Wriggins observed that the refugees he cared for lived "in a hiatus, rather like a patient with an unknown disease who waits anxiously for an unknowable diagnosis."[74]

5. Sites of Refuge and Angst

Consulates and Confinements

We do not want anyone's pity or help. I would like to work, but
nobody employs me.

In Germany and Nazi-occupied Europe, Jews watched nervously as their
public space shrank. "Forbidden to Jews" or "Jews not Wanted" signs proliferated.[1] Civil society, too, excluded Jews from clubs, restaurants, cafés,
libraries, and theaters, often well before the Nazis required it. In 1936, a
Jewish man from Breslau recorded: "My wife and I have not been out to the
theatre or to a concert, nor to a coffee house or to the cinema in three years."
In Nazi-occupied Warsaw, where Jews had already felt uneasy about public
space before the German invasion, Chaim Kaplan lamented in October 1939:
"Every public place shows hatred and loathing against Jews." Some Jews
began avoiding public spaces because of safety fears. Others refused to go
where they felt not wanted.[2] By contrast, in Lisbon, Jews could go anywhere,
without restrictions, curfews, or hostility. Lisbon was wide open.

Refugees wandered through the city's inviting public spaces, trying to
adjust to their new geographic realities. But they could not simply enjoy
Lisbon's streets or relax at the beach. They needed basic shelter and food.
Furthermore, securing both permission to stay longer and visas to leave
Portugal dominated their actions as Lisbon became the "great bottleneck of
Europe." While seeking these precious documents, they waited at consu-
lates, hoping to make it into the inner offices. These bureaucratic spaces,
signifying acceptance or rejection, became "depositories for feelings of pain

and anxiety."³ All too often, refugees swallowed bitter frustration as they emerged empty-handed. And those whose stays grew longer faced intern-ment. Detention in small villages, dubbed "fixed residences" (*residências fixas*) by the government, meant even more delays in acquiring a visa to leave Portugal, since consulates were mainly in Lisbon. And consulate delays meant possible jail time. A catch-22 ensued: none of these sites stood alone. One influenced another, and all heightened refugees' anxiety.

Seeking Shelter, Meals, and Spiritual Solace

Refugees prioritized the search for shelter and food. Thousands, probably up to ten thousand in mid-1940, required partial or complete subsidies from Jewish agencies and the Lisbon Jewish community. Their search for rooms proved daunting as they repeated the words " 'room with bath'; 'very well, without bath' . . .; 'what's the franc today?' " But many had endured worse. In June 1940, as tens of thousands fled France for Portugal, the American consul general explained that in the North "they are sleeping in barns, schools, or even on the ground!" A few months later, Eugen Tillinger reporting from Lisbon for the New York–based *Aufbau*, wrote: "For anyone who has known this city before, it's unimaginable how it has changed in such short time. . . . New émigrés from France and from German occupied territories arrive constantly. One hardly hears any Portuguese . . . in the middle of the city. . . . Lisbon is sold out."⁴

Rentals could run the gamut from run-down rooms in pensions to more spacious apartments. Portuguese families, and even some refugee fami-lies, offered accommodations. In one lodging, an "enormous number of people lived in four or five rooms, in the kitchen, in the dining room and in the bathroom." The Shadur family found two small rooms in the pension Madalena. The toilets, at the end of a corridor, felt "quite cold in winter," and family members "had to squeeze past the owners' chicken cages on the third floor to get there."⁵ Finding or preparing meals came next.

Until their flight, most had taken food for granted. If food had formerly provided pleasure, its absence during their escapes had caused not only hunger but also grave concern. For some, relief came at the Portuguese border. One man still smiled in 1999, remembering the smell of fresh rolls on the train through Portugal. A woman who had fed her famished child only sugar cubes as they climbed the Pyrenees wrote in 1942: "In Lisbon, the stores are full and there are still so many good things to eat. Our eyes popped when we saw such choice and abundance." While some refugees noted the multitude of hungry, impoverished Portuguese in the side streets of Lisbon and in nearby villages, others, such as the author Alfred Döblin, focused on their own immediate needs. He observed a "fantastic amount of food: thick, nutritious soup, fish, meat, and fruit, three times the quantity of a French meal. . . . We were so hungry that in the beginning that was all we cared about." Encouraging a friend to come to Lisbon in July 1940, the Austrian author Leopold von Andrian noted that the "food is very good . . . [and] gigantic portions."[6]

Refugees marveled at fruit. A German-Jewish eleven-year-old remembered, "We hadn't eaten fruit in years," and others reveled in "exotic fruits . . . . a true delight after the years of hunger." Shop windows displayed meat and sausages, although fish provided the main staple. One man remembered many versions of his mother's sardine dinners, "the main affordable food." Another recalled his allergic reaction to crayfish, which he bought because they cost so little, although he knew that Jewish dietary laws forbade eating them. Refugees ate salted dried cod, or *bacalhau*, Portugal's most popular food. Cooks boiled it and then sautéed it with potatoes, tomatoes, and onions. The Portuguese believed that "you can make a different version every day of the year." Still, central Europeans, unused to a constant fare of fish, appreciated meat on occasion. Letters that children arriving in New York sent to their parents in Lisbon "rave[d] about the amount of meat which they [got] to eat" at the social service reception center in New York.[7]

Some families cooked in their rooms or small apartments. Others found boardinghouses that offered modest meals or else ate with private Portuguese couples or more settled refugee families. One Jewish family, living in Portugal since the 1920s, had adapted to Portuguese staples. On Friday nights, however, they ate a "Jewish meal," including chicken soup and chicken. A German element also remained: cakes baked from "strictly German recipes," such as *Rahmtorte* (cream cake), *Bienenstich* (dough plus sweetened almonds, sugar, and butter), and *Mürbeteig* (sweet tart dough) baked with fruit. Adjusting to Portuguese customs allowed this family to acculturate and to buy more practical foods, but the craving for German pastries remained.[8]

Cafés, too, offered food, plus the opportunity to eat with other refugees. Those on tight budgets divided their portions into two meals, wrapping and taking their leftovers with them. Jews who observed ritual dietary restrictions cooked on their own or sought a kosher pension, of which there were at least two in Lisbon. They could also find kosher meat in Porto and Lisbon. Arriving in the city of Coimbra, one religious Polish-Jewish family ate vegetarian meals, except for fish, until another immigrant there learned the kosher method of slaughtering fowl. Then they ate chicken on occasion. This family found it "hard to keep kosher," but persisted, proud that they could uphold their traditions.[9]

Some opted to break the dietary laws, like Sig Adler, who decided he could "digress" a bit. Jews with insufficient incomes or those who had no cooking privileges trekked up the Lisbon hills at noon to receive a free hot lunch from the community's soup kitchen. Organized by COMASSIS and subsidized by the JDC, it served about five hundred kosher meals every day except Saturday. COMASSIS also managed to acquire the "Passover Biscuit" (matzot) to distribute to "refugees all over the country" during Passover week. The Jewish community held two Seders, the Passover ceremonial dinners, and also provided matzot for Jewish passengers sailing during the holiday.[10] These free meals symbolized a severe status loss, since these mostly middle-class people found themselves crowded into a charitable institution.

Some refugees needed more than food or shelter. The more observant sought spiritual solace, either by attending Portuguese synagogues or by creating a minyan (the quorum for prayer services) in rented spaces. The Pekelis couple attended services in the Lisbon synagogue. Although using a mostly Sephardic liturgy, derived from historical Spanish and Portuguese Jewish communities, the synagogue had adopted Ashkenazi influences. During prayers, Carla Pekelis could easily distinguish the Portuguese Jews from refugees: "The first had the indifferent and calm look of people at their ease and at home; the others, the timid, embarrassed manners of uninvited guests. During the services, there were those who could not control their sobs." In 1934, some Polish Ashkenazi Jews, mostly Orthodox, formed their own small synagogue in Lisbon, Ohel Jakob, using rooms of the small Zionist youth organization there. In Porto, Jewish refugees benefited from the solicitude of the Porto Jewish community, which invited them to its synagogue and provided matzot for Passover.[11]

In villages such as Ericeira and Caldas da Rainha, some refugees created Jewish spaces, organizing small prayer groups and improvising Seders in cafés. In Figueira, others established a small synagogue and also built a sukkah (a structure in which to celebrate the harvest festival of Sukkoth). And in Caldas, a few taught each other Hebrew and Yiddish, and

Bar Mitzvah in Caldas da Rainha, Portugal, 1940s (NY_03685, Courtesy of JDC Archives, New York).

Refugees sitting around the Passover table in Caldas da Rainha, 1940s (NY_03680, Courtesy of JDC Archives, New York).

studied the Torah. In addition, settled central and eastern European Jews who had come to Portugal earlier than other refugees invited some of the newly arrived to celebrate religious rituals in their homes. A family that had emigrated from Poland in 1933 regularly welcomed refugees to its Sabbath and holiday dinners. The man simply went to cafés and invited strangers. By contrast, the native-born Portuguese-Jewish community, which worked tirelessly to help refugees, rarely socialized with them, whether because of language constraints or because Portuguese Jews saw refugees as transient. Refugees hoping to reach out to other Jews turned to one another.[12]

Lines and Consulates Once Again: Sites of Angst and Disappointment

Refugees understood that Portugal would not shelter them indefinitely. Greatly relieved that they could walk and sit in public spaces, find shelter, eat at tables, and even frequent a synagogue, they nonetheless had to continue the paper chase. If they overstayed their ambivalent welcome, they feared imprisonment. They had spent frustrating days in their homelands lining up for necessary papers, and many had stood on similar lines in Marseille and then again at four border crossings before making it to Portugal. Now in Lisbon, they once again endured lines at consulates. Uncertainty magnified the stress of waiting. Even today, people on lines suffer stress and "that nagging sensation that one's life is slipping away"—and refugees had far more to lose.[13]

Many waited in front of the U.S. Legation and Consulate General in Lisbon, referring to it as the "consulate," "legation," or "mission." The lines there seemed to have "no end at all," raising an emotional trinity of anxiety, fear, and hope. By the fall of 1940, thousands in Lisbon were seeking to acquire U.S. transit visas or trying to submit immigrant or nonimmigrant visa applications. But the U.S. legation did more than attend to refugees. Hundreds of American citizens needed their passports amended or renewed in order to escape the war. The legation expedited business requests, cleared American vessels and crew lists, and gathered war information as well. But its staff grew at a snail's pace even as its work expanded exponentially. Until January 1941, it functioned with the minister, one secretary, and a clerk or two. By July 1941, it was employing three officers and seven clerks, but without additional office space. The United States raised the legation to the status of a full-fledged embassy only in June 1944, after most European Jews had been murdered.[14]

Other refugees tried the consulates of Latin American countries, Canada, and Britain. Husbands and wives frequently chose different lines in order to double their chances of getting into a consulate. Carla and Alex Pekelis approached many consulates systematically, while dividing up the work. Alex went out to "visit consulates, police commissioners, travel agencies . . . in search of a million things: travel permits, proofs of citizenship, money exchange, ship passage . . . and so on," and Carla "pounded out letters on the typewriter addressed to friends and relatives, especially in New York, with requests that went from a simple testimonial, authenticated by a notary, to the all-important 'affidavit' that would place the responsibility for [their] future on the shoulders of whoever acted as [their] guarantor." Carla recalled: "There were things that were now in our blood like a sort of poison. They were called 'work permits' and 'residence permits,' 'identity cards' and . . . 'temporary safe conduct and gasoline ration cards,' 'exit visas,' and 'transit visas,' and 'entry visas.'" The JDC office in Lisbon described the procedure as a "nightmare of securing 57 varieties of visas—exit, entrance, transit, expirations, renewals, revalidations," requiring applicants to wade "through oceans of red tape." Arthur Koestler, a well-known antifascist, feared for his life in Portugal. In October 1940, he told the British consul there that although he would happily die for a principle, he did not want to die because of red tape.[15]

Having devoted long hours and emotional stamina to gathering documents and lining up, the lucky ones made it into sterile waiting rooms— "those vestibules of heaven and hell!" Hermann Grab, who spent six months in Lisbon, wondered whether the receptionist at the U.S. consulate understood that his desk stood at "the threshold of the promised land." Alex Pekelis remarked, "One day someone will tell the story of these 'waiting rooms.'" He had met an old Yiddish-speaking man who had a heart attack on the same bench upon which he had waited for weeks, a young German-Jewish woman who later committed suicide after being repeatedly turned down, and a family that returned to Germany because they had run out of funds. Such a story "will be too late for those who fall by the wayside," he observed, "but it might bring catharsis to those who survive."[16]

Inside the consuls' offices, the situation barely improved. Miriam Stanton, a Polish citizen, appealed to the Polish consul in Lisbon for a visa to Canada or the United States. She decided to try a feminine tactic: "It was much more fitting for a young girl to be all smiles, humble and helpless." She failed to achieve her goal: "We thanked each other so graciously for nothing." While visiting the U.S. legation in Lisbon, Varian Fry complained that applicants "stood for hours in the waiting-room, stood again while the vice-consuls were questioning them." He protested their poor treatment: "One of the vice-consuls at Lisbon received applicants with his feet on his desk, pipe in mouth. He never got up from his chair, even for women." No such boorishness, however, appeared in a self-congratulatory postwar State Department report that described an overworked and understaffed legation, adding, "overtime was cheerfully given." Stefan Zweig summed up: "Human beings were made to feel that they were objects and not subjects, that nothing was their right but everything merely a favour by official grace. They were codified, registered, numbered, stamped."[17]

Even worse, U.S. consuls regularly added to their requirements. The Pekelis couple found that the American consul, a "young, elegant man of prosperous appearance . . . seemed friendly at first," but "began to enlarge his initial demands with the unthinking cruelty of a blackmailer. No sooner did we manage to secure a document, than he discovered that another was needed." He continually stifled their hopes as they repeatedly scrambled for new documents. Similarly, consuls relied on a 1930 directive banning immigrants "likely to become a public charge" to insist that close family or friends in America sign two affidavits of support for each refugee and deposit money in U.S. bank accounts. But the amount could vary depending on the suspicions or caprice of State Department officials. More perfidiously, after a lower-level U.S. bureaucrat in Lisbon showed Jan Lustig the telegram ensuring him a visa, the "young, blond consul" insisted that the telegram did not exist. With Lustig in tow, the consul confronted the same lower-level bureaucrat, who then stammered, "The dossier doesn't exist." The consul suggested that Lustig find another visa, after which the United States might reconsider his immigration: "Another visa? That's easy to say," responded Lustig. Curtly, the consul retorted, "Sorry." And then came the coup de grâce: if Washington turned down someone with all necessary papers, she or he could not appeal for six months.[18]

Fearing danger and grasping at any opportunity, most refugees persevered, repeatedly returning to these sites of frustration. Simultaneously, they desperately felt a need for speed, believing themselves to be "on the verge—of something," a tightening Nazi vise that might entrap and kill them. Their fears intensified if they held inadequate visas. Friedrich Torberg, who remained in Portugal from June through October 1940, possessed only a Haitian visa: "The relative ease with which I got it, makes me suspect it is worthless. . . . But even if it is legitimate, there are no direct ships that go to Haiti. . . . One would have to travel via Cuba, and the transit visa (there), if one could even acquire it, costs $200. So, I have to drop that plan. . . . What can I do now? . . . I have to wait." Highlighting the situation Jews faced since the 1930s, this "classic Jewish refugee joke" made it into a collection of Jewish humor in 1943: "A harassed attaché of the American Consulate at Lisbon told the story of a gray-faced little man who leaned over his desk one morning and anxiously inquired: 'Can you tell me if there is any possibility I could get entrance to your wonderful country?' The attaché, pressed by thousands of such requests and haggard from sleepless nights, replied: 'Impossible now. Come back in another ten years.' The little refugee moved toward the door, stopped, turned and, with a wan smile, asked, 'Morning or afternoon?' "[19]

Even sites intended to help refugees rarely quickened the process. One Quaker lamented, "Translated in human terms, this means a great increase in feelings of hopelessness on the part of the refugees and greatly reduced confidence on the part of those helping them. . . . Here the Portuguese *paciencia* would come in handy. But it is hard to ask them to be patient when they have already waited a year, or some as much as three years." The Quakers acknowledged, "We try all sorts of means to help the people with their emigration, but when you think you have found a way today—everything is turned over tomorrow." Upon appealing to the U.S. legation to aid a "racially" Jewish man who had converted to Catholicism, Howard Wriggins in Lisbon wrote to Quaker headquarters in Philadelphia, "We realize that possibilities for visas in such cases are as scarce as buttercups in January."[20]

Perhaps only a writer among the refugees could conjure up what the consuls themselves may have thought about the situation. Hermann Grab, originally from Prague, imagined, "These young men . . . graduates of the gentlemen's universities of Princeton or Yale . . . one or the other surely must have asked himself what he should do with this mass of humanity. . . . What should this new flashflood [made up] of the Children of Israel do on the shores of America?" More bitingly, the American author Stephen Longstreet reflected that "it is sad to think of all the poor honest little people who have to stay behind . . . all the little souls who have no drag with our State Department's men, or know no Cardinal or an Ambassador to smooth things over for their citizenship papers." Yet even knowing a former prime minister of Belgium, who vouched for him, did not ease Felix Oppenheim's concerns. When the U.S. visa finally arrived, "it still required much standing in line and much paperwork and having to cope with an unfriendly staff." Wriggins believed that his office mediated between refugees and Kafka's *The Castle,* where "authority was pervasive but unreachable." Carla Pekelis felt similarly: "It would have taken the pen of a Kafka . . . to depict the world of visas in all its surrealistic absurdity; that of a Dostoyevsky to render the nightmare of the petitioners' struggle for survival." In the end, refugees had only one "occupation": "waiting . . . waiting, waiting!"[21]

Kurt Israel and the American Visa

Kurt Israel's letters and his later memoir detailed how one man experienced the reality of waiting. His persistence and his increasing frustration after defeats at the U.S. legation provide insights into the state of mind of many refugees. None of their stories are exactly the same, but his encounters with the consulate highlight some of the obstacles and subsequent torment that others faced.

Born in 1909 in Hanover, Kurt Israel studied law, but Hitler's accession to power crushed that dream. The twenty-four-year-old law clerk fled early, in 1933, to Holland, where he found a job in a cousin's business in Rotterdam. With the German invasion of Holland on May 10, 1940, his life changed dramatically, and by May 15 he realized he had to flee again. A friend with connections offered him a safe haven in the Uruguayan Embassy, where Ambassador Carlos Maria Gurmendez had already taken in about sixteen Jews. But first the ambassador would have to interview him: "What am I going to say to this man who knows nothing of me, cannot possibly be interested in my fate and, moreover, to whom I have to talk in French, a language I have not used in many years?" He did not recall exactly what he said, but realized later, "I must have expressed my fear of being caught by the Nazis; I must have spoken of my mother in America who might never see me again— enough, the Ambassador appeared moved by whatever I stammered in halting French, and . . . he assured me I could stay in his house—and under his protection." Israel slept on a mattress in the attic and worked in the kitchen, washing and drying dishes, "a job that apparently never stops!"[22] With a safe conduct pass from Uruguay, he ran errands for the embassy as the ambassador's "valet."

Two months later, on July 17, 1940, representatives of the neutral countries, which included Uruguay, had to leave Nazi-controlled Holland. The ambassador headed for Lisbon, where he would represent Uruguay to Portugal. But first he negotiated with the Germans to be allowed to take the Jewish refugees in his embassy with him. Everyone received "genuine" Uruguayan passports for the ten-day trip. Israel joined the exodus from the embassy through Germany to Switzerland: "Here I am finally safe from the Nazis!" Getting to Lisbon on a bus with about thirty people aboard proved arduous. Southern France "[was] overrun by refugees from the North." Unlike most refugees, Israel noticed the beauty of the landscape around Portbou at the Spanish border: "on one side the majestic heights of the Pyrenees, while on the other we look straight down into the deep blue waters of the Mediterranean." The Spanish police, polite to the ambassador's family, scrutinized the entourage but let them through. They spent two nights in hot, overcrowded trains, arriving at the Portuguese border to face several more hours of passport control. He did not even mind turning in his Uruguayan passport once he reached a neutral country. Kurt Israel's real disappointment started in Portugal with the Americans. Upon arrival on July 27, 1940, he followed friends to Luso, north of Lisbon, where they entered a hotel, "a bedraggled group of exhausted refugees, badly in need of a bath, clean clothes, and a good long rest."[23]

A few weeks in Luso caused him to feel "topnotch" ("prima-prima") physically and in terms of his "nerves." But his first visit to the consulate in Lisbon, in August 1940, found him "trembling and shaking" as he stood before the consul. He submitted his papers, including birth certificates for himself and his brother Ernst, who was already in the United States and would vouch for him. Then he had to prove "financial resources" and provide details about the person who would support him. He soon realized he would have to move to Lisbon because "one has so many things to attend to at consulates, shipping offices, etc." There he found a German-Jewish couple who offered him room and board for $1 a day, and he discovered to his delight that the woman came from his mother's hometown and knew her well.[24] The comfort of the kind of home-cooked meals that he had grown up with—the intersection of physical and psychological well-being—buoyed him as his frustrations with the length of his stay grew. He did not need money from his family yet: "In all other respects I could and would have enjoyed my stay in Lisbon," but the government's policy forbidding refugees to work, which left him idle, and the "uncertainty concerning [his] future" made "any real enjoyment impossible." He carefully prepared for every appointment with the U.S. consul. His first interview went relatively smoothly, since the Uruguayan ambassador accompanied him. This allowed him to cut the long lines, and he gained speedy access to one of the vice-consuls, "beleaguered though they are by visa seeking crowds."[25] He had an immigration number, obtained in Rotterdam in 1938, and he handed in myriad other documents.[26] At first, the vice-consul seemed encouraging. But Israel needed to prove his "financial resources" before anything else could proceed. Still, he had "the definite impression that nothing will stand in the way of the visa if the material circumstances suffice."

However, he soon faced setbacks: "At subsequent appointments, a different consulate officer handles my case, a man who seems utterly indifferent to any pleading and at times even faintly hostile towards a would-be immigrant."[27] In September 1940, Kurt Israel thanked his brother for the $3,000 he had deposited in a bank account in Kurt's name, and Kurt believed optimistically that the consul would be impressed with this figure (the equivalent of $54,180 in 2019).[28] He expected his affidavits to have reached the consulate and looked forward to hearing good news any day. He understood that the consulate was "overburdened," but admitted disappointment, since he had expected a "quick processing."[29] Ten days later, Israel learned the bad news: the United States found his brother's income insufficient and would not accept his affidavit of support. The State Department had also rejected a second affidavit, from his uncle, because of the man's age. In addition, the Americans suspected that the bank account deposit in his name had been taken from his brother's account. Hence it would not suffice in case both men lost their jobs. The consul insisted that Kurt Israel's brother had to prove he still had money in his own account or find someone else willing to put up $2,500 (the average annual income in the United States in 1940 was $1,368) for an additional affidavit.[30] "Despondent," Israel could only request further help from his brother.[31]

That September, his feelings of frustration mingled with his longing for a well-ordered and vigorous life. Like so many other refugees, he had to worry about permission to remain in Portugal when, "more ardently than ever," he wanted "to stretch out his feet under [his] own table." He decried the "lazy vacation-life that was slowly but surely getting on [his] nerves."[32] As the U.S. visa process dragged on, he had to apply for extensions to stay in Portugal. Anxious about the police, who took "measures" against undocumented refugees, he could nonetheless understand that the authorities "were not enthusiastic about the overflowing capital city." He admonished himself regarding his exasperation at the Portuguese bureaucracies in charge of extending his residence permit. Uncritically accepting the stereotype of southerners as slow, he wrote: "if one is impatient by nature, one should not spend a long time in Portugal." Yet fears of an expanding war amplified his unhappiness with a "very inactive life": "The thought of waiting here with nothing to do while the future looks ever more menacing and uncertain is almost unbearable."[33]

While suffering this seemingly interminable wait, Kurt Israel still had a social life. He and his Dutch-Jewish friends celebrated Queen Wilhelmina's birthday at the Dutch consulate in Porto, and they met regularly. He also found new acquaintances in Luso and Lisbon, a city "teeming with foreigners, [where] one hears German, French, even Dutch." Among his new friends, who had "remarkable émigré fates," the conversation circled around the "eternal theme of 'visa.'"[34] In addition, "everyone talks about residence permits, . . . ship tickets and . . . politics." Although many refugees feared a German victory in 1940, immediately after Germany invaded France, his friends had no "doubts that England will win the war, but . . . the war will take many years." He also played bridge and read English, proudly informing his family that he had finished *Gone with the Wind*. In addition, he "rack[ed] [his] brains" trying to read Portuguese newspapers. Unlike most refugees, he took learning Portuguese seriously. To communicate, he spoke French or Portuguese and found himself like the "proverbial sailor who can say 'cheers' in 26 languages."[35]

By October 1940, three months after arriving in Portugal, he felt "damned to inactivity, an unhappy test of nerves," and "even the weather [was] cloudy and rainy." The combination confirmed his overall impression: "Leaving will not be hard for me." His room overlooked the harbor, where he "enviously watch[ed] the steamships and airplanes leave Europe." In mid-October, he wrote that the week had been bleak, "nothing but fruitless running around, sitting around and waiting, partly for permission to stay, partly for a visa." The former application had been so badly handled that he hired a Portuguese lawyer to prevent what he believed would be his expulsion. His lawyer solved the problem and refused to accept any payment. Israel hailed him "as a true Portuguese, he acted out of humanity!"

Americans, however, showed far less compassion. Exasperated, he reported that a declaration from a New York bank regarding the assets deposited in his name seemed to have vanished from the consulate. Eventually, the consulate found the declaration and gave him an appointment for the next week: *"Here one needs patience and strong nerves!"*[36] But once again the vice-consul dashed his hopes. The American questioned the finances of those signing for Israel and wanted more proof that his brother had not used his own money. Suddenly and sadly, Kurt Israel began to understand: "With all of this I am very afraid that the consul wants to make things difficult for me and will look for as many reasons to reject me as he can."[37]

In November, he shared his utter frustration with his mother and brother, sparing his friends in Portugal, since they, too, faced similar "chicanery, unnecessary delays, and unsubstantiated rejections." Yet another consular dispute had "deeply upset" him: "The disappointment at the consulate was too great!" He had expected that his papers would finally satisfy the Americans, but instead he "was all the more appalled when he learned his visa application had been turned down entirely" because of insufficient financial resources. When he vented his frustration to the consul—"This was inexplicable to me since I had done everything that I was told to do"— the man simply "shrugged his shoulders" and refused to give him any further information. In short, Israel realized, "any sum we could possibly pull together could again be considered inadequate," since the consul had known for months how much his family and friends could afford. He did not know that Breckinridge Long, the assistant secretary of state, had ordered the State Department to "postpone and postpone and postpone" the granting of visas a few months earlier. But he did recognize a policy. Despairing, he wrote: "I am completely convinced that they simply do not want to give me the visa, no matter what financial means we can prove."[38]

Observing the "limitless calamity" of refugees, he reflected, "How many will continue to come here and how many more can't even get here?" He realized that relatively few had actually succeeded in leaving German-occupied Europe and that he had to be thankful for his lot, which contrasted greatly with the misery of hundreds of thousands of others. Further, although he could live off the savings he had taken from Holland and had a brother who would help him if necessary, he knew of many refugees who had arrived with absolutely nothing. They all appeared to share one fate: the consuls strove to "always find new reasons not to give a visa."[39]

"Doomed to idleness and waiting," Israel hoped in the late fall of 1940 that connections, someone of "stature," might make a difference. In late

November, he appealed to the Uruguayan ambassador and to a "Committee"—most likely COMASSIS—and its chair, Augusto d'Esaguy. The Uruguayan ambassador provided a two-page handwritten letter recommending Kurt Israel to the Americans. "The letter is so lovely that I have had it photocopied," Israel wrote. Although not an American, this ambassador's statement praising Kurt's character may have helped him. The Lisbon Jewish Committee, too, gave him advice, suggesting that Israel find an American citizen to attest that he had not been politically active, that he would make a loyal citizen, and that he would never be a spy. He might even need a few more of these "moral affidavits," which his Dutch-Jewish friends could write, too. Optimistic that something good would come of these efforts, he nevertheless watched "with a heavy heart" as his last Dutch friends left Lisbon for Uruguay and Indonesia (then the Dutch East Indies): "I am the last of our circle still here."[40]

Israel's letters stop on November 28. We learn from his memoir that he received the visa at the end of December, but he could not ascertain whether the Uruguayan ambassador's letter or a "moral affidavit" sent by his brother's employer in the United States, or the simple fact that a different American official interviewed him had made the difference. On January 27, 1941, six months to the day after his arrival in Portugal, he boarded the *Lourenço Marques* for the United States. Those six months felt very long to him, since he did not know when or even if the United States would accept him. Although never in immediate danger, he worried about a spreading war, learned of deportations from Baden, Germany, to French internment camps, and wondered about friends in German-occupied Holland with whom he had lost contact. Joyously heading toward a family reunion, he recorded: "Never mind that I travel fourth class and share my quarters with some 80 very seasick people—I am on my way!"[41]

Fixed (or Forced) Residences: Congenial Confinement

The need for visas grew exponentially as Salazar's patience with refugees wore thin. After 1940, and more strictly starting in the summer of 1941, the Portuguese government attempted to alleviate overcrowding in Lisbon by interning refugees who stayed beyond their thirty-day Portuguese visas. Compelled to live in fixed residences in villages or towns some distance from the capital, refugees had to remain within three kilometers of the town centers.

Many refugees referred to these towns, including Curia, Luso, Figueira da Foz, Caldas da Rainha (often called Caldas), Cascais, and Ericeira, as "forced residences," as did social workers. These towns provided more freedom than jails, yet this spatial entrapment, even in pretty seaside towns, caused intense apprehension. Refugees needed special police permission for consular visits, and they could not travel to Lisbon regularly. It took three hours to travel the sixty miles to Lisbon from Caldas—on a new train.[42]

These sites, consulates and fixed residences, depended on each other but also created the catch-22 already mentioned. Living in a fixed residence made it harder to get to a consulate. Not acquiring proper visas from a consulate made it harder to leave Portugal. Aid workers understood that these sites kept refugees out of prison but multiplied their stress: refugees were "not badly accommodated, but all anxious, of course, to get their papers . . . to get out of Portugal." These organizations also noticed a drop-off in the numbers of applicants able to visit their offices: "Most of the work, support, counsel and emigration is carried out at arm's length by correspondence."[43]

From June 1940 onward, the Portuguese often sent trains with refugees directly from the border to these fixed residences. For example, the Czech people on Jan Lustig's train had to go to Figueira da Foz, and the French to Caldas da Rainha. On another train, police directed Austrians to Caldas, and Czechs and Poles to Porto. In August 1941, the government transferred 100 refugees who faced prison for overstaying transit visas to Caldas instead. That figure rose to 160 in November, including Jews without proper papers who had already served time in prison.[44]

One such group, the Arnholz family, spent one year in Lisbon before being forced to move to Caldas. The father, a fifty-four-year old banker, had applied for a U.S. visa in November 1938 but could not acquire it, because the State Department did not consider the affidavit from an American rabbi sufficient. Nor did the U.S. government believe that Mr. Arnholz could support his family. The family had suffered displacement since 1933, when they fled Berlin for Holland. In 1935, when the Dutch refused to grant Mr. Arnholz a work permit, they relocated to Belgium. That move, too, proved unsuccessful, and the family settled in Milan in 1938, only to face the Italian racial laws enacted that fall. Eventually, they made it to Portugal with a fake Panamanian passport. Both children had acquired excellent language skills on their journeys: the daughter, who had mastered English, French, German, Italian, Dutch, and Portuguese, along with shorthand and typing, worked for the

JDC; the son worked for the Unitarians in Lisbon. Still, they had no way of leaving Portugal, and the police grew impatient after a year. Sent to Caldas, they remained there until the end of the war.[45] Like the Arnholz family, many others in Caldas arrived exhausted, having spent months or years on the run.

Relatively few refugees spent long stretches in jail, an outcome the government threatened regularly but hesitated to pursue. The Jewish community and social work agencies interceded where they could. For example, in December 1942, Isaac Weissmann of the World Jewish Congress approached the secret police in hopes of freeing about two hundred Jews from prison by offering to assemble and supervise them in Ericeira. Others found themselves remanded to a beach resort: a spa, where they "played at being summer guests." The Gould family, sent to Ericeira, had to report daily to a "young man with a thin mustache," but the villagers there welcomed them with flowers: "It was a touching scene, all the more poignant because these people were shoeless and dressed in rags." The government released more undocumented aliens from the Aljube prison in January 1943, expecting them to remain in fixed residences as well. Not a prisoner, but not free, one refugee dubbed these residences "forced vacations," and another declared, "We are—let's say it openly—interned."[46]

Had refugees not suffered grief over loved ones left behind and anxiety about moving on, those detained in these villages might have enjoyed their attractions. For example, Caldas da Rainha, a spa, offered beaches lined with palm trees. Still, most chafed at the restrictions on their movements. The Quakers acknowledged this: "You get stale if you only have a radius of 3 kilometers." Some refugees spent their time walking through the weekly cattle fair, sitting in cafés, reading newspapers, and even gardening. Jewish children could attend school there, paid for by their parents or by Jewish agencies, and the JDC rented some land near Ericeira so that teenage refugees could train for agricultural employment in countries of immigration. During their long days, refugees deliberated: "the only thing that mattered was the chance of being admitted" to a safe country. Some refugees succumbed to depression; one young man "suffered physically and morally." A postcard from Caldas to the Quakers begged them to "snap up *any* visa you can possibly get for us, please."[47]

Living in small towns cost more than living in Lisbon, and international charities paid the steeper prices. But refugees found their small stipends insufficient, especially as the cost of living rose. They received $1 a day from the

JDC as well as clothing and medicine from the Lisbon Jewish community, also funded by the JDC. But the Quakers estimated the need at $2 a day by 1943, or $100 per month for a married couple. Refugees reported, "We were on the run continuously," moving to cheaper houses as their money no longer stretched to cover their rent. At one point, frustrated refugees joined together to ask the JDC for increased subsidies. Granted a small increase, they found it inadequate and requested more. Elias Baruel, vice president of the Lisbon Jewish community, saw their dissatisfaction as a sign of "unfriendliness and lack of consideration," whereas Joseph Schwartz of the JDC, realizing the exasperation and deprivation that refugees endured, agreed to another increase—also to avoid a possible demonstration by those interned in Caldas. Baruel later reported that Schwartz, referring to Jewish discontent, asked with a smile, "What do you want Dr. Baruel, to start a pogrom in Caldas?"[48]

Refugees referring to themselves as "Caldanesen" received packages from the Red Cross and from American Jews. Most lived in furnished rooms, barracks, or hotels, where Frank Arams ate "boiled chicken every day," which he described as "fine with me." He stayed in Caldas for three months in 1941 until his visa arrived. Others stayed years. One young man tried to occupy himself by taking long walks, brushing up on his math or economics studies, and playing table tennis or bridge. He wrote letters in the evenings. The Quaker recipient of his letters responded: "[It] was refreshing to hear a glad voice from out of the gloomy wilderness of Caldas. There is so much complaint and unhappiness issuing from the Queens' baths (Caldas da Rainha) that anything like your letter is to us a much-needed ray of sunshine."[49]

New York social workers visiting Caldas da Rainha worried that "fathers and children [were] idle" while mothers attended to laundry and mending. Alix Stiel Preece, a German non-Jewish woman forced to reside in Caldas after imprisonment in Gurs, concurred with this opinion. Employed by the USC to assist other refugees, she carefully observed several hundred mostly German-Jewish refugees and noticed gender divisions among them: "The women busied themselves in their households," but the men seemed bored. While some women cooked for others and received monetary compensation, men "sat around, played cards, listened to the radio." For them, "idleness was much harder and more harmful." Stiel Preece could not see whether there were tensions or altered gender roles inside the homes. In one case, however, a writer left a description of how he and his housemates divided the labor. His wife and another woman cooked. One man hauled potatoes and cleaned vegetables, two other men split firewood, and he made the beds, swept the rooms, and dried the dishes.[50] At least in this situation, the group shared chores, even if the women continued to cook.

Stiel Preece brought women together in knitting circles, with the USC providing wool. These groups sent warm items to people in internment camps as well as to the Portuguese Red Cross. She also organized volunteers to create activities for refugee children and to mail food packages to a Spanish camp where more refugees languished. In addition, the USC hired refugees to keep accounts, disburse allocations, and counsel one another. Refugees could also attend lectures and use USC lending libraries in both Caldas and Ericeira. These included mostly German books, but some in French and Portuguese as well. The Quakers also provided activities, in order to "stave [off] growing dislike on part of Portuguese for lazy, do-nothing refugees." They did not report such Portuguese attitudes, but hoped to keep them at bay. In 1942, the Quakers, too, resorted to forming knitting circles for women and added a farm for men.[51]

Refugees also organized themselves. Polish Jews in Caldas, numbering about two hundred, requested that the American Federation for Polish Jews send them two copies of its newsletter, *Polish Jew*. Refugees planned activities and courses as well, such as English-language classes, to distract those who had suffered "tragic losses of family members." Finally, snapshots of refugees on the beaches of these towns attest to some relaxing moments.[52] Nevertheless, villages like Caldas and Ericeira grew tedious as refugees hailing from largely urban environments tried to find a purpose in new, makeshift, temporary communities. Even if they sat in a local café with new friends, these were different cafés, different friends, and different times.

Because of their isolation, these seaside towns allowed for more intimate contacts between refugees and Portuguese neighbors. In fact, in some of these small villages, refugees made up a significant portion of the local population, especially in winter. Jan Lustig noted the warm reception his group received, but he also realized that refugees boosted the local economy and created jobs.[53] Most of the Portuguese of little or middling means seemed to appreciate the extra income they gained from refugees. Some may also have recognized the precarious legal situation of the newcomers, especially once some refugees began to speak a bit of Portuguese. As long as refugees did not compete for jobs, the local population welcomed them.

Nevertheless, as in Lisbon, cultural differences could irritate, and townspeople or the police sometimes expressed annoyance at refugee

women's dress and their enjoyment of public spaces. Less visible and therefore less irksome were the weekly stipends that refugees received from Jewish
charities, which exceeded the family incomes of many Portuguese. Still, the
fact that refugees spent hours in cafés made some Portuguese, who did not
know the rules prohibiting refugees from working, wonder about their idleness. Ilse Losa believed that most Portuguese knew very little about what the
refugees had faced before their arrival. She noticed that a few, perhaps more
informed than others, talked about the troubles of refugees, but also misunderstood their emotional style. The northerners may have felt despondent as
they shared their feelings in cafés. Yet a number of local Portuguese reacted
with, "If we were forced to leave our land, we'd spend our time crying and
not enjoying ourselves like these people."[54]

Misunderstandings notwithstanding, most small towns responded
warmly, aligning with the Portuguese kindness that refugees had already
found notable. In Curia, Friedrich Torberg met Portuguese pedestrians who
stopped him to ask what he was looking for and civil servants who seemed
pleased when their French or English allowed them to be helpful. "I have to
thank the Portuguese with my whole heart. . . . Their participation in our
destiny goes beyond bounds," Eugen Tillinger wrote to the *Aufbau* in
December 1940. Although nervous about being sent to a fixed residence in
Figueira da Foz, he found it to be an "enchanting bathing village directly on
the Atlantic" where the townspeople greeted refugees with buses to take them
to their residences, carried their baggage, and asked all the Portuguese men
who could speak French to interpret for them. Some refugees attended
evening movies for free, could speak French or English at the Department of
Tourism, read bilingual menus, and learned that the chamber of commerce
prohibited hotels from raising their prices. Villagers also took refugees shop-
ping, to the doctor, or to the police. One waiter even refused a tip.[55]

Small-town life encouraged acculturation and mixing. Alix Stiel Preece
admired the many refugees who attempted to learn Portuguese, especially the
women, recalling how "the housewife who shopped at the market had to learn
Portuguese, in order to 'discuss' the prices, because without bargaining no sale
takes place." She delighted in the Caldas market, the highlight of her stay in
Portugal, remembering "the blaze of color, the throngs, all the peasants come
in costumes with bright caps, they ride for hours on donkeys to sell their wares."
She also reflected on the Portuguese as "good-natured, very poor, modest
people . . . who live mostly from dried fish and green beans." Stiel Preece

assumed that Portuguese people noticed her and that they may have had feelings about refugees. Indeed, refugees overwhelmed the central squares in some towns. Yet instead of reacting to what could have been seen as an invasion of foreigners, small-town Portuguese welcomed them. She concluded, "It must be strange for the native people to see all these émigrés wandering around, but the stores and cafés were busy and if this invasion perturbed the amiable Portuguese, they didn't let us notice this in any way." Looking back, a Jewish refugee who had spent almost two years in Figueira da Foz remembered being invited for dinner in Portuguese homes and recalled that people in a café assisted refugees with filling out police forms. And when Ursula Leinung and her fiancé announced their engagement in Ericeira, "the whole village came to the engagement party, Jews and Portuguese." In 1994, she returned to Ericeira and recognized her old neighbors. They discussed the parties that Portuguese and Jews held when Jewish individuals or couples received their visas to go abroad, and the neighbors produced photos they had saved of these events.[56]

By late 1944, 700–800 refugees remained in fixed residences, with 300 housed in Caldas, about 125 in Ericeira, and the rest spread among other villages. By May 1945, the number in Caldas had only dwindled to 209. Even as the war wound down, the Portuguese police kept these refugees out of Lisbon, depriving them of easy interactions with consulates and aid groups. As of V-E Day, May 8, 1945, the Portuguese government intended to dismantle the fixed residences. But by July, the government had still not yet declared that refugees could leave them. Officially, the Portuguese police closed Caldas as a fixed residence at the end of August 1945, allowing most of the Caldas refugees to stay there as "free refugees" or to return to Lisbon. But the police could also refuse permission to individuals and sent some from Lisbon and Caldas to the fixed residence of Ericeira. In a rare case, the police arrested and held a twenty-three-year-old woman in Caxias prison for leaving her fixed residence without their permission at the end of 1945.[57]

A Tale of Fixed Residences: Trixie and Ferris, Feats and Frustrations
The situation of one couple illustrates the hopes and fears of two people forced to remain at these beautiful sites of frustration and poverty. Trixie and Ferris Ferrigo, young entertainers when they arrived in Portugal, had an extra reserve of optimism that kept their spirits higher than most. Yet even then, these attractive, energetic newlyweds experienced hunger, endured prison, and, at times, descended into despair.

Ferris Ferrigo, or Fridrih Goldstăjn, born in Istanbul in 1903, had two Jewish parents. His family's brief stay in Yugoslavia granted him Yugoslav citizenship, but he grew up in Berlin. With the Nazi takeover, his "race" and political affiliations with a Weimar-era peace movement forced him to flee. A tenor, he launched himself as an entertainer, finding employment in Holland, Belgium, and England by singing in variety shows. His repertoire included songs in English, German, Russian, French, Danish, Dutch, and more. While looking to establish himself in London and to hire a dancer and musician, he met Beatrice Jennet Gardner, or "Trixie," a young English Protestant ten years his junior. She played the accordion and danced, and he hoped to hire her for his "Orchestra of Nations." But Britain refused to extend his Yugoslav visa as war loomed, and he had to return to Europe. Trixie joined him in Antwerp in April 1939, and they performed together, along with an orchestra of Belgian women. They planned to marry on May 10, 1940, but the Germans invaded Belgium on that day. Instead, they managed hurried nuptials some weeks later, with Ferrigo asserting that he was Protestant and the Yugoslav Embassy affixing Trixie's photo to Ferris's passport. Despite that identification, Ferris warned his new wife, "You have a man without a country."[58]

Desperate to find a way out of Antwerp, they approached the consulate of El Salvador as a last resort. There they sought a Señor Lopes, who had spent many evenings at their show in Antwerp. He recognized them and happily gave them visas that would get them to Portugal, but not allow them to enter El Salvador. On September 28, 1940, they left Antwerp by train with Señor Lopes, traversing Belgium and France without incident. Still, they agonized: "What country would take us in?" Arriving at Vilar Formoso, the Salvadoran left them as he continued his trip, and they approached the Portuguese police. The police asked them to play their guitar and accordion. They performed the British and Portuguese national anthems, befriending the police. The chief then explained that they would have to find visas once they were in Lisbon. He offered them a two-week stay in his own apartment in Lisbon and then another two-week stay with a Church of England pastor. After that, they would have to join hundreds of refugees in a camp outside of Lisbon until they had a visa to go elsewhere.

Early on their first morning in Lisbon, they headed to the British consulate, where Trixie handed her passport to the consul general, hoping to get permission to return home with Ferris. To her shock and utter dismay, he confiscated her passport, explaining that by marrying a foreigner, she had forfeited her citizenship, according to British law. She had the option of divorcing Ferris and then returning to England, which she emphatically rejected. Steadfast, they continued to visit many consulates, but to no avail. They filled out applications to enter South Africa as entertainers; they applied for a Cuban visa. They also requested an emergency visa to the United States in the spring of 1941, just as the country was making it harder for all applicants by requiring "references from Americans who had known them for at least five years—or as long as possible." They knew no Americans. The Ferrigos then sought entry to Mexico, Brazil, Canada, Argentina, and Chile. They further applied—as foreigners—for visas to England or to "any land where we would be on British soil." In each case, they had to produce personal identity documents as well as letters of recommendation. For Brazil, for example, they needed a letter of application and letters of recommendation from the Quakers, the Yugoslav legation, and the British consul, all addressed to the consul general of Brazil. They met with either refusals or, in the case of Cuba, an impossible financial demand.[59]

Alongside trips to consulates, they began to offer concerts in order to raise their own spirits and those of others. They performed for British and Allied sailors at the British Seamen's Institute in Lisbon. They envisioned a concert that would bring together refugee musicians and singers, the proceeds of which would go to a Portuguese charity. They would title the program "Obrigado Portugal" (Thank you, Portugal), for the warm reception the Portuguese people had provided to refugees. As word passed among the refugee community, opera singers, concert pianists, dancers, a magician, and more musicians joined them. The theme song, "Obrigado Portugal," emphasized the kindness of the Portuguese people and the gratitude of refugees: "It warms the heart to meet a friend, / Before you reach your journey's end." Its English verses were intertwined with lines in Portuguese and with "thank you" in many languages:

> Muit' agradecido, you have all been very kind.
> Caros meus senhores Portugueses
> You have given us a welcome we didn't think to find.
> English, Poles and Czechs and Hollandeses.
> The debt that we shall owe you for your kindness
> We never shall be able to repay.
> But the least that we can do,
> Is to sing our thanks to you.

They expressed the longings of refugees for sanctuary in another song, "No Visa," in which one verse imagined an island where "all the policemen are smiling and bland, / they don't ask for visas—they beg you to land!"[60]

The concert, supported by a "commission of Portuguese ladies" and the newspaper *O Século*, co-owned by Moses Amzalak, head of the Jewish community and a close friend of Salazar, took place in December 1940.[61] They sold several hundred tickets and enjoyed a "great success." But immediately thereafter, the police arrested them—apologetically, but firmly. The Nazi regime had protested that Portugal, a "neutral" country, had accepted the thanks of refugees—people who had fled the Nazis. To reassert its neutrality, the Portuguese government arrested the concert's organizers.

The police informed them that of the three levels of prisons, they occupied "first class." Indeed, they had a tiny cell and could stay together. As the only woman in the prison, Trixie had a little bathroom to herself. All the men shared one shower and one toilet. British visitors brought them books, soap, writing pads, pencils, and a map of the world. While Ferris was dejected, feeling that he had put Trixie in this situation, Trixie was characteristically more optimistic. At one point, she climbed up to the tiny barred window and remembered a proverb: "Two prisoners of war looked through the same bars. One saw the mud, the other the stars."[62]

Released on their twenty-fifth day of captivity, Trixie and Ferris were sent to the fixed residence of Caldas da Rainha. They would live among several hundred other refugees, most of whom received support from one of the international agencies. There they slept and ate in barracks. The food consisted of dark bread, "soup with bits of an unknown meat floating in it," and Portuguese apples, which Trixie found "really delicious." But food "was not too plentiful," and at one point she thought an earthquake had started when in reality she was dizzy and needed "more healthy food." Nevertheless, determined to cast a positive light on their situation, Trixie pointed out that "none of us had hard work to do," and thus deemed the food supply "really sufficient." Quaker eyewitnesses, however, noticed that she was "growing thinner every day, [and] he paler for lack of food."[63]

Forbidden from any kind of work—"doing NOTHING," in Trixie's words—caused them and other forced residents the most frustration. This couple, however, invented something to do. They organized a library on the assumption that among hundreds of refugees, some had probably brought along a book. They hung up "Free International Library" signs and installed shelves in an old house. In October 1941, Trixie wrote Russell Richie of the Quakers to remind him to bring more books when he came to Caldas. They had over one hundred already, "and almost all are borrowed." At the end of that month, Richie commented, "The refugees are very grateful for any and all types of reading, for the winter evenings are drawing longer and colder." In November, they had four hundred books and needed to build another bookcase.[64]

The Ferrigos also interceded for less able refugees, taking up a collection for one man who needed shoes and then asking the Quakers to contact HICEM or the clothing closet in the British Repatriation Office. Another time, Ferris accompanied a sick refugee to a Portuguese doctor, who gave the man "expensive medicines, and charged *nothing*." They suggested that the Quakers write a thank-you to the doctor, who was "so kind to all the refugees." Ferris later reported on a suicide in Caldas. Expressing compassion, he wished he had known the man better: "He was lonely and this probably developed his depression to a crisis." Other refugees assisted in burying him.[65]

To boost morale among a bored and frustrated group and to lift their own spirits in the process, they gave concerts in Caldas. Ferris wrote: "We were so satisfied to be able to do a small bit from our past, and to cheer up people who [go] through the same pains and crises as we." By trying to keep busy, the Ferrigos enhanced not only their own stay in Portugal, but also those of refugees around them, and even of the Quakers. Writing to the central office in Philadelphia, a Quaker social worker commented: "Trixie dancing Scottish dances . . . or Ferrigo singing his Yugoslav songs, will not be easily forgotten by the people who have heard them during these difficult and nervous months."[66]

Like other refugees without papers, Trixie and Ferris had to apply and reapply for thirty-day extensions in order to remain in Portugal. The local police headquarters in Caldas granted permission, but the couple still grew increasingly miserable as their stay stretched into months. "Is there any hope, please?" Trixie inquired of the Quakers in April 1941. In addition, as with all refugees residing in Caldas, the Ferrigos needed special police permission to go to Lisbon to approach consulates and aid organizations. She appealed to the Unitarians and the Quakers, and Ferris addressed the Jewish organization, HICEM, even though he identified as a "Protestant of Jewish parentage." The Quakers contributed for incidentals and coordinated the search for affidavits to the United States and other countries.[67] The Ferrigos showed enormous gratitude in every correspondence with the Quakers, thanking them for their hard work even as they asked for their weekly allowance and inquired about the progress of their appeals to various consulates.

The Quakers liked this "brave young couple" very much: "splendid young people," with a "strong appeal." Aware of "Obrigado Portugal," the Quaker representative quoted the words of two of its songs, trying to entice Americans to sponsor the couple. Ferris had composed these two songs, which were "the talk of Lisbon." The Quaker continued: "It seemed to me that . . . the great hosts of refugees have found their voice in them. . . . The . . . brave voice . . . of sufferings past and . . . faith for a future. . . . If I were the head of a Propaganda Campaign I would send a flying boat post haste for these two who understand and express so eloquently the aspirations, the faith of the refugees." Visiting Lisbon for one day in June 1941, the Ferrigos waited— the first people in line—at the U.S. mission. The consul explained that for the United States, Ferris's birth in Turkey, not his Yugoslav citizenship, counted. He fell under the Turkish quota of 226 per year. Trixie, who remained British in the eyes of the Americans, could enter the United States under the much more generous English quota (65,721 per year) once she had the proper paperwork in place. Refusing to separate from Ferris, Trixie wrote the Quakers, "Have you any more chances . . . or hopes you can give us? Or should we prepare ourselves for a new disaster!? Don't think we are pessimists because we naturally wonder what is going to happen to us."[68]

Despite the couple's efforts, the police grew impatient with the Ferrigos, who had not found a visa by July 1941, nine months after their arrival. Once more they faced jail in Lisbon, this time in late July. Prison officials allowed them to visit consulates from prison, accompanied by a policeman. In addition, the Ferrigos could buy their own food—a privilege, according to Trixie. Correspondence begging the Quakers to mail money for meals—"we find it dearer to live in prison than in liberty"—ensued.[69] In addition, they asked for some clothing and books. Promising—again—to find a visa, the Ferrigos gained their freedom about eleven days later, with the stern warning that they would face prison once more if they had no visa within thirty days.

Trixie wrote a brief note to the Quaker office after their incarceration, adding her usual gloss: "We feel well, thank you, although we both spent three days in bed. The doctor said it was nervousness (perhaps after the prison)." Ferris, on the other hand, was beside himself. He, who usually had Trixie write because of his flawed English, took up a pen to address the Quakers in his own words: "It is unimaginable to describe what feelings and impressions where in us, when we left our prison to go to Caldas—directly from the half dark atmosphere of our 11-day detainment into the sun—wonderful fields, mountains of this wonderful land." The first days in jail, he stated, "were not so bad, friends come, brought help, confidence, cheered us up." Commenting on the Portuguese people he had met, he added: "This people is good in his heart, willing to understand the pains and suffering of us—refugees. . . . You know how deeply . . . when our neighbor—a tailor . . . comes with tears in his eyes to visit us in prison." But now he fully understood "the danger of our actual situation." The police had told him that he could be sent back to Yugoslavia, and English "ladies" who visited them in prison suggested that Trixie leave for England without him. Ferris had suggested the same plan to her earlier, but she had responded that "she would better finish her life than leave me alone." He reminded the Quakers that he had been "pushed from land to land since 1933 . . . as one of the millions of sacrifices . . . longing to found a home. . . . I know that one person don't count in this world struggle and one life is not more important than a stone." He concluded that he had been "punished for his only crime, to be a homeless refugee!"[70]

All of a sudden, their luck changed. The Quakers had found sponsors willing to sign affidavits, and Washington had approved. When they returned to the consul on December 7, 1941, they heard of the bombing of Pearl Harbor and learned they had to ready themselves to leave immediately, since the United States would declare war. HICEM paid one fare, and the Quakers the other. They sailed for the United States on the *Guine* on December 18, 1941. Later, they performed for American troops, traveling over twenty thousand miles by 1943 under the auspices of the USO, an organization that provided live entertainment to boost the morale of the armed forces.[71]

ӘѴС

Waiting on consulate lines heightened anxiety and dejection. Many refugees began to feel that no country wanted them. Black humor made the point: A refugee enters a travel agency and says he'd like to go to any country in the world. The agent brings out a globe, and the customer studies it carefully, finally asking, "Is that all you have to offer?" He really needed the "island" that Ferris and Trixie had imagined, where "they beg you to land." Instead, refugees' homelands had terrorized them, and myriad consulates had caused grave disappointment. But they had lost even more. Besides roots, Simone Weil believed that humans require the need to feel useful to others.[72] Unlike the Ferrigos, whose performances and volunteer work made them feel useful, most adult refugees biding time in Portugal lived lives of frightened waiting. Their hopes for a distant future on a new continent mixed with fears of more immediate unknowns. They tried to assuage anxieties by sharing news and feelings with others in complex spaces. They wrote letters to loved ones abroad to reaffirm friendships and family bonds, but, as we will see, these letters also stirred fears. Similarly, although new friendships in cafés provided moments of relief, they also reminded refugees of all they had lost.

6. Sharing Feelings in Letters and in Person

Those messages felt like a lifeline, and the ones that were not
harrowing were comforting.

Separated from their former selves and from family and friends, refugees needed to find support during their indefinite stays in Portugal. Two approaches helped them maintain old relationships and create new ones: writing to and receiving letters from loved ones, and forming new friendships in cafés. Letters attempted to preserve deeply rooted relationships torn apart by war. Cafés fostered the creation of temporary and contingent "Jewish spaces" for those brought together by war. Epistolary spaces, the fragile threads that held families and friends together, stirred up private and intimate emotions, longing and love. And physical spaces, permeated with the aroma of coffee, offered venues where refugees forged emotional connections with new acquaintances.[1] Shared anguish and cherished moments of relief sustained both letter writers and café patrons.

Epistolary Spaces: Letters and Packages of Love and Care

Refugees' letters to and from Lisbon reveal constant worries about loved ones. Difficulties tracking the changing addresses of friends and families in areas under Nazi domination left those in Lisbon bewildered. Mail from war-torn Europe, intermittent and censored, meant temporary relief or sharp agony to readers in Portugal. Such correspondence provided a lifeline, a desperate attempt to hold on to human solidarity in the face of persecution and war. A brief note from a friend in London to Lisbon stating, "How happy I am that you and your husband have escaped hell," made its recipient,

Hannah Arendt, "very happy." Miriam Stanton, hoping to leave Lisbon and desperately lonely for her family and her fiancé, "lived for those letters."[2]

After long days of wrestling with consuls and charities, most refugees spent fretful hours writing letters and waiting at the post office for news from loved ones. They wrote frequently to safe lands asking for help, in the form of money or visas. Many visited Lisbon's central post office daily, but they thought about it continually. The author Alfred Döblin noticed that "people came here morning or evening, many came both morning and evening." They located the general delivery windows, "pressed to the wall, as we ourselves were." Observing other refugees, he wrote: "Many of them asked their questions numbly and then numbly left." Postal officials assisted refugees in sending letters, telegrams, and cables. In villages, too, refugees headed for the post office. In Figueira, for example, the formerly sleepy post office saw traffic "from morning to night" as postal agents transmitted hundreds of communications to "every corner of the earth." Refugees also observed "mountains" of general delivery letters waiting to be picked up by other refugees.[3]

Scholars have recently written on the "performative [and] fictive . . . dimensions of letter-writing" as well as on the discursive practices of different eras. These features are seen in letters from Nazi areas. Indeed, these letters are more performative than typical letters, since their writers, aware of Nazi censors, "performed" for both recipients and censors.[4] Letters from Lisbon, too, took Allied censors into account. And all the letters contain cultural formulae and conventions. But rather than emphasizing the constructed character of these letters, my goal is to read them to understand their emotional salience for their writers and their recipients, and the effect of these epistolary spaces on refugees' daily lives and their milieus.

The letters of Kurt Israel from Portugal provide an example of writing as a means of maintaining familial intimacy. Yet all correspondents had to be careful about what they wrote: Israel commented at the beginning of his second letter of September 1940: "*nota bene*, opened by British Censor." In stark contrast with his inhibitions about describing political circumstances, the thirty-one-year-old had no compunction about expressing his feelings, which could be expansive. He emphasized how much he missed his mother and brother, already in the United States. Longing for his family, he wrote, "The promise of a motherly welcome-embrace has never felt as dear as now." And if he did not receive a letter every ten to fourteen days, he grew "very nervous" from "endless" waiting. When a letter arrived, he read it "with great delight" and "frequent repetitions." He declared: "I cannot tell you how happy I always am to receive your reports." Reading and rereading letters helped him reimagine his family, feel close to them, and reduce the time separating them, not just the space.[5]

Writers like Israel express how deeply they felt the loss of loved ones. For Israel, family topped all other concerns. His extended family had lived in Hanover for generations and had scattered to the United States, South Africa, Mandate Palestine, and England. Israel's letters asked about the entire family. Upset about his mother's eye operation, he attempted to console her because she would not be able to read or write for some time. He sympathized with relatives whose son had committed suicide and wondered about people still in occupied Europe and those in England and Canada. Most of all, he longed to see his mother's and brother's faces again soon.[6] For "faces," he used the Judeo-German (Western Yiddish) word *Ponim* rather than the standard German word, probably a linguistic means of showing affection and invoking an intrafamily dialect occasionally used by German Jews.

Letters from parents to children poignantly communicated their despair after sending children ahead to safety. Many wrote that "children became letters" (*aus Kindern wurden Briefe*) as they ached for word from them.[7] After two hundred refugee children left Portugal for the United States on children's transports, separations grew longer than most parents or children had anticipated. Parents spent long months—sometimes years—upset, waiting to receive letters, as wartime postal services slowed mail deliveries and children's new lives distracted them. Even after the war, some families could not reunite quickly, because of restrictions imposed by the United States. Letters detailing children's daily lives created imaginary spaces where parents could feel close to them, providing at least some comfort. Yet children's letters also provoked mixed feelings: they assuaged anxieties but created intense longing.

Parents had been responsible for their children's social, cultural, and emotional development. Once they sent children abroad, they could not even choose the families, the most intimate environments, into which the agencies placed their children. Letters from refugee parents in Lisbon to aid organizations in America often sound anguished as they ask for word of their children. They worried in particular about the smallest children, who could not yet write for themselves. A few parents tried to exert at least some influence on their children's environments from afar. In January 1943, a refugee rabbi in Lisbon sent his son to the United States with USCOM. The well-meaning foster family, headed by a rabbi, enrolled him in an Orthodox Jewish school to prepare for the rabbinate. But the boy did not want to become a rabbi, and his father interceded for him. The European-Jewish Children's Aid reassured the father that it had "carefully investigated" the curriculum of the yeshiva and declared that the boy would not receive rabbinical training. In addition, the father was upset that his son lived in a dorm rather than with a family. The agency comforted him, suggesting that the youngster "seemed to like the idea better than living with a family," although it, too, "hope[d] . . . he will find his place again with a family unit."[8]

Similarly, Rachel Librowski's parents, still in Lisbon after sending her to the United States six years earlier, wrote the European-Jewish Children's Aid to express their hope that she would go to college. In Europe, they might have expected that she would pursue higher education, but U.S. agencies dissuaded refugee children from this goal, especially girls. The social worker explained that "very few children totally dependent on social welfare agencies . . . have the opportunity to attend college, completely supported by the agency." They realized that it was "difficult for Mr. and Mrs. Librowski to bear the separation and not to participate in the educational plans of their child, but this unfortunately is one of the conditions over which neither they nor we have any control." Similarly, some Orthodox parents could not guarantee that their children would have kosher food to eat. One family learned that despite promises to provide their daughter with kosher meals and attempts by American social workers to do so, she had angrily rejected a ham sandwich, forbidden by Jewish dietary laws, offered her on the ship to the United States. Most parents had to endure losing any semblance of control over their children's lives.[9]

Parents expressed relief that their children had left Europe and landed safely in the United States. Yet as the length of their separation increased, fear of losing contact with their children forever replaced relief. One father wrote the Quakers from a fixed residence: "As I sent my child over, I was told, I should follow her rather soon . . . now we are separated for seven months and no prospect to see her again?" Others lost all touch with their children, uncertain about what the young ones needed. In 1947, the European-Jewish Children's Aid wrote to one set of parents, still in Portugal, about future plans for their son, who had arrived in the United States four years earlier. Acknowledging that "it is difficult for you to make such a decision, for you have now been separated from him so long, and probably don't know what he himself would want to do," the agency nonetheless urged them to "come to a decision of some kind," since their son had "become quite Americanized and if you wanted him to return to your care, it should be done quickly before it becomes too difficult for him to do so."[10] Children's temporary safety could estrange them from their parents.

Sometimes children simply did not write or moved to new addresses without informing their parents. The Quakers in Lisbon wrote to an agency in New York in March 1943, requesting that the new addresses of certain children be cabled to them as soon as possible: "The parents on this end are most anxious for this information and will continue to besiege us until we have [it]." The Quakers also asked a New York agency about correspondence from the son of a Mrs. Kroll. The boy had left Lisbon six months earlier, on March 2, 1943, and "she has never received a written word by him." Indeed, she "comes in and weeps practically every week." And a few parents learned to their horror that their children lived in unhealthy circumstances. Powerless to do more than protest, one father wrote that his son described living in "filth" with an elderly lady, and pleaded that the child be placed with other children. He was. Some parents received reports from the foster parents. But the terror that their children would not remember them and that their family life would remain disrupted forever haunted many. Social workers realized that most parents wished for "their own child's handwriting, a photo, anything which will show the parents the child has not forgotten them."[11]

Children too, but less often, sought mail contact with their parents. Most believed that their parents, who had sent them ahead for safety, faced danger. When the postal service returned a letter that Richard Rosenberg, a thirteen-year-old, had sent to his parents in Lisbon, stating they no longer lived at that address, he panicked. The boy begged the agency that had placed him to find out where they lived; he was "exceedingly worried over his parents."[12]

It may be worth noting the contrasts and similarities between these letters and some written to and from European migrants who sought better lives in North America in the nineteenth and twentieth centuries. Differences stand out.[13] Migrants provided details of their new lives. Writers who fled to Portugal voiced impatience to get on with their lives. And those under Nazi domination concealed information, aware of censors and hoping not to make the recipients overly anxious. Also, earlier migrants expressed optimism even as they met daunting obstacles, whereas the letters from Portugal to loved ones in safe lands expressed exasperation, and those sent to Lisbon from Germany and German-occupied lands convey powerlessness and resignation.

French-Jewish refugee children writing letters to parents, Parede, Portugal, 1940s (NY_03588, Courtesy of JDC Archives, New York).

Similarities appear as well. In all cases, the letters reinforce ties and sustain essential relationships that were torn apart. The writers express the pain of separation and document how they feel about their unpredictable situations. Some migrants, not unlike victims of the Nazis, saw their letters as a form of "therapy," a "means for self-preservation." And although letters require historical context and cannot "speak for themselves," they can convey feelings poignantly.[14] In all cases, letters provided a space in which to connect.

Three very different sets of letters offer insight into the meaning of correspondence for both the writers and, by inference, the recipients. First are the evocative letters of twenty-one-year-old Peter Schwiefurt to his mother, later published by the filmmaker Claude Lanzmann. They depict the struggles of a young man without proper papers to gain a foothold in Portugal as well as to maintain intimacy with the family he left behind. The unpublished correspondence between a mother in Lisbon and her two children sent ahead to the United States offers a window into her feelings of loneliness, but also of relief, similar to what many parents experienced after their "children became letters."[15] And then there are a variety of letters addressed to friends and family in Lisbon that remained unread until I opened them, as well as a small cache of postcards sent from Warsaw through Lisbon. Many of these missives shared a practical purpose: they asked for food. But they also revealed an intensely emotional purpose: to connect with the receivers. Although the Schwiefurt and Losser letters and those from Nazi Europe cannot represent other individuals or groups, all share a similar motivation. The correspondents, cut off from loved ones and uncertain of meeting them again, used these epistolary spaces to reach out to comfort and embrace each other.

Peter Schwiefurt: A Young Man Reports to His Mother
Peter Schwiefurt's sixty letters to his mother, all but the last one written between December 1938 and March 1941, reveal complex emotional reactions to his refugee experience.[16] Peter, whose mother was born Jewish, declared himself a Jew at the age of twenty-one and fled to Portugal, although his parents had urged him to stay in Germany, where his father and stepfather, both non-Jews, believed they could protect him. Arriving in late October 1938, probably after Portugal instituted the thirty-day tourist visa, he had hoped to travel on to Brazil. Instead, he found himself penniless, looking for employment, and applying to remain in Portugal. He offered German and English lessons in the village of Faro and lived with a Portuguese family.

Peter wrote his mother both with a sense of adventure and with loneliness. He shared his joy with her when he found employment in a sardine factory as a translator of English, German, and French: "I've great news: I'm working! . . . The boss is a nice man and has taken a fancy to me—so far." Proudly, he noted that "our sardines are so much fatter" than those from Morocco. He liked his employer's family of six children, adding that his "wife is ravishing, but he is unfaithful to her, as is the custom." Additionally, he offered a glimpse of his daily life, spent with a family that raised small farm animals. He enjoyed the children and even played "Father Christmas," giving out small gifts. When he got up in the morning, "a whole farmyard . . . besieges me as Hannibal did poor Rome." His meal consisted of bread and margarine: "That's my breakfast and it never varies. It's already a long time since I forgot the taste of butter." At night he tried to read in bed, listing such authors as Stendhal, Goethe, and Shakespeare.[17] In addition to the reassurance and intimacy provided by his letters, his demand for letters describing the specifics of his mother's and two half sisters' days illustrate his attempt to maintain closeness through the details of everyday life, even from afar.

More than the specifics of daily life, however, he prioritized accounts of the family's emotional well-being. He was frantic about the safety of his mother and half sisters in Germany and later when they hid in the open as Christians in Bulgaria. About two months after he left home, he asked his mother, "What is your state of mind? Are you bearing up all right?" and a month later noted again, "I'm terribly worried about your nervous depression even though you say you've got the better of it." When his mother and sisters quarreled, he requested that the children be kinder to their mother. Powerless to intervene in person, he wrote: "Just think what Mother gives you compared with what she gets from you in return." Deep concern for his mother's anxieties recurred throughout the letters, along with his own love and need for her: "Mother dear, you mustn't be distressed. . . . Oh, how I long to talk to you!" Despite his growing fluency in Portuguese, Peter underlined his loneliness. Only the humanity of the Portuguese people—"never once has anyone been rude to me"—raised his spirits.[18]

Out of his familial and cultural milieu, Peter experimented with his own identity. First, he decided to convert to Judaism, causing no end of agitation for his Jewish mother, who had married three non-Jewish men, passed as a German, and would soon convert to Russian Orthodoxy in Bulgaria. He did not intend to become observant, but hoped to "bear witness" to this "form of Jewish life." He admonished his mother, who had never told his half sisters of their Jewish lineage: "Don't disown or condemn your and your own children's Jewishness. It's your whole strength." He reminded her, "I've always felt a deep affinity with all things Jewish," and angrily responded to one of her remonstrances: "I don't want to shed my skin, like you. I'm not adopting a new religion . . . *I am a Jew and I say so*, just as I have always done." He "had to smile" at the way Portuguese Jews reacted to his wish to convert. A member of the Sephardic Jewish community told him, "We don't accept anyone." Peter quipped to his mother, "He must be a very good Jew." Then he rejected his Germanness: "I owe Germany nothing but my mother tongue—which is, I admit, a lot, and the only thing which I am able or willing to preserve."[19] The resolution of both matters eluded him, since the Jews he approached refused to convert him, and the German consulate would not provide the passport with the red letter *J* that he requested.

In 1939, exactly one year after his arrival in Portugal, with many frustrations behind him, he wrote his mother that he had obtained an identity card. Ostensibly, this card meant he would not face expulsion for five years. But something went awry, and the Portuguese arrested and imprisoned him

that December. After his release fourteen weeks later, in March 1940, probably with the financial help of his mother and the local Jewish community, he
fled to Athens. The "Jewish Committee," most likely the Lisbon Jewish
community, paid his fare and his three-week journey. Temporarily safe, with
a Greek visa in hand, Peter wrote his mother: "Subsistence is not the problem
at the moment. It's the future that's the problem." Like other Jewish refugees, he wanted to get on with his life, but faced huge obstacles. Still, Peter
remained determined: "My one goal is to leave Europe. I never lose sight of
it. I'm thinking about it all the time."[20]

That goal changed dramatically in December 1940 when the twenty-
three-year-old joined the Free French Forces after having also applied to the
British Army. He fought in Syria, Libya, Tunisia, Italy, and France. Three and
a half years of fighting later, he confided to his mother that he only regretted
"the time that has been wasted, all the years that have been stolen from me,
and that it won't be easy to make up . . . but I don't at all regret having done
. . . my duty."[21] Peter's letters stopped when he was killed near Alsace, only
months before the end of the war.

Lily, Gaby, and Yutta: A Mother Connects to Her Children Abroad
Three years of correspondence between Lily Losser, a widow, and her two
children sent ahead to the United States evoke the desires of a mother to stay
close to her children.[22] Losser's family had moved from Essen, Germany, to
Portugal in 1933. Her husband died there, as did her mother-in-law. As a
widow with a command of German, Portuguese, and English, and good
typing skills, Losser got a job as a secretary at the JDC offices. A refugee who
would otherwise have been forbidden to work in Portugal, she thus had the
rare opportunity to support her daughters and her father, who had joined
them in 1940, as the war spread.

In January 1943, Losser reluctantly decided to put Gaby (age seven)
and Yutta (age ten) on a children's transport out of Lisbon, fearful that
"something will happen here politically" and that "you are not safe." Moreover, she did not see a "future" for the girls in Portugal. She sent them to
America "to do something good," putting aside her own feelings, "I have not
thought of my sad loneliness. Mothers are not allowed to only think of themselves." Her letters valiantly attempted to "parent at a distance,"[23] inquiring
into details of their daily lives, advising them, and admitting to intense loneliness as time passed and they remained apart.

The sisters stayed together, living in the Jewish Children's Home in Newark, New Jersey, and in two Jewish foster homes nearby. They reported dutifully, although infrequently, about their schoolwork and adjustments. But Losser did not receive all the letters. Indeed, she received none the first year. To her relief, a foster mother occasionally wrote about their progress. Losser also asked the Quakers to check on the children six months after they left, since she had received no communications from them. The Quakers in Phila-delphia sent back a reassuring report in December 1943, noting that the smaller child had adjusted more easily, and that the older one had been promoted twice in school and would soon be with girls her own age.[24]

The girls' letters, written at first in Portuguese or German, rapidly turned to English as they picked up that language. Their mother made the communication easier for them by typing her letters in English. In November 1943, ten months after they had left, she wrote: "I guess you are already real American good children, and I would like to know whether you know still a little Portuguese and German." Realizing that the children had given up their native German reassured her that they had successfully acculturated, but also indicated that they had moved linguistically away from their upbringing. For Losser, words of endearment still came out in German: "My beloved sweet good *goldene liebe Darlingskinder.*"[25]

She tried to mother them by writing weekly, asking whether they conducted themselves politely and performed well in school. She wondered whether they liked their teachers and asked about what they read at home. And, did they have some good friends? She urged them to behave as quintes-sentially good girls, to help their foster mother wash dishes, to make their own beds, and to clean up their rooms: "no clothes on the chairs, no shoes on the floor, and all your things in their places." In October 1944, she asked whether her older daughter liked piano lessons, dancing, and books. She wondered whether she studied "a lot" and ate "much at mealtimes." She worried about Yutta's feet and her teeth. She acknowledged that she wanted to know every-thing about them: "I could ask you much more questions, but there is not paper enough to write them down." To little Gaby, she asked about her dolls—"Are they well?"—and about her friends: "Do you play with them every day?"[26]

Occasionally, Losser referred to Jewish holidays, describing a Hanukkah party (1943) in Lisbon and assuming the girls had had such a party as well. The following year at Passover, Yutta wrote, "We have been eating matzo all week and not any bread." That fall, their mother reminded both girls of the approach of "our most important holidays, Rosh Hashonoh," and "hope[d]" that they would "go to the Synagogue and that you know what these holidays mean for us all." She, too, would attend synagogue services. She wished them a "happy new year," one in which they would "be reunited soon."[27]

Lily Losser wrote to the foster mothers of her daughters, appreciatively acknowledging their responses. She wondered whether the first foster mother, who had two children of her own, realized that Yutta and Gaby were good children but, after all, still children? In May 1943, she expressed the hope "that my two babies do not annoy you too much," adding, "They are children like all children, with their good and their bad sides. I did my best to educate them to make them as reasonable as possible. I can't tell you how grateful I am if you give them a little bit of love, that is the most important that children need." She recognized that her daughters would need help with school: "Both are not too good pupils, but with better teachers and much patience there will be some success." In June 1944 she learned that a new foster home awaited her children. This new couple had earlier adopted two children who had since grown up. As of July 1944, Lily maintained a correspondence with the new foster parents, receiving assurance from their adopted son that "this is a family that loves children" and that "the photograph of yourself with the girls is standing on the radio in our living room."[28]

Losser mailed the girls inexpensive little gifts such as ribbons, vests, blouses, baskets, dried roses, and a photo album of "the time of our happiness" in Portugal. She made special stationery, at times gluing prints of little dogs on it. She often shared how much she missed them. She urged them to write her regularly and told them about their friends, children of Jewish refugees, still in Portugal. She also made sure to report that some of their friends, also in America, did not write their parents in Portugal often enough, which agitated their parents, indeed made one mother sick. When she received rare photos of them, she expressed overwhelming joy: "I look at them and look at them a thousand times. . . . Your sweet good darling faces so happy looking are all my joy now and I have the pictures always with me . . . you know how much I longed for those pictures."[29]

Reading and rereading, looking again and again, helped diminish the space and also the time apart, but only slightly. It bridged the distance and simultaneously reminded her of the physical separation. In one of many attempts to both cheer herself and create a moment of intimacy with "her baby darling," Gaby, on her ninth birthday, she "prayed to God" that they would be together on her tenth birthday and made plans for many celebrations together in the future. She told Gaby the story of her birth in Lisbon, detailing the delight expressed by Gaby's deceased father, by Yutta, and by herself. She hoped that Gaby would eat some cake or "even ice cream" on her special day. As she sent Gaby a "million kisses," she promised to keep Gaby in her thoughts all day and also to eat some ice cream herself.[30]

The children, too, found this separation wrenching, even if they did not write as regularly as their mother. Both girls tried to share small moments in their lives. Little Gaby wrote in three-quarter-inch-high block letters in May 1944. She asked about her mother ("Mommy") and grandfather ("Opa" in German) and added that she had a friend across the street and "liked school very much." That same day, the older daughter wrote, "My darling good mom" and added, "Hi! (that means hello)." She reported that she and her sister had grown, and mentioned photos they had sent. She assured her mother that "school is fine!" and that she might enter seventh grade in the fall. Indeed, the children wrote cheerful letters, though a later interview with the younger one indicated stressful situations in both foster homes, heavy burdens on the children.[31]

Lily Losser's letter of October 1944 notified the children that their grandfather who had lived with them had died. She now visited three graves in Lisbon, their father's, their grandmother's, and their grandfather's. "All alone now in our apartment," she still hoped that she would secure a visa "soon." A hearing had taken place in Washington, but "we have to be prepared to get the refusal." She stopped cooking after her father's death, but reassured the girls, "I hope that soon I will be with you darlings, then I make for you and me good meals and we all eat together."[32] A letter of January 4, 1945, found her still in Lisbon, repeating "we must be patient" three times. Loving spaces created by this mother's letters may have provided some consolation and threads of connection on both sides, but the thousands of miles of distance had an effect letters could not overcome.

Losser eventually came to the United States in 1946, three years after sending her girls abroad, but faced disappointment again. When she arrived that winter, social service agencies decided she could not support her children and could not live with them. She visited them regularly, but they were reunited only in the summer of 1949. They had lost six crucial years of family life. In response to correspondence she received in 1980 from the foster "brother" of the second family, Lily Losser emphasized that the children had suffered by growing up without their mother: "Only one comment I have: the children were *not* only 'lightly bruised' by our tragedy."[33] She understood the necessity of safety but underlined its emotional costs.

Unopened Letters and "Packages of Love"

An unusual set of sources, a cache of 290 unopened letters and unread post-cards from twenty-nine countries, reveals the love and trauma that bound Jews separated by war.[34] These unopened correspondences came from safe lands such as the United States and England as well as from Nazi Europe. A smaller batch of forty-five postcards, eventually delivered to the recipients, came to Lisbon from the Warsaw Ghetto.[35] The writers reached out to loved ones to strengthen bonds of family and friendship, fighting dispersion with pen and paper. The letters from across the Channel or the Atlantic report on strange new experiences, ask about the plans of those in Lisbon, and offer encouragement. These letters, had they been read at the time, could have told the recipients that their families and friends had found safe havens, even if they might also have caused loneliness.

The tragic correspondence from Germany and eastern Europe, however, alerts us to much more. It provides the partial knowledge and hints that informed refugees in Portugal about the mounting terror in Nazi-controlled areas and allows us to understand the worries that refugees suffered and shared with one another. These letters and cards arrived in Lisbon in 1941 through the spring of 1942, when genocide in Nazi-occupied Europe was escalating.[36] They highlight failed attempts at emigration and an increasing sense of powerlessness. Writers note steamship schedules and the costs of ocean voyages. They describe the anxiety of waiting to hear from consulates, the frustrations as America raised its requirements, and the despair when Germany forbade further emigration in October 1941. Refugees in Lisbon had been in regular correspondence with these letter writers; the letter writers frequently thank them for recent letters or packages of food. But this particular collection of letters never reached the recipients. They had moved on from Lisbon.

Yet even if the intended recipients in Lisbon did not read these letters, the correspondence provides a lens into the kinds of information that refugees in Lisbon gleaned from previous letters and offers insight into the emotional bonds between those who fled and those left behind. As refugees read more details, their grief, concern, and, perhaps, guilt multiplied. One

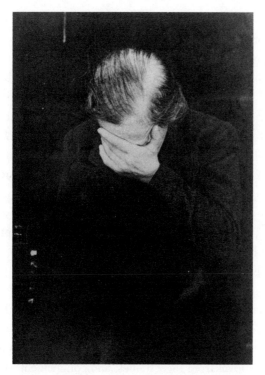

Refugee in Lisbon in deep grief, 1940s. (Photograph by
Roger Kahan, NY_06717, Courtesy of JDC Archives,
New York).

woman who had made it to Lisbon by climbing the Pyrenees may stand in for
many others. Learning about conditions at home, in Prague, made her feel
"so sorry for my mother, remaining there alone. I never saw her again."[37]
Escape was not free of sorrow.

The same letters provided their writers with a momentary refuge in
which to remember better times and to escape the grueling present. Their dire
situations notwithstanding, the writers often tried to comfort others. One letter
asked the recipient, headed for Havana, to assure a friend there that the friend's
parents in Antwerp remained in "good condition." Another, writing from
Poland in April 1942 and referring, presumably, to Passover, insisted: "We had
everything we needed for the holidays [yontef] as always." Some of these writers
attempted to minimize their tragic situation, saying, for instance, "Don't worry,
we are healthy." They also expressed curiosity—"Do you have acquaintances
there?"—or offered advice, for example, on how to prevent seasickness, and
briefly identified with hopeful journeys, not likely to be their own.[38]

These undelivered letters reveal the vital importance of maintaining intimate contact in the face of terrifying conditions. The writers relate feeling great joy when letters arrive and beg fervently for more. As their lives descended into chaos and fear, just a few words from Lisbon could raise spirits. A card from Poland requested that the recipient write every week. When a letter arrived, the writer reported, "I really perked up." Others thanked their relatives or friends for sending good news from Lisbon, eagerly anticipating even more letters.[39]

The act of sustaining contact took a great deal of time and commitment, becoming a consuming and creative act of connection. In April 1942, a young Berliner wrote his mother and sister in Lisbon after a day of forced labor. He had just finished supper "after returning home exceptionally tired." He wanted to have a "conversation with them" in order to "cheer himself up." Using the only means possible, correspondents could participate in a shared epistolary experience that bound them to each other. Love, longing, and memories of joy mixed with the brutality of everyday life, even when writers and recipients understood that the censors, too, read these letters.[40]

Mindful of censorship, writers understated the adversities of daily life, forced labor, removal from their homes, and confinement to ghettos. They employed innuendo and told fragmentary stories. They hinted at the dire state of affairs by bringing up their feelings and the effects these had on their bodies or their work. For example, a writer from Berlin to a close friend in Lisbon on March 25, 1942, amidst ongoing deportations to the East, guardedly shared his dread of deportation after losing his job: "I was [recently] fired . . . and you must know what that means. For the time being, I am heading into an uncertain future, still hoping despite it all, that I will see my beloved wife and children again. . . . I am trying to steady my nerves and retain hope so that I can hang on mentally, emotionally, and physically." A letter from a Berlin woman in April 1942 reported that her son had made it to Canada, but hinted that her friends had been deported: "At the moment, I am still at my old job, whereas Ludwig [and] Grete Bernst., also Feo Rabinowitz . . . are gone. Personnel changes incessantly and one constantly [toils] with new workmates. Naturally that doesn't make the work, which is strenuous in itself, any easier."[41]

Jews in Portugal knew that many of their loved ones suffered under forced labor, cramped housing, war, and occupation. They followed the war as closely as they could. It is not clear how refugees in Lisbon, who had few reliable sources of news, understood these kinds of letters or what they learned about shootings or deportations to concentration and extermination camps. Although "what remains unsaid can be eloquent," these letters do not prove that most Jews in Lisbon fully grasped the horrors of the situation in Germany and Nazi-occupied Europe.[42] They may have sensed an impending catastrophe from the letters, but still not have comprehended genocide.

Hunger was another matter. The letters cried out straightforwardly and urgently for food parcels from Lisbon and expressed deep appreciation for provisions previously sent. That the writers faced serious deprivation could not have been clearer. A Viennese woman wrote a contact in Lisbon that her friends received weekly food packages from Lisbon and asked for "coffee, tea, canned goods, condensed milk, etc.," since "everything is so scarce now"—an allusion to the diminished rations allowed to Jews. Portugal seemed "the only land from which one can still send something abroad," so another writer begged for food for an uncle in Galicia. A telegram from Noe, an internment camp in France, asked a friend in the Bronx for food "through Lisbon." Another letter from France requested oil or biscuits. Yet another expressed appreciation for marmalade and wondered where one found the sugar to make it. Describing the destitution in Warsaw, a woman wrote that the situation had returned to a "state of nature." Referring to a "battle for survival," she concluded, "The only daily worry is [finding] a bite of food."[43]

Refugees and members of the Jewish community in Portugal sent food parcels to Jews in Nazi-occupied Europe. Groups of volunteers from the Jewish community worked intensely, mailing packages to strangers. *Hechawer* (Hebrew, "friend"), a Zionist Jewish youth club, received names and addresses from Jewish aid organizations, and its members filled packages every day after school. One of its members, then sixteen years old, recalled that for her, the "war stopped everything, it was more important to help out than to go to school." She added that others came by to lend a hand after work. This project provided emotional gratification both from the relief mailed to starving Jews and from the camaraderie that ensued. Still, refugees suffered "heart pain" from trying to find and help their own families trapped in Europe. They wanted to maintain family ties but also to send a sign that those ensnared by Hitler were not forgotten. Friedrich Westheimer, active in the Lisbon Jewish community's refugee aid committee, recorded the dozens of food packages that he sent to friends languishing in the Gurs camp in Vichy France between 1940 and 1941. In his small handwritten notebook, chocolate topped his list of foods, followed by sardines, cheese, and canned meat.[44]

Sardines ranked as the most nutritious food sent eastward by the Lisbon refugees. Sealed in airtight cans, they served as a good source of proteins and calcium. An escapee from Gurs believes to this day that the sardines posted by her parents from Lisbon in 1941 saved her and her husband's lives, since they shared the fish with important officials at the Gurs camp when deportations eastward began in July 1942. Packages mailed from Lisbon to individuals in Terezin (also called Theresienstadt), the concentration camp near Prague, consisted to a large extent of canned fish and other canned foods.[45]

Recipients gratefully acknowledged these "love packages" or "love gifts" (*Liebesgaben*). Why did they use these odd terms? During World War I, Germany had permitted civilians and the Red Cross to send such "gifts of love" to soldiers at the front or in hospitals and to prisoners of war.[46] Again in World War II, Germans mailed parcels to their soldiers. The Nazis also allowed small packages to be sent to Jews in Germany and in German-occupied lands as "love gifts," although not all of them arrived at the designated addresses.

Some of these parcels made it to the Warsaw Ghetto, and their reception there indicates what they meant on the ground. A secret report of November 1941 written by the U.S. vice-consul in Poland observed that the Germans permitted small packages of food, weighing slightly over one pound, to be relayed to Poland as "gifts" (*Liebesgaben*). The report did not distinguish between Polish and Polish-Jewish recipients, but concluded that "the most effective form of relief in Poland at this time are the small food packages sent in from Portugal." Such packages cost 18 escudos, or less than $1 ($17.50 in 2019) to mail. People in the United States (until it entered the war) could pay for food or clothing gifts—packaged in Portugal—to be sent to Nazi-occupied eastern Europe and to Gurs. Private businesses that advertised, for example, in the refugee newspaper *Aufbau* expedited these gifts.[47]

By 1941, Jews in the Warsaw Ghetto were subsisting on an average of 1,125 calories a day, and this amount dropped until the summer of 1942, by which time almost all of them had been murdered. Having escaped from Poland to New York, one woman sent food packages from Portugal to her children and grandchildren in Warsaw throughout 1941 and into early 1942, when the Germans forbade shipments there. A grateful grandson who survived the ghetto later described her as the "big heroine in our family," noting that she spent all of her earnings on these packages of sardines, coconut butter, and Lipton tea. The tea "was worth its weight in gold" because one could trade it for bread and other commodities.[48]

In a small batch of postcards written from January 1940 through July 24, 1942, from the Warsaw Ghetto to Lisbon, there are similar requests for food and also for more letters. Ghetto inhabitants eagerly received sardines and assured senders that the food caused "great happiness and great relief." Most of these cards came to Tamara Frimmer in London from her mother, father, and close relatives in the ghetto. Because mail could not be sent from occupied Poland to the United Kingdom, the cards went to Frimmer's friend, a Polish diplomat in Lisbon. He then carried or sent the postcards in his diplomatic pouch to England. The theme of the mother-daughter exchanges circled on love. In one the mother wrote, "Finally, finally your sweet lines. I kiss (literally!) your signature!" She hoped her daughter had found "someone who loves and cares for [her]," and urged the young woman not to "feel guilty": "You've done everything possible."[49] Other cards revealed that writers and senders did not always know each other; some from Warsaw were addressed to an expediting firm in Lisbon that Tamara Frimmer had paid. The recipients of packages wrote extremely formal salutations and farewells, listing the foods received and writing in the only two allowed languages, German or Polish. Unusually, the writer of one such postcard hinted at a deportation by suggesting that people in Lisbon no longer needed to send food to one woman, because "she's gone away."[50]

Several writers from Warsaw asked for more than provisions, desiring a personal connection: "I find it very distressing that I receive a package without even a brief line." Most likely, the senders in Lisbon could not include letters or even short messages in these packages, because of censorship, but the recipients, not knowing this, longed for communication. Although desperate for food, the trapped Jews also needed emotional connections. Still, for many, a gift of food lifted their spirits. Indeed, a Jewish newspaper from Warsaw, referring to packages received in the ghetto, underlined their psychological effect: "The contents of the packages . . . often move people to tears with their proof of deep feeling, attention, and remembrance on the part of somebody on the other side of the world." Similarly, in Terezin, Ruth Bondy recalled that these packages "strengthened those who received them, both physically and mentally, gave them a few hours of happiness, and provided them with hope."[51]

Their intense efforts notwithstanding, individuals and groups in Lisbon neither initiated nor relayed the lion's share of these packages—although at the time some may have thought they had. Organizations from other neutral countries such as Sweden, Yugoslavia, and Switzerland also sent packages to diverse recipients. The British and the American Red Cross, for example, sent parcels to their POWs. The Unitarians shipped food packages to concentration camps in France, and Polish and Czech exile groups dispatched parcels to occupied Poland and Czechoslovakia. And the Czech consul in Lisbon bought packages of sardines and figs to send to Czech Jews in Terezin. Further, groups serving national constituencies packed and shipped from Lisbon.[52] Moreover, Jewish international organizations arranged for a large portion of the shipments sent to other Jews, fearing that the Nazis would starve Jews to death—before news of their annihilation had spread. For example, the World Jewish Congress, aided by the Portuguese Red Cross, and the JDC sent packages to Jews interned in Holland, in southern France, and in eastern Europe, including in ghettos and camps, starting in 1941.[53]

The U.S. Treasury Department and the British Treasury exercised stringent control over these packages, starting with licenses allowing the relief agencies to buy food in Portugal, and directed that Jewish and other organizations deliver food packages only to individuals, not en masse.[54] In addition, the Allies blocked any products (including food and medicine) that could be sent to Axis-occupied territories to help German war efforts. Even so, Jewish and other aid organizations successfully pressed for the right to ship food, but the JDC in Lisbon warned the New York headquarters that "publicity would be most undesirable." It was mailing food "quietly" as late as 1944, hoping not to antagonize the Allies.[55] By that time, however, Germany and its collaborators had already murdered most Jews. Nevertheless, as late as the winter of 1944–45, inquiries arrived at the JDC in Lisbon regarding sending food packages to the Bergen-Belsen concentration camp in northern Germany.[56]

A significant percentage of packages never reached the addressees during the war. Aware of this, the Unitarians in Lisbon wrote, "We here cannot guarantee a single thing about any order, not even that the package can be started on its way, still less that it can be delivered." Nazi bureaucrats tracked these packages carefully and allowed only a portion of them to reach their destinations. In August 1943, for example, a report to Adolf Eichmann listed the number of packages that the Red Cross in Geneva had sent from

Lisbon to Terezin.[57] Tens of thousands of packages went missing, some confiscated and used by the SS—exactly what the Allies had feared. Other packages dispatched to French camps came back marked "deceased" or "escaped."[58] Had the Nazis not stolen a single package, however, it is clear in retrospect that these parcels could never have prevented the mass starvation of Jews. Still, determined people sent hope and love—emotional sustenance. And committees insisted that "the preservation even of single individuals is momentous."[59] In Portugal, refugees had made the emotional decision to do something to help and did not allow the potential futility of sending packages to deter them.

Sharing Space, Sharing Feelings: The Café

Letters and packages, however, could not replace the day-to-day need for human contact. Portugal's ubiquitous cafés therefore played an essential role in most refugees' lives, offering an opportunity to meet others who struggled with the same hopes and fears. Avid café regulars in Vienna, Prague, and German cities found that this new city of cafés offered a semblance of normalcy—one called the café "the only place where I could feel at all as if I belonged"—a place where they could remember their former status and feel recognized by others from their previous worlds.[60]

Whether living in camps or among local populations, refugees often "re-create viable societies to the extent that they are allowed to do so." Central European refugees gathered in cafés that reminded them of home, creating serendipitous, ephemeral, and sometimes sustaining communities of waiting. While reading the daily news in a variety of languages at kiosks or waiting on consulate lines, "they couldn't help running into each other." Then they "gather[ed] to console one another" in cafés, bonding over their histories and uncertain status while offering each other comfort. Some cafés, like the Café Palladium on the Rossio, seemed "filled with refugees."[61]

Cafés offered spaces where they could share the same "psychic hell" and create emotional and social networks. They had left "relatives in the Polish ghettos and our best friends . . . in concentration camps, and that [meant] the rupture of our private lives." Jews in these cafés connected quickly, mulling over "problems . . . anxiety, what happened to other members of the family." Stretching their drinks for hours, women and men found familiarity at outdoor tables or in smoky, densely packed rooms where patrons spent their last escudo. Arthur Koestler described café patrons in his novel about refugees in Portugal: "Some of the tables were occupied by mixed groups of men and women . . . foreigners, exiles in transit from countries overrun by the war. They talked in low voices with little nervous tics in their faces, putting their heads together over the table like crows in a thunderstorm. . . . The exiles here were tied together by their common fate." The historian Barbara Rosenwein wrote that "people have a way of finding (or carving out) little islands for themselves—communities that work for them, that make them comfortable."[62] Cafés served precisely this purpose. They furthermore provided a brief return to the middle-class comforts of urban European life, to an experience continuous with the refugees' past and their sense of self.

No strangers to coffeehouses, European Jews first encountered them in the German and Italian states in the seventeenth century. In the modern era, many male Jews, especially in major cities like Berlin, Vienna, Venice, Budapest, Prague, and Paris, began to incorporate cafés into their lives. In the nineteenth century, Jewish and non-Jewish men congregated there, sometimes playing games, making business deals, or debating politics. Cafés offered secular "irreplaceable arenas" for "cultural refinement among intellectual elites and circles of the bourgeoisie." Hebrew and Yiddish modernist writers turned many European cafés into "substitutes for a real 'home,' community, or the traditional 'house of study.' "[63]

Aside from the women who brewed and served coffee, cafés remained male spaces until the mid-nineteenth century. Women, too, enjoyed meetings over coffee, but these took place at home, at a gathering known in German-speaking lands as the Kaffeeklatsch. Housewives would visit one another in the late afternoon to share coffee, cake, and conversation. In 1856, Viennese coffeehouses were opened to women, and some decades later unaccompanied women as well as families began to appear in certain cafés in Vienna, Paris, and Berlin. By the 1920s, women and men met in cafés in mixed groups. In Germany, cafés also served as a Sabbath treat, and some Jews in irreverent Berlin pointed to the Café Loy, near the liberal Neue Synagoge (New Synagogue), as the place to have a good dinner in a secluded room on the fasting holiday of Yom Kippur.[64]

The Viennese in particular embraced cafés, which functioned as "natural annexes" to crowded and chilly apartments and rented rooms. In fact, many Viennese saw the café as a "Jewish space," depicted in this well-known stereotype: "The Viennese spend most of their time in a coffee house, the Jews spend all of their time there; it follows that Viennese Jews cannot exist without coffee houses." In 1935, the Viennese author Stefan Zweig visited a New York café that welcomed literary and theater people. He wrote he could as easily have traveled to Warsaw or Leopoldstadt (a Jewish section of Vienna) to see "the same smart, sharp, but wan faces of our nation."[65]

When Hans Sahl decided to leave Nazi Berlin in 1933, he paid a last visit to the Romanisches Café. Small groups of Jewish literati and political activists had formerly gathered there. He noticed some old-timers "sitting there, wondering why they were still sitting there." Others "bent over maps or wrote letters to relatives who had previously emigrated."[66] Jews could still patronize cafés in 1933, but as "Jews not Wanted" signs proliferated, they lost those venues.

As refugees, they found cafés again in France, Spain, and Portugal, the kind of "Jewish spaces" they recognized and whose customs they understood. In Bordeaux and Marseille, they stood or sat with cups of coffee that tasted like "acorns, dried peas and possibly mud, plus one bean of coffee per 50 cups—or thereabouts," and the usual accompaniments were missing: "There is no milk. For sugar, there is saccharine." Anna Seghers's narrator drank his coffee standing up, listening to Marseille's "harbor gossip": "All around me I heard people talking. It was as if the counter where I was drinking stood between two pillars of the Tower of Babel. Nevertheless, there were occasional words I could understand . . . Cuba visa and Martinique, Oran and Portugal, Siam and Casablanca, transit visa and three-mile zone."[67]

Cafés served as crucial hubs of information. In 1940, Eugen Tillinger reported for the *Aufbau* on the Café Tortoni in Bordeaux. Whereas some cafés appealed to French politicians, intellectuals, reporters, or entertainers, the Tortoni overflowed with central Europeans "who had the luck to come this far." Everyone there knew that they had to leave France quickly, and the "wildest rumors circulated." On one occasion, groups rushed from the café to the Brazilian consulate, having heard of visa possibilities. They came back a half hour later, disappointed. Then "someone suddenly brought the . . . solution: Portugal." But Portugal would give only transit visas, so they needed an additional solution: "A rumor arose that Haiti would provide 30 day visitors' visas." The café crowd rushed to the Haitian offices and with those visas in hand approached the Portuguese. Tillinger concluded: "The Tortoni indirectly saved all of our lives. Without it we would never have known that it was at all possible to get a visa." Aiming for Lisbon, a young man received excellent advice: "Ask directions to the largest coffee house in the center of town."[68]

Since refugees could never be certain of the accuracy of the censored news or letters they read, they looked to café rumors—also known as the "refugee telegraph"—for information. "Wherever there are refugees, there are also rumors," recalled Kurt Lenkway, whose parents had dodged police checks as a result of café hearsay. And as café customers "hatch[ed] little plots to get precious tickets on steamships and clippers to America, rumors provided hints as to which shipping agencies had come across extra tickets." On occasion, the café could provide more than rumors or information. Sometimes kindhearted helpers found visas for those in need. Yitzchak Wakman, for instance, born in Poland and resident in Portugal from 1931, began to visit cafés once refugees began flooding in. When he met people in need of visas, he either interceded for them with the proper aid agencies to acquire genuine visas or found forgers. According to his daughter, the Jewish community knew forgers but had to be careful. Wakman "took a chance" and provided Latin American visas.[69]

Notwithstanding the kindness of many Portuguese and the extraordinary efforts of the Portuguese-Jewish community, most adult refugees sought out other refugees with similar losses and needs. Cafés meant far more than sociability, card games, or an occasional dance. Refugees "droop[ed] over sidewalk café tables," sharing their anxieties about dear ones and themselves. Many whiled away their entire days in cafés, only sleeping in their rooms. The café provided "a place where at least it was possible to get away from the small room and the other people with whom one was living." In addition, cafés were "warm and cheap and there were different people to meet and to talk with." Hans Sahl summed up, "One lived in the café, slept in the café, [and] wrote farewell letters in the café."[70]

Chance meetings in cafés brought old friends together. People who thought they had lost each other accidentally reconnected. Heading toward a café for her first breakfast in Lisbon, Elisabeth Bab ran into good friends who had climbed the Pyrenees: "What a reunion that was!" She and her family immediately moved to the pension where her friends lived. But moments of joy could turn into tears as people realized how sick or transformed their friend looked, and as they exchanged somber news. The physical effects of trauma on a young friend whom she had not seen in two years dismayed Erika Mann: "Her once soft face was hard and small, her full, childlike mouth appeared like a line."[71]

Cafés also brought strangers together, emerging as new international and temporary "homes" for a vast variety of European Jews. This corner of their new urban landscape offered a setting where they could speak "the language we hungered for." Eugen Tillinger, writing in German, dubbed the café Chave de Ouro, where he heard overwhelmingly Czech, a branch of the Czech consulate during the war. Generally, however, German and French dominated these multilingual locations for refugees from eastern and western Europe, and the refugees, "although usually speaking in German, nevertheless found it wise to replace the words Portugal and Portuguese with Greece and Greeks, which would attract less attention when their conversations were overheard" by waiters who might be spying on them. They worried that some waiters worked for the state police. Indeed, on occasion, the police swept down on cafés and arrested those with inadequate papers. They detained two thousand people in one such roundup, but let them go when the Jewish community agreed to identify the individuals.[72]

Despite intermittent dangers, cafés served as a "momentary rendez-vous, a passing station," on refugees' "never-ending escape through life." There they created fluid communities, since many stayed for only a few weeks or months, until they acquired their documents. And since they were headed for diverse destinations, most did not assume they were making new lifelong friendships. Carla Pekelis made precisely this point when she wrote: "Then suddenly some visas—owing to the whim of a consul, the distraction of another, the corruption of a third—flung one family to the United States, one to Brazil, one to Argentina, like leaves driven by the wind." Nevertheless, friendships among refugees did occur. When the fortunate ones finally left Lisbon, those remaining behind endured the "loss of precious ties." They gathered in crowds at the pier, waving white handkerchiefs in farewell.[73]

Given the importance of even short-term attachments, political disagreements among friends or strangers seemed a luxury of the past. The writer Valeriu Marcu, who had moved to Nice in 1933 after fleeing Germany and Austria, sat on the terrace of a Lisbon café in early 1941 and "without seeking it, met Europe's past: Acquaintances, friends, opponents of various parties. Once these . . . people would have considered it blasphemous to speak to one another. . . . Today Hitler has pushed them literally to the edge of the continent. One more step and they would be in the water! Now they sit peacefully, ... scarcely mention politics and are interested only in who will get to New York first."[74]

Class remained a divide for some, since the wealthiest refugees chose fancier hotels in Lisbon or seaside resorts for their stay. Lisbon cafés, however, accepted everyone. Tillinger noticed refugees from very different economic and social classes brushing elbows at cafés: "The Polish Minister [sat] at the same coffee table as the little Jewish Polish emigrant, who formerly lived somewhere in the Warsaw Ghetto, owned a small wretched shop and who would have heard about the Minister only from newspaper reports." He described the "colorful" assortment of refugees sitting near one another, including a newspaper publisher from Paris, a haircutter from Nice, poets from Prague, Dutch merchants, Belgian artisans, and students, among many others. Class may have endured, but these cafés served as spaces of mutual experience, a kind of diasporic homeland. Hermann Kesten, who saw cafés as "waiting rooms for poetry," endowed them with symbolic meaning: "In exile, the café becomes home and homeland, church and parliament. . . . Exile creates loneliness and kills. Of course, it also enlivens and renews. The café becomes the only site of continuity. I sat in a dozen lands of exile in a café and it was always the same café. . . . I only have to sit in a café and I feel at home."[75]

These café "homelands" offered creative but emotionally complicated spaces. Built on a foundation of mourning, they provided distractions but rarely relief. Refugees could invent "families" and develop friendships, but new social circles could not replace the longing for loved ones or the long-time relationships they had treasured at home. The space itself evoked a past, a blurred image of previous friends and café encounters. The experience of constant loss lived just below the surface of these new relationships.

Many expressed the connection between space and mood, feeling power-less as they sat in cafés, "consumed by waiting." Ilse Losa compared cafés to "waiting rooms in train stations, only there one waited for something concrete, namely a train, whereas in the bleakness of the cafés one waited full of weari-ness for something undetermined or for nothing." Jan Lustig summed up his impression of the departure-obsessed inhabitants of cafés: "The emigrants sit in cafés with hollow cheeks and rimmed eyes, stick their heads together and talk, talk. Day and night, day and night. One says with a sigh: '. . . visa . . .' Another smiles ironically and bitterly: '. . . visa . . .' The third gives a long, excited speech, but one understands only: visa . . . visa . . . visa . . ."[76]

Stressful and tedious boredom, similar to depression, could set in. The reporter Eric Sevareid observed: "Daily the same routine: the general delivery window to ask for a letter; the American consulate; the newsstand to speculate on Hitler's next move; back to the café." Repetition without results underlined how refugees had lost control of their lives. Social workers from the JDC sympathized with refugees "sitting around and gossiping, repeating horror stories, and waiting, waiting." Elizabeth Dexter of the USC deemed "enforced idleness" to be "the most demoralizing factor in refugee life." And focusing on men, Lawrence Parrish of the Quakers wrote in his diary: "Most of them are terribly anxious to be able to work again." He decried the idling of refugees' expertise: "[A] great amount of talent going to waste here—highly trained technical men, doctors, businessmen—marking time for three or four years. . . . It is surely a short-sighted policy . . . when they could contribute so much in almost any society." The refugee narrator of Seghers's *Transit* highlighted the pain of idleness: "They talk about fatal wounds and fatal illnesses: they also speak of fatal boredom. I assure you, my boredom was deadly."[77]

Friendships alleviated this boredom, but these could also be strained and sometimes alienated relationships. By sharing angst and empathy, café patrons bonded, yet they were also rivals enveloped in their own misery. They depended on one another for friendship and support, but they also competed for scarce visas and insufficient space on ships. Sharing hope, they needed to repress disappointment and envy when someone else succeeded. When one woman received her American visa, the café in which she passed her days first erupted in a flurry of questions: "What kind is it, a visa to immigrate or an emergency visa? Where did you get it? Certainly not here? When do you leave?" Only then did her colleagues celebrate. Erika Mann observed that while these café goers all rejoiced for the lucky woman about to embark for the United States, "all were jealous of her."[78]

Besides temporary friendships, fleeting love or sexual liaisons added to the emotional complexity of café life. Such relationships provided comfort to some, including a few forced to separate from their spouses during their escapes. Extramarital affairs may have assuaged the loss of companionship and self-respect in shifting, often humiliating circumstances. But gossip spread, challenging the calm of the café and possibly targeting women more than men. Yet Howard Wriggins of the Quakers observed that those who found short-lived relations "seemed to survive with greater vigor and better health" and that the "solitaires, men and women, did less well." A few couples even reconciled just in order to travel abroad together. Another marriage had clearly come apart while the couple was in Portugal, but they were reunited when the husband received his visa for the United States. Jan

Lustig commented, "Hunger and love accomplish a great deal in this world. But a visa accomplishes even more."[79]

Miriam Stanton at the Café Palladium

Miriam Stanton's reliance on cafés in Lisbon exemplifies the importance of these sites for many refugees' emotional stability, and her friendships highlight some of the types of relationships that could be created there. Born in 1916 in Poland, Stanton immigrated to France with her parents and two brothers in 1930. Ten years later, the family escaped from Paris, ending up in southern France. She left for Portugal on March 31, 1941, expecting her parents and siblings to join her shortly thereafter. Engaged to a man in England, she planned to stay in Portugal for two weeks. But neither the visa from England nor her family arrived as she had hoped.

At the beginning of her sojourn, the twenty-five-year-old felt lucky to have found a room on the seventh floor of a walk-up building above the Café Palladium, "very popular indeed amongst the refugees." Stanton met "old hands" there who shared important information, along with recent arrivals who brought news. She thought that "everyone sooner or later seemed to come to Lisbon, and everyone who came to Lisbon sooner or later seemed to come to our café." Her daily routine included visiting the English and Polish consulates, telephoning her parents, stopping at the post office to check on the elusive visa and to send food parcels to her parents, and "hanging around cafés . . . waiting." The café offered her a "melting pot for news, ideas, help and comfort."[80]

Stanton understood that cafés offered refugees a chance to get away from roommates or family, but for her—as for so many others—they also provided her with her only companionship. After setbacks, she headed to the Palladium. There, she wrote letters and shared information from the letters she received. When her money started to run out, she asked her landlady for three rolls at breakfast. She ate one in the morning, one at noon, and one for dinner. She went to the café and drank warm coffee after the noon and evening "meals." The café provided her "daily diet and [her] daily variety." She also made friends there. When she finally got her visa to England, she invited them for a good-bye coffee. They accompanied her to the harbor, but then consoled her when the British consul unexpectedly denied her access to the ship.[81]

In the cafés as elsewhere, small tense groups tended to gossip. Stanton's friendships with single men led her to worry about her reputation. "If I so much as sat and talked with a man," she commented, the gossips seemed to know "for a fact that the man was my lover." The talk about her behavior continued even when she befriended single women and married couples. In retrospect, she appears to have understood this chatter: "We were all so anxious and there were so many of us living all near each other that such gossiping was unavoidable."[82]

The sense of looking out for one another, which could sometimes turn into gossip, had a positive side, allowing refugees to feel known and be part of a community. Cafés provided refugees with a place to celebrate Jewish holidays, for instance. When Passover approached, Miriam Stanton first just wanted "to be left alone with [her] thoughts"; she missed her family and fiancé. But when the holiday arrived, her café acquaintances decided to hold a traditional Seder there, since they had no space in their small rented rooms. About thirty people gathered, sharing matzot. When the man leading the ritual arrived at the traditional question, "Why is this night different from all other nights?" spoken in Hebrew, he broke down and cried. He had lost his wife and only child. In trying to console him, the group grew closer to one another and, for that moment, "felt like a family." They hired a passing street musician and taught him some Jewish songs, which they sang: "This is how we spent the first Seder night of our wandering life."[83]

The café also served as the site of one of the more remarkable moments of Stanton's refugee saga. She sat among many Polish refugees at the Palladium, "sharing with our co-sufferers our sorrows" and "drinking one cup of coffee after another." Toward the end of November 1941, many refugees at the café—like most refugees in Lisbon—received letters from the Portuguese government informing them that if they did not leave the country within two weeks, it would transfer them to a "forced residence." Not sure what that term meant, some panicked, fearing a concentration camp. Out of their gloom, Stanton heard someone say, "It's Churchill's birthday very soon, let's send him a birthday telegram, wishing him great success in his efforts to win the war, and long life, and . . . begging him to send us to any country in the world under the British flag. Signed by all Polish Jews in Lisbon."[84] The refugees collected money for the telegram and appointed the man who had suggested it, a Belgian doctor, to compose it. Then they walked to the post office together to mail it.

They hung a calendar on the wall of the café and crossed off the days as they waited for an answer. Twelve days went by; on the thirteenth day, the Polish consul in Lisbon wrote that they should appear at his consulate with their passports. The café broke out in cheers—"Everybody was there, full of excitement, shouting, screaming, kissing each other"—until they realized that no one knew what the consul wanted. They all arranged that they would meet on day fourteen outside the Polish consulate, and they promised to follow the motto "one for all and all for one." The café solidarity they had forged over many unhappy months held fast as two hundred of them crowded into the waiting room, where the Belgian doctor spoke for them. They learned that the British government, reversing a previous policy of keeping refugees out of its colonies, had agreed to send several hundred mostly Polish-Jewish refugees to Jamaica, and that the JDC would pay for their trip and their stay.[85] The Portuguese government allowed these delighted refugees to remain in Lisbon until their boat sailed in January 1942, whereas many other refugees lacking proper papers had to move to fixed residences. Whether this policy came about as a result of the telegram from the café, as Miriam Stanton suggests, or, more likely, as a result of discussions already in progress, it gave the refugees a sense of agency that thrilled them.[86] They remained in Jamaica until the end of the war. Then most moved to the United States or Britain, and Miriam joined her fiancé in England after seven years apart.

Having left home and family far behind, refugees headed to the nearest café, the one place that proved indispensable to people suffering one disappointment after another. Sipping coffee implied continuity with the past and gave the momentary illusion of a normal life. These spaces accommodated transient yet meaningful communities that offered refugees solace and advice. Meanwhile, refugees attempted to sustain deeper bonds through letter exchanges with loved ones they had left behind in Nazi-occupied Europe. But even as they exchanged mutual affection and care, refugees learned that Jews in war-torn Europe faced forced labor and starvation. Neither these epistolary spaces nor cafés could provide safety or relief. For that, they had to pursue ship tickets to new worlds and new lives.

7. Final Hurdles

*The boats are bigger, but they are also very crowded, with 300 to 400
people on fishing boats made for 40 or 50 [people].*

Refugees lucky enough to acquire their crucial visas needed ships to journey
on. But decreasing shipping options caused more long lines, jammed shipping
offices, and heightened exasperation. This shortage had already grown dire as
the United States limited shipping to and from nations at war in November
1939. Italy's entry into the war in June 1940 meant fewer ports, and a smaller
number of ships available from France meant higher prices. Additionally, by
1942 word of the mass murder of Jews had begun to leak into Portugal. Some
knew; others suspected. Waiting in Portugal, refugees viewed ships as sites of
final rescue, but once they set sail, they experienced these vessels as sites of
conflicting feelings. Sadness about leaving Europe and all it had represented
vied with relief at escaping war and persecution. An adage of the Viennese
Jewish author Arthur Schnitzler, "A departure always hurts, even when one
has long looked forward to it," resonated for many.[1]

Crowded Shipping Offices and Scarce Ships
Starting in the summer and fall of 1940, refugees "fervidly engaged in the
battle for ship tickets" with "ever more urgent assaults on agencies and
offices, naturally armed with papers." Writing to colleagues in New York,
Morris Troper of the American Jewish Joint Distribution Committee (JDC)
in Lisbon prefaced his description with "it is impossible to realize [the situa-
tion] unless one actually is on the spot." He described refugees with tickets
who learned through "the rumor mill" that their ship would not leave but

another one would. Frantically, they tried to get refunds and buy new tickets: "travel offices and bureaus are mobbed" and those refugees who still had some money but lost it through delays became "a burden on the local committee." Then the paper chase had to start from scratch. Hannah Arendt likened her own relatively short ordeal in leaving Lisbon to the German children's game Mensch ärgere Dich nicht, akin to the American board game Sorry! Just as one's pawn was nearing the goal, someone could bump it back to "start." As a result, in 1940 HIAS scrambled to get Jews on a ship, "whatever it costs," before their three-month U.S. visas ran out.[2]

Often visas did expire before the ship on which passage was booked sailed. In mid-1941, some ships ran "half empty because those booked cannot get their visas in time to reach their boats." Particularly after Pearl Harbor, when American steamship lines interrupted operations and Spanish lines suspended sailing to the United States, the inability to coordinate visas with ship departures caused delays. This happened to Ella and Elizabeth Hirsch, mother and daughter. They held visas that lapsed on January 23, 1942, but their ship left on January 24. The United States refused an extension. They finally got a new visa after Mrs. Hirsch's son, already in America, contacted his congressman. The visa came five months later, on June 15, but in the meantime they lived on subsistence in Lisbon. Similarly, when a sealed train transport of three hundred people from Germany arrived in Lisbon, fifty passengers watched their visas run out because the ocean liner they had booked postponed sailing for ten days. One of these, a doctor, could not simply apply for a new visa. American requirements had escalated. It took him another two and a half years in Lisbon, and he needed to ask for charity while there.[3]

If a visa expired after someone had boarded the ship, or while they sailed on the high seas, problems still arose. A woman traveling with her child on that sealed train boarded the delayed ship on the very day her visa lapsed, but the ship postponed leaving for yet another day. She endured an increasingly nerve-racking voyage. No one could predict whether the United States would allow her in. The worried ship's officials "said that they would never take such a risk again, because if the immigration authorities in N.Y. should rule that she was not on the high seas when her visa expired, they would send her and the child back to Europe." The company would have to pay the fare and a fine of $2,000.[4]

Evelyn Blumberg found herself in an even worse dilemma. She arrived in Lisbon with her papers in order, only to learn that the agency in charge of her passage had given her ticket to someone else. The aid workers thought she would be late and miss the boat, and a crush of passengers needed tickets. Her visa expired on April 20, 1941. The Americans denied a new visa because they had created a "close family" rule in June 1941, which meant that applicants whose immediate family lived in Germany or German-occupied territories would be refused entry. Blumberg's parents still lived in Vienna. By January 1943, the Nazis had deported her parents to "Poland address unknown," and she no longer received communication from them. Still, she did not have a visa, and the Portuguese police remanded her to the fixed residence in Caldas. It took five years before the Quakers could acquire a visa for her.[5]

The vast majority of refugees sought ship tickets, because tickets on Pan Am's *Yankee Clipper*, popularly known as the "flying boat," which landed in Lisbon harbor and flew to New York, cost far too much. Refugees could not afford the price of its "luxury travel": a one-way ticket for the twenty-five-hour flight cost about $375 ($6,772 in 2019 dollars). Inaugurated in May 1939, it carried almost a ton of mail, but too few passengers, and flew infrequently. In addition, the tiny Clipper fleet of two that flew between Lisbon and the United States gave priority to U.S. military needs even before Pearl Harbor, and no longer served civilian purposes thereafter. As early as 1940, George Warren, executive secretary of the President's Advisory Committee on Political Refugees, pronounced a "desperate need for finding means of transportation." Two shipping companies remained: the Companhia Colonial de Navegação and the Companhia Nacional de Navegação.[6]

Yet even on board a ship, refugees experienced delays and frustration. The S.S. *Quanza* left Lisbon in August 1940 with 317 passengers and arrived in New York, where 196 people held papers acceptable to U.S. authorities. The ship then headed to Mexico, where only 35 found a haven, and the remaining unlucky passengers faced a return to Europe. During a stopover to refuel in Virginia, a local Jewish lawyer sued the shipping company, as did some passengers. While the ship waited for the courts to proceed, a State Department official, at the behest of Eleanor Roosevelt, allowed the refugees to disembark. This "happy ending"—unlike that of the previous year's S.S. *St. Louis* calamity—caused Assistant Secretary of State Breckinridge Long to declare he would never allow another case like the *Quanza* to happen again.[7]

As the Committee on Political Refugees saw it, the rescuers had the funds but not the ships. Eventually, the JDC chartered some ships on its own or reserved blocks of tickets to secure definite spaces for the refugees and also to keep prices down. Further, HICEM and the JDC had contracts with Portuguese shipping firms; in June and August 1941, these agencies chartered the S.S. *Mouzinho* to take refugees from Lisbon to New York. Estimates suggest that about 2,000–3,000 refugees, mostly Jewish, left each month in the first half of 1941. Some ships even left for Shanghai from Lisbon.[8]

After the attack on Pearl Harbor and the U.S. entry into the war, American ships no longer took on civilians, making matters worse. On December 15, 1941, one man and his family were stranded: "Unnecessary to give you a picture of our morale," he wrote. The *Guine* and the *São Tomé*, the last Portuguese vessels to leave Europe with an American flag on their sides, that is, under American auspices, left in early 1942. After that, they sailed with Portuguese identification. Still, in the months between January and July 1942, the JDC managed to book spaces for 4,000 people on eight ships sailing to the United States. But these did not suffice. Spanish lines, too, suspended trips from Spain to the United States, sending refugees waiting to leave for Cuba into a frenzy. Eventually, some Spanish ships continued erratically, but the refugees fearfully labeled them "subordinates" of the Gestapo. In all, about a dozen ships, mostly Portuguese, and occasionally a Spanish ship, remained in operation.[9]

Refugees still in Lisbon felt increasingly perplexed and exasperated by the shortage of ships. Visiting Lisbon's Cook Travel Agency in early 1941 to look for any spot on any ship, some refugees wondered how the huge U.S. liner *Manhattan* could advertise for Hawaiian tourist cruises when people desperately sought to escape war-torn Europe. In the United States, the German-Jewish *Aufbau* noted that refugees with U.S. visas had been waiting for months for ship reservations: "One cannot understand why America doesn't send a larger ship . . . at least once a month." Moreover, ships sold out well in advance; refugees had bought up ten thousand tickets from the American Export Line by the spring of 1941, meaning that when *Life* magazine displayed photos of refugees jamming into the American Export Line office that spring, tickets had already been sold out until February 1942. When Alfred and Anna Eisinger arrived in Lisbon a month after the *Life* photo, in May 1941, with a U.S. visa that expired eight days later, they, too, could not book a ship. They wound up stranded for six years.[10]

Some wrote friends in desperation, and others even staged a protest once. Having arrived in Lisbon in February 1941, the German-Jewish writer and film theorist Siegfried Kracauer wrote friends in New York a few days

Woman with luggage, waiting in Lisbon, 1940s. (Photograph by Roger Kahan, NY_06718, Courtesy of JDC Archives, New York).

later, begging them to help him find ship tickets. He had learned that despite the tickets he had paid for months ahead of time, HICEM was prioritizing bookings for those whose U.S. visas would lapse before his. But if he did not get to New York quickly, he would lose the job awaiting him at the film library of the Museum of Modern Art. The general situation turned so bleak that dismayed refugees caused a furor that April when they learned that the Portuguese authorities had reduced the number of tickets for one ship, the *Serpa Pinto*, from 600 to 450, though refugees had already bought and paid for their tickets. Police quelled the unrest.[11]

An American newsreel best illustrates the feelings of some who made it into a ticket office. Taken sometime in 1942–43, the film depicts lines of men and a few women waiting in front of the American Export Lines office. They move restlessly from foot to foot. Then they go into the office, which has a huge American flag on one wall. They find a small reception area, where about six people at a time can fill out applications at a counter. They smoke, search for documents in their coats, and jostle for space. All look tense. A young man visibly gulps.[12]

Refugees may not have realized that American neutrality laws meant that its ships had to avoid combat areas, including much of Europe's coast. Yet the historian David Wyman argued that sufficient shipping existed: "When the Allies wanted to find ships for nonmilitary projects, they located them." But "when it was a matter of transporting Jews, ships could almost never be found." By November 1943, Breckinridge Long, the assistant secretary of state who had purposely delayed visas to needy refugees, could hypocritically claim that this alleged lack of shipping explained the State Department's disinclination to issue more visas.[13]

Returning from shipping agencies empty-handed, refugees beseeched aid committees for spots aboard the few ships still sailing from Lisbon. When the physicist Sergio DeBenedetti finally received his U.S. visa, delays meant that he had only two days to find a departing ship before his visa extension expired. He implored every shipping company in Lisbon, but none had a berth available: "It seemed that I would never leave Portugal." Before heading back to his fixed residence in Coimbra, he stopped at the HICEM office, where he heard a commotion: "Seven emaciated Jews had appeared, one of them an old lady who could hardly stand. They had walked across the Pyrenees and taken a train to Lisbon. There were painful scenes, telephone calls, old ladies crying. . . . They had valid American visas, which would expire in a week. If they did not leave immediately, they would lose their only hope of going to America." Someone found eight berths on a ship about to leave. DeBenedetti, with his "brand new visa, . . . would take the eighth berth." Then HICEM drove the eight people to consulates and offices for all the necessary papers.[14]

Refugees generally thought that aid organizations moved too slowly. These groups offered relief, but triggered exasperation. Some refugees suspected favoritism and feared that they lacked the connections that might help them with these agencies. A few German Jews believed that HICEM favored eastern European Jews. One journalist complained: "In general, the group of German refugees . . . are discriminated against everywhere." He provided no proof for his assertion, but remained bitter that "we who have sat in internment camps have no extra shirt, no coat, nothing." Hannah Arendt resented appearing as a supplicant over and over again. "I do not know how long we will have to stay here. We have no transportation at the moment, and I will have to hassle with HICEM, which hasn't gotten nicer with time," she wrote a friend. HICEM had paid for her mother's ship tickets, and the Emergency Rescue Committee would do the same for Arendt's and her husband's tickets, yet "a true battle rages over places on the ship."[15]

Personnel at aid organizations had feelings, too. Starting in 1940, Lolita Goldstein interpreted for the JDC. She had fled from Berlin to Portugal with her family, supporting them by tutoring in Spanish, German, French, English, and Portuguese. When the JDC opened its European headquarters in Lisbon, its director, Joseph Schwartz hired her: "Being American, they hardly spoke any languages," she observed. At the age of twenty-three, she made arrangements for the JDC with the Portuguese police, the post office, the phone company—anything that required Portuguese-language skills. She also chartered liners and allotted beds and cabins by using diagrams of the ships. She emphasized the "very complicated and time-consuming work" involved. With about twenty-five other JDC employees, she toiled long, intense hours: "The office never closed." Nevertheless, she depicted a lively atmosphere with good "esprit de corps," since "everyone felt their work was important." Remembering a special indulgence that raised spirits, she described afternoon breaks when Schwartz ordered "wonderful Portuguese coffee" and "a big tray of these wonderful . . . cakes and cookies" from the Imperium, a fancy café across the street. None of them could otherwise have purchased such treats. Small pleasures aside, all understood ships to be a "lifeline" for refugees.[16]

Frustratingly for refugees and social workers, the cost of this "lifeline" skyrocketed as demand exceeded supply and as insurance firms required higher premiums to cover each ship because of the expanding war. Shipping and insurance companies made huge profits. The Quakers estimated there were about sixty ticket agents and "many, many more sub-agents" in Portugal; HIAS suggested that the refugees found themselves "at the mercy of every little agent." Lolita Goldstein saw Portuguese companies making a "windfall, from almost no business to overwhelming business." Many companies, not only Portuguese, demanded double the prewar fees. On the American Export Line, the fare for one bed in a three- or four-berth cabin equaled the price of a prewar single cabin on a luxury liner. Between September and December 1940, the price of a third-class ticket rose from $200 to $320 (about $5,779 in 2019).[17]

That month, Elisabeth Bab and her husband, having booked a private cabin on the *Siboney*, found that ticket costs had jumped so high that their payment covered only passage, but not a room. They slept on cots in a large space with men on one side of the room and women on the other. Similarly, because of the length of Sergio DeBenedetti's wait in Lisbon, the money he had paid in Bordeaux for a first-class ticket could purchase only half the value of a third-class ticket in Lisbon. Hence, HICEM had to pay the other half. Prices continued to climb. Moreover, when Germany invaded Greece in April 1941, passengers could no longer hope for a cheaper spot on the Greek ship *Nea Hellas,* which had charged about $250. They needed to pursue more expensive Portuguese ship accommodations, starting at $350. From May 1941, the *Siboney* served the U.S. army, transporting troops, which left only three American ships to carry refugees. By June 1942, legitimate tickets cost around $500 and HICEM paid about $420 per person for destitute Jews. Elizabeth Dexter of the Unitarians labeled this steep rise in prices a "special history of gangsterism."[18]

Observers noticed that ticket agents "had lost all sense of compassion." In February 1941, the Romanian writer Valeriu Marcu approached clerks in a steamship company to buy a ticket for the United States, only to be met with incredulity and disdain: "[They] looked at me in surprise, as though I had come to ask for their daughters' hands. I want something quite normal and I am regarded as a madman." He notified them that if he had to wait as long as they suggested, his American visa would expire, but "the gentlemen behind the counter refused to listen to me any longer." When he could not afford a ticket priced at three times its worth, the agent responded, "In that case, you will probably have to walk to New York."[19]

A black market in tickets thrived.[20] It provided some refugees with the coveted tickets, but cheated others. Refugees might acquire ship tickets from people at cafés. Frank Furth, for example, tried to purchase a legitimate ticket in late 1940, but knew that "one solution was to go and buy one in a coffee shop." Similarly, as Valeriu Marcu grew utterly desperate to find a ship ticket, he knew he had to resort to "go-betweens . . . found in . . . cafes": "They carry their offices in their pockets." They asked "double or triple fare," more if they could. Even children traveling alone "witnessed some of the ticket sale transactions and still worse, heard the . . . rumors about the bribing." In May 1941, a black-market ticket sold for an extra $150, as reported to the National Shipping Agency, a governmental organization. A few lucky individuals paid that $150 as a simple bribe. Frank Furth, who found it "almost impossible to get a legitimate berth or cabin," went to a shipping office in Lisbon run by a Spanish line with service to Havana. There a clerk told him that a ticket would be "hopeless . . . but for $150 American dollars he'd get me on the boat." Furth got a spot near the stokers. Some fake agencies and corrupt bureaucrats sold tickets that did not permit the holder to embark. A few refugees got into the act, although with real tickets. A man who had provided ship tickets to a political refugee realized that he could buy tickets and sell them at a much higher price if a worker in a Lisbon travel agency cooperated. They would split the profit. This "business" helped him pay for his stay in Lisbon and his own tickets when he finally received his visa.[21]

On Board: Dangerous Waters and "Floating Hell"

Even after refugees boarded ships to carry them far from war-torn Europe, they did not feel secure. Ships entered dangerous waters. Earlier in the war, in October 1939, passengers sailing from England to the United States signed statements that accepted responsibility for their decision to leave: "I am aware of the dangers of crossing the Atlantic at the present moment. . . . But . . . I wish to depart at my own risk." By 1940, Germany's submarines were prowling the seas, and passengers on neutral liners like those belonging to Portuguese or American companies worried. Further, ships whose passengers aimed for illegal entry into Palestine faced the possibility of being caught and turned back by British ships. The attack on Pearl Harbor meant the end of American neutrality. Peter Lax, then a fifteen-year-old from Hungary, later recalled that the American vessel they took from Lisbon on December 4, 1941, kept its flag illuminated to prove its neutral status. One night, all of a sudden, the crew turned the light off. The Japanese had just bombed Pearl Harbor. As a result, the American crew felt vulnerable to attack. After Pearl Harbor, Germany's U-boats did attack ships along the East Coast of the United States, in the Gulf of Mexico, and in the Caribbean, which meant precarious passage from Europe to the Americas.[22]

Portuguese ships, protected to some extent by Portuguese neutrality, faced fewer attacks than most. Refugees boarding or waving to friends at the Lisbon port noticed that painted on a ship's hull would be a large Portuguese flag, the ship's name, and "Portugal," in huge letters. Bright spotlights aimed at the names to show the ship's nationality at night: "German submarines were allegedly plentiful in the Atlantic." Indeed, German ships stopped some

Portuguese liners on the high seas, and a German submarine sank a Portuguese merchant ship in June 1942, despite its identification.[23] Acquiring the precious tickets, boarding with one's meager belongings, and setting sail did not guarantee arrival at the desired destination. Although a journey could take as few as ten days from Lisbon to New York, many ships took longer, stopping at Casablanca, Bermuda, or Havana. Others set out on unpredictable routes, faced serious delays, and traversed stormy seas.

Some ships under way for America had to return to Europe or Casablanca, for a variety of reasons. In the spring of 1941, Hugo Marx and his wife started their voyage from Lisbon. Their ship sailed along the northwest African coast. Because of the war, they had to lay anchor at Dakar, on the coast of Senegal. The narrow confines and the heat, but mostly the uncertainty whether they would have to turn back, plagued them. To their horror, the ship returned to Casablanca, and they dreaded that they might have to dock in Marseille, under German surveillance. But the ship turned toward Lisbon and then headed to the United States.[24]

Such delays and uncertainties were common. In the spring and summer of 1940, many ships hastily left ports when Germany invaded France. In London, the *Times* reported: "In the Tagus, fishing boats and squat freighters disgorged a . . . mass of humanity." Another ship, the *Dora*, left Marseille in July 1940 with about fifty passengers, aiming for Casablanca. But a naval battle between Britain and (Vichy) France near Oran meant that it was ordered to sail for Lisbon harbor, where it waited for three weeks. The travelers ran out of food and water and needed assistance from the Portuguese Maritime Police. None of the passengers had proper papers, since they had not intended to land in Lisbon, so the Portuguese eventually interned all of them. They wound up in the Caxias prison. Although the Portuguese authorities treated them "humanely," according to a letter they sent to the American-Jewish newspaper *Forverts,* the internees begged Jews in the United States to rescue them. With the JDC's assistance, twenty-six had found new destinations by September, and Portugal set the others free.[25]

On board, conditions ranged from elegant for the very few to unhygienic and overcrowded for most. On December 28, 1940, Kurt Teller, heading to the Dominican Republic, boarded the *Serpa Pinto* in Lisbon. The JDC representatives in charge of his group appeared horrified when they inspected the refugees' quarters on board, which Teller described as suited for "livestock ready to be slaughtered." Shipping agencies regularly overbooked and overloaded their vessels, sometimes at the request of aid organizations. Still, refugees preferred overcrowded ships to no ships. The week in 1941 that Nazi Germany invaded the Soviet Union, the *Villa de Madrid,* a Spanish passenger and cargo ship intended for 225 passengers, departed Barcelona for Lisbon. There, it took on more passengers, for a total of 617 people. For twenty-one days, passengers crowded the decks and public rooms or found space in the hold, "which was a mess." Three hundred people slept two to a bunk between the decks in separate compartments, one for men and the other for women. Rats "were no novelty in the 'tween deck section," according to a passenger.[26]

Another Spanish freighter, the *Navemar,* first stopped in Seville and then Lisbon, heading for Cuba and the United States. The JDC, HICEM, the Unitarians, and the Quakers supported many of its passengers. In normal times, the ship could hold about 800, but many passengers possessed soon-to-expire U.S. visas. As a result, the shipping agency let them crowd on, adding extra two-tiered bunks in the cargo hold, which had previously stored coal. The *Navemar* left Lisbon with 1,100–1,500 passengers in the summer of 1941. Because of conditions on board, six passengers died and eight others disembarked in Bermuda, too ill to go on. While passengers dubbed the ship the "S.S. Nevermore," Joseph Schwartz of the JDC in Lisbon referred to it as a "floating concentration camp," and the *Aufbau* called the ship a "floating hell." Kurt Weishaupt, aboard the *Navemar,* had different worries: "The sea was wild," and he slept at the "bottom of the ship . . . just on top of the water," with about 300 other men. More frighteningly, a German submarine stopped the ship temporarily before it reached New York.[27]

The better-appointed *Serpa Pinto* left Lisbon in November 1941 with 1,200 passengers, about four times its usual load. Lisa Fittko on the S.S. *Colonial,* heading to Cuba right before the attack on Pearl Harbor, described the appalling conditions: "So many people one can hardly move. . . . We sleep way below decks in a dark, enormous room without hatches, normally used to stow baggage. Men on one side . . . women and children on the other. Almost all are seasick; we others are nauseated by the stench. . . . I see a fat rat running back and forth on the girder directly above my head." Passengers on other ships also experienced crowding, cold, sometimes hunger, and even antisemitism from crew members.[28]

After the attack on Pearl Harbor, crowding grew worse. The Aal family, with tickets for an American ship in hand, learned that they had to pay for a

Portuguese ship instead. On December 11, they sailed on the *Guine*, a vessel meant for 186 people that had more than 400 jammed on board. For twenty-six days, they made their way from Lisbon to Casablanca and then to Cuba, Bermuda, and up the East Coast of the United States to New York. "Every ship seemed to be the last one—but none really was the last!" remarked the *Aufbau*, describing Lisbon as the "Jewish civil Dunkirk," an allusion to the Battle of Dunkirk, which ended in the evacuation of British and Allied forces from Europe by ship and boat.[29]

In Lisbon, the JDC continued to fill non-American ships with refugees. In June 1942, the thirteenth ship since Pearl Harbor left Lisbon for New York, with 677 passengers. By then, the Quakers had decided that the war had made "emigration for the United States from Europe practically impossible." Throughout the rest of the war, fewer ships, facing greater danger, continued to depart from Lisbon.[30]

Many refugees remembered the ships that made the most trips, such as the *Nea Hellas, Nyassa, Guine,* and *Serpa Pinto,* all Portuguese. The journey usually took from twelve to seventeen days, depending on weather and docking sites. Memories of the ships evoked sadness. Carla Pekelis, whose four-month stay in Lisbon felt like "a single, interminable moment filled with anxiety," believed that the *Nea Hellas* "oozed a gloomy exhaustion." Traveling to Palestine, some recalled the *Nyassa.* For this ship to arrive safely, the JDC needed the permission of the British Foreign Office as well as clearance by both the Allied and the German governments. Only three shiploads, with a combined total of 875 passengers, managed to sail from Lisbon to Palestine during the war.[31]

The *Serpa Pinto,* built in 1914 and described by its captain as "one of the best, if not the best Portuguese passenger ships," often journeyed between Lisbon, New York, and Rio de Janeiro. It made more transatlantic crossings during the war than any other civilian ship. As a result, it acquired the nickname "Ship of Destiny." On the route westward, it usually carried 700–800 passengers, despite having been built for 350–500. Between 1941 and 1944, the JDC either financed or subsidized about a dozen of its voyages, often made in submarine-infested waters. Returning to Lisbon, it carried Germans from abroad, or *Auslandsdeutsche,* particularly Germans living in Brazil who wanted to help the Nazi regime. A neutral vessel, it flew a large Portuguese flag that remained illuminated at night. Still, German, American, and British ships repeatedly stopped the *Serpa Pinto* for inspections. One of the most nerve-racking voyages for Jewish passengers occurred immediately after Pearl Harbor. On the high seas when the Japanese attacked Pearl Harbor and the United States declared war, the ship continued to the Dominican Republic, Cuba, and Mexico. Terror gripped the travelers as they passed along "wild rumors" of being forced back to Europe, but as the ship sailed on, "hopes grew," and they landed safely in New York. Still the *Serpa Pinto* continued to face confrontations. In May 1944, a German U-boat forced 385 passengers and crew members to abandon the liner as it headed west. They sat in lifeboats all night while the Germans awaited orders to torpedo the ship. When they did not receive the orders and left the area, the passengers returned to the *Serpa Pinto,* although two crew members and sixteen-month-old Betty Trapunski drowned during the ordeal. The ship did not cross again until the end of the war. Such conditions notwithstanding, refugees continued to prefer overcrowded, perilous voyages to remaining in Europe.[32]

What They Knew as They Left

Refugees

Refugees first learned about deportations from letters written by friends and relatives in Nazi-occupied Europe, starting in the fall of 1941. But at that stage, even those directly under Nazi rule were not sure what "deportations" meant. Nazi euphemisms regarding "resettlement in the East" (*Umsiedlung*), "evacuation" (*Evakuierung*), and "departure" (*Abwanderung*) gave some hope that they might survive "hard labor," whereas others "looked upon arrest and deportation as spelling their end." By 1942, suspicions of murder circulated among Jews in Germany and Austria. On January 13, 1942, Victor Klemperer in Dresden wrote: "Rumor, but it is very credible and comes from various sources—evacuated Jews were *shot* in Riga . . . as they left the train." Some weeks later, on March 1, he concluded that "concentration camp is now evidently identical with a death sentence." And suicides rose, especially before deportations. Historians have concluded on the basis of written and oral records that by 1943, the suspicion of mass murder had turned into a certainty among most Jews in Germany.[33]

In Portugal, however, the deportations between late 1940 and late 1942 confused those Jewish refugees who remained there after most had departed.

They knew that relatives in Berlin, Vienna, or Warsaw faced starvation. They could also read between the lines when letters shared fears of losing jobs or information about friends who had "left." But they did not have regular access to a free press or to international radio programs. So we do not know whether those facing delays in Portugal heard the Nobel Prize winner Thomas Mann speaking on a BBC broadcast in September 1942, warning of the "extermination" of Jews, or whether they were informed of the announcement in November 1942 by the New York rabbi Stephen Wise that two million Jews had already been murdered. Many refugees in Portugal received only partial information and could not grasp the entirety of the Final Solution, even though they lived in dread for their loved ones' safety. And even when one refugee in Portugal did hear BBC reports of mass murders, she assumed them to be propaganda: "We didn't believe what they said." This was true even for someone as astute and as experienced in fascist brutality as Hannah Arendt. In 1943, she first registered her shock regarding the mass murders in eastern Europe. Safely in New York, neither she nor her husband initially believed the reports.[34]

Still others, especially people like Heinz Wisla, who had survived the Oranienburg concentration camp and escaped to Lisbon, knew from their own experience and from rumors what the Nazis were capable of. In the summer of 1943, the German postal system returned all his recent letters to his parents and brother in Berlin, stamped "Address Unknown." Thereafter, a German neighbor wrote him: "One early morning all remaining Jews were herded together and sent to the East." Wisla commented: "Since everybody knows now what happens to the deported Jews in Poland, I am in deep shock and spend days walking lonely along the beaches here, listening to the pounding surf of the waves, watching the sea gulls."[35]

International and Local Agencies

International agencies had better sources of information than the average refugee. Yet they also displayed confusion or disbelief about the news coming in from the Reich. They recognized the desperate hunger, cold, and forced labor that many Jews faced, and they heard rumors of the worsening situation in Nazi-occupied Europe. Lisbon's small Zionist Federation, in contact with the Jewish Agency in Geneva, received regular reports in 1942 on the deteriorating condition of European Jews. The Quakers in Lisbon, too, received reports in June and July 1942 "of awful things happening in France."

They worried about rumors regarding roundups, but did not understand what "roundups" led to. On August 7, 1942, a woman came to the Quakers, "inquiring about rumors heard from BBC on deportations of 10,000 Jews from France to Germany for workers." Howard Wriggins responded that he "knew nothing and did not believe rumors until [he] had some better proof," but he noted in his diary that "this is not the first of these rumors, and this may be true." These speculations referred to roundups, however, not murder.[36]

News of atrocities came most directly to international organizations within Europe. Hence, many aid workers may have known, and some must have known. Indeed, information about concentration camp conditions sent to the Red Cross and to Jewish organizations in Switzerland "was often transmitted through Lisbon" to London, Jerusalem, New York, and Istanbul. But organizations and governments continued to resist believing what they heard. The "Riegner Telegram" of August 8, 1942, sent by Gerhard Riegner of the World Jewish Congress in Geneva to the U.S. State Department and the British Foreign Office, confirmed the Nazi resolve to "exterminate" up to four million Jews. Yet the governments dismissed this message as "rumors." A few months later, on November 22, 1942, the Jewish Agency published a statement about the Nazi murder of Jews in Europe—about a month before a similar Allied broadcast. And by early 1943, the murder of European Jews appeared in the American-Jewish press, demonstrations occurred in cities with large Jewish populations, and church groups, women's clubs, and labor organizations tried to pressure the U.S. government to rescue Jews. Yet doubts persisted. When Wriggins heard rumors of extermination camps, he could not imagine the Nazis would "waste their energies—and scarce railroad cars—on non-military objectives" and recalled the exaggerated propaganda both sides had disseminated during World War I.[37]

A few nonetheless drew the correct conclusions. For example, Donald Lowrie of the YMCA in Geneva wrote to colleagues in the United States in August 1943: "We probably know more than you do at home about the unspeakable atrocities accompanying this slaughter of millions." Lowrie's observation notwithstanding, Herbert Katzki at the Lisbon JDC insisted in an interview in 1995 that the JDC in 1943 did not have "that information." He continued: "The curious thing is this: People thought that since I was in Lisbon . . . we knew all about what was going on with the stories that were coming out from the concentration camps, which later became known. We did not—I did not know that in Lisbon." He clarified that the information from Riegner in Geneva went to Washington, which suppressed it because "they wanted proof," but in Lisbon "we didn't know . . . because the Portuguese papers certainly didn't carry it. . . . So the information wasn't generally known."[38]

Whatever Katzki and Wriggins may have known, refugee workers inside the Lisbon Jewish community, particularly those who had fled central and eastern Europe, appear to have had some access to more information—or simply believed it. Fred Mann, who escaped from Leipzig, worked with new arrivals. Mann learned about starvation and "wanton killing" from men who had suffered through concentration camps in Germany. Toward the end of 1940, he heard that the Nazis had created a sealed ghetto in Warsaw. In addition, he found out in September 1941 that Jews in Germany had to wear the yellow Star of David, the same month the Nazis began requiring it. He further claims in his memoir that he was aware of mass killings of Jews near Vilna and "all over German-occupied southern Russia." Similarly, Rabbi Diesendruck, originally from Vienna and working for the Lisbon Jewish community, listened to refugees' frightening reports and asked the director of the Lisbon JDC, Joseph Schwartz, to urge the Jews of Lisbon to consider rescuing Jews trapped in France rather than merely offering relief for refugees in Portugal. But Schwartz, himself a rabbi, responded, "Rabbi, it's your community, why don't you straighten it out?"[39]

Mann and Diesendruck probably learned more details from the newcomers than native Portuguese Jews did. Portuguese Jews had access only to short articles in the censored press. One of Lisbon's local papers, the *Diário de Notícias*, depicted refugees departing on ships for the Americas, but nowhere in it would one have read about mass murder. This lack of information included Portuguese Jewish leaders. Augusto d'Esaguy, head of COMASSIS, for example, had no idea that in September 1940 the Gestapo had commanded that all Jews leave Luxembourg. Even as late as 1943, when a Jewish woman who had escaped France and arrived illegally in Portugal came to the accountant of the Jewish community to ask for help, he asked her "Madam, why did you leave Paris?" This man apparently had no knowledge of the mass deportation of Jews either from Paris or from other parts of France in the summer of 1942. Rabbi Diesendruck believed that Portuguese Jews simply did not understand what was happening in central and eastern Europe.[40]

Leaving Portugal with Mixed Feelings

Despite obstructions and circuitous journeys, by mid-1942 most refugees from the largest influx (in 1940) had managed to emigrate. Still, as we have seen, refugees continued to arrive, caused by later developments in the war, just as departures grew more infrequent. In January 1944, the *American Jewish Year Book* estimated that about 1,100 Jewish refugees remained in Portugal, mostly of German and Austrian origin, but also Polish, Belgian, French, Dutch, Czech, Yugoslav, and Hungarian. In the spring of 1944, the Quaker Philip Conard wrote: "If visas were to be had, everybody would go to the United States. Many would accept Canada as a poor second choice. A few would go anywhere and gladly."[41]

Enough refugees remained during the war years to crowd piers and wave good-bye to their lucky friends or relatives. One of those unlucky ones standing at the pier gazing at a liner protested, "I'm tired of waving!" He lamented that the *Nea Hellas* would leave the following day—without him. An American observed those watching "with longing" as ships left the harbor and concluded, "They are trapped. There is no 'green frontier,' as they call any border they can sneak across. Only the ocean."[42]

Those fortunate enough to find tickets left others behind. An article published in a Portuguese newspaper in January 1941 depicted one such departure:

> In the middle of the afternoon on the quayside . . . there was an endless, confused movement of people and final preparations for departure. It was a sad crowd . . . with the air of apprehension and resignation of those who are forced to leave due to fate, and are leaving the remains of broken lives and pieces of their own souls in some far off place. The luggage . . . which the cranes were raising up into the hold of the . . . ship . . . were the remains of those bitter existences, and spoke of painful wanderings throughout bloody Europe. . . .
>
> . . . The steamer was about to cast off. . . . It was full of people and along its rails one could see sad silhouettes . . . faces with an expression of bitterness, contemplating the beloved city in acknowledgement. . . .
>
> . . . The ship slowly pulled away . . . and sometime later was sailing offshore, on its way to the New World.

In Remarque's novel *The Night in Lisbon*, his character saw the ship as the ark at the time of the Flood: "It was an ark. Every ship that left Europe in 1942 was an ark."[43]

The lucky ones, sailing mostly for North and South America and for Palestine, encountered a cacophony of languages. On one journey, for example, the 741 refugees heading for Palestine aboard the *Nyassa* represented twenty-one nationalities. Even in 1943, as the war raged on, an American newsreel filmed for CBS depicted hundreds of refugees with earnest faces watching others ascend the gangplank. Wishing the travelers farewell, they waved white handkerchiefs. The camera then focused on the palpable anxiety of the passengers as they waited at a table to pick up their final papers. Among those who left, a few children smiled, but most boarded hurriedly. They waved to those left behind. This film crew could not capture a joyful departure.[44]

On board the coveted ship, refugees endured ambivalent feelings. This new space provided an escape from a "rotten" Europe. Yet frightening memories and fear continued to haunt many, even as they also experienced relief. On the *Nea Hellas* in October 1940, Franz Werfel wrote his parents: "This ship is full of fates that far surpass ours in horror. Misfortune is so widespread, that one should really not complain." Young Isaac Bitton, heading for Palestine, observed the "permanent anxiety" of other passengers, worrying about what their families in Europe faced. And they traveled with guilt. As Hugo Marx's ship started its motor in 1941, he breathed a sigh of relief that he had managed to cut his ties with this "continent of horrors," but also felt like a traitor to those who remained imprisoned there. Indeed, many carried this guilt with them into their new lives. In New York, the poet Alfred Farau wrote of the "guilt of having left behind people very dear to oneself in their dreadful misery; and a strange disgust of oneself for having survived it mixed with the feeling of one's own safety."[45]

That moment of embarkation forced passengers to face another reality. They had become emigrants, exiles, and permanent refugees. For many, this awareness had come earlier, in the face of discrimination and violence in Germany, or as they tried to stay ahead of the German army, or as they read papers about the war and heard rumors of murders while waiting to leave Portugal. Others, such as Hugo Marx, had not confronted their status until the moment the ship departed: "As long as we were in Europe, we didn't actually feel like emigrants. We felt more like refugees, a concept that . . . offered the logical possibility of a return to the . . . *Heimat* . . . [and] also allowed us emotionally not to see this separation from our *Heimatland* as final. . . . The departure from Europe was intimately connected with the feeling that we had transformed from refugees to émigrés."[46] Freedom felt bittersweet.

Adults in particular worried about the countries they were heading toward and whether they could make a living there and not burden those who had vouched for them. Annette Finger recalled that her mother left reluctantly. Coming to the United States meant "coming to the totally unknown." She had been very happy in Portugal, her "little place in heaven." Siegfried Kracauer and his wife, like so many others, would depend on aid organizations and good friends for their upkeep. Boarding the *Nyassa* en route to New York, his thoughts turned toward his recent past and his fears for the future: "It is terrible to arrive like us—after eight years of an existence that doesn't earn that name. I've grown older, also inside me. Now the last station, the last chance arrives that I can't gamble away, otherwise all is lost. I can only recognize this last chance if I get a first [chance] in New York—because I am arriving poor, poorer than I ever was, and so it is impossible to take those first steps entirely on my own." Even younger refugees, more optimistic in general, expressed sorrow when leaving, but for different reasons. Eighteen-year-old Anita Wakman, who had lived in Portugal for eight years, remembered peacefulness in Portugal. Yet her parents, fearing a possible German invasion, chose to flee. "I was heartbroken to leave Portugal," she recalled, where she had led a "beautiful life."[47]

Many mourned their loss of Europe, their "Europeanness," their native languages, and the countryside in which they had grown up. Fourteen-year-old Mara Vishniac, daughter of the photographer Roman Vishniac, felt an "immense sadness" about "leaving Europe." Hans Sahl grieved for the "words that I spoke as a child," the "music of the countryside," and the world he had been born into. On board, Hugo Marx choked up: "What did it mean to be a European, to what extent were we? and what would it take to become something different?" The Jewish author Eugen Tillinger and the non-Jewish author Heinrich Mann evoked the feelings of many who focused on European history and culture. In 1944, Mann described the sorrow that came with his last glimpse of the port of Lisbon. It appeared "indescribably beautiful"—"a lost lover is not more beautiful"—he reminisced: "Everything that was given to me, I had experienced in Europe, the joy and pain of my era." In addition, he felt a connection to European history. His farewell felt "exceptionally painful." Tillinger watched the port of Lisbon disappear and remembered "the most beautiful scenes from the European past, baroque and gothic . . . the towers of Prague, the sweet Austrian landscape, Paris—a whole life spent in Europe." In stark contrast, Valeriu Marcu voiced his anger. He recounted the story of a German refugee about to immigrate to Australia: "Why so far?" asked a surprised friend. The émigré responded: "Far? Far from where?"[48]

By early 1944, most of the thousands of refugees to Portugal had transmigrated. By war's end, about 1,000 remained. The Lisbon Jewish community expedited their voyages, but some did not receive visas until as late as 1951.[49] These statistics hide the many trials and errors and the frustrated attempts to escape Europe. Nevertheless, as a result of the refugees' persistence, the help of relatives and aid agencies, and countries that reluctantly accepted refugees, the huge numbers that had entered Portugal, with or without legal documents, had dwindled to a few. Still, these ocean liners did not represent sites of pure joy. Refugees had clambered up gangplanks with suitcases and with hope, but they had left whole lives and families behind.

Conclusion

Exile . . . is the unhealable rift forced between a human being and a native
place, between the self and its true home.

In his otherwise masterful study of Portugal, Salazar, and the Jewish refugees, Avraham Milgram writes that the refugees led "totally ordinary lives."[1]
In fact, refugees experienced their lives as precisely the opposite of ordinary.
As they lined up to acquire shelter, visas, and ship tickets, they experienced
the abnormal as routine, even depressingly boring, but never "ordinary."
Formerly citizens with rights, stable lives, family networks, and friends, they
had faced previously unimaginable losses—personal, political, economic,
and social. And although immeasurably luckier than Jews caught up in the
Nazi genocide, few refugees knew that at the time. They realized that friends
and family trapped in Europe suffered, but they could not predict mass
murder, nor did they realize until later that Portugal had saved their lives.

Refugees formed part of the Jewish experience of the Holocaust.
Hindsight and comparisons with those who endured or fell victim to Nazi
atrocities should not obscure that fact. By the time refugees reached neutral
Portugal from Nazi-occupied Europe, their external and internal worlds had
been turned upside down. Indeed, refugees' daily lives and feelings, their
objective escapes and subjective fears, are part and parcel of the Holocaust
and can expand our sense of its range and impact.

Portugal and its heart, Lisbon, represented a point where time and
place, the pace of war and the geography of Europe, intersected. Time
seemed to be running out as refugees dashed through Europe with the
German army at their backs. No one, certainly not the refugees, had a clear
idea of when the German army might appear at the Portuguese border.

Anxiety surged when Germany achieved military successes, but rarely diminished when it suffered setbacks. Those Jews who remained in Portugal in 1943 and 1944 began to recognize that Germany might lose the war, but also knew that refugees continued to flee over the Pyrenees. Most refugees felt relief only after crossing the ocean, and some only on V-E Day. Some may never again have found inner security.

Jewish refugees constantly traversed liminal spaces, physically and psychologically. These sites of anxiety could range from the massive scale of the nation to the micro scale of the visa office. The nation of Portugal offered safety if one could depart quickly, but imprisonment or fixed residences if one stayed too long. Refugees faced dreadful time pressures as they rushed to leave before their welcome wore out. They needed to obtain the proper papers within tight deadlines, yet were forced to wait on long lines and deal with intransigent and capricious bureaucrats. Those who failed to get their papers in good time suffered "deadly" boredom and prolonged apprehension. Some even endured prison. The fateful and shifting combinations of time and place created a whiplash of emotions; hope vied with despair during an anxious life in limbo.

Harsh rejections and obstacles notwithstanding, refugees acted as protagonists in their own dramas. With the outbreak of war, individuals brave and lucky enough jumped the daunting hurdles between their countries of origin and the Portuguese coastline. Escaping the Nazi invasion of France with millions of others, a former Viennese haberdasher en route to Lisbon recalled that "thousands of people . . . went through the garbage . . . in Marseille," as he did. Refugees waited at borders in "hot, dusty, half-freight, half-passenger train[s]" full of fearful people with or without the proper papers. They suffered physical and mental anguish, but they persisted and continued onward. Trying to leave Portugal, many encountered what Remarque portrayed as "a jungle of consulates, police stations, and government offices . . . bureaucratic red tape, loneliness, homesickness, and withering universal indifference."[2]

In the face of fierce impediments, some refugees lost the ability to function or even succumbed to suicide. Most, though, clung to hope, showing remarkable resilience despite intense frustration. They approached their situations energetically, but in shock, seeing their new interim life as strange and foreign, even if it became depressingly routine. Although fear overcame them at points, even the most panic-stricken tried to figure out rational responses to their predicaments.[3] Their story is not only one of violent loss, confusion, and deprivation. Individuals also created communities that connected them. There they could acquire information, confidence, and temporary friendships. Further, Jews played an active role in organizing and advocating for their own escape, demonstrating courage and endurance. Once inside Portugal, they strategized means of escape, enlisted the help of aid organizations, advised and encouraged each other, and simply did not give up. Alf Lüdtke, a historian of the German working class, coined the term *"Eigen-Sinn,"* self-affirmation or agency, to describe how laboring people became active agents in their worlds, how they resisted outside forces, not always successfully, and how they pushed against boundaries. Recounting workers' sense of self-preservation and their self-presentation, he noted "the innumerable small ways in which [they] created and defended a sense of self, demarcated a kind of autonomous space, and generally affirmed themselves in a hostile and limiting world."[4] He could have been writing about Jewish refugees. Within intimidating political, social, and cultural structures, Jews acted not only as victims but also as agents: they deciphered events, defended themselves, and often succeeded.

In 1936, as the refugee crisis began to escalate, the *Manchester Guardian* summed up the situation for Jews, quoting Chaim Weizmann, president of the World Zionist Organization: "The world seemed to be divided into two parts—those places where the Jews could not live and those where they could not enter." Portugal, however, quietly allowed hundreds of Jews to settle there until 1938 and then made a temporary haven available for tens of thousands of Jews in transit. Indeed, Portugal provided the only mass escape route from western Europe after the spring of 1940. Refugee accounts highlight the generosity of Portuguese people as well as the absence of racialized antisemitism. Still, this is a complicated picture. Portugal raised barriers against Jewish immigration and delayed bringing in Sephardic Jews claiming Portuguese citizenship, condemning many of them to death. Yet its government, and even more so its people, also helped Jews. Although the government jailed some refugees lacking necessary credentials or forced others into fixed residences until they had the visas needed to leave Portugal, in 1942 the American Jewish Committee concluded that "the visitors . . . are well treated." The following year it reported, "This country again opened its doors to the oppressed." At the end of 1944, a Quaker representative could justly laud Portugal's treatment of Jewish refugees.[5]

Portuguese governmental reactions to Jewish refugees add an important dimension to the word "neutrality" as nations understood it in the 1940s. Several countries besides Portugal, such as Spain, Sweden, Switzerland, Ireland, and Turkey, declared "neutrality" in the midst of the war, basing their status on the 1907 Hague Convention forbidding military help to either side, but allowing noncombatants to trade with both sides. None of the declarations in 1907 referred to refugees. Portugal's behavior as a noncombatant meant carefully maneuvering between the Allies and the Axis with regard to trade. And yet Portugal admitted tens of thousands of refugees fleeing the Axis—silently (and ambivalently) challenging the 1907 definition of "neutrality." Of all neutral nations, Portugal accepted the most Jews. One grateful refugee concluded, "What Portugal did, no other country did."[6]

Aid organizations functioned as unsung heroes during this refugee crisis. A poor country like Portugal, with a population bereft of many essentials, could not have sustained an influx of penniless transmigrants. International and Jewish aid groups came to the rescue. They paid for refugees' basic needs and also negotiated with Portuguese authorities to ensure the safety of refugees. They assisted with food and ship tickets, interceded with governments, and sent supplies to fixed residences. In the process, they saved lives.

These refugee experiences held distinctive meanings for young and old. Young people adjusted more quickly, saw new challenges as adventures, tried new foods, and enjoyed the freedom to roam public spaces that Nazi Europe had denied them. Children and teenagers differed from their elders in their ability to maintain some conventional behaviors, such as attending school or heading to a local movie theater. They more easily retained optimism, looked forward, and appeared more flexible. Still, older teenagers acknowledged the trauma of fleeing familiar surroundings and being forced to take on adult responsibilities early. In retrospect, Margit Meissner reflected that she had "had no adolescence" and "grew up from one day to the next." Her time in Portugal stamped the rest of her life: "Being a refugee [was the] fundamental formative experience of my life without any doubt. The most important facet of who I am. . . . I started this emigration . . . as one person and I came out another person."[7]

Older refugees, their universe in turmoil, spent seemingly endless hours in cafés, those "meeting [places] of refugees from all over the world." After "applying for visas to go anywhere," they sustained communities of waiting in cafés, sharing feelings and information.[8] As they slowly sipped their strong coffee, they revealed the estrangement they felt from their old worlds, their efforts at figuring out their new environments, and their irrepressible distress—but also hopes—about the future.

Jewish women and men experienced a fluctuation in gender roles that had begun in their homelands. There, as men faced more physical danger, women took on serious role reversals. They intervened for men with governmental officials, often acted as breadwinners, and exerted enormous energy to get husbands and sons out of concentration camps. During their time in Portugal, traditional gender roles also made little sense, but extreme role reversals subsided. Both women and men had lost status and the comforts of home, and both genders pleaded with police, stood in consulate lines, and stretched tight budgets. The stereotypes of women as more emotional, more subject to panic and grief than men no longer held fast.[9] Men and women shared these feelings, although they might have expressed them differently. And although women had also left full lives and loved ones behind and struggled to maintain themselves in Portugal, apprehensive of what was to come, they rarely felt a career loss as men did or suffered as much from their diminished public status.

The strangeness and disbelief with which men and women, old and young, approached their fate as refugees gradually turned into uneasy acceptance. While in Lisbon, many had time—too much time—to reassess their identities. They had become refugees. Within the limited emotional and cultural spaces available to them, they created makeshift communities and safe havens: letters kept relationships with loved ones alive as long as possible, and cafés offered new connections. Practicing a hard-won perseverance while lining up to appeal to welfare organizations and consulates, they refined some of the skills they might need in new lands for which they had inadequate language, few skills, and even less money.

Life in limbo has at its core anxiety and fear, but also courage and resilience. Most refugees in Portugal showed strength and stamina as they faced unimagined challenges. For them, Lisbon emerged as a site of temporality and transition, a "no-man's-land" between a painful past and a hopeful future.[10]

Epilogue

The story of Jewish refugees in Portugal exemplifies the terrible odysseys of many refugees who fled before and after them. Since a focus on feelings opens an unusual lens onto the hardships of all refugees, I hope that this history of refugees' daily lives and emotions can add to studies of refugee crises, whether historical or contemporary. Even if each refugee crisis is historically specific, studying refugees' feelings helps transform statistics into people, faceless masses into men and women, boys and girls. Individual stories can help personalize refugee crises.

Studying refugees' feelings helps us understand them as individuals with a treasured past and a precarious present. When the public or the media discuss refugees in transit, they often concentrate on refugees' current identity rather than on what came before: the homes they fled, the families in which they grew up, the careers they pursued, or their civic and emotional attachments to their homelands. They can all too easily miss the obvious: most refugees would stay home if they could, rather than flee persecution over treacherous terrain to seek asylum in unwelcoming places. In 1951, the Refugee Convention of the United Nations classified a refugee as someone who "owing to a well-founded fear of being persecuted for reasons of race, religion, nationality, membership of a particular social group or political opinion, is outside the country of his nationality and is unable, or owing to such fear, is unwilling to avail himself of the protection of that country; or who, not having a nationality and being outside the country of his former habitual residence as a result of such events, is unable or, owing to such fear, is unwilling to return to it." We need Warsan Shire, the first Young Poet Laureate of London, to explain this even more strikingly: "no one leaves home unless / home is the mouth of a shark." She emphasizes that one leaves home only when "home won't let you stay."[11]

Focusing on individuals gives us entrée into their era, whether in the 1940s or today. There are significant differences, of course. First, the Nazis dubbed Jews their enemy par excellence even as they persecuted communists, Roma, homosexuals, physically and mentally disabled individuals, and others who did not fit their political or racial ambitions. By contrast, at the time of this writing, more than 65.3 million people, the "highest level of displacement on record," have fled their homes. Not generally targets of their own governments because of their putative racial identities, they are escaping from conflicts, wars, and terrorism. Half of them are children.[12] Second, numbers matter. Hundreds of thousands of Jews tried to find safety across the Atlantic, although countless were turned away. The millions today overwhelm nations willing to absorb them and create resistance to acceptance in other nations. Their numbers stun the organizations attempting to assist them. Third, the

Jewish refugee crisis and the Holocaust did not make major headlines in most Western papers, which saw reports of those atrocities as "beyond belief." Today's crisis, however, appears daily in traditional newspapers and journals, and is amplified on television news, Internet websites, and social media. Additionally, refugees lived very differently in the 1940s than they do today. In Portugal, Jewish and nonsectarian aid organizations provided shelter in houses and apartments, offered sufficient (though not ample) food, and gave ship tickets to those who had run out of money. Most of these Jewish refugees were privileged compared with today's refugees, who often travel in flimsy boats and dangerous vehicles and who, upon arriving at a safe destination, make do in plastic tents on the streets of Paris, in crowded makeshift shelters in a dismantled Berlin airport, or out in the open after the French government razed the "camp" at Calais and forbade charities to offer tents to refugees. Millions of others live in camps under "temporary protection" in Turkey or Jordan, or continue their seemingly endless treks away from harm.[13] Finally, Jewish refugees escaped from western and eastern Europe to the Iberian Peninsula and later farther west, finding languages, cultures, and religions fairly familiar to them. Today's refugees linger in camps, and the longer it takes to find a new home, "the tougher and tougher [it is] for refugees to survive . . . unite their families and begin to rebuild their lives."[14] Those who do manage to find safety come from entirely different parts of the world with languages, religions, and cultures often misunderstood or even vilified in Europe and the Western Hemisphere.

Similarities exist too. The epigraphs at the beginning of each chapter highlight a particular moment in a refugee's odyssey. They could have come from the memoirs and letters I used. But they come, instead, as mentioned in the preface, from refugees today, quoted in newspapers or by aid organizations. Their voices, like those from the 1940s, express frustration with their own idleness, appreciate help, and yearn for families back home. Then and now, refugees risked their lives to escape death. Then and now, we find widespread distress but also surprising energy, dislocation but also persistence. We also find community making, whether in cafés at the Rossio in Lisbon then or on Sonnenallee in Berlin now, where Syrian refugees make friends while sharing food that reminds them of Damascus.[15] There are many parallels.

Governmental reactions to refugees display resemblances as well. We have seen the Portuguese government's ambivalence toward refugees and its people's generous embrace of them. Similarly, today the United States and many European governments—with Germany a major exception—resist an influx of homeless and distraught individuals and families, even as they tolerate or instigate right-wing nativism. And yet large swaths of public opinion in these countries welcome refugees. In the United States, governmental bans targeting refugees from certain Muslim countries provoked mass demonstrations against the policy at airports in the winter of 2017.[16]

The United States played a major role then and continues to do so. The Great Depression had caused sustained, widespread joblessness in the country, and its workers feared job competition in a stalled economy. Today, too, we hear that immigrants may squeeze Americans out of jobs or lower their wages by working for less. This despite the country not being in a depression, unemployment levels at record lows, and evidence that immigrants are "integral to the nation's economic growth." In the 1930s and 1940s, "wariness toward refugees . . . outweighed sympathy" in the United States. Then, opponents of Jewish immigration, afraid of "Trojan horses" who might undermine their societies, dubbed them "so-called Jewish refugees," "communists," or "Nazis." Nowadays, politicians seeking to stir up anti-immigrant fears and cater to their white supremacist base cast Latino immigrants as criminals and Muslim immigrants as "terrorists" or, once again, "Trojan horses." "They're dangerous and different" grew into a refrain then and now.[17]

Bureaucratic obstructionism plagued refugees in the 1940s and does so today, especially tormenting those fleeing from war, who often had no time to gather birth certificates, citizenship papers, visas, or other such documents. Then and now, refugees learned that documents mattered—and matter—far more than the individual. And they all shared the anxiety and boredom of waiting for unseen bureaucrats to determine their fates. In the 1940s, a German political refugee spoke out for refugees then and now: "We are the victims, without rights, without passports, without a fatherland, the burdensome foreigners, whom one arrests and maligns. . . . We are really nothing but sand strewn by the winds of history."[18]

Notes

Abbreviations

Archives

AFSC, Phila.	American Friends Service Committee Archives, Philadelphia, Foreign Service, Country Portugal. For more AFSC files, see USHMM, below.
Andover-Harvard	Andover-Harvard Theological Library
CAHJP	Central Archives for the History of the Jewish People, Jerusalem
	Two major collections within the Lisbon Jewish Community Collection:
	Secção, CAHJP: Secção de Refugiados (Refugee Section)
	Comissão, CAHJP: Comissão Portuguesa de Assistência aos Judeus Refugiados (Portuguese Commission to Assist Jewish Refugees)
Digibaeck	Leo Baeck Institute, digital archive
DLA Marbach	Deutsches Literatur Archiv Marbach, Germany
Estoril Museum	Espaço Memória dos Exílios, Estoril, Portugal
FVA	Fortunoff Video Archive for Holocaust Testimonies, Yale University Library
	This archive truncates the last name of an interviewee.
Houghton	Manuscripts by various authors in the collection titled "My Life in Germany Before and After 1933," BMS Ger 91, 1940, Houghton Library, Harvard University.

JDC   American Jewish Joint Distribution Committee
                             Archives, New York City Records, 1933–45. Many
                             of the records consulted for this book refer to
                             Records of the AJJDC, Countries: Portugal
                             general 1933; 1939–42, file 896 or 897; cited as file 896
                             (or 897), JDC, with the proper folder and document
                             numbers.

JHI   Jewish Historical Institute, Warsaw
                                 Its collection of forty-five postcards sent from the
                                 Warsaw ghetto to Lisbon is posted at cbj.jhi.pl/
                                 collections/658182.

JLC, Tamiment   Jewish Labor Committee Collection, Tamiment
                             Library and Robert F. Wagner Labor Archives,
                             New York University

LBI   Leo Baeck Institute, archives, New York City

MJH   Museum of Jewish Heritage, New York City
                                 Lisbon Coll., MJH: Letters to Lisbon: Gift of
                                 Oscar Schreyer, Yaffa Eliach Collection, donated
                                 by the Center for Holocaust Studies, Museum of
                                 Jewish Heritage

NARA   National Archives and Records Administration,
                             College Park, Maryland
                                 Draft Histories, RG-59, NARA: War History
                                 Branch, Draft Histories of Embassies (entry
                                 A1-716), box 29, "Lisbon," 1946 August,
                                 RG-59, 46

Portuguese   Arquivo Nacional da Torre do Tombo, Lisbon
   National Archive

RIHS   Rhode Island Historical Society, Providence

RSCL OxOn   Refugee Studies Centre Library, University of
                             Oxford, at Forced Migration Online

Shoah   University of Southern California Shoah
                             Foundation, Visual History Archive, Los Angeles

USC   Unitarian Universalist Service Committee,
                             "Holocaust Rescue and Relief," at Andover-Harvard
                             Theological Library, digitized at library.hds.harvard.
                             edu/collections/digital/holocaust-rescue-and-relief

USHMM   United States Holocaust Memorial Museum,
                             Washington, DC

AFSC, 2002.296: American Friends Service Committee Refugee Assistance Case Files. The overall collection record for 2002.296 is at https://collections.ushmm.org/search/catalog/irn42486.

"Church Mouse": Martha Sharp, "Church Mouse to the White House," box 30, folder 3, RG67.017, accession number 2010.180

Goldstajn: Fridrih Goldstajn, file 7060, AFSC, 2002.96

Wiener Lib.	Wiener Library for the Study of the Holocaust and Genocide, London
WRB	War Refugee Board. Microfilmed archives at the USHMM.
Yale	Manuscripts and Archives, Yale University Library Schauffler, Yale: Schauffler Family Papers, MS 1389, box 55 "Refugees"
YIVO	YIVO Institute for Jewish Research, New York City YIVO, RG 249: RG 249 (German-Jewish Children's Aid collection, 1933–53). This archive truncates names.

HIAS-HICEM archives: series I, file no. XII-Portugal A-2, "Report of the HIAS-ICA Activities in Lisbon, July 1, 1940–Dec. 18, 1941," finding guide no. 245.4, HICEM/HIAS Lisbon Coll., series 1–12, call no. 245, microfilms 15. 30–15.36. Cited as 245.4, section I, file no. XII-Portugal A-2, microfilms 15.30–15.36, HIAS-HICEM, YIVO.

Journals and Wire Services

AHR	*American Historical Review*
AJH	*American Jewish History*
AJYB	*American Jewish Year Book*
JC	*Jewish Chronicle*
JTA	Jewish Telegraphic Agency
JSS	*Jewish Social Studies*
LBIYB	*Leo Baeck Institute Year Book*

Unless otherwise indicated, all translations are by the author.

Introduction

1. Perhaps 7,000–10,000 Jews traveled through Morocco. My thanks to Daniel Schroeter for this estimate (email to the author, Mar. 16, 2017); see also S. Miller, "Passage to Casablanca."

2. For the "largest number," see Y. Bauer, *American Jewry*, 47; "100,000" in "Review of the Year 5704," *AJYB* 45:238. Varying wildly, the numbers lie somewhere between Yehuda Bauer's estimate of 40,000 Jews passing through Portugal in 1940–41 (61) and the 100,000 suggested by Michael Marrus (*Unwanted*, 265). Avraham Milgram argues for around 15,000 (*Portugal, Salazar, and the Jews*, 61). Jewish sources, however, cannot tell the whole story, since Jews also passed through Portugal without the assistance of Jewish organizations. Some left Lisbon by air at their own expense (Weber, *Lisbon Route*, 13). Using Jewish and non-Jewish sources, Irene Pimentel suggests 60,000–80,000 refugees ("Refugiados," 103), and Patrik von zur Mühlen suggests 80,000 (*Fluchtweg*, 124, 151–52). Zur Mühlen estimates that Jews accounted for 90 percent of all refugees and states that German Jews made up about two-thirds of Jewish refugees. For estimates of 200,000, see Wriggins (*Picking Up the Pieces*, 18) and "200,000 Have Fled via Lisbon," *New York Times*, Aug. 19, 1941, 4.

3. Following their treks closely, but not addressing their emotions, Debórah Dwork and Robert Jan van Pelt describe refugee reactions and "emigration psychosis" in *Flight from the Reich*. For examples of adaptation to new countries, see Lowenstein, *Frankfurt on the Hudson*; Berghahn, *German-Jewish Refugees in England*; M. Kaplan, *Dominican Haven*.

4. Knowles et al., *Geographies of the Holocaust*. For how historians use space as an analytical category, see Akbari et al., "AHR Conversation." For space and emotions, see Davidson and Bondi, "Spatialising Affect"; Anderson and Smith, "Emotional Geographies"; see also the journal *Emotion, Space and Society*.

5. These were not "Jewish spaces" as such, but became "Jewish" at certain times, especially in 1940 and 1941; see Lässig and Rürup, *Space and Spatiality*.

6. Hagit Lavsky defines refugees as people "forced to leave under immediate threat to their lives," and argues that German Jews did not become refugees until late 1938 (*German-Jewish Diaspora*, 3–4). I maintain that relentless governmental, social, and personal persecution, as well as physical assaults, caused anguish, fear, and refugee flight. Violence under the Reich increased Jewish suicides even in 1933; see Goeschel, *Suicide in Nazi Germany*, ch. 3.

7. Yehuda Bauer cites 8,000 for the end of 1940, a figure that includes only people supported by the JDC (*American Jewry*, 47). The figure of 14,000 comes from d'Esaguy, *Repaying a Debt* and JDC, file 896 (2 of 3), June 4, 1941, 2; zur Mühlen lists 14,000 for Nov. 1940 (*Fluchtweg*, 152).

8. The sum comprises 21.3 million refugees, 3.2 million asylum seekers, and 40.8 million people internally displaced within their own countries (as of June 2016); see "Refugees and Migrants" at http://refugeesmigrants.un.org/%E2%80%98unprecedented%E2%80%99-65-million-people-displaced-war-and-persecution-2015-%E2%80%93-un; "Refugee Planet," commondreams.org/news/2016/06/20/refugee-planet-there-have-never-been-many-displaced-people-earth; Wyman, *Paper Walls*.

9. Gemie, Reid, and Humbert, *Outcast Europe*. They look at "little peoples" (255), but not specifically Jewish refugees.

10. Those refugees who wrote memoirs for "My Life in Germany" between 1939 and 1940 had entered a contest initiated at Harvard (Liebersohn and Schneider, *My Life in Germany*). For terms like "refugee," see Arendt, "We Refugees" (1994).

11. For the struggle to forget, see Nutkiewicz, "Shame, Guilt, and Anguish." Interviews present their own set of problems; see Langer, *Holocaust Testimonies;* Brison, *Aftermath;* Waxman, *Writing the Holocaust;* Shenker, *Reframing Holocaust Testimony.*

12. Horváth, Thomassen, and Wydra, introduction.

13. Baumel, "Gender and Family Studies," 111. For refugees, see Milgram, *Portugal, Salazar, and the Jews;* M. Kaplan, *Dominican Haven;* Ephraim, *Escape to Manila.*

14. Matt, "Current Emotion Research"; Ikegami, "Emotions."

15. Cole, *Holocaust Landscapes;* the quoted material is from Knowles et al., *Geographies of the Holocaust*, 1, 4. On the "spatial turn" more generally, see Kümin and Usborne, "At Home."

16. Knowles et al., *Geographies of the Holocaust*, 4; Cole, *Holocaust Landscapes.*

17. Knowles et al., *Geographies of the Holocaust*, 3; Cole, *Holocaust Landscapes*, 99–126. The mention of railroad cars is in Cole, *Holocaust Landscapes*, 2.

18. Brauch, Lipphardt, and Nocke, *Jewish Topographies;* quoted material in Katz, *How Emotions Work*, 1.

19. Tillinger, *Aufbau*, Sept. 6, 1940, 1. The *Aufbau* was a New York–based German-Jewish newspaper.

20. Most liberal Western states tried to—and did—send some refugees back to Germany, and when a public outcry arose, they simply increased their border

patrols radically to prevent refugees, even those with visas, from entering (Caestecker and Scuto, "Benelux"). Thank you to Frank Caestecker for further explanations (email to the author, Oct. 20, 2017). Switzerland, too, turned away some 20,000 refugee Jews. What is not as well known is that even Denmark deported some Jews (Rünitz, *Danmark*).

21. There is a vast literature on this subject, from Niederland's "Clinical Observations" (1968) to more recent work such as Papadopoulos, "Refugees, Trauma, and Adversity" (2007). Quoted material in Papadopoulos, "Refugees," 301.

22. "Historians" in Reddy, *Navigation of Feelings*, 315–20, and Plamper, *History of Emotions*, 12; "female" in Biess, "Feelings in the Aftermath," 31; Anderson and Smith, "Emotional Geographies," 7; Ikegami, "Emotions," 340; "masculinity" in Kessel, "Gefühle."

23. Grossman, "10 Questions."

24. See Stearns and Stearns, "Emotionology" and Peter Gay's five-volume series *The Bourgeois Experience*. For hundreds of works published since 2008, see "Institute Publications: History of Emotions (2008–)," https://www.mpib-berlin.mpg.de/en/research/history-of-emotions/publications; see also Frevert, "History of Emotions." Plamper showed that in the field of experimental psychology, specialists offered ninety-two definitions of emotions between 1872 and 1980 (*History of Emotions*, 11). Frevert underlined the variability of the concept and the importance of cultural and historical context; see "Defining Emotions" in *Emotional Lexicons*, 4, 10, 24–31; see also Gammerl, "Felt Distances," and Ikegami, "Emotions."

25. I am following Plamper's example and not using "affect," which he describes as a term "influenced by neurosciences," one that "has assumed the idea of physical, prelinguistic, unconscious emotion" (*History of Emotions*, 12).

26. The idea that genes may have a memory is a shortcut for asking whether trauma can be passed down transgenerationally through genetic expression; see Shonkoff, Boyce, and McEwen, "Neuroscience," and Rothstein, Cai, and Marchant, "Ghost in Our Genes."

27. Frevert, "Gefühle"; Lerner et al., "Emotion and Decision Making," 799, and the bibliography for the article, 817–23; see also Reddy, "Self and Emotions"; Benthien, Fleig, and Kasten, *Emotionalität*, 9.

28. "Stress" in #213 (card), from Siegfried Israel (last name unclear) in Berlin to Leopold Bloch, Mar. 25, 1942, in Lisbon Coll., MJH. For the reference to gambling, see Anita Walker, interview by the author, Brooklyn, N.Y., Dec. 26, 2016 (hereafter cited as Walker interview). Her father told her not to

"judge" the ones who went to the casino, since they had lost families; see also Lässig and Rürup, "What Made a Space."

29. "Same emotions" in Berlant, "Thinking About Feeling Historical," 4; "epochs" in Plamper, *History of Emotions,* ch. 2; Rosenwein, "Problems and Methods."

30. Zur Mühlen, *Fluchtweg,* 124, 151–52. Blum and Rei claim that 45 percent of Jewish refugees in Portugal came from Germany, 4 percent from Austria, 14 percent from Poland, and 7 percent from France ("Coming to America," table 4).

31. "Cultural contexts" in Plamper, "History of Emotions." "Fate" was a term used by many Germans but also by German Jews after World War I to affirm their group identity (Baehr, *Caesarism, Charisma, and Fate,* 128).

32. There is growing research in this area; see, for example, Barak and Szor, "Posttraumatic Stress," and Gillick, *They Had a Country.*

33. Pellew, "Home Office," 369; Marrus, *Unwanted;* "too many to count" in Crossette, "Century of Refugees."

34. A vast literature exists on the topic of refugees from the 1930s to the present, focusing on all refugees as well as on Jews. For an overview, see Dwork and van Pelt, *Flight from the Reich,* 382–84.

35. This figure is for "Germans" after the annexation of Austria; see "Refugees," in Holocaust Encyclopedia, USHMM, at ushmm.org/wlc/en/article.php?ModuleId=10005139.

36. Strauss, "Jewish Emigration from Germany, I." As many as 10,000 may have returned because of their inability to find work in safe countries. In early 1935, the German government threatened to arrest them if they returned, ending the return migration (Strauss, "Jewish Emigration from Germany, I," 357).

37. Meyer, *Fatal Balancing Act,* 29, 30–31, 68; "coffers" in M. Kaplan, *Dignity and Despair,* ch. 2; Barkai, *From Boycott to Annihilation,* 173.

38. "Money to leave" in Barkai, *From Boycott to Annihilation,* 140; "eastern lands" in Y. Bauer, *American Jewry,* 48. Around 8,500 Jews still managed to escape after Oct. 1941 (Strauss, "Jewish Emigration from Germany, I," 327). Beate Meyer cites Herbert Strauss's figures but also offers ones larger than those Strauss believed to be true: 1933–35, 112,500; 1936–38, 101,400; 1939, 68,000, with a total up to Oct. 1941 of 352,696 (*Fatal Balancing Act,* 90n87). Strauss came up with the following figures: 1933–35, 81,000; 1936–38, 88,000; 1939–Oct. 1941, 101,000, totaling 270,000 ("Jewish Emigration from Germany, II," 326).

39. M. Kaplan, *Dignity and Despair*, 118, 189. In Austria, too, at the end of 1940, two-thirds of those remaining were women, of whom 80 percent were older than forty-five (Y. Bauer, *American Jewry*, 59).

40. For Austria and Czechoslovakia, see Laqueur, *Holocaust Encyclopedia*, 49, 78. On Vienna, see Joseph Loewenherz, letter of Jan. 9, 1941, from Lisbon, Joseph Loewenherz Coll., AR25055, Digibaeck.

41. Diamond, *Fleeing Hitler*, 30, 35–36, 150, 163. She estimates that there were 1,800,000 Belgians on the road.

42. Gold, *Crossroads Marseilles*, 144. On July 14, 1938, Germany's Denaturalization Law revoked the citizenship of Jews naturalized in Germany. On Sept. 27, 1940, Germans decreed that Jews who left the Occupied Zone could not return (Diamond, *Fleeing Hitler*, 157, 165). On November 26, 1941, the Eleventh Decree to the Reich Citizenship Law deprived any German Jew outside Germany's borders of citizenship.

43. Fry, *Surrender on Demand*, 16.

44. I am not engaging in the debate about whether there is a "refugee experience." Those in Lisbon referred to themselves as refugees, although distinctions surely existed then and today; see Malkki, "Refugees and Exile."

45. Arendt, *Origins of Totalitarianism*, 295–96; Werner Goldberg folder (written Mar. 1941), Lisbon AF series, AFSC, 2002.296, USHMM; see also DeGooyer et al., *Right to Have Rights*.

46. Bourdieu, *Distinction*.

47. "Life or freedom" in Caestecker and Moore, *Refugees from Nazi Germany*, 7, 249, 315–16, quoted material on 316. There were also Jewish political refugees. "Aversion to refugees" in Reginbogin, *Faces of Neutrality*, 21.

48. France, where refugees from Syria, Turkey, Bulgaria, Hungary, Russia, Italy, Spain, and Armenian territories had found asylum during and after World War I, placed "first among refugee-receiving countries," accepting 25,000 refugees from Germany in 1933 alone (Dwork and van Pelt, *Flight from the Reich*, 22, and Caron, *Uneasy Asylum*, 2).

49. Dwork and van Pelt, *Flight from the Reich*, 92–94. European neighbors took 25 percent, and Palestine absorbed 15 percent.

50. "Spy hysteria" in Strauss, "Jewish Emigration from Germany, I," 349–50. Labor unions concerned about competition also supported restrictions. The 1924 act targeted those from southern and eastern Europe and virtually all Asians; see FitzGerald and Cook-Martin, *Culling the Masses*.

51. Strauss, "Jewish Emigration from Germany, I," 349–50; the quoted phrases are from Laughlin, *Immigration Control Law*, 6, 100.

52. Even after the violence of the Austrian annexation, 67 percent of Americans did not want to let in more refugees. The United States had eleven million unemployed that year (Harwood, "American Public Opinion," 202).

53. Estorick, "Evian Conference," 136; Laffer, "Jewish Trail of Tears"; "declined the invitation" in Milgram, *Portugal, Salazar, and the Jews,* 60n3.

54. Welch, "American Opinion Toward Jews," 14.

55. Percentages of the quotas filled for German and Austrian immigrants to the United States are as follows: 1933, 5.3 percent; 1934, 13.7 percent; 1935, 20.2 percent; 1936, 24.3 percent; 1937, 42.1 percent (Strauss, "Jewish Emigration from Germany, II," 359).

56. "Wrong one" in M. Kaplan, *Dignity and Despair,* 59, from Mally Dienemann, 25, Houghton; "so is every heart" in Dembitzer, *Visas for America,* 201.

57. Figures for the United States are in Laffer, "Jewish Trail of Tears," 388. He gathered data from 1933 to 1945 and assumed that additional thousands of Jewish refugees found shelter in places like South Africa, Japan, Spain, and Portugal.

58. Laffer, "Jewish Trail of Tears." His statistics included, in addition, Canada 5,000; Australia 15,000; Switzerland 22,000; Shanghai 18,000; and Sweden 12,000, for a total of 565,000. To enter Great Britain, 14,000 Jewish women agreed to work as domestic servants (Dwork and van Pelt, *Flight from the Reich,* 150). Even some in transit through the United States to Canada faced hostility, since many Americans saw them as enemies rather than as victims; see Les Perreaux, "Serpa Pinto: Voyages of Life and Death," *Toronto Globe and Mail,* Apr. 24, 2009, theglobeandmail.com/news/national/serpa-pinto-voyages-of-life-and-death/article1196753/?page=all.

59. See Steedman, *Dust,* for some healthy skepticism about the "truth" in archives; Montaigne, *Essays,* ch. 4.

60. Historians of early modern history have expanded the category of "ego-documents" to include judicial, administrative, and economic records that give a glimpse into a person's self-understanding, fears, or values; see Lindemann, "Sources in Social History," and Dekker, "Egodocumenten"; see also Schulze, *Ego-Dokumente,* 28; Rutz, "Ego-Dokument."

61. Garbarini, *Numbered Days;* Zim, *Consolations of Writing.*

62. The journal *History and Memory,* begun in 1989, contributed to this discussion. For a bibliography of the topic, see Ollila, *Historical Perspectives on Memory,* particularly her article "History as Memory and Memory as History"; see also LaCapra, *History and Memory.*

63. "Agency of ordinary people" in M. Kaplan, "Revealing and Concealing"; "additional information" in Zalc and Bruttmann, "Microhistory of the Holocaust," 4; "they are telling" in Fritzsche, *Life and Death*, 9.

64. "Raw material" in Le Goff, *History and Memory*, xi; "(and healthy) forgetting" in Stern, *Five Germanys*, 10; "experience of an emotion" in Plamper, *History of Emotions*, 290.

65. Stanislawski, *Autobiographical Jews;* N. Miller, "Ethics of Betrayal," 44.

66. Frevert, "History of Emotions," 79; Eustace et al., "AHR Conversation." Jack Katz warns that scholars actually study how people talk about their emotions, not the emotions as such (*How Emotions Work*, 4).

67. Kolmar quoted in Jäger, *Gertrud Kolmar*, 57. "Anxiety for another" in Bourke, *Fear*, 6–9, 73–75, 90, 289–90, esp. 190.

68. "Heart of language" in Ochs and Shieffelin, "Language Has a Heart," 8–10, 15, esp. 22. See also Krauss, Chen, and Chawla, "Nonverbal Behavior," esp. the bibliography; Ikegami, "Emotions," 337.

69. For a bibliography of studies of the connections between psychological suffering and physical reactions, see Zajonc and McIntosh, "Emotions Research"; "mouth was very dry" in Stanton (née Sandzer), *Escape from the Inferno*, 133–34; Demos, *Unredeemed Captive*, 108.

70. Friedländer, *Years of Extermination*, xxv.

71. "Continuity and optimism" in Berlant, "Thinking About Feeling Historical," 4; "right to eat" in M. Kaplan, *Dignity and Despair*, 61.

72. M. Kaplan, *Dignity and Despair*, ch. 5.

73. Jewish responses to war may also have been less gendered; see Adler and Aleksiun, "Seeking Relative Safety."

74. Meissner, *Margit's Story*, 118.

75. For Alexievich's work, see Gessen, "Memory Keeper."

76. M. Kaplan, *Dignity and Despair*, 7; "worthy of public notice" in Norich, "Family Singer," 99.

77. Histories of emotions, too, reflect on many lives to make more general points; see, for example, Stearns and Stearns, *Anger*, and P. Stearns, *Jealousy*.

1. Escaping Terror and the Terror of Escaping

Epigraph: Um Eddine, age thirty-two, from Daraa, Syria, "Syrian Refugees: In Their Own Words," *Guardian*, Apr. 2, 2012, https://www.theguardian.com/world/2012/apr/02/syrian-refugees-their-own-words.

1. Zur Mühlen, *Fluchtweg*, 93.

2. "Refugee families" in Dr. Robert Kauffmann to James McDonald, Oct. 17, 1934, in McDonald, *Advocate for the Doomed*, 512–13.

3. "No antisemitic feelings" in Pimentel and Heinrich, *Judeus*, 34; "cork and sardines" in interview with Ruth Arons, in Schnabel, *Lisbon: Harbour of Hope*.

4. The figure for Portuguese Jews in Lisbon is in d'Esaguy, *Repaying a Debt*, 1, and JDC, file 896 (2 of 3). Zur Mühlen estimates that there were about 1,000 in Lisbon, Porto, Far, and Braganza combined (*Fluchtweg*, 125).

5. Milgram, *Portugal, Salazar, and the Jews*, 26–33. The 3,000 Jews lived among a Portuguese population of approximately 7 million. Jewish statistics did not include small clusters of conversos, who lived in northern Portugal (Robinson, *Contemporary Portugal*, 31). Converso Jews also lived in Belmonte, where their descendants emerged from secrecy in the 1990s and a museum about them opened in 2017; see Rachel Nolan, "After 500 Years in Hiding, Jews Bring Prosperity to Iberian Town," *Forward*, Jan. 2, 2008, http://forward.com/news/12391/after-500-years-in-hiding-jews-bring -prosperity-t-01065.

6. D'Esaguy, *Repaying a Debt*, 1, 12; The first chair of COMASSIS was Adolfo Benarus, also a leader of Lisbon's Jewish community and Zionist Federation; the figure 650 in Leshem, "Rescue Efforts," *LBIYB*, 236–37.

7. AJJDC, *World Refugee Organizations*, 66; the list of small businesses is in *Korrespondenzblatt über Auswanderungs-und Siedlungswesen*, Aug. 1934, 12; Sept. 1935, 22; see also Bitton, oral history (1990), RG-50.030*0027, USHMM, (shoemaker), and Pimentel and Ninhos, *Salazar, Portugal*, 467 (dressmakers); the reference to Jews being allowed to work for Portuguese firms is in Joseph Schwartz to Philip Conard, memo, Feb. 14, 1944, doc. 404 in Sutters, *Archives of the Holocaust*, 2:492, and "Portugal and the Refugee Problem," 1, JDC, file 897 (2 of 2).

8. The reference to Jews working as representatives of German or American companies is in Kalischer, *Vom Konzentrationslager*, 151, and zur Mühlen, *Fluchtweg*, 122–23. Kalischer changed his name to "Howard Heinz Wisla" when immigrating to the United States from Palestine. His memoirs and journal under the name Wisla are digitized on Digibaeck. Pimentel writes that after April 1939, only foreigners who had passed the equivalency exams by the previous February could practice medicine ("Refugiados," 103).

9. "Laundry in Porto," along with other examples, is in Pimentel and Ninhos, *Salazar, Portugal*, 467; see also Hess, "Was Portugal," 178.

10. The account of the Blum family in Portugal is in Fritz Blum, "The Story of My Parents' Lives, 1881–1992," 12–17, Digibaeck (hereafter cited as Blum, "My Parents' Lives"). They left in April 1941.

11. Irene Shomberg (née Westheimer), interview by the author, Dec. 6, 2013, New York City (hereafter cited as Shomberg interview).

12. Hess, "Was Portugal," 174–76. The article refers to Wolf and Anna Delmonte and family; see also Correia, "Abschied von Europa," 28.

13. "*Bolas de Berlin*" in Gouveia, "Lisbon"; "Hungarian pastries" in Pimentel and Heinrich, *Judeus*, 166; Davidsohn's shop is in Heinrich, Winterberg, and Kirkamm, *Lissabon*, 11.

14. Wakman's watch business comes from Walker interview; the Augusts' story is in Blaufuks, *Under Strange Skies*. They remained in Portugal for the rest of their lives. Brodheim's Montessori school is in Antunes, *Judeus em Portugal*, 339–53. Montessori methods had been introduced in a Lisbon neighborhood in 1920, but the Salazar regime generally opposed them for being too liberal (Sapega, *Consensus and Debate*, 94–95).

15. Losa in Pimentel and Ninhos, *Salazar, Portugal*, 467; for German refugees working in Portuguese films, see https://www.berlinale.de/en/archiv/jahresarchive/2013/02_programm_2013/02_Filmdatenblatt_2013_20132252.html#tab=filmStills. Thanks to Nicholas Baer for alerting me to the film *Gado Bravo*. Schwerin's story is in a written statement by him, Lisbon, Aug. 25, 1944, USC, Exec. Director, bMS 16007_Box 20_folder 10, RG-67.028, USHMM.

16. D'Esaguy, *Repaying a Debt*, 1; Brodheim in Antunes, *Judeus em Portugal*, 352.

17. Hess, "Denn unser Leben." Hess interviewed Noemi Gelehrter Ricca Gonçalves (born 1919, Berlin).

18. Obtaining Portuguese nationality was possible because of an accord signed by Germany and Portugal in 1926 (Pimentel, "Refugiados," 103). A fake marriage, for example, gave a seventy-year-old woman the right to live in Portugal; see Hermine Shocron, AFSC, 2002.296, USHMM; the figure of 600 Jewish refugees is in zur Mühlen, *Fluchtweg*, 123; mostly German and Polish Jews came in the first wave (Correia, "Abschied von Europa," 28–29).

19. "Vistos feitos por russos, polacos, heimatlos, indivíduos de nacionalidade diferente do país que os documentou, assírios e libaneses": see nos. 3 and 8, Apr. 7 and 18, 1936, in MC 480, Sector PVDE, Lisboa, no.F. 13, no PT 7/21 NT 352, Portuguese National Archive.

20. The recommendation for mandatory visas is in Correia, "Abschied von Europa," 31. A few months after November 1938, the civil governor of

Funchal (Madeira) requested that Jews be allowed to remain there because they might stimulate trade and tourism; see civil governor of Funchal, to Ministério do Interior, Gabinete do Ministro, Jan. 29, 1939, MC503 Caixa 61, Liv.3 PV/Fl no.3, p. 8 of file, and from Funchal on Nov. 29, 1938, pp. 11–14 of same file, Portuguese National Archive.

21. For Circular #10, see Pimentel, "Refugiados," 103, and Milgram, *Portugal, Salazar, and the Jews,* 66; the reduction of visa lengths is in Pimentel and Ninhos, "Portugal, Jewish Refugees, and the Holocaust," 104. In spite of Portugal's stricter immigration regulations, a Viennese Jewish paper announced twice in 1939 that Portugal would grant permanent residence to the parents of German refugees who were living in Portugal before March 1938 (*Jüdisches Nachrichtenblatt,* Feb. 10, 1939, 5, and May 12, 1939, 6).

22. Hess, "Denn unser Leben," 62–65.

23. The family's story is in Blum, "My Parents' Lives," 14; the Protestant pastor is in d'Esaguy, *Repaying a Debt,* 13.

24. For Spanish refugees from the civil war, see "Portuguese Recall Wartime Tales of Aid to Their Neighbors," *New York Times,* Oct. 28, 1999, nytimes.com/1999/10/28/world/portuguese-recall-wartime-tales-of-aid-to-their-neighbors.html. Scholars estimate that thirty thousand Spaniards fled to Portugal.

25. "Fascist custody" in Meneses, *Salazar,* 198–99; the *Chicago Tribune* article is quoted in Stelmach, "We Can't Have Reds," 127–28; "anti-Semitic motives" in AJJDC, World *Refugee Organizations,* 66.

26. "German offensive" in *AJYB* 42 (1940–41): 336; Morton, *17 Carnations,* 160; Borden, *Curious George;* Döblin, *Destiny's Journey,* 212.

27. Davidson and Bondi, "Spatialising Affect," 373–74; Anderson and Smith, "Emotional Geographies," 7–10.

28. "Counsellors and suppliants" in Boas, "Shrinking World," 260; Dwork and van Pelt, *Flight from the Reich,* 120.

29. "Bombers overhead" in Sharp, *Journey to Freedom,* 12; Bodley, *Flight into Portugal,* 40; Rudolf Graf (1995), #508, seg. 46 and 48, Shoah.

30. Rony, *This, Too,* 222–23.

31. Bodley, *Flight into Portugal,* 45–46.

32. Cahors in Sharp, *Journey to Freedom,* 13; "place to eat" in Morris Troper to JDC, July 8, 1940, quoted in Y. Bauer, *American Jewry,* 43; Werfel quoted in Abels, *Franz Werfel,* 124.

33. Fry, *Surrender on Demand,* 14; the account of police roundups is in Gold, *Crossroads Marseille,* 232; Gestapo in Fry, *Surrender,* 51.

34. Art. 19 of the Franco-German Armistice of June 25, 1940, available from the Avalon Project, http://avalon.law.yale.edu/wwii/frgearm.asp; "enemies in disguise" in Fry, *Surrender on Demand*, xi.

35. AFSC quoted in Marrus and Paxton, *Vichy France*, 165; Ryan, "Vichy and the Jews," 191.

36. M. Feuchtwanger, "Émigré Life"; L. Feuchtwanger, *Devil in France*, 248–50.

37. Mahler-Werfel, "Alma & Lisbon."

38. Kantorowicz, *Exil*, 187, 228; Marx, *Die Flucht*, 121–22, 150; "the hours sociably" in Christine Morrow, *Abominable Epoch* (private pub. [1972]), 27, quoted in Gemie, Reid, and Humbert, *Outcast Europe*, 122.

39. Waitstill Sharp, 1940, memo of Aug. 13–14, 1940, 6, bMS 16114/4 (63) USC Lisbon, Andover-Harvard, http://nrs.harvard.edu/urn-3:DIV.LIB. USC:4907147?n=18.

40. Bromberger, "Family Flight from Antwerp," 14.

41. Marx, *Die Flucht*, 148.

42. "French ships" in Klein, *Flüchtlingspolitik*, 284. In mid-1941, the British refused passage to one ship and the French blocked two others, all heading for Martinique. The Allies captured other ships, such as the S.S. *Normandie* (in New York Harbor). Sahl, *Das Exil*, 261; "Gibraltar" in Ryan, "Vichy and the Jews," 265.

43. Ships from Spain, irregular and frequently canceled, often stopped at Lisbon. Thank you to Pedro Correa Martín-Arroyo for this information. "Illegal immigration" in Meyer, *Fatal Balancing Act*, 38–40. See also Bilbao, ship leaving as of July 2, 1941, and Gothenburg, ship supposed to leave in mid-Sept. 1941, Legation of Sweden to State Dept., Aug. 19, 1941, and Holocaust and World War II victims records, 1939–45, 1994.A.0342 Reel 48, USHMM.

44. Fittko, *Escape Through the Pyrenees*, 105.

45. Bodley, *Flight into Portugal*, 64.

46. Sharp to Robert Dexter, Aug. 18, 1940, 2, USC Lisbon, Andover-Harvard, bMS 16114/4 (63), http://nrs.harvard.edu/urn-3:DIV.LIB. USC:4907147?n=25.

47. "Traumatic parting" in M. Krauss, *Heimkehr*, 19; "mosaic" in Schlör, "Man Lässt," 102; Hilberg, *Politics of Memory*, 43; Eschelbacher, *Der Zehnte November*, 77, as he left Germany, quoted in Schlör, "Man Lässt," 105n9.

48. For private donors, see Ryan, "Vichy and the Jews," 276. HIAS was founded 1881, and HICEM developed from the merger in 1927 of HIAS, the ICA (the Jewish Colonization Association, based in Paris and acting as a British

charity), and EMIG-Direct (a refugee relocation program in Berlin that closed in 1933). HICEM ended in 1945, and HIAS took over its programs.

49. Mason, *Social Policy,* 242; the figure is for 1938.

50. Oberfinanzdirektion Berlin (Fasanenstrasse), Haupttreuhandstelle Ost, Sonderabt. Altreich, file 10998 (Regina Spindel), USHMM. Spindel had spent RM 2,000 a year earlier to ship home furnishings to Antwerp and on to the United States. Thanks to Martin Dean for bringing this case to my attention.

51. U.S. vice-consul H. Francis Cunningham Jr. to Regina Spindel, in Oberfinanzdirektion Berlin (Fasanenstrasse), Haupttreuhandstelle Ost, Sonderabt. Altreich, file 10998 (Regina Spindel), USHMM; see also Zucker, *In Search of Refuge.*

52. See examples of the forms in the Nordman file or the Henri Gutwirth file, Lisbon AF series, AFSC, 2002.296, USHMM; "tired and harassed" in Michael Wurmbrand, Report of 1940, "Lissabon, die Tür Amerikas zu Europa," 245.4, section I, file no. XII-Portugal-A23, microfilms 15.30–15.36, HIAS-HICEM, YIVO.

53. "Loosened considerably" in Fahrmeir, "Governments and Forgers," 219–20, and in Lucassen, "Many-Headed Monster," 252–55, both in Caplan and Torpey, *Documenting Individual Identity*; "free flow across their borders" in Lucassen, "Many-Headed Monster," 254–55; "enormous increase" in Torpey, "Great War," in Caplan and Torpey, *Documenting Individual Identity,* 257. For Imperial Russian attempts to control Jews through identity documents, see Avrutin, *Jews and the Imperial State.*

54. L. Feuchtwanger, *Devil in France,* 253; Brecht, *Fluchtlingsgespräche,* 7–8; Zweig, *World of Yesterday,* 411.

55. Examples are in R. Kaplan, *Varian and Putzi* (film). Other groups included the Quakers as well as many political, trade union, and Christian groups, although Jewish organizations had handled the "bulk of refugee aid" (Marrus, *Unwanted,* 182).

56. For the necessity of proof of entry, see Ernst Hofeller (1995), #937, "Refugee," 9, 24, LBI. Of the countless such passports with myriad visa stamps, see the one belonging to H. Ginsburg of Belgium, in the Friedman Family Coll., 1996.A.0426, USHMM; Fittko, *Escape Through the Pyrenees,* 94.

57. The prefect of the *département* (unit of local government) around Marseille, the Bouches-du-Rhone, had to issue exit visas. But the central government at Vichy, not the department, decided whether to grant such exit papers to people from Greater Germany, and until January 1941 it refused to do so; see

Klein, *Flüchtlingspolitik,* 284, 290. For the German occupation of Vichy, see Ryan, "Vichy and the Jews," 265, 268, 279; see also Wischnitzer, *Visas to Freedom,* 178–79.

58. For the letters threatening jail, see Kantorowicz, *Exil,* 156–57; "entry visa" in Ryan, *Holocaust and the Jews,* 130.

59. Rony, *This, Too,* 238; Lustig, *Ein Rosenkranz,* 60–61; Bodley, *Flight into Portugal,* 52.

60. W. Gallagher, "See You in Lisbon," 190–92; Felix E. Oppenheim, "Recollections" (Jan. 9, 1993), 23–24, RSCL OxOn.

61. "Forced to strip" in Lustig, *Ein Rosenkranz,* 61; "internal bodily examinations" in Eva Marx, interview (June 1955), Ref: P.III.i no. 105, Wiener Lib.; "Borders meant danger" in M. Krauss, *Heimkehr,* 22–24; Remarque, *Night in Lisbon,* 186. Remarque wrote the book in 1962. Although he had not been in Lisbon, he brilliantly evoked the atmosphere of that time.

62. For Löwenherz's meeting with Brunner, Apr. 12, 1940, see Joseph Loewenherz Coll., AR25055, box 1, folder 6, 846–47, Digibaeck.

63. Zur Mühlen provides the figure of 15,000 refugees in 1940 (*Fluchtweg,* 37). He suggests there were 8,000 for 1941, but the Central Association recorded only 5,945 from November 27, 1940, until the end of October 1941, statistik-des-holocaust.de/Emigration-Bericht2-6a.jpg. Thanks to Beate Meyer for alerting me to this site.

64. The figure for twenty-five transports is in statistik-des-holocaust.de/Emigration-Bericht2-6a.jpg; "prisoners' train" in Herbert Jonas, oral history (1983), 5 RG-50.156*0025, USHMM. It took five days for the trains to go from Vienna to Portugal (Wachstein, *Too Deep Were Our Roots,* 200). For a horrific contrast with trains heading toward extermination camps, see Cole, *Holocaust Landscapes,* 99–126. "Gestapo forced transports" in *Aufbau,* Dec. 20, 1941, Nussbaum-Koch Family Coll., RG-10.255, USHMM; see also "Bericht ueber die Mitteilungen von Frau A.B. geb. Loewengard aus Wiesbaden" (Oct. 1955), DOC REF 047-EA-0500, Ref: P.II.b. no. 166, Wiener Lib. For a similar locked or "sealed" train, see "An Octogenarian's Records of His Life and Experiences as a German Jew," ref. P.II.f.No.972 (1958) [author: M.M., from Freiburg im Breisgau], cited as "An Octogenarian's Records," Wiener Lib.; see also F. Mann, *Drastic Turn of Destiny,* 171 (for trains through 1941), and Bazarov, "HIAS and HICEM," 73.

65. Meyer, *Fatal Balancing Act,* 31, 76, 283.

66. Reichsvereinigung der Juden in Deutschland, Abt. Abwanderung, "Ausreise über Spanien und Portugal," Feb. 1941. Thank you to Herbert Lenk,

Sarasota, Florida, who shared this document that his parents, Richard and Martha Lenk, received.

67. E. Neumayer, Vienna, to Mary Rogers, Philadelphia, June 28, 1941, file Therese Pollack, AFSC, 2002.296, USHMM.

68. "As many as half" in Y. Bauer, *American Jewry*, 46, and Fry, *Surrender on Demand*, 39–55, 197; "buy fake Portuguese passports" in Martins, *Judaísmo e Anti-semitismo*, 95; "Cook sold" in Fittko, *Escape Through the Pyrenees*, 95; "currency of survival" in Zahra, *Lost Children*, 21.

69. Fry, *Surrender on Demand*, 39–55; Frucht, *Verlustanzeige*, 167; Sahl, *Das Exil*, 102 (Mar. 17, 1941); "toothpaste tubes" in Skwara, "Hans Sahl," 100. For fake stamps, visas, and passport, see also Kurt Lenkway, "This Small Piece of History: The Lenkway Family's Escape from Germany, 1938–1941," (1991), 29, RG02.065*01, USHMM; hereafter cited as Lenkway, USHMM.

70. Fry quoted in Subak, *Rescue and Flight*, 188; K. Mann, *Briefe*, 114; Fry, *Surrender on Demand*, 170.

71. "Naturally one did" in Alice Baerwald, 73, 75, Houghton; Mann is quoted in Fry, *Surrender on Demand*, 65. The Manns left Marseille on September 12, 1940. For Jewish defiance, see Gruner, "Germans Should Expel."

72. Fittko, *Escape Through the Pyrenees*, 101, 113; "shoot trespassers" in Fry, *Surrender on Demand*, 122.

73. Mahler-Werfel, "Alma & Lisbon," and *And the Bridge*, 266.

74. Eva Lewinski Pfister, unpublished memoir (1979), 70–71, quoted with the kind permission of her children, Peter, Katherine, and Thomas Pfister; see also Pfister, Pfister, and Pfister, *Eva and Otto;* "Security reasons" in Sahl, *Das Exil*, 263.

75. JTA archive, Nov. 23, 1942, jta.org/1942/11/23/archive/emigration-of-refugees-through-portugal-continues-hias-announces; "dogs and alpine soldiers" in Correa Martín-Arroyo, "Iberian Peninsula," 184–95.

76. Vigée, *Wintermond*, 111, 126, 129–31. This was published first in French as *La lune d'hiver* (Paris, 1970).

77. "Three Belgian Jews" in Amipaz-Silber, *Sephardi Jews*, 296–97; the estimate of 80–100 illegal crossings is in Wriggins, "January Report," Jan. 8, 1943, 1, Foreign Service, 1943, and letter of Jan. 16, 1943, from Philip Conard, both in Portugal, AFSC, Phila.; the estimate of over 150 crossings is in memo of Jan. 10, 1943, Refugee Service, Portugal, AFSC, Phila.; "Forgers carefully duplicated" in Amipaz-Silber, *Sephardi Jews*, 204, quoting Avni, "Zionist Underground," 567.

78. Fanny Stern-Lazego, video at the museum of Camp des Milles, Aix-en-Provence, France. Thank you to Page Delano for sharing this story with

me. For a description of escapes over the "Freedom Trail" in the central Pyrenees (mostly by anti-Nazi French and British troops), see Stourton, *Cruel Crossing.*

79. J. Jacobs, "Ein Freund," 3, 28; Frucht, *Verlustanzeige,* 168. Varian Fry's guides worried about the Spanish concentration camp at Miranda (Fry, *Surrender on Demand,* 202); Karp, *Maquis Connection,* 81–82, 98, 104; Giselle Karp quoted in Wimmer, *Strangers at Home,* 88–94.

80. Eva Lewinski, speech, quoted with permission of Peter, Katherine, and Thomas Pfister, see also Pfister, Pfister, and Pfister, *Eva and Otto.*

81. Arendt quoted in Taussig, *"Benjamin's Grave"*; "really tough walk" in Stourton, *Cruel Crossing,* 7.

82. Rother, "Franco als Retter," 123. Spain announced neutrality early in the war, but declared "non-belligerence" on June 10, 1940 (when Italy entered the war) and then proclaimed neutrality again on October 1, 1943. Marquina, "The Spanish Neutrality During the Second World War," 171, 181.

83. "Treatment at the borders" in Anna Geyer, memoir (written after 1940 but during the war), 3–4, JLC, Tamiment; Fry, *Surrender on Demand,* 85, and *Assignment,* 95. The Spanish government continued to hand over Jewish refugees to the Germans until the summer of 1944, both from borders and from Spanish territory more generally (Correa Martín-Arroyo, "Iberian Peninsula," 184–95).

84. *Chicago Tribune,* Feb. 2, 1941, 6; the description by the refugee couple is in Bagger, *For the Heathen,* 178–79.

85. M. Feuchtwanger, "Escape," 273, and "Émigré Life," 3:1028; Stanton, *Escape from the Inferno,* 133–34.

86. Mahler-Werfel, *And the Bridge,* 266–67; the German brothers' story is in Lenkway, 29, USHMM; Paetel, *Reise,* 247.

87. "Sold entry permits" in Marrus, *Unwanted,* 260–61, and Fry, *Surrender on Demand,* 65, 67–68, 74; Friedman Family Coll., 1996.A.0426, USHMM. Willem Friedman's journey occurred in September 1940. Ryan suggests a correlation between affluence and the ability to exit France (*Holocaust and the Jews,* 113).

88. Eiland and Jennings, *Walter Benjamin,* 671; Mauas, *Who Killed Walter Benjamin.* The film raises the question whether he killed himself or died of a stroke or heart attack. (On the French exit visa, see the film at 11:39–12:00.) Experts and witnesses stated that at least one high-level Gestapo officer and possible undercover Nazi agents patrolled Portbou at that time. (See the film at 19:14 and 43:08–43:59.) Arendt, Introduction, 18.

89. Geyer, memoir, 3–4, JLC, Tamiment; they started in October 1940. "Icy wind" in Robert Groetsch, memoir (n.d.), 3, JLC, Tamiment.

90. Franco's unreliability is in Fry, *Surrender on Demand*, 85, and *Assignment*, 95; Sequerra quoted in Amipaz-Silber, *Sephardi Jews*, 226, 252; "thorny and rocky" in Groetsch, memoir, 2, JLC, Tamiment; Paul K. (Aug. 2, 1999), #T-3927, FVA; "felt hopeless" in Groetsch, memoir, 3.

91. Annette Baslow Finger (née Szer), #6981, Shoah.

92. For Margosis, see Photo Archives, w/s #57898, USHMM; for brutality at the Miranda camp, see Y. Bauer, *American Jewry*, 48. The newspaper article (probably from an American paper) detailing Egon Bamberger's escape headlined the story "You Have to Bribe Your Way out of Nazi Europe" (Julius Bamberger folder at AFSC, 2002.296, USHMM).

93. Rother, *National-Spanien*, 104–5; Payne, *Franco and Hitler*; "Masonic conspiracy" in Dauner, "Franco, Nazi Collaborator," 17.

94. "Through the country quickly" in Rother, *Spanien und der Holocaust*, 337, and "National-Spanien," 104. Franco compiled a list of Spanish Jews for the Nazi regime in 1941 at the behest of Heinrich Himmler; see Giles Tremlett, "General Franco Gave List of Spanish Jews to Nazis, *Guardian*, June 20, 2010, https://www.theguardian.com/world/2010/jun/20/franco-gave-list-spanish-jews-nazis. "Possible doom" in Robert Philpot, "Was Franco the 'Good' Fascist?" JC, Nov. 23, 2015, thejc.com/comment-and-debate/comment/149674/was-franco-good-fascist. Patrick Bernhard has found instances in which Jews were sent back by the Spanish border police during the war (email to the author, Sept. 5, 2017).

95. "Majority of Jews" in Rother, "Franco als Retter," 123; the figures for refugees who crossed Spain are in Rother, *Spanien und der Holocaust*, 5. Historians on the panel on Spain at the "Lessons and Legacies of the Holocaust" conference suggested the figure of 35,000 (Boca Raton, 2014).

96. "Jewish volunteers" in Herbert Katzki, oral history, compiled by Ellen Lewis, rec. 5/99, 59, 62, JDC (hereafter cited as Katzki interviews, JDC); "passengers hiding under the seats" in Lenkway, 29, USHMM; "sealed trains" in Alfred Lieberman (1926–2012), "A Tale of Many Cities," private memoir (Jan. 1996), 9, used with the permission of his daughter, Diane Sadel, transmitted to the author by Daniel Lee; "indescribable poverty" in "An Octogenarian's Records," 36, Wiener Lib.; "no bread" in Friman, "Von Wien," 32.

97. "Everyone would cry" in Gisela W. (Apr. 26, 1992), #T-2079, FVA; see also Kohn, "Naturally Berlin," 31; "give up their bread" in Paula Phillips,

oral history (1989), RG-50.477*1252, USHMM; see also Rony, *This, Too,* 246–47. Paul K. recalled that in Spain, "starvation and poverty [were] worse than occupied Europe" (#T-3927, FVA).

98. "Bombed out and collapsed" in Lenkway, 31, USHMM; Bagger, *For the Heathen,* 177; Mahler-Werfel, *And the Bridge,* 268; "heap of rubble" in Lustig, *Ein Rosenkranz,* 62.

99. Rony, *This, Too,* 245; Paetel, *Reise,* 250–51; see also "An Octogenarian's Records," 36, Wiener Lib.

100. "Spanish customs-house officers" and "locked up in their carriages" in Bodley, *Flight into Portugal,* 57; Elisabeth Bab, memoir, 215, LBI; the British Embassy official is in Wisla, memoirs/journal, Digibaeck, 58.

101. Lustig, *Ein Rosenkranz,* 62, 64–67; Marguerite Douhaerdt to Manfred George (editor of the *Aufbau* from 1939), Oct. 31, 1940, A: George 75.2439/1–2, DLA Marbach.

102. Other refugee trains, too, stood locked for many hours. For further information about Luxembourger Jews in Spain and Portugal, see JDC archives, Subcollection 4: Countries and Regions, record group 4.40, Luxemburg [*sic*], file 742, Luxemburg [*sic*], Emigration, http://archives.jdc.org/our-collections/finding-aids/new-york-office/1933–1944/countries-and-regions-abyssinia-philippines.

103. Ernest P. (Mar. 17, 1988), #T–1224, FVA.

104. Baer, "Oma Clemens," 116. Thank you to Alejandro Baer for sharing this document with me.

105. Oppenheim, "Recollections," 26, RSCL OxOn; "capture upon landing" in Pimentel and Heinrich, *Judeus,* 125–26; Graf, #508, Shoah.

106. Nadia Gould Coll., Acc. 1994.A.0265 RG-02.141, 4–6, USHMM.

107. "Report on Arrival of *Serpa Pinto* Children—arrived 1–25–43," YIVO, RG 249, folder 478; "parents whispered" quoted in Amipaz-Silber, *Sephardi Jews,* 244; Kluger, *Still Alive,* 15.

108. Doctors created the OSE in 1912 in St. Petersburg as a Jewish health organization. In 1923, it fled to Berlin and in 1933 to Paris. The OSE ran orphanages for Jewish children and smuggled them to neutral countries. Other organizations such as HIAS and the German-Jewish Children's Aid, formed in 1934, also paid for and settled some children. By 1941, the National Refugee Service had taken over both functions.

109. "Rhodes Scholarship" in Zahra, *Lost Children,* 68; Conard letter, prepared by Wriggins, Refugee Services, Portugal, Nov. 24, 1943, AFSC, Phila.; "first excellent meal" in Dr. and Mrs. Chomski to Robert Lang, Director,

USCOM, June 26, 1941, Isaac and Masha Chomski Papers, RG-10.206.01, USHMM.

110. Morris C. Troper to Mrs. Franklin Roosevelt, June 7, 1941, YIVO, RG 249, folder 357; Conard to his wife, June 15, 1941, AFSC, 2002.296, USHMM.

111. Chomskis to Lang, June 26, 1941, RG-10.206.01, USHMM. They referred to João Pereira da Rosa, the "director" of the newspaper. The paper was co-owned by Moses Amzalak (see ch. 2).

112. "Erase the imprints" in Troper to Roosevelt, June 7, 1941, YIVO, RG 249, folder 357. The three groups together included 311 children; see Photo Archives, w/s #16197, USHMM.

113. Wriggins to M. Schauffler, Feb. 18, 1943, Schauffler, Yale; Conard, "Brief Report on the Lisbon Office of the AFSC, May to August '41" (Aug. 23, 1941), 9, Schauffler, Yale.

114. Edel is in Photo Archives, w/s #6361, USHMM; the JDC's work is in Dwork and van Pelt, *Flight from the Reich*, 213.

115. Weissmann's methods are detailed in Rosensaft, *World Jewish Congress*, 38; "relatives in the United States" in Segev, *World Jewish Congress*, 147–53. Segev provides details of the smuggling of up to seven hundred children.

116. His name appeared among the first thirty-three people whom the Nazis stripped of citizenship in 1933; see Gumbel, *Freie Wissenschaft*, 268, and Brenner, *Gumbel*.

117. For Gumbel's escape journey, see Neilson, *We Escaped*, 44–45, 52–53, 51, 56–57; for his wife, see Emil J. Gumbel Coll., LBI microfilm, at https:// www.bsb-muenchen.de/mikro/lit277.pdf. Gumbel arrived in the United States in October 1940.

118. "Chaos that was Marseille" in Meissner, *Margit's Story*, 111; "bordello" in Margit Meissner, interview by the author, Washington, DC, Nov. 19, 2014. In her book, she referred to the place as a "flophouse" (*Margit's Story*, 111).

119. Meissner, *Margit's Story*, 111–19; "multiple exiles" in Frank, "Budapest–Berlin–New York," 204–6.

2. *The Exasperations and Consolations of Refugee Life After 1940*

Epigraph: From the story of a woman, age eighty-two, giving shelter to Syrian refugees in Idomeni, Greece; see Nima Elbagir and Dominique van Heerden, " 'Ordinary' Greek Grandmother's Extraordinary Kindness to Refugees," CNN: World, May 4, 2016, cnn.com/2016/05/04/europe/greece-grandmother-syria-refugees.

1. Querg, "Spionage und Terror," 191.

2. Wyman, *Paper Walls,* 150. Many refugees had useless visas to Curaçao and Costa Rica. They could not reach these destinations from Lisbon, because consuls at transit hubs like the United States refused to issue transit visas (Bazarov, "Racing with Death," 25).

3. "Refugee harvest" in Gramling, *Free Men,* 26; Packard and Packard, *Balcony Empire,* 361.

4. Circular #14 in zur Mühlen, *Fluchtweg,* 156; "Jews expelled" in *Spared Lives,* 68. Also in March 1940, Portugal refused entry to Jews with valid visas for Brazil and Argentina (Wasserstein, *Ambiguity of Virtue,* 102, 105–6).

5. "Tickets to a third country" in *Spared Lives,* 12; Circular #23 in zur Mühlen, *Fluchtweg,* 156, and JDC archives, Subcollection 4: Countries and Regions, record group 4.40, Luxemburg [*sic*], file 742, Luxemburg [*sic*], Emigration, http://archives.jdc.org/our-collections/finding-aids/new-york-office/1933–1944/countries-and-regions-abyssinia-philippines; "dumping ground" in zur Mühlen, *Fluchtweg,* 156; "still open shops" in Pimentel and Ninhos, *Salazar, Portugal,* 467.

6. The actions of d'Esaguy are in Milgram, "Portugal, Consuls, and Refugees," 23; "on their train for a week" in Ernest P., #T-1224, FVA.

7. Pimentel and Ninhos, "Portugal, Jewish Refugees, and the Holocaust," 106.

8. "Lifted that ban" in Wasserstein, *Ambiguity of Virtue,* 106, 109; "suspended transit visas" in "Review of the Year 5702," *AJYB* 44, 232; "irregular intervals" in Pimentel and Ninhos, *Salazar, Portugal,* 490; Walker, "All Refugees in Portugal"; "refugees continued to arrive" in "Review of the Year 5703," *AJYB* 45, 297.

9. Salazar's stance on Portuguese colonies is in Milgram, *Portugal, Salazar, and the Jews,* 107–9; "Angola and Mozambique" in Stein, *Extraterritorial Dreams,* 30–36; "Portuguese collective identity" in Milgram, *Portugal, Salazar, and the Jews,* 108.

10. "Civilize the colonies" in G. Santos, "Birth of Physical Anthropology." Rarely did the Portuguese government react as vehemently as when a couple arrived in May 1941 with a false visa for Mozambique (Fred Altman, letters of June 13, 1942, and Aug. 22, 1941, file 6646, AFSC, 2002.296, USHMM). As late as the spring of 1943, Salazar refused to let two hundred refugees heading to Palestine from the Iberian Peninsula transit through Mozambique unless Britain guaranteed that they would not outstay their four-week visas (Correa Martín-Arroyo, "Iberian Peninsula" 214–18).

11. "Fire escape" in *A Tale of Two Worlds* (1941), USHMM, RG-60.2225, film I.D. 2305. This book cannot discuss all of the organizations that smuggled refugees into Portugal. Obviously, "many rings were involved," including criminals; see Dwork and van Pelt, *Flight from the Reich*, 213; Shirer, *Berlin Diary* [entry for Oct. 15, 1940], 542.

12. "Shot out of the ground" in Losa, *Unter fremden Himmeln*, 97; "enormous rooming house" in Ernst Hofeller, "Refugee," 29, unpublished memoir, LBI; "only a cellar room" in the *Ottawa Citizen*, Nov. 9, 1940, 7; Tillinger, *Aufbau*, Oct. 18, 1940, 5; Koestler, *Scum of the Earth*, 275.

13. The JDC cites 8,000 Jews in Lisbon (Y. Bauer, *American Jewry*, 47), as did James Reston (*New York Times*, Dec. 15, 1940). Wriggins suggests that there were 10,000 Jews in Lisbon in late 1940 (*Picking Up the Pieces*, 24). "Expenditures for refugees" in d'Esaguy, speech, June 4, 1941, 2, file 896 (2 of 3), JDC; "Britain stood alone" in Beevor, *Second World War*, 223. He points to troops from Britain's colonies as well as to Polish and Czech airmen who aided Britain.

14. In January 1942, the JDC supported 600 of 800 remaining refugees; see draft of report, Jan. 8, 1942, file 896 (3 of 3), JDC. For the figure 10,000 (late 1942), see HIAS Report for 1942–1943, quoted in Amipaz-Silber, *Sephardi Jews*, 295; the figure 1,000 for mid-1945 is in zur Mühlen, *Fluchtweg*, 163.

15. "Precarious economic situation" in Rosas, "Portuguese Neutrality"; Draft Histories, RG-59, NARA.

16. "Democratic ideas" in Pinto, *Modern Portugal*, 27, 35; "destabilize his regime" in *Dossier sobre Emigração*, Ministério do Interior, Gabinete do Ministro, MC 486, PVDE, Lisboa, Nov. 1937, Liv 1-PV/L No. 96, NT 359–1 No. F. 20, Portuguese National Archive; see also "Portuguese Recall Wartime Tales of Aid to Their Neighbors," *New York Times*, Oct. 28, 1999, nytimes.com/1999/10/28/world/portuguese-recall-wartime-tales-of-aid-to-their-neighbors.html; pamphlet quoted in Sapega, *Consensus and Debate*, 17–18.

17. "Race in its colonial empire" in de Matos, *Colours of the Empire;* "dangerous consequences" in Pimentel and Heinrich, *Judeus*, 41; "constricting the actions" in Pimentel, "Refugiados," 109.

18. Salazar's telegram quoted in Correia, "Abschied von Europa," 28n1; "enjoy equal rights" in JTA, "Portugal Protests"; "Hitler, drunk with victory" in Robinson, *Contemporary Portugal*, 87.

19. "Blue Shirts" in Milgram, *Portugal, Salazar, and the Jews*, 11, 43; "synagogue of Tomar" in Stuczynski, "Digging Portugal's Jewish Past."

20. In addition, the Unitarians referred to a "Polish and very orthodox" syna-
gogue in Lisbon in 1944 (USC Lisbon to Rebekah Taft, executive director of
USC Boston, June 14, 1944, USC, bMS 16007_Box 20_folder 11, RG-67.028,
USHMM).

21. "Jews facing danger abroad" in James Mann Report, Aug. 30, 1944, 18–19,
WRB, USHMM. For accusations that Amzalak believed the Nazis were
defending Europe from communism and leaned toward them, see Tom
Segev, "How We Missed Out on the Swiss Option," *Haaretz*, Nov. 29, 2007,
haaretz.com/weekend/magazine/how-we-missed-out-on-the-swiss-
option–1.234249, and "The Jew with a Nazi Medal," posted to YouTube by
EszterPictures, May 3, 2010, youtube.com/watch?v=5RcQ_WzmvLA.

22. "Children's camp" in *O Século*, June 1941, Chomski Papers,
RG-10.206.01*05, USHMM; "tried to limit news" in Pimentel, "Salazar
impediu," 22–23; "false or no papers" in Dr. Baruel to the PVDE, Lisbon,
May 11, 1943, Correspondência 1941–1956, file 390468, Code: HMB, Origin:
PO/Li, AII–12a/4, CAHJP; see also *AJYB* 44, 232.

23. "Two alternatives" in Miriam Stanton, unpublished manuscript, quoted in
Bartrop, "From Lisbon to Jamaica," 52; "competition from Jewish refugees"
in Pimentel, "Refugiados," 106. Portuguese emigration figures are in *Korrespondenzblatt über Auswanderungs-und Siedlungswesen*, Aug. 1934 (Berlin), 12.
This exodus occurred until Brazil placed restrictions on immigration in 1933,
when only 9,000 people left Portugal (*Korrespondenzblatt über Auswanderungs-und Siedlungswesen*, Sept. 1935, 22). Statistics for 1940 are from Nuno
Valério, compiler, *Estatísticas Históricas Portuguesas*, vol. 1 (Lisbon: Instituto
Nacional de Estatística, 2001), 37.

24. Originally the tax was $12 per passage, but grew in Feb. 1941 to more than 5
percent of the transportation cost (Mary Rogers to Schauffler, Feb. 21, 1941,
Schauffler, Yale).

25. "Inflation" in Meneses, *Salazar*, 310. A case of sardines cost 100 escudos at
the start of the war, but 280 in 1944 (Robinson, *Contemporary Portugal*, 91).
"Black market" in Alexander, "Nazi Offensive in Lisbon," 16; "rationing
staples" in report, May 18, 1944, 4, file 897 (2 of 2), JDC.

26. The Salazar-Franco agreement is in Robinson, *Contemporary Portugal*, 87;
"self-interested noncombatant" in Petropoulos, "Co-Opting Nazi
Germany"; "handsome dividends" in Leshem, "Rescue Efforts," 235. Salazar's trade balance improved from a deficit of $90 million in 1939 to a surplus
of $68 million in 1943; see Reginbogin, *Faces of Neutrality*, 126. "Renewed in
1899" in Meneses, *Salazar*, 278; "commercial relationship" in Sideri, *Trade*

and Power. He argues that Britain reaped far more benefit than Portugal did from the partnership. Glyn Stone, in *Oldest Ally*, addresses that relationship from the British diplomatic and strategic perspective.

27. "American oil" in Hull, *Memoirs*, 1:1334. On the importance of tungsten, see Wheeler, "Price of Neutrality," 107–27; the price of tungsten, a scarce mineral, soared by 1,700 percent in the first fifteen months of the war (Louçã and Schäfer, "Portugal and the Nazi Gold," 106).

28. Gold came from German-occupied territories (from national banks, private businesses, and individuals); see Lochery, *Lisbon*, ch. 25. Moreover, Portuguese tungsten helped prolong the war (Reginbogin, *Faces of Neutrality*, 129). The U.S. secretary of state, Cordell Hull, worried about exactly this possibility (*Memoirs*, 2:1336). "Looted gold" in Louçã, *Nazigold;* see also Simons, "Nazi Gold."

29. "Gestapo men" in Bayles, "Europe's Bottleneck," 79–80; "Gestapo roamed Lisbon" in JTA, "Gestapo Gangs"; Schellenberg, *Memoiren*, 268, and *Labyrinth*, 41.

30. Kennan, *Memoirs*, 143 (quotation), and "Diplomatic-Military Collaboration," 131; for Josephine Baker, see Ramalho, *Lisbon*, 98–100.

31. *Life*, Feb. 19, 1951, 130. Graham Greene, who had joined MI6 in 1941 to investigate counterespionage on the Iberian Peninsula, later based *Our Man in Havana* on a double agent in Lisbon. "Mélange of mistrust" in Nigel Thompson, "Checking Out the James Bond Spy Society in Estoril," *Mirror Online*, Jan. 7, 2012, updated July 22, 2015, mirror.co.uk/lifestyle/travel/city-breaks/checking-out-the-james-bond-spy–171152; Sevareid quoted in Schroth, *American Journey*, 179; see also Sevareid, *Not So Wild a Dream*, 180; "passengers appear" in Rev. Henry Smith Leiper, "Lisbon: Oasis in Chaos," *Living Church*, Aug. 30, 1942, file 896, JDC.

32. Torga, *La Création*, quoted in Fralon, *Good Man in Evil Times*, 43; "contest between us" in Schellenberg, *Labyrinth*, 117. Additionally, some Portuguese double agents worked for both the Nazis and the Allies (Wheeler, "In the Service of Order," 8, 10).

33. "Satellite in the police" in Pimentel, *Espiões em Portugal*, 167. Pimentel sees a leaning toward Germany (166–69). "German advisers" in Hess, "Was Portugal," 172, quoting Soares, *Portugal*, 19; RSHA in Correia, "Abschied von Europa," 32–34.

34. Pimentel and Ninhos, *Salazar, Portugal*, 252, 273. In April 1939, the National Assembly passed a law prohibiting doctors who had not passed the Portuguese equivalency exam by February 1939 from practicing (ibid., 466). "Revolutionaries and undesirables" in ibid., 414.

35. "Without a clear conscience" in Correia, "Abschied von Europa," 34; PVDE in Wheeler, "In the Service of Order," 11; "carefully following" in Wheeler, email to the author, Dec. 4, 2014.

36. Gisela W. (1992), #T-2079, FVA; similar observations can be found in Lilly Lewis (1996), #12696, seg. 44–47, Shoah. On the Gestapo, see Frieda Leitner (1995), #1741, seg. 51–53, Shoah; "I could not take" in Heinz Wisla, memoirs/journal (n.d.), Digibaeck, 61–62.

37. "English and German papers" in Tillinger, *Aufbau*, Oct. 18, 1940, 5; "identical size" in Alexander, "Nazi Offensive in Lisbon," 15; "very strange sight" in Lenkway, 38, USHMM; "A Visita do 'Deutschland'" and "A Visita Oficial da 'Home Fleet'" are in Blaufuks, *Under Strange Skies*, 1:48–1:57.

38. Fry quoted in zur Mühlen, *Fluchtweg*, 147; Pimentel, *Espiões em Portugal*, 166–69; "neutral collaboration" in Baiôa, Fernandes, and Meneses, "Political History of Twentieth-Century Portugal"; "presumed winners" in Correia, "Abschied von Europa," 32. In June 1944, two days before D-Day, Portugal refused to deliver tungsten to either side. Weber devotes an entire chapter, "Wolfram by Day," to this (*Lisbon Route*, 277–92); see also Meneses, *Salazar*, 304–16.

39. Wheeler, "In the Service of Order," 6–9.

40. "Fifth columnists" in McDonald, *Refugees and Rescue*, ch. 9; Roosevelt, "Fireside Chat 15"; "nativist and restrictionist" in Breitman and Kraut, *American Refugee Policy*, 127, and Long, *War Diary*, 173–74; "spy hysteria" voiced by Margaret Jones, AFSC, quoted in Breitman and Kraut, *Refugee Policy*, 131.

41. "American interest" in "New Rule Will Bar Immigrants Unless Entry Is for Good of U.S.," *New York Herald Tribune*, June 15, 1940, 1A, ProQuest Historical Newspapers; "We can delay" in Assistant Secretary of State Breckinridge Long to State Department Officials, memo, June 26, 1940, available at "Americans and the Holocaust," USHMM, https://exhibitions.ushmm.org/americans-and-the-holocaust/personal-story/breckinridge-long.

42. The legation and the consulate general did not become an embassy until June 1944, although refugees usually referred to both as "the consulate"; see Draft Histories, RG-59, NARA. The United States and Portugal had had diplomatic relations since 1791. From the mid-nineteenth century, America sent an "Envoy Extraordinary and Minister Plenipotentiary" there. Only in June 1944 did it raise this representative's status to "Ambassador Extraordinary and Plenipotentiary" and the legation to an embassy. See U.S. State

Department, Office of the Historian, "Chiefs of Mission for Portugal," https://history.state.gov/departmenthistory/people/chiefsofmission/Portugal, and "A Guide to the United States' History of Recognition, Diplomatic, and Consular Relations, by Country, Since 1776: Portugal," https://history.state.gov/countries/portugal.

43. Fry, "Our Consuls at Work," 507. Fry referred to events in August 1940. He may not have known that Schiaparelli had an American daughter, but some Jews, too, had close family in the United States. "Refuse to grant" in Breitman and Kraut, *American Refugee Policy*, 135–36; Joy quoted in Subak, *Rescue and Flight*, 56.

44. "Upright character" in Klein, *Flüchtlingspolitik*, 117. In some cases, the United States required this moral affidavit earlier; see Kurt Ibson, letter of Nov. 28, 1940, private coll. The Russell bill of July 1941 (named for Senator Richard Russell, D-Ga., chairman of the Senate Immigration Committee) gave consuls the power to refuse visas to people suspected of being foreign agents (Wyman, *Paper Walls*, 141, 192, 195). "Man of high moral character" in Mary Rogers to U.S. Consul, Lisbon, regarding Gadiel, Mar. 8, 1941, file 5768, AFSC, 2002.296, USHMM.

45. "Relatives in Europe as Hostages" in McDonald, *Refugees and Rescue*, ch. 10; "Explanation of New Regulations and Restrictions Affecting Immigration to the United States," National Coordinating Committee for Aid to Refugees and Emigrants coming from Germany, July 23, 1941, Schauffler, Yale; "expired visa" in Wischnitzer, *Visas to Freedom*, 171.

46. "800 people" in statistik-des-holocaust.de/Emigration-Bericht2–5.jpg (written around Nov. 1941); "more entangled" in Conard to his daughter Lois, Oct. 12, 1941, Conard files, AFSC, 2002.296, USHMM; Fry quoted in Isenberg, *Hero of Our Own*, 232.

47. Although the United States took about 130,000 Jewish refugees before the end of 1941, it had left 110,000 available quota slots unfilled by that year. When war broke out, in 1939, 310,000 German nationals, mostly Jews, were waiting for U.S. visa numbers (Katznelson, "Failure to Rescue," 51); see also Breitman and Lichtman, *FDR and the Jews;* quotation in Wriggins, *Picking Up the Pieces*, 12.

48. "Portugal's elites" in Milgram, *Portugal, Salazar, and the Jews*, 90–91; "Jewish 'problem'" in Ninhos, "What Was Known."

49. Sousa Mendes quoted in Marrus, *Unwanted*, 263; "crimes of the Inquisition" in Hess, "Was Portugal," 187, quoting Afonso and Pescada, *Um Homem Bom*, 96.

50. "Remembering the Inquisition" in Meneses, *Salazar*, 238–39; d'Esaguy, *Repaying a Debt*, 11.

51. Y. Bauer, *American Jewry*, 44–53. For current estimates of the number of Jews saved by Sousa Mendes, see the website of the Sousa Mendes Foundation, http://sousamendesfoundation.org.

52. Several other consuls also saved hundreds, perhaps thousands of lives. They include Dr. Feng-Shan Ho, consul general of China in Vienna, 1938–40; Francis Foley, British vice-consul in charge of visas in Berlin, 1938–39; Abdol Hossein Sardari, Iranian consul in Paris, 1942; Jose Castellanos, Salvadoran consul in Geneva, 1941–44; Carl Lutz, Swiss vice-consul in Budapest, 1942–45; and Sempo Sugihara, the Japanese consul in Kovno, 1940. Lutz may have saved more Jews than Sousa Mendes.

53. "German tanks" in Meneses, *Salazar*, 237–39. Portugal did not stand alone in punishing "insubordinate" consuls who signed visas. Switzerland officially "reprimanded" Carl Lutz, and the Japanese consul Sempo Sugihara had to resign for "insubordination" at the end of the war.

54. Bitton, *Letters to the Editor*, 102, and oral history, Bitton (1990), minutes 1:05:59–1:08, RG 50.030*0027, USHMM; "paid his medical bills" in Baruel, Lisbon, to HIAS, Paris, Aug. 30, 1949, Lisbon, Correspondência geral, Code HMB/1584, Origin PO/Li, AII–12a/12, file 400763, Secção, CAHJP. Information about an American organization dedicated to honoring Sousa Mendes can be found at http://sousamendesfoundation.org.

55. "Thousands of people" in Milgram, *Portugal, Salazar, and the Jews*, 73–91, and Bartrop, "From Lisbon to Jamaica," 50. Without a U.S. transit visa, Steinberg could not deplane, and so he returned to Italy. After a brief internment there, he collected all the necessary documents to leave from Lisbon a year later (Lalli, "Descent from Paradise").

56. "Casanova" in Milgram, "Portugal, Consuls, and Refugees," 28; see also Magno and Casanova in Martins, *Judaísmo e Anti-semitismo*, 97–98; "Embassy in Budapest" in Milgram, *Portugal, Salazar, and the Jews*, 260–83, esp. 280.

57. "Temporary shelter" in Ramalho, *Vilar Formoso*, 14, 80, 88; for the English businessmen, see Bagger, *For the Heathen*, 184, and Bodley, *Flight into Portugal*, 60.

58. "Racial nationalism" in *O Valor da Raça* (*The Value of Race*, 1915). As an example of this concept, the author António Sardinha demanded that race and nation be equated, excluding Jews, "negroes," and "foreigners" (Benz, *Judenfeindschaft*, 287). *Protocols* in zur Mühlen, *Fluchtweg*, 138. Two other books addressed alleged Jewish transgressions: Paulo de Tarso, *Crimes da*

Franco-maçonaria Judáica (The crimes of Jewish Freemasonry, 1924), and Mário Saa, *A Invasão dos Judeus* (Invasion of the Jews, 1925). The *Protocols* surfaced again in 1937 and 1939, this time in four volumes (Benz, *Judenfeindschaft*, 287). "Trinity" in Martins, *Judaísmo e Anti-semitismo*, 186–87; "gained traction" in Benz, *Judenfeindschaft*, 287–88, and Martins, *Judaísmo e Anti-semitismo*, 191.

59. *A Voz* correctly noted that Porto Jews had received funds for their synagogue from Jews abroad. They had even named the building after the main donor, Sir Elie Kadoorie, who lived in London. And the Portuguese-Marrano Committee in London, founded in 1926, supported the Porto synagogue's building fund (Melammed, *Question of Identity*, 147–48). In 1937, Barros Basto faced dishonorable discharge from the army; he died in 1961. In 2015, the Porto Jewish community requested his full reinstatement to the rank of colonel; see JTA, " 'Portuguese Dreyfus' Cause Taken Up by Candidate," *Forward*, Nov. 5, 2015, http://forward.com/news/breaking-news/324119/portuguese-dreyfus-cause-taken-up-by-leading-candidate/?attribution=home-breaking-news-headline-3.

60. Martins, *Judaísmo e Anti-semitismo*, 177–80.

61. For example, David Bitton—the father of young Isaac, who helped in the Jewish soup kitchen—became assistant chief of police in Lisbon, and David Bitton's godfather, Chaym Attias, served as secretary to President Carmona, who had named himself president of Portugal in 1926 and nominated Salazar as prime minister in 1932 (Bitton, *Letters to the Editor*, 73).

62. Benarús, *O Anti-semitismo*, 76; letter to Salazar in Isaac Bitton, microfiche, RG-19.011*06 and translated by Bitton, 1990, original letter in Isaac Bitton Coll. 1990.205.01–15, USHMM. Maximiliano Azancot delivered the letter (in late 1939?) and claimed, years later and without proof, that this appeal induced Salazar to issue orders limiting antisemitic propaganda.

63. "Homeless people" in *República* (Nov. 12, 15, and 27, 1938), *A Voz* (Nov. 11, 1938), *Novidades* (Nov. 19, 1938), and *República* (Dec. 7, 1938), all quoted in Pimentel and Ninhos, *Salazar, Portugal*, inserts after 256; "mostly children" in Bitton Coll. 1990.205.01–15, USHMM; "secret police" in *Diário de Notícias*, Jan. 24, 1944 (Bitton's translation), Bitton Coll., RG-19.011*06, USHMM.

64. In 1938, the government's official paper, *Diário da Manhã*, asserted this; cited in *Das Jüdische Volk*, a Zionist paper in Berlin, Feb. 4, 1938, 2.

65. Oppenheim, "Recollections," 26, RSCL OxOn.

66. "Spoke with one's hands" in *Jüdisches Nachrichtenblatt* (Vienna), Nov. 15, 1940, 1; Reston, "Lisbon's Refugees," *New York Times*, Dec. 15, 1940; "never

felt antisemitism" in Bitton, oral history, RG-50.030*0027, USHMM; see also Kalischer, *Vom Konzentrationslager,* 151.

67. Pimentel and Heinrich, *Judeus,* 45. Similarly in Spain, the Catholic Church opposed the Nazis' racism and murderous eugenics (Ben-Dror, *La Iglesia Católica,* 43–53, 61, 73–74, 102).

68. "Church" in T. Gallagher, *Portugal,* 126; for the encyclical, *Saeculo Exeunte Octavo,* see the English translation at vatican.va/holy_father/pius_xii/encyclicals/documents/hf_p-xii_enc_13061940_saeculo-exeunte-octavo_en.html; "clerical-conservative" in Bruneau, "Church and State in Portugal," 463.

69. "Bad people" in Walker interview; "go to church" in Shomberg interview.

70. The ambassador's letter quoted in Milgram, *Portugal, Salazar, and the Jews,* 77–78; "people of color" in de Matos, *Colours of the Empire;* "racial mixing" in Sapega, *Consensus and Debate,* 126; "did not face expulsion" in Pimentel and Heinrich, *Judeus,* 40.

71. Isaac Weissmann to Dr. Arieh Tartakower, World Jewish Congress (WJC) in New York, Jan. 5, 1944, regarding Weissmann's activities in Portugal on behalf of the WJC, doc. #8, Isaac Weissmann Archive: Documentation of the World Jewish Congress in Lisbon, item 3690143, Yad Vashem Digital Archive, https://portal.ehri-project.eu/units/il–002798-p_3.

72. "Deportations firsthand" in Laqueur, *Terrible Secret,* 65–100. Salazar heard of mass executions from the Portuguese ambassador in London and from Portuguese military missions in Germany (Pimentel and Ninhos, "Portugal, Jewish Refugees, and the Holocaust," 107); see also Meneses, *Salazar,* 224. Eden's speech is in Schulze, *"Heimschaffungsaktion,"* 54.

73. Schulze, *"Heimschaffungsaktion,"* 50–54; "to avoid delays" in German Foreign Ministry, Brussels, to Portuguese Consul, Brussels, Feb. 10, 1943, Ministério Negócios Estrangeiros Holocausto, reel 13, #8, RG-42.001M, Acc.2000.170, USHMM.

74. "Opportunity to save" in Stein, *Extraterritorial Dreams,* 119; "stalling until May" in Pimentel and Ninhos, "Portugal, Jewish Refugees, and the Holocaust," 107–8.

75. "Necessary documents" in "Portuguese Jews Expelled from France Reached Portugal," Sept. 21, Oct. 14, and Nov. 16, 1943, file 897, JDC. The delay regarding Greece may have saved Jews, since they were later liberated—although acceptance by Portugal would have rescued them from danger sooner; see a cable regarding Portuguese Jews in Greece (excerpt of cable sent by Reuben Resnik, JDC, Beyoglu, Turkey, to Joseph Schwartz, JDC,

Lisbon, Apr. 24, 1944, "A Small Group Portuguese Nationals Remain Greece May Be Deported Poland Unless Intercession By Portuguese Government"), Correspondência, Refugiados, Code HMB, PO/Li, AII–12a/3, file 390018, CAHJP. "Efforts to repatriate" in Milgram, *Portugal, Salazar, and the Jews,* 252, 259, and Schulze, *"Heimschaffungsaktion,"* 62, 64.

76. "Less restrictive" in Schulze, *"Heimschaffungsaktion,"* and Rother, "Die Deutsche Judenverfolgung," 218. Moreover, Turkey decided to strip some Jews of Turkish nationality who were still in Nazi-occupied lands just when they needed it most. And Turkey blocked Jewish refugee ships traveling to Palestine from refueling in its ports (Guttstadt, *Turkey, Jews, and the Holocaust,* chs. 5–7). The USHMM cites 16,000 Jews who made it to Palestine by "passing through Turkey": "Escape from German-Occupied Europe," Holocaust Encyclopedia, https://www.ushmm.org/wlc/en/article.php?ModuleId=10005470.

77. Dauner, "Franco, Nazi Collaborator," 17.

78. In 1944, Salazar's chargé d'affaires in Hungary, Branquinho, brought Salazar news documenting atrocities in Auschwitz (Martins, *Judaísmo e Anti-semitismo,* 96). *"A Voz"* in Pimentel and Ninhos, *Salazar, Portugal,* 803; "accessible to him" in Meneses, *Salazar,* 224.

79. Milgram, *Portugal, Salazar, and the Jews,* 260–83, esp. 280, referring to Spain, Switzerland, and Sweden; Martins, *Judaísmo e Anti-semitismo,* 98.

80. Conard, "Brief Report on the Lisbon Office of the AFSC, May to August '41" (Aug. 23, 1941), 12, Schauffler, Yale; "Police pressure" in doc. 392, Sutters, *Archives of the Holocaust,* for Jan. 10, 1943; "JDC officials" in Sharp, *Journey to Freedom,* 10; the JDC's observation in zur Mühlen, *Fluchtweg,* 161. The historian Irene Pimentel also concluded that Portugal did not extradite or return refugees to Germany (Pimentel and Heinrich, *Judeus,* 127). "Quakers corroborated" in memo of Nov. 6, 1944, from Marjorie ("Marnie") Schauffler, Conard Coll., AFSC, 2002.296, USHMM; see also Sutters, *Archives of the Holocaust,* 494, Joseph Schwartz to Philip Conard, memo, Feb. 14, 1944.

81. WJC in Mann Report, Aug. 30, 1944, 25–26, WRB, USHMM. The JDC promised to pay for the costs of recuperation; see F. Lichtenstein, Jewish Agency for Palestine, to Dr. Baruel, June 28, 1945, Correspondência 1941–1956, Lisbon, Code: HMB, Origin: PO/Li, AII–12a/4, file 390395, Secção, CAHJP.

82. Anny Coury, interviewed by Ramalho, in *Vilar Formoso,* 88.

83. "Flood" in Rony, *This, Too,* 248–49; Pekelis, *My Version,* esp. 132.

84. "Pots of soup" in Ramalho, *Vilar Formoso*, 89, 95; "smiling villagers" in M. Bauer, *Beyond the Chestnut Trees*, 105–6.

85. "Very genial" in Prutsch and Zeyringer, *Leopold von Andrian*, 711; "very nice in every respect" in Janina Lauterbach (1995), #1138, seg. 36–41, Shoah; see also Leopold von Andrian to Andrée Wimpffen, July 2, 1940, A: Andrian, NZ. 78.2.740, DLA Marbach.

86. "Bitter pill" in Döblin, *Destiny's Journey*, 212; "flat broke" in Torberg, *Eine tolle*, 123; "loaf of bread" in Schnabel, *Lisbon: Harbour of Hope*, 21:20–22:15; Döblin, *Destiny's Journey*, 213–14, 235. For the story of another generous conductor, see Yvette Davidofe in Heinrich, Winterberg, and Kirkamm, *Lissabon*, 8.

87. "No Portuguese" in Trixie (Ferrigo) Robins, 014_letter_robins—"An English Girl's Impression of Portugal," Personal Collection of Melodie Pelloni-Robins, with thanks to her for sharing a copy with me and the USHMM; Shadur, *Drive to Survival*, 100–101; Stanton, *Escape from the Inferno*, 144–45; "In Coimbra" in Pimentel and Heinrich, *Judeus*, 135.

88. "Hat that she liked" in Robins, "English Girl's Impression"; Meissner interview; Rony, *This, Too*, 252–53; "very generous" in Lucy Frucht (1995), #7156, seg. 40, 51, Shoah.

89. Meissner interview; Hess, "Was Portugal," 192–93, quoting Friman, "Von Wien," 32.

90. "Portuguese Recall Wartime Tales of Aid to Their Neighbors," *New York Times*, Oct. 28, 1999, nytimes.com/1999/10/28/world/portuguese-recall-wartime-aid-totheir-neighbours.html. At Figueira da Foz, for example, locals welcomed the "refugees of war" (Tillinger, *Aufbau*, Sept. 6, 1940, 2); see also Pimentel, "Die Portugiesen und die Flüchtlinge," in Heinrich, Winterberg, and Kirkamm, *Lissabon*, 21.

91. "People of Portugal" in Rony, *This, Too*, 253; "greater empathy" in Lutz and White, "Anthropology of Emotions," 415; Stellar, et al., "Class and Compassion," 449–59; see also Grewal, "Wealth Reduces Compassion."

92. "Unforeseen events" in Nussbaum, *Upheavals of Thought*, 315; she describes Rousseau's awareness that one's own vulnerability is necessary for pity; see also ch. 6 on compassion and empathy; Weissmann in WJC, New York, to Dr. Arieh Tartakower, Jan. 5, 1944, doc. #8, Isaac Weissmann Archive: Documentation of the World Jewish Congress (WJC) in Lisbon, item 3690143, Yad Vashem Digital Archive, https://portal.ehri-project.eu/units/il-002798-p_3#desc-eng-il_002798_p_3_10661031_eng. A Jesuit priest, meeting a refugee on the train, offered the Jewish man the use of his library (Furth testimony, #1990, v.39, tape 3 of 5, MJH).

93.   Whereas a few hotels took advantage of the refugee influx to raise prices, most refugees reported the opposite (Lochery, *Lisbon*, 104). Mahler-Werfel, *And the Bridge*, 268–69; "In Curia" in Torberg, *Eine tolle*, 124; Sergio DeBenedetti, "Between Fascism and Freedom: The Education of Sergio DeBenedetti," 1941, ch. 8, 3, accession 2004.57, USHMM.

94.   Leopold von Andrian to Andrée Wimpffen, July 2, 1940, Andrian, NZ. 78.2.740, DLA Marbach; Döblin, *Destiny's Journey*, 214.

95.   Bagger, *For the Heathen*, 185.

96.   Gelehrter quoted in Hess, "Denn unser Leben," 65.

97.   "Half as urban" in da Silveira et al., "Population and Railways," 41, 43; "sacred Portuguese family" in Ferreira, "Home Bound," 142; Salazar quoted in Sadlier, *Question of How*, 2–3.

98.   "As regards women" in Sadlier, *Question of How*, 121; "minimum wages" in Pimentel and de Melo, *Mulheres Portuguesas*, 221, 240; "gender restrictions" in M. Santos, "Women's Studies in Portugal"; "permission to marry" in Sapega, *Consensus and Debate*, 95n13; see also Pimentel and de Melo, *Mulheres Portuguesas*, 245, 259–62, 327–28.

99.   "To be a wife" in Sadlier, *Question of How*, 120; literacy rates in Pimentel and de Melo, *Mulheres Portuguesas*, 181, 241, and Cova and Pinto, "Women Under Salazar's Dictatorship," 132, 137.

100.   "Worked in agriculture" in Cova and Pinto, "Women Under Salazar's Dictatorship," 132; "served as breadwinners" in Sapega, *Consensus and Debate*, 4, 105n25; "markets and groceries" in "Pocket Guide to Portugal," Office of Strategic Services, Aug. 17, 1943, 80, Richard Baker Coll., RIHS; workforce statistics in Pimentel and de Melo, *Mulheres Portuguesas*, 300–301. In official statistics, the concepts of "domestic" and "housewife" varied, and many women who were rural workers were placed in those categories (*Mulheres Portuguesas*, 297).

101.   "Selling fruit" in Dijn, *Das Schicksalsschiff*, 191; quoted material in Robins, "English Girl's Impression"; "Lisbon—Gateway to Warring Europe," *National Geographic*, Aug. 1941, Bitton microfiche, RG-19.011*05, USHMM; see also Parrish diaries, 7, Refugee Services, Portugal, 1943 AFSC, Phila.

102.   "No tea shops" in Bodley, *Flight into Portugal*, 94; "unaccompanied ladies" in "Pocket Guide to Portugal," 82, Baker Coll., RIHS, and Sapega, *Consensus and Debate*, 59–60; Hahn quoted in Ramalho, *Vilar Formoso*, 133.

103.   "Cafés of the Rossio" in Sadlier, *Question of How*, 4, quoting Garnier, *Salazar*, 6. The statement referred to the situation in the early 1950s, but not

much had changed in the previous ten years. Losa's comment in Nunes, *Ilse Losa*, 87; "refused to seat" in Pimentel, "Refugiados," 106; "young girls" in Lenkway, 32, USHMM.

104. "Hermetically sealed" in Guggenheim, *Out of This Century*, 279; "most liberal father," "eagle eye," and "chastity is not expected" in "Pocket Guide to Portugal," 81–84, Baker Coll., RIHS. In fact, despite refugees' frustrations, Portugal did not lag drastically behind other nations. For example, local community norms throughout the United States dictated the dress, hairstyles, and behavior of female teachers; see "That Typical American— The School Teacher," *New York Times*, June 26, 1938, 104, ProQuest Historical Newspapers.

105. Wisla, memoirs/journal, Digibaeck, 62–63.

106. Nunes, *Ilse Losa*, 24; "Ericeira" in Schnabel, *Lisbon: Harbour of Hope*.

107. "Shocked some Portuguese" in Shomberg interview and Nunes, *Ilse Losa*, 92; "wear a hat" in Hess, "Denn unser Leben," 64; see also Pimentel, "Refugiados," 105.

108. The arrest was in October 1940 (Lustig, *Ein Rosenkranz*, 104–5); see also Bayles, "Lisbon," 80; "hat and gloves" in Pimentel and Heinrich, *Judeus*, 167.

109. "Bathing-suit styles" in Pimentel and Heinrich, *Judeus*, 171; "During the summer" and "tactless police" in Bodley, *Flight into Portugal*, 96; M. Feuchtwanger, "Émigré Life," 3:1038–40; Guggenheim, *Out of This Century*, 280.

110. "Lisbon was like a village" in Ruth Arons, interview by Gouveia, in "Lisbon"; "middle-class Portuguese women" in Pimentel and Heinrich, *Judeus*, 136; "One not only" in Ernst Levy to Irene Shomberg, n.d. (but postwar), copy in author's possession.

111. "*À Refugiada*" in Pimentel, "Refugiados," 107; she refers to the authors Alves Redol, Ilse Losa, and Suzanne Chantal. "Blonde women" in Ramalho, *Vilar Formoso*, 136; Babo in Pimentel and Heinrich, *Judeus*, 168.

112. E. Mann, "In Lissabon gestrandet," 151.

113. Zur Mühlen, *Fluchtweg*, 163.

114. *AJYB* 43, 203–4, 325; Chantal in Pimentel, "Refugiados," 109; "German Embassy" in zur Mühlen, *Fluchtweg*, 128, and Pimentel and Ninhos, "Portugal, Jewish Refugees, and the Holocaust," 110.

115. Wisla, memoirs/journal, Digibaeck, 62–63; "when we left Lisbon" in Bromberger, "Family Flight from Antwerp," 19. Years later he visited Portugal with his wife and tried to find the old acquaintances.

116. Some Portuguese men entertained the idea of befriending refugee women but, with few exceptions, never marrying them, according to Ruth Arons, who did marry her Portuguese husband (Pimentel and Heinrich, *Judeus*, 169).

117. Libermann and Renee Silbermann (who married a young doctor who cared for her family in Caldas) are both in Ramalho, *Vilar Formoso*, 149–50. For others who stayed, see Schnabel, *Lisbon: Harbour of Hope;* Blaufuks, *Strange Skies;* Losa in Nunes, *Ilse Losa*, 80; Losa, *Unter fremden Himmeln*, 83.

118. "Children without worries" in Ruth Arons interview in Gouveia, "Lisbon"; Shomberg interview.

119. The figure of fifty refugees is according to Blaufuks, *Strange Skies;* Ruth Arons interview in Gouveia, "Lisbon"; "canasta group" in Blaufuks, *Strange Skies*.

120. "Well-placed bribe" in Stephanie Krantz, née Wieser, oral history (1991), RG 50.477.1011, USHMM; "It wasn't integration" in Schnabel, *Lisbon: Harbour of Hope*, 28:28.

3. "Lisbon Is Sold Out"

Title: "Lisbon Is Sold Out" is from Tillinger, *Aufbau*, Oct. 18, 1940, 5.

Epigraph: Tedros Abraha as told to Ryan Lenora Brown, "Looking for Legal Status," *New York Times Magazine*, Aug. 5, 2016, https://www.nytimes.com/2016/08/07/magazine/looking-for-legal-status.html.

1. Bodley, *Flight into Portugal*, 91.

2. Remarque, *Night in Lisbon*, 3, 27; "rolling hills" in Wriggins, *Picking Up the Pieces*, 16; "old-fashioned capital" in "Pocket Guide," 61–62, Baker Coll., RIHS; Chantal, *Portugal*, 10.

3. Sharp, "Church Mouse," ch. 17, 2; Joy quoted in Subak, *Rescue and Flight*, 54; "blowing their horns" in Alexander, "Nazi Offensive in Lisbon," 16.

4. Döblin, *Destiny's Journey*, 212, 215, 227; "parades, or fiestas" in Sharp, "Church Mouse," ch. 17, 2; "mosaic patterns" in Corkill and Almeida, "Commemoration and Propaganda," 382.

5. Seghers, *Transit*, 242; Döblin, *Destiny's Journey*, 214; "very beautiful and busy" in Berthold Rosenthal to Ernst Rosenthal, Dec. 6, 1940, Correspondence 1940–1961, box 1, folder 1, Berthold Rosenthal Family Coll., AR 25248, LBI; "locked Lisbon" in Jansen and Schmidt, *In steter Freundschaft*, 140.

6. Remarque, *Night in Lisbon*, 8; "three million Portuguese" in Corkill and Almeida, "Commemoration and Propaganda," 384; "Portugal's history" in Buch, Contreras Zubillaga, and Silva, *Composing for the State*, ch. 8; see also

photo of buses leaving from the Rossio to the Expo. do Mundo Português, Cota Actual: photo collection: Dp6/SI1/Arm2, Empresa Pública Journal *O Século* 1880/1979, Álbum no. 076 [Letra O–4a Parte], [number on photo: 2381–0], Portuguese National Archive.

7. H. Mann, *Ein Zeitalter*, 448.

8. "We hardly needed" in F. Mann, *Drastic Turn of Destiny*, 159; Gay, *My German Question*.

9. "In Portugal, Pope Proclaims Two Fátima Siblings Saints," *New York Times*, May 13, 2017, https://www.nytimes.com/2017/05/13/world/europe/in-portugal-pope-proclaims-two-fatima-siblings-saints.html; "Popular religiosity" in Manuel, "Marian Apparitions," 11.

10. "Indescribable poverty" in Pimentel, "Refugiados,"105; "children begged" in Shomberg interview; Paetel, *Reise*, 253; Beauvoir, *Mandarins*, 96–98; see also Booth and Buck, *Lisbon*, 11.

11. "Freedom and peace" in "An Octogenarian's Records," 36, Wiener Lib.; "sleep better" in Marian Back (1996), #14542, seg. 34, Shoah, and Pekelis, *My Version*, 324; F. Mann, *Drastic Turn*, 156.

12. "Only pleasure" in Lily Losser to her children, Aug. 3, 1944, Gabrielle Greenberg Collection, LBI; see also Back, #14542, seg. 34, Shoah; Felix Bauer, memoir, 30, LBI; Felix Bauer, oral history (1992), RG-50.166*0002, USHMM; "paradise" in Else Melchior to her daughter, Ruth, Apr. 4, 1941, in Gisela A. Weil Coll.; AR 25391, box 1, folder 1, LBI.

13. "Not in luxury" in Nordman (starting with #881), 1945, AFSC, Phila. Male workers earned twice as much as women, and it took about 48 escudos (about 25 cents) a week to cover basic needs (Pimentel and de Melo, *Mulheres Portuguesas*, 279). Troper, Lisbon, to JDC, New York, Nov. 4, 1940, file 896 (1 of 3), JDC. By 1943, aid groups were estimating that it cost $60 a month to care for a child, $100 a month for a married couple, and $120 for a family of three (Refugee Services, Portugal, 1943, AFSC, Phila.). The costs in Spain could be twice as much.

14. COMASSIS, supported by several wealthy Jewish families, still needed financial support from the JDC and coordination with HICEM. D'Esaguy served as president until September 1941, and was followed by Dr. Baruel (deputy president of the Lisbon Jewish community and head of Refugee Relief). Thereafter, the Comité da Comunidade Israelita de Lisboa, headed by Moses Amzalak, aided refugees who remained in Portugal during the war.

15. "Inexpressible joy" in d'Esaguy, *Repaying a Debt*, 17; "Israelite Hospital" in Martins, *Judaísmo e Anti-semitismo*, 95. The hospital was built in 1916. In the

first three months of 1941, five Jewish refugees died (d'Esaguy, *Repaying a Debt*, 13, 18).

16. Ernst Levy to Irene Shomberg, n.d., copy in author's possession. Born in 1922, Levy remained in Portugal for fifty-five years. Davidofe quoted in Heinrich, Winterberg, and Kirkamm, *Lissabon*, 13–14; Lucy Frucht, #7156, seg. 40, 51, Shoah.

17. D'Esaguy, speech, June 4, 1941. file 896 (2 of 3), JDC; see also "Review of the Year 5702," *AJYB*, 232.

18. Dr. Baruel to the PVDE, May 11, 1943, Code HMB, Origin: PO/Li, AII–12a/4, Correspondência 1941–1956, file 390464, Secção, CAHJP. Hundreds of these exchanges regarding permissions are in Correspondência com Direção da Polícia Internacional e Defesa do Estado, Code HMB, Origin: PO/Li, AII–12a/7, Lisbon Coll., Secção, CAHJP. Friedrich Adler, an Austrian-Jewish Socialist, hid with the help of Augusto d'Esaguy. He headed toward the Sintra airport but did not leave, and thereafter used the last name "Herzl" (Pimentel and Heinrich, *Judeus*, 125–26).

19. "Arrest or worse" in Director of PVDE to Dr. Baruel, Feb. 10, 1943, and Dr. Baruel to the PVDE, Lisbon, May 11, 1943, Code HMB, Origin: PO/Li, AII–12a/4, Correspondência 1941–1956, file 390464, Secção, CAHJP. As late as 1949, Baruel was helping about 118 refugees hoping to transmigrate. Into the 1950s, Baruel corresponded with the police, refugee organizations, and refugees still in Portugal as well as with those who had left Lisbon. See, for example, Correspondência geral, Code HMB, Origin: PO/Li, AII–12a/12, files 400400–400745 and 400889–400896, Secção, CAHJP; for the 118 refugees, see file 400813.

20. The JDC occasionally referred to "self-sustaining" refugees, and the Polish and Czech national committees in Lisbon assisted some of their nationals; see Nussbaum of the JDC, Lisbon, report of Oct. 8, 1941, file 896 (2 of 3), JDC.

21. "USC's efforts" in Subak, *Rescue and Flight*, 82; see also Michelle Bates Deakin, "Unitarian Couple Honored for World War II Heroism," *UU World*, Dec. 12, 2005, uuworld.org/news/articles/2453.shtml. "Lisbon Jewish community" in Martha Sharp (USC) to Dr. Baruel, Apr. 4, 1945, thanking him for a gift of matzot, Code: HMB, Origin: PO/Li, AII–12a/3, 1941–48, file 390269, Comissão, CAHJP. Sharp's group supported Youth Aliyah, which was run by Hadassah (Subak, *Rescue and Flight*, 177–79).

22. "February 1941" in Conard Report, July 26, 1945, AFSC, Phila.; "wandering Jew" in Conard Report on Work of AFSC, 1941–44, 20, AFSC, Phila.; "Jewish ancestry" in Wriggins, *Picking Up the Pieces*, 17; "Unknowns" in

(no name, probably Conard) to Mary Roger, Phila. Pa., July 20, 1942, letter #355, MS 1389, box 55, Schauffler, Yale; Karl Glauber folder in AFSC, 2002.296, USHMM.

23. When the Viennese Jewish community asked whether the JDC would pay for "not Mosaic," that is, converted, Jews, the JDC demurred; see Joseph Loewenherz Coll., meeting of Jan. 25, 1941, AR25055, 55, Digibaeck.

24. "Not endangering" in JDC, Lisbon, to JDC, New York, telegram, Aug. 28, 1940, file 896 (1 of 3), JDC; "anxious to avoid" in "Conversation with Baerwald," memo of Nov. 5, 1940, file 896 (1 of 3), JDC; "no refugee" in Hyman, New York, to João de Bianchi, Washington, DC, May 16, 1941, file 896 (2 of 3), JDC.

25. Dwork and van Pelt, *Flight from the Reich*, 234. Bazarov estimated that the HIAS (HICEM) office, established in Lisbon on June 26, 1940, helped over 11,000 refugees leave Portugal between then and the end of 1941 ("Racing with Death," 24). HICEM maintained contact with agencies in New York and in Axis-occupied countries (Bazarov, "HIAS and HICEM," 74); Sahl, *Das Exil*, 277.

26. "A few steps ahead" in *Footnotes: The Newsletter of the JDC New York Archives*, Dec. 1999: 2. Katzki, secretary of JDC's European Executive Council, and his coworkers slept in fields in France before getting to Lisbon. Schwartz, a rabbi and Yale Ph.D. in Semitic studies, was vice-chair (1940–41) and chair (1942–49) of the JDC's European Executive Council. Schwartz took over as director of European operations when Morris Troper joined the army once the United States entered the war. Manny Rosen handled emigration (Katzki interviews, 55, JDC). Katzki and Lou Sobel returned to Lisbon in November 1942 when they believed the Germans would not invade Portugal; see also *Footnotes*, Dec. 1999: 3. Joseph Schwartz joined the U.S. Army in early 1942.

27. "JDC supported 1,500" in Y. Bauer, *American Jewry*, 47; "main support" in Katzki interviews, 67, JDC; "wholesale business" in Herbert Katzki, oral history (1995), RG-50.030*0337, USHMM, and Bazarov, "HIAS and HICEM," 76; "Affidavits" in Katzki interviews, 67, JDC; "reserves of the refugees" in Nussbaum of JDC, Lisbon, report of Oct. 8, 1941, file 896 (2 of 3), JDC.

28. "Accepted deposits" in JDC and AFSC files; see also remittances in O. Trilling to the Portuguese Jewish community, Apr. 24, 1943, promising $100 a month for H. Anschel in Lisbon, Code: HMB, Origin: PO/Li, AII–12a/3, 1941–48, file 390138, Comissão, CAHJP; memo about matzot, Mar. 6, 1941,

file 896 (2 of 3), JDC; "Memo about Matzoth," Apr. 14, 1942, file 896 (3 of 3), JDC; memo, Apr. 15, 1943, file #897 (1 of 2), JDC; Passover special grant of Apr. 1, 1944, file #897 (2 of 2), JDC.

29. Bill of Mar. 15, 1943, from Horowitz to the JDC, Lisbon, Code: HMB, Origin: PO/Li, AII–12a/3, 1941–48, file 390185, Comissão, CAHJP. In 1942, the JDC shipped 357 such cartons (file 390207, bill of lading, Feb. 9, 1942, to Moses Amzalak) at a cost of $4,500 (file 390209, bill of Jan. 27, 1942, from B. Manischewitz Co.); see also the first shipment of 4,200 pounds of matzot and 1,000 pounds of matzah meal in 1941: cable, Mar. 6, 1941 (refers to "Matzoth" and "Easterbread"), file 896 (2 of 3), JDC. Dollar-value conversions at Inflation Calculator, accessed July 5, 2019, at http://www.in2013dollars.com/us/inflation/1940?amount=1.

30. Conard, report of Nov. 25, 1941, AFSC, 2002.296, USHMM; "trying to give assistance" in Schauffler to Ambassador Weddell, memo, Mar. 22, 1941, regarding transportation from Lisbon, Schauffler, Yale; "clients seemed inconsolable" in Blumberg, letters of Jan. 12, 1943, and June 10, 1946, AFSC, 2002.296, file 2692, USHMM; "exaggerated feminism" in USC Lisbon to Rebekah Taft, USC Boston, June 14, 1944, USC, Exec. Director, bMS 16007_ Box 20_folder 11, RG-67.028, USHMM; "flood of tears" in RWR to LKC [initials only], Apr. 18, 1945, Cases, 1945, AFSC, Phila.

31. Lawrence Parrish, diaries, Oct. 24, 1943, 13, Refugee Services, Portugal, 1943, AFSC, Phila.; Troper, JDC, Lisbon, to JDC, New York, Nov. 4, 1940, file 896 (1 of 3), JDC; "Refugees are grateful" in Kurt Haut, Caldas, to E. Dexter, Nov. 24, 1944, USC, bMS 16007_Box 20_folder 10_066, RG-67.028, USHMM; Field quoted in Subak, *Rescue and Flight*, 179.

32. "Amzalak" in James Mann Report, Aug. 30, 1944, 18, WRB, USHMM; d'Esaguy, *Repaying a Debt*, 15; "sweet" in Memo of Conversation with Baerwald, Nov. 5, 1940, file 896 (1 of 3), JDC. On bribes, see also Stephanie Krantz, née Wieser, oral history (1991), RG50.477.1011 transcript, 40, 44, USHMM. Douglas Wheeler stated that the PVDE was "open to bribes" (email to the author, Dec. 4, 2014). "Retaliate by refusing" in James Mann Report, WRB, USHMM; "Letters from the JDC" in Lisbon, Correspondência com Direção da Polícia Internacional e Defesa do Estado, Code: HMB/, Origin: PO/Li, AII–12a/5, Comissão, CAHJP; for examples, see files 400482–400550.

33. Conard to his family, Oct. 12, 1941, and note from Lois Conard Gassler, 1981, Conard Coll., AFSC, 2002.296, USHMM.

34. "Isaac Weissmann" in Y. Bauer, *American Jewry*, 213–14; "Robert Dexter" in James Mann Report, WRB, USHMM; Elizabeth Dexter in oral history

project at the Hebrew University, quoted in DiFiglia, *Roots and Visions*, 28; "baby kangaroo" in the file "Portugal. Lisbon. Letters from, 1944–1945," USC, RG-67.028, USHMM; "work troika" in zur Mühlen, *Fluchtweg*, 191.

35. Joseph Schwartz to Moses Amzalak, Dec. 16, 1941, offering JDC money for "direct relief, for medical service," and for office expenses, and giving full control to COMASSIS as of Dec. 18, 1941, file 896 (2 of 3), JDC; see also Bernstein of HICEM to Amzalak, Lisbon, Dec. 16, 1941, Code: HMB, Origin: PO/Li, AII–12a/2, 1941–42, Comissão, CAHJP, and Amzalak to Joseph Schwartz, Dec. 22, 1941, Code: HMB, Origin: PO/Li, AII–12a/4, 1941–56, Comissão, CAHJP. The JDC openly transferred $22,500 to the Lisbon Jewish community for January–March 1942 via its London bank account, just a few weeks after Pearl Harbor; see Amzalak and Baruel to the JDC, Dec. 22, 1941, and Louis Rosner, chief accountant (JDC), to Amzalak, Dec. 22, 1941, Code: HMB, Origin: PO/Li, AII–12a/3, 1941–48, Comissão, CAHJP. HIAS, too, transferred funds and gave the names of the leadership of the Lisbon Jewish community to the State Department; see Bernstein, HIAS, to Amzalak, Jan. 20, 1942, Code: HMB, Origin: PO/Li AII–12a/6, Folhas de cobrança, 1942–43, Secção, CAHJP.

36. "Transfers" in Y. Bauer, *American Jewry*, 198.

37. HICEM also let the Lisbon Jewish community take over its office space; see Bernstein to Amzalak, Dec. 16, 1941, Code: HMB, Origin: PO/Li, AII–12a/3, 1941–48, Comissão, CAHJP; "working overtly" in zur Mühlen, *Fluchtweg*, 187.

38. Shepherd, *Wilfred Israel*, and Nir, *The Essential Link: The Story of Wilfrid Israel* (film).

39. "Joined the Nazi Party" in Pimentel and Heinrich, *Judeus*, 63, 65; "German Colony" in zur Mühlen, *Fluchtweg*, 124, 136–37; Schickert and Denk, *Die Bartholomäus-Brüderschaft*, 259–77. Katzenstein returned immediately after the war. "Nazi Party meetings" in Pimentel and Heinrich, *Judeus*, 64. The newsletter ceased publication with the outbreak of war.

40. "Anti-Bolshevik" in Alexander, "Nazi Offensive in Lisbon," 15; "knew exactly where" in Pimentel and Heinrich, *Judeus*, 63.

41. Pimentel and Heinrich, *Judeus*, 61, 66.

42. Nunes, *Ilse Losa*, 25; "Nazi anthem" in Pimentel and Heinrich, *Judeus*, 62–63, 66; "French instruction" in Ramalho, *Lisbon*, 145; "*liceu*" in Shomberg interview; Aberle in Pimentel and Heinrich, *Judeus*, 62, 66.

43. "Nazi organizations" in Pimentel, "Refugiados," 103, and Schickert and Denk, *Die Bartholomäus-Brüderschaft*, 261; "anniversary of Salazar's

revolution" in Ramalho, *Lisbon*, 145; "ardent enthusiasts" in Pimentel and Heinrich, *Judeus*, 63, 65.

44. "Vast assortment" in Pekelis, *My Version*, 137; "arrived overdue," regarding English papers, in Archives National (France): AJ38 988, Reel 175 from June 17, 1941, RG-43.023, USHMM; "American newsreels" in Pimentel, "Refugiados," 108; Sahl quoted in Blaufuks, *Strange Skies;* see also Kalischer, *Vom Konzentrationslager*, 148–49.

45. Von Andrian to Andrée Wimpffen, July 2, 1940, A: Andrian, NZ. 78.2.740, DLA Marbach; Israel to relatives in the United States, Aug. 25, 1940, private collection of Ralph Ibson (shown to the author); Douhaerdt to Manfred George, Oct. 31, 1940, A: George 75.2439/1–2, DLA Marbach; Salomon Berenholz (1996), #14294, seg. 70–79, Shoah; Saint-Exupéry, *Lettre à un Otage.*

46. "German invasion" in 254.4, section I, file no. XII-Portugal A-2, microfilms 15.30–15.34, 6, HIAS-HICEM, YIVO; Davidsohn family in Heinrich, Winterberg, and Kirkamm, *Lissabon*, 11; Fritz Blum memoir, 18, LBI.

47. Sharp, *Journey to Freedom*, 10; "inaccurate rumor" in Sharp to Seth Gano, Sept. 14, 1941; "completed cases" in Sharp to Harry Hooper, Sept. 17, 1941, both letters in bMS 16135 USC Lisbon, box 3, folder 22, Dexter correspondence, 1941, Andover-Harvard; Shirer, *Berlin Diary* (entry for Oct. 15, 1940), 542; Sevareid, "Escape Hatch," 93.

48. "All Lisbon" in Lotte Marcuse, "Arrival of Children on S.S. *Nyassa,* on April 23, 1941," 1933–1953, YIVO, RG 249, folder 478; Conard, "Brief Report on the Lisbon Office of the AFSC, May to August '41," Aug. 23, 1941, 16, AFSC, 2002.296, USHMM, and Schauffler, Yale; "Everyone was so certain" in Katzki interviews, 56 (referring to Dec. 1941), JDC; "case of nerves" in Conard, to his family, Jan. 3, 1942, AFSC, 2002.296, USHMM.

49. "Germany no longer" in Wriggins, *Picking Up the Pieces*, 45, 54–55; "occasional victories" in Wisla, memoirs/journal (n.d.), Digibaeck, 63; "practice blackouts" in Parrish diary, Oct. 16, 1943, 10, Refugee Services, Portugal, 1943, AFSC, Phila.; "German submarines," seen in 1941, in Legião Portuguesa, Comando Geral, 2nd Repartição, Proc. 1566/15-B5, #290, and Legião Portuguesa, Comando Geral, #288, Portuguese National Archive; "stop with Spain" in Fry, *Surrender on Demand*, 73, 76; "British Embassy" in Potworowski, "Evacuation of Jewish Polish Citizens," 163.

50. Minutes of the Wannsee Conference available in English translation at the Holocaust Research Project, holocaustresearchproject.org/holoprelude/Wannsee/wanseeminutes.html; Thies, *Hitler's Plans;* "demands of war" in Fritzsche, *Life and Death*, 165.

51. *Life,* July 29, 1940, 65; *Saturday Evening Post* quoted in Alexander, "Nazi Offensive in Lisbon," 15; "organic" in Pinto, *Modern Portugal,* 24, 27, 30–38. Pinto argues that Salazarism, "dominated by Maurrasian and Catholic thinking," had more in common with Vichy, Dollfus, and Franco than with the Nazis. "Provincial elites" in Sapega, *Consensus and Debate,* 2, 9, 11.

52. "Low-key terror" in T. Gallagher, "Controlled Repression," 386; Gumbel, "Nazi Activity in Portugal," 3–4, Emil J. Gumbel Coll., series 3, box 2, folder 14, LBI; see http://archive.org/stream/emiljgumbelb002f014#page/n12/mode/1up/search/Portugal.

53. Marcu, *Ein Kopf,* 205; von Andrian in Prutsch and Zeyringer, *Leopold von Andrian,* 709.

54. F. Mann, *Drastic Turn of Destiny,* 173; "impatient" in Grab, *Hochzeit in Brooklyn,* 57; "recalled this torment" in Schnabel, *Lisbon: Harbour of Hope,* 54:30–56:23; Stanton, *Escape from the Inferno,* 146; "cold sweat" in Hess, "Denn unser Leben," 65.

55. Visa prices shown on visas issued by the Consulate of Portugal in Marseille, Oct. 5, 1942, and police extensions, Oct. 15, 1942, Zweigenthal family, Access. 1998.A.0210, USHMM; "police did not harass" in Pimentel and Heinrich, *Judeus,* 142.

56. "Official agencies" in Martins, *Judaísmo e Anti-semitismo,* 90; "kindly set free" and "wholesale internment" in Comissão, Lisbon, to JDC, Paris, Dec. 22, 1939, file 896 (1 of 3), JDC.

57. "Sent back home" in Grab, *Hochzeit in Brooklyn,* 57; Lion Feuchtwanger's flight and "risk of abduction" in M. Feuchtwanger, "Escape," 266, but she offers no proof; Lewis, #12696, seg. 44–47, Shoah.

58. Varian Fry charged that the Gestapo had kidnapped ten refugees in Portugal, but offered no details (JTA, "Gestapo Gangs").

59. Wheeler, "In the Service of Order," 11–12. Pimentel and Ninhos cite at least two other cases of Jewish men who were expelled from Portugal but managed to remain, thanks to the intercession of the Jewish community (*Salazar, Portugal,* 456). "Raiding cafés" in Heinrich, Winterberg, and Kirkamm, *Lissabon,* 17.

60. "Attempts to intercede" in Correspondência com Direção da Polícia Internacional e Defesa do Estado Lisbon, Code: HMB, Origin: PO/Li, AII–12a/5, all folders in this category, Secção, CAHJP; lists of workers in Correspondência 1941–1956 (see, for example, Baruel to the PVDE, Jan. 5, 1943), Code: HMB, Origin: PO/Li, AII–12a/4, Secção, CAHJP; Wriggins,

Picking Up the Pieces, 24–25; "We came to Portugal" in (unnamed writer) to Dr. J. Schwarz, JDC, Lisbon, Apr. 7, 1941, file 896 (1 of 2), JDC.

61. "As many as half" in Heinrich, Winterberg, and Kirkamm, *Lissabon,* 13; "Aljube prison" in Hess, "Was Portugal," 183; Quakers quoted in "Prisons for foreigners in Portugal" (undated report), Schauffler, Yale; Wisla, memoirs/journal, Digibaeck, 60–61.

62. Wisla, memoirs/journal, Digibaeck, 63; "overcrowded cages" in Wriggins, *Picking Up the Pieces,* 18–19.

63. Lenkway, 33–35, USHMM; "remained in Caxias" in memo, Nov. 6, 1944, 8, Conard Coll, AFSC, 2002.296, USHMM; Dexter to Edward Crocker, Feb. 14, 1944, Doc. 405, Sutters, *Archives of the Holocaust,* 2:498.

64. "Jail was very nice" in Leitner, #1741, seg. 51–53, Shoah; "guards in the prison" in Frucht, #7156, seg. 51–70, Shoah.

65. Wolfsohn's story is in Pimentel and Heinrich, *Judeus,* 127; Winter's account is in his letters to the AFSC, Mar. 15, 1940, and June 9, 1941, file 3886, AFSC, 2002.296, USHMM.

66. Isaac and Sara Glozer folder, AFSC, 2002.296, USHMM. These files refer to May–Aug. 1941, after which the family left for Cuba; "prison guards" in Lenkway, 36–37, USHMM.

67. The teenager's story is in Bromberger, "Family Flight from Antwerp," 18; Stanton, *Escape from the Inferno,* 146–47.

68. Letter headed "Jewish refugees from ship *Dora,*" AOS/CO/IN–8B (1940), Doc. 1. Cota Actual: Arquivo Salazar, IN–8B, c. 331, pt. 1, Portuguese National Archive.

4. Emotional Dissonance

Epigraph: Interview with Beatrix Bücher, CARE, on Syrian refugees in Jordan, care.org/emergencies/syria-crisis/interview-urban-refugees-are-struggling-more-and-more-survive.

1. Arendt to Salomon Adler-Rudel, Feb. 17, 1941, available (in German) at hannaharendt.net/index.php/han/article/view/72/108; see also Bertolt Brecht, "We hear the screams from the camps wherever we are," in "Über die Bezeichnung Emigranten," written in 1937 in Paris.

2. "Cut from the security" in Reichmann, *Deutscher Bürger,* 279; see also Adler and Hamilton, *Homes and Homecoming,* 2.

3. Tuan, *Space and Place,* 33; Marcus, *House as a Mirror;* Feuchtwanger quoted in Schlör, "Menschen," 44.

4. Massey, *Space, Place, and Gender.*
5. "Spacial identity" and "similar to mourning" in Fried, "Grieving for a Lost Home," 365, 369; "connected to a place" in Amato, *Rethinking Home,* 4.
6. Allen, *Home.*
7. Auslander, "Coming Home," 237, and Easthope, "Fixed Identities," 69; see also Anthony, "Return Home."
8. Musil, *Man Without Qualities,* 4, 6. The novel, which takes place at the end of the Austro-Hungarian monarchy, was written between 1930 and 1943. Arendt, *Origins of Totalitarianism,* 145.
9. "Linked to ideas" in Frevert, "Trust as Work," 100, and "Does Trust Have a History," 8.
10. "Losing equal citizenship" in Rürup, "Lives in Limbo," 123–24. The "Eleventh Decree" (*Elfte Verordnung zum Reichsbürgergesetz*), enacted on November 25, 1941, automatically deprived Jews of their German citizenship if they resided outside Germany on or after November 27, 1941 (Reichmann, *Deutscher Bürger,* 279). "dispossessed, uprooted" in "An Octogenarian's Records," 37, Wiener Lib.
11. Weil, *Need for Roots,* 6–8; Hobsbawm, "Exile," 64, 59.
12. "Emotional citizenship," in Frevert, "Does Trust Have a History," 8; "home as a political space," in Auslander, "Coming Home," 259; "ever truly been theirs" in Améry, *At the Mind's Limits,* 50; "loving relationship" in Malkki, "National Geographic."
13. "We didn't emigrate" in Brecht, "Über die Bezeichnung Emigranten"; "World War I veterans" in M. Kaplan, *Dignity and Despair,* 65–66, and Winkle, *Der Dank des Vaterlandes;* "Habsburg Austria" in Rozenblit, *National Identity,* 162.
14. Lambert, *Diary of a Witness,* Oct. 19, 1940, 23; see also Cohen, "Jewish Leader in Vichy France," 292.
15. "Communal memory" in Moltke, *No Place like Home,* 227, quoting Williams, *Country and City,* 297; "thoroughly romanticized" in Dodman, "Before Trauma." On smells and wind, visit (in person) the Emigration Museum, Ballinstadt, Hamburg; see also Boym, *Future of Nostalgia.* Thanks to Marcella Simoni for reminding me that Italian Jews in Israel also missed their homeland, the "historic buildings . . . art, and . . . landscape"; see Fallaci, "Italiani di Israele." The anthropologist T. M. Luhrmann similarly noted people's connection with place ("How Places Let Us Feel," A19).
16. "Primeval woodlands" in Schama, *Landscape and Memory,* 83–85, 89; Caspar David Friedrich in Schama, "Homelands," 21–22; Gay, *My German Question,* 117.

17. "Mountains, and forests" in Scheiber, *Politische Berge,* and Lehmann and Shriewer, *Der Wald;* "mobility and dislocation" in Moltke, *No Place like Home,* 230.

18. Losa titled two of the novels *The World in Which I Had Lived* (1949) and *Under Strange Skies* (1962); they were translated into German in 1990 and 1991. Nunes, *Ilse Losa,* 110; for similar examples, see Easthope, "Fixed Identities," 61–82; H. Mann, *Ein Zeitalter,* 448; see also Voigt, quoting Mann, in *Heinrich Mann,* 54.

19. "Viennese Jews" in Rozenblit, *Jews of Vienna,* 17–21. In 1871, about 70 percent of the Jews in Germany lived in the countryside. Forty years later, about 70 percent resided in cities, but only 21 percent of non-Jews did (Ruppin, *Die Juden der Gegenwart,* 42, 44); see also Lowenstein, "Rural Community," and Thon, *Die jüdischen Gemeinden,* 73.

20. "Regional identities" in Applegate, "Europe of Regions"; "*Heimatlos*" in Schnabel, *Lisbon: Harbour of Hope,* 3:58–4:10.

21. Refugee audiences in New York and in mostly Jewish Catskill mountain hotels enjoyed these carefully chosen memories into the 1950s; see N. Jacobs, "Soirée bei Kohn," 200–202. Kafka quoted in Wagenbach, *Kafka's Prague,* 7.

22. "Place of remembering" in Pfanner, *Exile in New York,* 139; "Old Vienna" in Weiss and Leopoldi, *Leopoldi und Möslein,* 66–67, 77–78, and Traska and Lind, *Hermann Leopoldi,* 254; see also Spitzer, *Hotel Bolivia.*

23. Weiss and Leopoldi, *Leopoldi und Möslein,* 71–73. Leopoldi and his musical partner, Helly Möslein, offered "a Viennese Rendezvous" in a variety of cafés; see an advertisement for Eberhardt's Café Grinzing (*Leopoldi und Möslein,*" 78). There are also ads and photos in Klösch and Thumser, *"From Vienna,"* 19, 20, 22, 24, 25, 29–30, 32. "Overlooked disease" in Dwork and van Pelt, *Flight from the Reich,* 317, quoting Lothar, *Das Wunder des Über-lebens,* 313; see also Stella Kadmon's "insane homesickness for Vienna" in Tanzer, "Performing the Symbiosis"; Mann quoted in Sprecher, *Thomas Mann;* Anderson, *Imagined Communities;* "Janus-faced" and "bitterness of rejection" in Spitzer, *Hotel Bolivia,* 143–44 and ch. 5.

24. Bab quoted in Pfanner, *Exile in New York,* 149. Only about one-third of German Jews had lived in Berlin, whereas the vast majority of Austrian and Czech Jews came from Vienna and Prague; hence, the difference in attitudes toward Berlin.

25. Adorno, *Minima Moralia,* 87; Ellis, *Encountering the Jewish Future,* 172, quoting Arendt, "What Remains," 13, and "Hannah Arendt im Gespräch mit Günter Gaus," 37:16; Reichmann, *Deutscher Bürger,* 267; Stern, *Five Germanys,* 514.

26. "Considered going back" in a talk by Robert Dexter, Feb. 18, 1944, Doc. 406, Sutters, *Archives of the Holocaust*, 2:499; "the more optimistic" in Wriggins, "January Report," Jan. 8, 1943, 4, Foreign Service, 1943, Portugal, AFSC, Phila. Some Jews did return to these countries and to central Europe after the war; see Lühe, Schildt, and Schüler-Springorum, *"Auch in Deutschland"*; Koch, "Home After Fascism"; and Wilder-Okladek, *Return Movement of Jews*.

27. Saint-Exupéry, *Lettre à un Otage*.

28. "Set one's heart" in Marianne Gilbert Finnegan, *Das gab's nur einmal: Verloren zwischen Berlin und New York* (Zurich: Diogenes, 2007), 42, quoted by Schlör, "Man Lässt," 103; "express similarities" in Auslander, "Jewish Taste"; "convey to others" in Auslander, "Coming Home," 238; see also Blunt and Dowling, *Home*, and Vansant, *Reclaiming Heimat*.

29. "Stand-ins for losses" in Wallen and Pomerance, "Circuitous Journeys," 257; "Reichmann, *Deutscher Bürger*, 267; Levi, *Survival in Auschwitz*, 27; "loss of heritage" in Auslander, "Coming Home," 238.

30. "Biographies" in Auslander, "'Jewish Taste,'" esp. 300–302, 315; see also Kopytoff, "Cultural Biography of Things," 67; "tangible reminder" and "towel" in Körte and Axelrod, "Bracelet, Hand Towel, Pocket Watch," 109–11; "loss of these keepsakes" in Auslander, "Coming Home," 238; see also Parkin, "Mementoes," and Hoskins, *Biographical Objects;* "memories of one's personhood" in Parkin, "Mementoes," 309; "part of who we are" in Luhrmann, "How Places Let Us Feel," A19; see also Marcus, *House as a Mirror*, 241; "Doris' shoes" in Schauffler to Conard, July 31, 1942, Gaertner file 6801, AFSC, 2002.296, USHMM.

31. "1940s Hats History," http://vintagedancer.com/1940s/1940s-hats, and "History of Hats for Women," http://vintagefashionguild.org/fashion-history/the-history-of-womens-hats. Thank you to Flora Cassen for sharing Zandmer's story and photos and for granting permission to publish them (emails to the author, July 9, 2014, July 4, 2016, and July 11 and 13, 2018). "Leather baggage" in Losa, *Unter fremden Himmeln*, 83; "This is it" in Schrag and Schrag, *Europe Was a Prison Camp*, 265.

32. Jansen and Schmidt, *In steter Freundschaft*, 118.

33. "Slower pace" in Ernst Levy to his cousin, Irene Shomberg, regarding life in Portugal (n.d., copy in author's possession); "check your watch" in Schnabel, *Lisbon: Harbour of Hope*, 3:31–3:40; "memory spaces" in Wise, "Home"; "soft voices" in M. Kaplan, *Jewish Middle Class*, ch. 1.

34. Kracauer in Jansen and Schmidt, *In steter Freundschaft*, 119; "fur coats for sale" in Bayles, "Europe's Bottleneck," 80; "had no possessions" in Fernanda

de Castro, *Fim da Memória* (Lisbon: Verbo, 1986–87), quoted in Pimentel and Heinrich, *Judeus*, 137–38; Stephanie Krantz, née Wieser, oral history, 40, 44. USHMM.

35. Werner Goldberg to "Mrs. Shcauffler" [*sic*], AFSC, Mar. 8, 1941, AFSC, 2002.296, USHMM; Bernhard, AFSC, 2002.296, USHMM.

36. Döblin, *Destiny's Journey*, 219; "heavy wool garments" in E. Mann, "In Lissabon gestrandet," 151; H. Paul to Wriggins, Dec. 16, 1942, Paul file 8703, AFSC 2002.296, USHMM.

37. "Bewildered looks" in Fry, *Surrender on Demand*, 4; Mahler-Werfel, *And the Bridge;* social worker, USC Lisbon, to Irene O. Hay, Jan. 10, 1945, USC, Exec. Dir., bMS 16007_Box 20_folder 10, RG-67.028, USHMM; Arendt, "We Refugees" (1994), 114.

38. Margit Meissner, oral history (1992), USHMM, and Meissner, interview; see also "Forgotten Designer Nelly de Grab," *Couture Allure Vintage Fashion Blog,* Mar. 20, 2013, http://coutureallure.blogspot.com/2013/03/forgotten-designer-nelly-de-grab.html; "kosher meals" in Joseph Sucher, "Luck was on our Side," ms. 818, 10–11, LBI; "Czech cartoonist" in Alexander, "Nazi Offensive in Lisbon," 15; Marguerite Douhaerdt to Manfred George, Oct. 31, 1940, *Aufbau,* A: George 75.2439/1–2, DLA Marbach.

39. Political prisoner quoted in Wriggins, journal entry, Sept. 10, 1942, box 1, folder 30, 1942, RG 67.008, USHMM; Arendt, "We Refugees" (1994), 110.

40. "It is pitiful" in JDC, Lisbon, to JDC, New York, Nov. 4, 1940, file 896 (1 of 3), JDC; Arendt, "We Refugees" (2007), 269, and "We Refugees" (1994), 111.

41. "Parables of increasing self-loss" in Dagmar Barnouw, *Der Jude als Paria* (1986), 44, commenting on Arendt, cited in Nunes, *Ilse Losa,* 26; "Nobody here knows" in Arendt, "We Refugees" (1994), 115. Arendt was hardly the only refugee writer in Lisbon. Roda Roda (Sandor Rosenfeld), Ulrich Becher, Henry William Katz, Siegfried Kracauer, Soma Morgenstern, Balder Olden, Hans Sahl, Maximilian Scheer, Siegfried Thalheimer, Otto Zoff, and Kurt Wolff, among many others, also waited there in 1941. Teixeira, "Warten," 15; Losa, *Unter fremden Himmeln,* 124.

42. Gay, *Bourgeois Experience;* "degradation ritual" in Loewenberg, "*Kristallnacht,*" 309–23; Arendt, "We Refugees" (1994), 114.

43. Kessel, "Balance der Gefühle," 32–33; see also Kessel, "Das Trauma," 156–58.

44. "Success in the nineteenth century" in Kessel, "Balance der Gefühle," 234, 237–39, 244, 255; "public respect" in Heinrich Fonfé to AFSC, Apr. 12, 1942, Heinrich Fonfé file, AFSC, 2002.296, USHMM; "upward mobility" in

M. Kaplan, *Jewish Middle Class,* 52; "valued their work" in Orbach, "Work Is Where We Live"; "travel to any country" in Fonfé to AFSC, April 12, 1942; motto in Kessel, "Whole Man," 4, 20.

45. Frevert, "Honor, Gender and Power," 234–40, 245–47; Rürup, "Jüdische Studentenverbindungen"; Zwicker, "Performing Masculinity"; Dunker, *Frontsoldaten.*

46. Quoted in Y. Bauer, *American Jewry,* 55.

47. "Loyal and enterprising" in Dina Moore Bowden to Schauffler, report, Apr. 18, 1941, Schauffler, Yale; "to urge emigration" in M. Kaplan, *Dignity and Despair,* chs. 2, 3, 5; Lasch, *Haven in a Heartless World;* "enthroned fixture" in Hareven, "Home and Family," 235–36.

48. Tec, *Resilience and Courage,* 10; "more emotional" in Kessel, "Gefühle," 40; "November Pogrom" in M. Kaplan, *Dignity and Despair,* 125–45.

49. Arendt, "We Refugees" (1994), 119. Stefan Zweig, though not in Lisbon, echoed this sentiment: "I have decided not to change myself . . . to remain loyal to those who have remained loyal to themselves" (Zweig and Zech, *Briefe,* 151). "Could not forget" in Bodley, *Flight into Portugal,* 106; Koestler, *Arrival and Departure,* 19; Saint-Exupéry, *Lettre à un Otage,* 16.

50. "Most of us" in letter to Dr. J. Schwarz, JDC, Lisbon, Apr. 7, 1941 file 896, JDC; Stanton, *Escape from the Inferno,* 178; DeBenedetti, "Between Fascism and Freedom," ch. 8, 3, accession 2004.57, USHMM; "supported and guided" in Leshem, "Rescue Efforts," 240.

51. "Pills for anxiety" in Sahl, *Das Exil,* 277. It is likely these were barbiturates, among which Veronal had also been used to commit suicide in Germany (López-Muñoz, Ucha-Udabe, and Alamo, "Barbiturates"). On suicides, see M. Kaplan, *Dignity and Despair,* 181–84. "Breakdowns" in Bitton, oral history (1990), minute 1:10:41, RG 50.030*0027, USHMM. One such case is in Comissão, Lisbon, to JDC, Paris, Dec. 22, 1939, file 896 (1 of 3), JDC; Zweig in Fuechtner, *Berlin Psychoanalytic,* 133–34; "dammed up feeling" in Vansant, *Reclaiming Heimat,* 51.

52. Fry, *Surrender on Demand,* 13, 103; "morale boosting" in report of June 9, 1944, USC, Exec. Dir., bMS 16007_Box 20_folder 11, RG-67.028, USHMM; "often feel" in DiFiglia, *Roots and Visions,* 25, quoting the USC worker Herta Field.

53. Wriggins, *Picking Up the Pieces,* 22; Paul, report of Dec. 1, 1942, file 8703, AFSC, 2002.296, USHMM. The Pauls arrived in June 1941 and left in March 1943.

54. No one used the term "post-traumatic stress disorder" then. Only in 1955 did psychologists recognize that refugees, too, not only concentration camp

survivors, had mental health and social problems (Murphy, *Flight and Reset-tlement*). The man eventually reached the United States, where he completed a medical degree, according to the AFSC; see Conard, memo of work done by AFSC 1941–41, 4, Refugee Services, Portugal, 1943, AFSC, Phila., General Files, USHMM.

55. "Past trials" in Dina Moore Bowden to Schauffler, report, Apr. 18, 1941, Schauffler, Yale; suicide rates in M. Kaplan, *Dignity and Despair*, 179–84, and Goeschel, *Suicide in Nazi Germany*, ch. 3; Koestler, *Invisible Writing*, 423, and Cesarani, *Arthur Koestler*, 169; "American consul" in Blaufuks, *Strange Skies*, quoting Hertha Pauli; see also Lewis (1996), #12696, seg. 44–47, Shoah.

56. "Fearfully desperate" in [unknown writer] to Margaret Jones, Dec. 20, 1942, Rosenfeld file 6031, AFSC, 2002.296, USHMM; Dembitzer, *Visas for America*, 212; Lustig, *Ein Rosenkranz*, 91; Arendt, "We Refugees" (1994), 112–14.

57. "Beg for relief" in Conard, Report on Work of AFSC, 14, Foreign Service, 1945, AFSC, Phila.; "stream of people" in Dina Moore Bowden to Schauf-fler, report, Apr. 18, 1941, Schauffler, Yale; "guts" in Nicholas Farkas folder, 2002.296, AFSC, USHMM; Conard's observations in Conard to AFSC, Phila., Oct. 9, 1941, AFSC, 2002.296, USHMM; "human greatness" in Bowden to Schauffler, Apr. 18, 1941.

58. Bodley, *Flight into Portugal*, 51–52; Seghers, *Transit*, 31.

59. "Reports from a neurologist" in Boas, "Shrinking World," 256–57 and n92; "fought with their reluctant parents" in M. Kaplan, *Dignity and Despair*, ch. 4.

60. Hilberg, *Politics of Memory*, 43; Rosy S. (1993), #T-2684, FVA; Shadur, *Drive to Survival*, 95–97, 102.

61. Hilberg, *Politics of Memory*, 43; Sucher, "Luck was on our Side," LBI, 11, Gould Coll., RG-02.141, 7, USHMM.

62. F. Mann, *Drastic Turn to Destiny*, 155–56; unaccompanied teens in Lotte Marcuse, director of placement of the European-Jewish Children's Aid, "Reception of children who arrived on April 15th," and [no name], "Arrival of 3 children on the SS Siboney—March 27, 1941," YIVO, RG 249, folder 478.

63. Irene Shomberg to the author, Nov. 8, 2013.

64. Henri Deutsch (1995), #10463, seg. 57–65, Shoah; Albert Lichter (1996), #12774, seg. 40–49, Shoah; F. Mann, *Drastic Turn to Destiny*, 172; "in love" in Bromberger, "Family Flight from Antwerp," 18.

65. "Stephanie Flakowicz Marks, the fifteen-year-old, quoted in Ramalho, *Vilar Formoso*, 148; Photo Archives, W/S #28936, Margit Meissner, USHMM, and

Meissner interview; "Portuguese husband" in Stephanie Krantz, née Wieser, interview, 42–47, RG 50.477.1011, USHMM.

66. Liny Pajgin Yollick, oral history (1990) transcript, 14, RG-50.030*0265, USHMM; Stephanie Krantz, née Wieser, interview, 42–47, RG 50.477.1011, USHMM; Lenkway, 31, USHMM.

67. M. Bauer, *Beyond the Chestnut Trees*, 104; Margit Meissner, oral history (1992), RG-50.233*0087, minutes 81–82, USHMM; Arnholz, file 3728, folder II, AFSC, 2002.296, USHMM.

68. Shadur, *Drive to Survival*, 103; Gould Coll., RG-02.141, 11, 13, USHMM; Edith Jayne Personal Coll. 1784, Accession # 2009/13, Wiener Lib; Finger, #6981, Shoah.

69. Nicholson in Lotte Marcuse, report, Jan. 16, 1943, YIVO, RG 249, folder 485.

70. "Expect their children" in Lotte Marcuse, report, Jan. 16, 1943, YIVO, RG 249, folder 485; "anguished mother" in Wriggins, *Picking Up the Pieces*, 48; see also Howard Wriggins to Evelyn Wriggins, Jan. 16, 1943, Individuals, Foreign Service, Portugal, 1943, AFSC, Phila.; "indefinite time" in Lotte Marcuse, report, Jan. 16, 1943.

71. Lotte Marcuse, report, Jan. 16, 1943, YIVO, RG 249, folder 485. The Jewish refugee children were helped by USCOM, the National Refugee Service, and the European-Jewish Children's Aid. (In November 1942, German-Jewish Children's Aid, formed in New York in 1934, changed its name to European-Jewish Children's Aid.) The United States accepted 1,035 children between 1934 and 1945 (Zahra, *Lost Children*, 68). For the State Department's refusal to take more children, see Baumel, *Unfulfilled Promise*, 76.

72. "Poor parents" and "individual garments" in "Arrival of 3 children on the SS Siboney—March 27, 1941," YIVO, RG 249, folder 478; "styles differed" and "parents' efforts" in [unknown writer] to USCOM, New York, July 30, 1943, YIVO, RG 249, folder 245; "as parents hoped" in Valeska Menges to USCOM, Sept. 12, 1943, Foreign Service, Portugal, USCOM, 1943, AFSC, Phila. On suitcases, see Schlör, "Menschen," 42; see also Auslander and Zahra, *Objects of War*.

73. "You know I feel" quoted in Wriggins, journal entry, Sept. 10, 1942, box 1, folder 30, 1942, RG 67.008, USHMM. Studies of refugees from more recent disasters conclude similarly, namely, that they "felt like a stranger everywhere" (Parkin, "Mementoes," 315).

74. Wriggins, *Picking Up the Pieces*, 58.

5. Sites of Refuge and Angst

Epigraph: Salwa, from Latakia, Syria, quoted in "Syrian Refugees: In Their Own Words," *Guardian*, Apr. 2, 2012, https://www.theguardian.com/world/2012/apr/02/syrian-refugees-their-own-words.

1. Space is never neutral. Power is distributed spatially, and all spaces have rules regarding who uses them and how. The literature on space is vast; sources that speak directly to my topic include Harvey, *Spaces of Capital* and *Spaces of Hope;* Kümper, *Makom;* and Brauch, Lipphardt, and Nocke, "Exploring Jewish Space."

2. "My wife and I" quoted in Bajohr, *Unser Hotel,* 60, and Miron, "Lately, Almost Constantly"; see also, Zadoff, *Next Year in Marienbad,* on "bourgeois experiential spaces," and Borut, "Struggles for Spaces," esp. 331, on Breslau; see also M. Kaplan, *Dignity and Despair,* chs. 1–2; Chaim Kaplan quoted in Tec, *Resilience and Courage,* 22; "refused to go" in Maurer, "From Everyday Life," 335, 337; see also Wildt, *Hitler's Volksgemeinschaft,* and Miron, "'Lately, Almost Constantly.'"

3. "Bottleneck of Europe" in Conard, memo of work done, 1941–42, 2, Refugee Services, Portugal, 1943, AFSC, USHMM; "depositories for feelings" in Smith, *Emotion, Place, and Culture.* In different circumstances, the same place can cause pleasure as well as anxiety; see David Sibley, "Geographies of Difference" (1999), quoted in Parr, "Emotional Geographies," 480.

4. Yehuda Bauer claims that there were 8,000 Jewish refugees in Lisbon at the end of 1940, but that figure included only those supported by the JDC (*American Jewry,* 47). Even 10,000 seems low, given the work of non-Jewish groups. "Room with bath" in Treanor, "Lisbon Fiddles," 82; "sleeping in barns" in Sharp, "Church Mouse," ch. 17, 2; Tillinger, *Aufbau,* Oct. 18, 1940, 5.

5. Several refugees mentioned bedbugs in pensions and hotels: Horst Wagner, "Wohin gehen wir?" (1975), 10, LBI; Lily Alexander (1997), #25993, seg. 94, Shoah; Hofeller, "Refugee," 29, LBI; and letter to the Lisbon JDC, Sept. 9, 1941, about Pension Capitão's bedbugs, and the JDC's response, Oct. 21, 1941, claiming that owners of pensions and hotels did their utmost to fight this "plague," file 896 (2 of 3), JDC. "Enormous number" in Lustig, *Ein Rosenkranz,* 98; Shadur, *Drive to Survival,* 102.

6. "Fresh rolls" in Liane Reif-Lehrer, oral history (follow-up to video interview of 1989, part 1 of 5), RG50.549.02*0043 (1999), USHMM; "In Lisbon" in

letter, Nov. 28, 1942, quoted in Karp, *Maquis Connection,* 104; Döblin, *Destiny's Journey,* 215; Leopold Andrian to Andrée Wimpffen, July 2, 1940. A: Andrian, NZ. 78.2.740, DLA Marbach; see also Marian Back, #14542, seg. 34, Shoah; Paul K., #T-3927, FVA; Wisla, memoirs/journal, Digibaeck, 62; Hans Kaichen (1996), #17727, seg. 46–47 (referring to 1941), Shoah.

7. "Hadn't eaten fruit" in Eva Arond (1995, referring to 1940), #13552, seg. 78–80, Shoah; "exotic fruits" in Dijn, *Das Schicksalsschiff,* 191; "meat and sausages" in Pimentel and Heinrich, *Judeus,* 142; "main affordable food" in Henri Deutsch (1995), #10463, seg. 57–65, Shoah; "crayfish" in Ernst Levy to Irene Shomberg, n.d.; "different version" in Shomberg interview; "amount of meat" in "Report on Arrival of *Serpa Pinto* Children—arrived 1–25–43," YIVO, RG 249, folders 478 and 485.

8. "Modest meals" in Paul K., #T-3927.28, FVA; "strictly German recipes" in Shomberg interview.

9. "Taking their leftovers" in Pimentel and Heinrich, *Judeus,* 138; "kosher pension" according to the Reichsvereinigung der Juden in Deutschland, Abt. Abwanderung, "Ausreise über Spanien und Portugal," Feb. 1941 (sent to me by Herbert Lenk, whose parents received it in 1941); "kosher meat" in Joseph Sucher, "Luck," MS 818, 10–11, LBI; "hard to keep kosher" in Walker interview. Ericeira seems to have had a butcher shop that could slaughter according to Jewish ritual (Ramalho, *Vilar Formoso,* 178).

10. Sig Adler (1997), #25626, seg. 19–20, Shoah; "soup kitchen" in Reston, "Lisbon's Refugees"; "subsidized by the JDC" in zur Mühlen, *Fluchtweg,* 162; "kosher meals" in Katzki to JDC, New York, May 10, 1943, file 897 (1 of 2), JDC; "except Saturday" in Troper, Lisbon, to JDC, New York, Nov. 4, 1940, file 896 (1 of 3), JDC; "two Seders" in d'Esaguy, "Report on the First Quarter of 1941," file 896 (2 of 3), JDC.

11. Pekelis, *My Version,* 141. "Ashkenazi influences" in Ernst Levy to Irene Shomberg, n.d. Ohel Jakob, still the only Ashkenazi synagogue in Portugal, is connected with the European Union of Progressive Judaism as of 2016. "Matzot for Passover" in letters of Feb. 24 and Mar. 2, 1941, Synagogue Kadoorie Mekor-Haïm, Acc. # 2013.212, RG-42.003, USHMM.

12. "Prayer groups," in "Review of the Year 5704," *AJYB* 45, 239, and Photo Archive, NY_03691, JDC; "Seders in cafés" in NY_03680, JDC; "sukkah" in Ramalho, *Vilar Formoso,* 136; "Torah" in Jason and Posner, *Don't Wave Goodbye,* 103, quoting Michel Margosis; "celebrate religious rituals" in Leshem, "Rescue Efforts," 237; "invited strangers" in Walker interview; "turned to one another" in Shomberg interview.

13. Alex Stone, "Why Waiting Is Torture," *New York Times*, Aug. 18, 2012, nytimes. com/2012/08/19/opinion/sunday/why-waiting-in-line-is-torture.html.

14. "No end at all" in E. Mann, "In Lissabon gestrandet," 150. After Pearl Harbor, the staff grew from twenty-six people in Jan. 1942 to fifty-one that July, and an extra building was added; see Draft Histories, RG-59, 3–4, NARA.

15. Pekelis, *My Version*, 134–35; "57 varieties" in Rosen, "New Neighbors," 476; Koestler described in Cesarani, *Arthur Koestler*, 170.

16. "Heaven and hell" in Remarque, *Night in Lisbon*, 186; Grab, *Hochzeit in Brooklyn*, 65; Pekelis, *My Version*, 148–49.

17. Stanton, *Escape from the Inferno*, 157; Fry, "Our Consuls at Work," 507 (referring to Aug. 1940); "State Department report" in Draft Histories, RG-59, 11, NARA; Zweig, *World of Yesterday*, 411.

18. Pekelis, *My Version*, 136, 138, 141. The Hoover administration based its 1930 directive on the Immigration Act of 1882, which denied entry to persons "likely to become a public charge." Lustig, *Ein Rosenkranz*, 96; "could not appeal" in note of Oct. 9, 1942, Rosenfeld, file 6031, AFSC, 2002.296, USHMM.

19. "On the verge" in Kathleen Stewart, *Ordinary Affects* (2007), quoted in Berlant, "Thinking About Feeling Historical," 5; Torberg, *Eine tolle*, 129, 139; "classic Jewish refugee joke" in Raskin, "Far from Where," 143.

20. "In human terms" in [no name, probably Conard] to Mary Roger, Phila., July 20, 1942 (letter #355, covering Jan.–July 1942), Schauffler, Yale; "turned over tomorrow" probably referred to a new State Department rule that all decisions had to be made in Washington, DC; see letter of June 28, 1941, in Pollak, file 7901, AFSC, 2002.296, USHMM; Wriggins to headquarters, Dec. 3, 1943, Rubensohn, file 6282, AFSC 2002.296, USHMM.

21. Grab, *Hochzeit in Brooklyn*, 69; Longstreet, *Last Man Comes Home*, 184; Oppenheim, "Recollections," 28, at RSCL OxOn; Wriggins, *Picking Up the Pieces*, 30; Pekelis, *My Version*, 148–49.

22. Ibson, "Reminiscences" (1974; hereafter cited as memoir), 3–4, private coll. Kurt Israel changed his last name to Ibson. Many thanks to his son, Ralph Ibson, for sharing the memoir and letters with me and for granting permission to quote from them.

23. Ibson, memoir, 7, 9, 11.

24. Ibson, letters, Aug. 25 and Sept. 20, 1940.

25. Ibson, memoir, 11–12.

26. Ibson, letter, Sept. 2, 1940.

27. Ibson, memoir, 12.
28. Ibson, letter, Sept. 2, 1940. Monetary equivalences calculated at Dollar-Times, dollartimes.com/inflation/inflation.php?amount=3000&year=1940.
29. Ibson, letter, Sept. 10, 1940.
30. Annual income figure in Diane Petro, "Brother, Can You Spare a Dime?" *Prologue* 44, no. 1 (Spring 2012), archives.gov/publications/prologue/2012/spring/1940.html.
31. Ibson, letter, Sept. 20, 1940.
32. Ibid., Sept. 2, 10, and 26, 1940.
33. Ibid., Sept. 10 and 26, 1940.
34. Ibid., Aug. 25, Sept. 2, and Nov. 3, 1940.
35. Ibid., Aug. 25, Sept. 2, and Oct. 20, 1940.
36. Ibid., Oct. 9 and 17, 1940; emphasis in the original.
37. Ibid., Oct 24, 1940.
38. Ibid., Nov. 3 and 20, 1940.
39. Ibid., Nov. 3 and 8, 1940.
40. Ibid., Nov. 20 and 28, 1940.
41. Ibson, memoir, 13.
42. "Forced residences" in Stanton, *Escape from the Inferno,* 193, and Lawrence Macgregor, memo, July 27, 1945, 2, Foreign Service, Portugal, 1945, AFSC, Phila.; "police permission" in Ramalho, *Vilar Formoso,* 140; "three hours" in Wriggins, journal entry, Aug. 2, 1942, box 1, folder 30, RG 67.008, USHMM.
43. "Not badly accommodated" in Conard to his family, Aug. 12, 1941; "work, support, counsel" in Schauffler to AFSC staff, memo, Nov. 6, 1944; both in Conard Coll., AFSC, 2002.296, USHMM.
44. "Trains with refugees" in Hess, "Was Portugal," 191. Lustig noted that this occurred on June 25, 1940 (*Ein Rosenkranz,* 66); "Austrians toward Caldas" in M. Bauer, *Beyond the Chestnut Trees,* 105; "Poles to Porto" in zur Mühlen, *Fluchtweg,* 158; "time in prison" in "Review of the Year 5702," *AJYB* 44, 232.
45. Arnholz, folder II, file 3728, AFSC, 2002.296, USHMM.
46. Segev, *World Jewish Congress,* 139; "Review of the Year (1942–43)," *AJYB* 45, 297. In October 1943, the Quakers counted 180 refugees still in Ericeira; see Parrish diaries, 10, Refugee Services, Portugal, 1943, AFSC, Phila. "Summer guests" in Lustig, *Ein Rosenkranz,* 68; Gould Coll., 11, 13, RG-02.141, USHMM; "Aljube prison" in Kalischer, *Vom Konzentrationslager,* 149–50 (referring to 1943); "forced vacations" in Tillinger, *Aufbau,* Sept. 6, 1940, 1; "let's say it" in Lustig, *Ein Rosenkranz,* 75.

47. "You get stale" in Thumwood to Conard, Feb. 7, 1945, Nordman file 8028, AFSC, 2002.296, USHMM; for images of refugee life in Caldas, see "Refugees in Caldas da Rainha," outtakes from "Portugal—Europe's Crossroads," a March of Time newsreel, RG 60.0788, USHMM; available at https://collections.ushmm.org/search/catalog/irn1000585; "attend school there" in zur Mühlen, *Fluchtweg*, 160, and "Review of the Year 5704," *AJYB* 45, 239; young people preparing for work in Palestine in fields near Ericeira in photo archive, NY_03697, JDC; the JDC-subsidized Ericeira Jewish school in photo, NY_03692, JDC; "only thing" in M. Bauer, *Beyond the Chestnut Trees*, 115–16; "succumbed to depression" in Thumwood to Conard, Mar. 21, 1943, Nordman file 8028, AFSC, 2002.296, USHMM; "snap up" in Trixie Ferrigo to Russell Richie, postcard, Aug. 3, 1941, emphasis in the original, Goldstajn, USHMM.

48. Cost-of-living comparison in file 896 (3 of 3), AR33/44, JDC; see also Nussbaum, JDC Lisbon, report, Oct. 8, 1941, file 896 (2 of 3), JDC. That month it cost 50 escudos for a single person in Lisbon and 70 in Caldas. "$1" in Kalischer, *Vom Konzentrationslager*, 151; "married couple" in HW to MF [initials only], Lisbon, Aug. 10, 1943 (letter #583), Schauffler, Yale; "on the run" in Wilhelmer, *Transit-Orte*, 223; "moving to cheaper houses" in Pimentel and Heinrich, *Judeus*, 137; Baruel, memo (quoting Schwartz), Jan. 1948, Code: HMB, Origin: PO/Li, AII–12a/3, file 390444–446, Correspondência, Refugiãdos 1941–1948, Comissão, CAHJP.

49. Arams (1998), #40598, seg. 55, Shoah; for the Quaker, see Johnson to Beer, Feb. 11, 1943, and Beer to Wriggins, Mar. 3, 1943, file 2092, 2002.296, AFSC, USHMM.

50. "Fathers and children" in Lotte Marcuse, report, Jan. 16, 1943, YIVO, RG 249, folder 485; Alix Preece (née Stiel), Re P.III.i. No. 582 (recorded May 1957, covers 1941–45), Wiener Lib. This observation is consistent with the behavior of Jewish families in Germany in the 1930s (Kaplan, *Dignity and Despair*, ch. 2). "Wife and another woman" in Lustig, *Ein Rosenkranz*, 70–71.

51. "These groups" in Elizabeth Dexter, Lisbon, report, Nov. 2, 1942, Code: HMB, Origin: PO/Li, AII–12a/3, 1941–48, file 390232, Comissão, CAHJP; "USC hired refugees" in DiFiglia, *Roots and Visions*, 28; for the libraries in Caldas and Ericeira, see USC, Exec. Dir., bMS 16007_Box 20_folders 13_052 and 13_053, project reports, RG-67.028, USHMM; "growing dislike" in Wriggins, journal entry, Aug. 2, 1942, box 1, folder 30, 1942, RG 67.008, USHMM.

52. The figure of two hundred is in *Polish Jew*, May–June 1943, 1.2.7.2/82170545 #1; the request for newsletters is in *Polish Jew*, July–Aug. 1940, 1.2.7.2/

82171073#1, both at ITS Digital Archive, USHMM. For photos of refugees on the beaches, see "Moshe and Rachel Engelhard," Photograph #99690, USHMM, and photo exhibit at Estoril Museum.

53. "Especially in winter" in Pimentel and Heinrich, *Judeus*, 138; Lustig, *Ein Rosenkranz*, 67–68.

54. "Public spaces" in Lustig, *Ein Rosenkranz*, 104–5; "weekly stipends" in Pimentel, "Refugiados," 107; Losa, *Unter fremden Himmeln*, 97; "forced to leave" in Pimentel and Heinrich, *Judeus*, 169.

55. Torberg, *Eine tolle*, 125; Tillinger, *Aufbau*, Sept. 6, 1940, 1–2.

56. Preece, Re P.III.i. No. 582, 6, Wiener Lib; "police forms" in Pimentel and Heinrich, *Judeus*, 136; Ursula Leinung, #2632, seg. 58–67, Shoah, and Leinung in Schnabel, *Lisbon: Harbour of Hope*, 28:28–31.

57. "Late 1944" in Schauffler to AFSC staff, memo on Caldas, Nov. 6, 1944, Conard Coll., AFSC, 2002.296, USHMM, and "Portugal and the Refugee Problem," report, file 897 (2 of 2), JDC; "May 1945" in Caldas, monthly report for May 1945, USC, bMS 16007_Box 19_folder 22_002, RG-67.028, USHMM; "by July" in Lawrence Macgregor, Foreign Service, Portugal, memo, July 27, 1945, AFSC, Phila.; "fixed residence of Ericeira" in J. C. Wavrek to Mrs. Sharp, Aug. 6, 1945, USC, bMS 16007_Box 19_folder 22, RG-67.028, USHMM; "Caxias prison" in letter from Paul and Thomas Arnholz, Lisbon, Feb. 4, 1946, AFSC, 2002.296, file #3728, IV. The family claimed that fixed residences no longer existed when the police arrested her.

58. Robins, *Quest of Love*, 134.

59. "Handed her passport" in Robins, *Quest of Love*, 134–44; "references from Americans" in Trixie Ferrigo to Russell Richie (of the Quakers), July 28, 1941, and the Ferrigos to Mrs. Bowden, U.S. consulate, June 1941 [approx.]; "Brazil, for example" in Trixie Ferrigo to Richie, Sept. 5, 1941 [approx.]; "case of Cuba" in letters of May 10, 12, and 14, 1941, Aug. 7, 1941, and Oct. 16 and 25, 1941. All of the above in Goldstajn, USHMM.

60. "Allied sailors" in Trixie Ferrigo to "Dear Sir," Apr. 19, 1941; letter and songs in Goldstajn, USHMM; "entitle the program" in Robins, *Quest of Love*, 151.

61. Song sheet and flyer in Goldstajn, USHMM.

62. Robins, *Quest of Love*, 152–54.

63. "Food consisted of" in Robins, *Quest of Love*, 151–58; "paler for lack" in Miss Bowden to Mrs. Morgenthau, Apr. 14, 1941, Goldstajn, USHMM.

64. "Most frustration" in Robins, *Quest of Love*, 155; Richie's comments in Richie to AFSC Phila., Oct. 30, 1941, Schauffler, Yale; details of the books and bookcases in Trixie Ferrigo to Richie, Oct. 7, 1941, and Trixie Ferrigo to

Richie, postcard, Oct. 25, 1941, and Ferris Ferrigo to Richie, Nov. 5, 1941—
all in Goldstajn, USHMM.

65. "HICEM" in Trixie Ferrigo to Richie, postcard, Oct. 12, 1941; "Portuguese
doctor" in the Ferrigos to Richie, Oct. 11, 1941 (emphasis in the original);
"developed his depression" in Ferris Ferrigo to Richie, Sept. 10, 1941—all in
Goldstajn, USHMM.

66. "We were so satisfied" in Ferris Ferrigo to Richie, Sept. 10, 1941; Quakers,
Lisbon, to Phila., memo regarding Ferrigo, n.d. [approx. July 1941]—both in
Goldstajn, USHMM.

67. Trixie Ferrigo to Richie, Apr. 23, 1941, and AFSC Immigration Inquiry, both
in Goldstajn, USHMM. Ferris's Protestant marriage certificate is in the
personal collection of Melodie Pelloni-Robins; my thanks to her for sharing
her copy with the USHMM. HICEM gave the Ferrigos 110 escudos weekly
and 150 monthly (for rent), and the Unitarians gave 130 weekly; see Trixie
Ferrigo to Mrs. Price, Aug. 14, 1941, asking whether the Quakers could also
help them, Goldstajn, USHMM.

68. "Brave young couple" in Miss Bowden to Mrs. Morgenthau, Apr. 14, 1941;
"hosts of refugees" in Quaker office (unsigned), Lisbon, to Mrs. Morgenthau, Apr. 26, 1941; "any more chances" in Trixie Ferrigo to Richie, Aug. 13,
1941—all in Goldstajn, USHMM.

69. "July 1941" in Trixie Ferrigo to Richie, July 16 and 27, 1941, and "dearer to
live" in Trixie to Richie, July 23, 1941, all in Goldstajn, USHMM; "their own
food" in Trixie Ferrigo to her parents, Sept. 18, 1941, personal coll. of
Melodie Pelloni-Robins.

70. "We feel well" in Trixie Ferrigo to Mrs. Price, Aug. 14, 1941; Ferris Ferrigo to
Mrs. Bowden, Aug. 2, 1941; both in Goldstajn, USHMM.

71. "Quakers had found sponsors" in Conard to AFSC, Phila., Sept. 18, 1941,
Goldstajn, USHMM; *Guine* in Ferris Ferrigo to AFSC, Phila., Jan. 7, 1942,
Goldstajn, USHMM; see also "U.S.O. Entertainers Sang Way out of
Europe," *Charleston (S.C.) Evening Post*, June 8, 1943.

72. The refugee joke is in Raskin, "Far from Where," 143. Besides work, Weil
listed equal respect as a human being, honor, and truth (*Need for Roots*, 6–8).

6. Sharing Feelings in Letters and in Person

Epigraph: Wissam al-Hajj, a refugee in Toronto, referring to WhatsApp messages
from relatives in Syria, in Jodi Kantor and Catrin Einhorn, "What Does It Mean to
Help One Family?" *New York Times*, Oct. 22, 2016, nytimes.com/interac-
tive/2016/10/22/world/americas/canada-refugees-syria.html?emc=eta1.

1. Lässig and Rürup, "What Made a Space"; 2. Redford, *Converse of the Pen;* Smith-Rosenberg, "Female World of Love," 3. Although much narrower in time and space, these café relationships show similarities with Barbara Rosenwein's "emotional community," which consisted of "social groups whose members adhere to the same valuations of emotions and their expression" (Rosenwein, "Problems and Methods," and "Worrying About Emotions," 842); see also Biess et al., "History of Emotions."

2. "Constant worries" in Leopold Andrian to Andrée Wimpffen, June 25, 1940, A: Andrian, NZ. 78.2.740, DLA Marbach; "very happy" in Arendt to Adler-Rudel, Apr. 2, 1941, hannaharendt.net/index.php/han/article/view/72/108; Stanton, *Escape from the Inferno,* 162; see also Dwork and van Pelt, *Flight from the Reich,* 245–63.

3. Döblin, *Destiny's Journey,* 217–18; "letters, telegrams, and cables" in Dijn, *Das Schicksalsschiff,* 194; "mountains" in Tillinger, *Aufbau,* Sept. 6, 1940, 2.

4. "Dimensions of letter-writing" in Decker, *Epistolary Practices,* intro.; "Nazi censors" in Garbarini, *Numbered Days,* 66–70.

5. Redford sees such letters as a "campaign for intimacy" (*Converse of the Pen,* 10). Ibson, letters of Sept. 2, Sept. 26, Oct. 17, and Nov. 3, 1940, private coll.

6. Ibson, "Unsere Familie in Hannover," (1980), LBI, AR4910; Ibson, letters of Sept. 2 and 3, 1940, private coll.

7. M. Kaplan, *Dignity and Despair,* 116–17, 235.

8. Lotte Marcuse to MD [name protected], Jan. 13, 1944, YIVO, RG 249, folder 357.

9. "Very few children" in Lotte Marcuse to Joel Sequerra, Lisbon, Jan. 19, 1949, YIVO, RG 249, folder 357. Social workers usually provided kosher food for children who needed it; see "Reception *Nyassa* Group," YIVO, RG 249, folder 484.

10. Social workers thought that parents sent children to the United States "primarily" for educational opportunities. I believe parents sought safety first. "Landed safely" in "Report on Arrival of *Serpa Pinto* Children—arrived 1–25–43," YIVO, RG 249, folder 478; "sent my child" in Albert Rzezak to AFSC, Nov. 30, 1943, Rzezak, file 8756, AFSC, 2002.296, USHMM; "it is difficult" in Lotte Marcuse to Mr. and Mrs. R. [name protected], Lisbon, Oct. 21, 1947, YIVO, RG 249, folder 357.

11. "Parents on this end" in YIVO, RG 249, folder 486; "filth" in Lowy, file 9644, AFSC, 2002.296, USHMM; "child's handwriting" in AFSC, Lisbon, to USCOM, New York, Dec. 13, 1943, YIVO, RG 249, folder 245.

12. Lotte Marcuse to Herbert Katzki, Lisbon, Sept. 21, 1943, YIVO, RG 249, folder 245.

13. In contrast to migrant collections that contain letters from both sides of the correspondence, I have found, with one exception, only one-sided correspondence from refugees, so we have to infer what the other side wrote from the responses in the letters at hand.

14. "Therapy" in Antonio Gibelli, *La grande guerra degli italiani, 1915–1918* (Milan: BUR Rizzoli, 2014), quoted in Cancian, *Families, Lovers, and Their Letters,* 11; "speak for themselves" in David Gerber, *Authors of Their Lives: The Personal Correspondence of British Immigrants to North America in the Nineteenth Century* (New York: NYU Press, 2006), quoted in ibid., 7.

15. Gabrielle Greenberg Coll., AR 25528, LBI.

16. Schwiefert, *Bird Has No Wings.* Thanks to Hannah Aschheim for recommending this book.

17. Ibid., 10–14, 27, 37–39.

18. Ibid., 16, 40, 106–10.

19. Ibid., 5, 11, 21, 30; emphasis in the original.

20. Ibid., 74, 77.

21. Ibid., 58, 66, 121–24.

22. Thank you to Gabrielle Greenberg for sharing these letters and for filling me in on the details (interview with the author, New York City, Dec. 11, 2012). The letters are now available at the LBI and at Digibaeck.

23. "Parent at a distance" in Garbarini, *Numbered Days,* 103.

24. "Her own age" in AFSC, Lisbon, to Losser, Dec. 27, 1943, Losser, file 20120, AFSC, 2002.296, USHMM.

25. Letters of Nov. 16, 1943, and Apr. 6, 1944.

26. "Not paper enough" in letters of Nov. 16, 1943, and Oct. 30, 1944; "play with them" in letter of Nov. 16, 1944.

27. "Matzo all week" in letters of Dec. 23, 1943, and Apr. 13, 1944; "happy new year" in letter of Sept. 4, 1944.

28. Letters of May 13, 1943, June 13, 1944, and July 7, 1944.

29. Letter of Apr. 6, 1944.

30. Letter of Aug. 20, 1944.

31. One foster mother even read the letters they wrote (Greenberg interview).

32. Letter of Oct. 21, 1944.

33. "Six crucial years" in Greenberg, email correspondence with the author, Mar. 9, 2013; "lightly bruised'" in letter of May 4, 1980.

34. Oscar Schreyer File, Yaffa Eliach Collection, Lisbon Coll., MJH.

35. Thanks to Megan Lewis at the USHMM for alerting me to the postcards from the Jewish Historical Institute (JHI) in Warsaw. These cards either went

directly to Lisbon or to the London-based daughter of a correspondent by way of a Polish diplomat in Lisbon. The daughter donated them to the Warsaw museum.

36. The letters and cards were addressed to Lisbon and Barcelona. For this book, I used only those sent to Portugal. Thanks again to Bonnie Gurewitsch and Esther Brumberg at the MJH for alerting me about them. The collection also contains letters from the United States and other safe havens.

37. Quoted in Subak, *Rescue and Flight,* 73.

38. "Good condition" in [illegible], Switzerland, to L. Rosenzweig, Feb. 1, 1942, item #142; "everything we needed" in Sara Krieger, Poland, to Leitner, Caldas da Rainha, Apr. 21, 1942, item #267; "we are healthy" in G. Esriel, Tarnów, Generalgouvernement [Poland], to Dr. Alexander Halberstam, June 12, 1942, item #158; see also item #156—all in Lisbon Coll., MJH.

39. "Perked up" in card from Poland to H. Leitner, Caldas da Rainha, Mar. 12, 1942, item #216; For thanks, see examples in items #112, #217, and #225, Lisbon Coll., MJH.

40. "Cheer himself up" in Kurt Israel Joachimsthal, Berlin, to Isabella Rosenthal, Lisbon, card, Apr. 8, 1942, item #237; awareness of censors in Yosette Schmit, Luxembourg, to Blanchy Binchy, Lisbon, Mar. 20, 1942, item #1371, Lisbon Coll., MJH.

41. "You must know" in Siegfried Israel [last name unclear], Berlin, to Leopold Bloch, Lisbon, card, Mar. 25, 1942, item #213; "At the moment" in Asta Sara Jacob, Berlin, to Paul Mayer, Lisbon, Apr. 7, 1942, item #236, Lisbon Coll., MJH.

42. Eustace et al., "AHR Conversation," 1498.

43. "Coffee, tea, canned goods" in Yosette Schmit, Luxembourg, to Blanchy Binchy, Lisbon, Mar. 20, 1942, item #137; "diminished rations" in Jenny Sara Goldstern, Vienna, to Herr Torn, Lisbon, Mar. 30 [probably 1942], item #198; "send something abroad" in [illegible], Switzerland, to L. Rosenzweig, Feb. 1, 1942, item #142—all in Lisbon Coll., MJH. "through Lisbon" in Ludwig Bauer, telegram, Mar. 1941, #2009.A.356, MJH; "oil or biscuits" in Joseph Erson [unclear], Camp du Récébédou [France], to Kulner, Lisbon, Jan. 23, 1942, item #110; "sugar to make it" in Isabel, [near Cascais], to Monica Smith, Lisbon, Feb. 12, 1942, item #154, both in Lisbon Coll., MJH. "Battle for survival" in Stanislav Albrecht to T. Frimer, card, July 24, 1942, JHI. Thanks to Natalia Aleksiun for translations of the cards at JHI from Polish.

44. "War stopped everything" and "heart pain" in Walker interview. Westheimer's notebook is on display at the museum, #1851.90.1–4, MJH. See

also a note from Zimmerman (in Gurs) to Westheimer, asking for salted butter, hard sausage, chocolate, cocoa, and canned foods and offering that his brother in Buffalo would pay Westheimer (#693.92 1–2), and also the note from Siegel (in Gurs) to Westheimer (1850.90). Stores advertised that they would send packages with coffee, chocolate, and cocoa to Spain, France, Poland, Belgium, Italy, and Germany; see advertisement of Oct. 5, 1940, in Pimentel, "Refugiados," 106.

45. "Sardines ranked" in Helena Steinmetz, Poland, to Jakob Scheffer, Caldas da Rainha, card, Mar. 31, 1942, item #217, Lisbon Coll., MJH. An inexpensive staple for the Portuguese, "sardines" referred to a variety of small fish. "Escapee from Gurs" in Ruth Hellman, interview by the author, Mar. 24, 2014, New York City. See the labels from packages sent to Terezin (Theresienstadt), ID #1900.91–1904.91, 1907.91–1912.91, MJH; see also Láníček, "Arnošt Frischer," 37, and *Frischer and Jewish Politics,* chs. 5 and 6.

46. "Love packages" (*Liebespaketchen*) in Rakowski, Kalisch [Poland; German, Wartheland/Warthegau], to "Dear Friend" [Natan Schwalbe], Lisbon, June 20, 1942, item #235, and Krieger, Kańczuga [bei Jaroslaw; Poland], to Jakob Schaffer, Caldas da Rainha, Jan. 30, 1942, item #157, both in Lisbon Coll., MJH. "Love gifts" (*Liebesgaben*) in Ines Rebhan-Glück, " 'Liebesgaben' an die Front und Lebensmittelpakete in die Heimat," http://ww1.habsburger. net/de/kapitel/liebesgaben-die-front-und-lebensmittelpakete-die-heimat.

47. Engelking and Leociak, *Warsaw Ghetto,* 374; "form of relief" in T. H. Chylinski [U.S. vice-consul], "Poland Under Nazi Rule," confidential report (declassified in 2001), Nov. 13, 1941, 32, https://www.cia.gov/library/readingroom/docs/POLAND%20UNDER%20NAZI%20RULE%201941_0001.pdf; *Aufbau,* Feb. 14, 1941, 6.

48. Calorie counts at "Warsaw," Holocaust Encyclopedia, USHMM, https:// www.ushmm.org/wlc/en/article.php?ModuleId=10005069; "big heroine" in George Topas, oral history (1992), RG50.233*0136, 19–21, USHMM.

49. "Received sardines" in Ewa Lebenhaft to Maria Werner, card, July 19, 1942; "great relief" in Ewa Lebenhaft to Tamara Frimer, card, Apr. 7, 1942, both in JHI. Ewa Lebenhaft, originally from Lodz, was murdered around the age of forty-five; see the Yad Vashem record at http://yvng.yadvashem.org/nameDetails.html?language=en&itemId=443390&ind=0. "Finally, finally" in Ester Lebenhaft to Ewa Tallin [intimate: Meine Allerliebste!], card, Sept. 29, 1941, JHI; "feel guilty" in Aimee Amiga, "Rare Postcards from Warsaw Ghetto Surface in Poland," *Haaretz,* Nov. 4, 2015, at haaretz.com/jewish/news/.premium-1.684238.

50. "Expediting firm" in Ewa Lebenhaft to "Frau Maria Werner," card, May 4, 1942; B. Lebenhaftowa to T. Frimer, card, May 4, 1942; Lebenhaft to "the firm Maria Werner," card, June 2, 1942; Lebenhaft to Maria Werner, card, July 19, 1942; "gone away" in E. B. Lebenhaft to Ewa Tallin [formal, using "*Sie*"], card, June 9, 1941—all on the JHI website.

51. "Very distressing" in Lebenhaft to Tallin, card, June 9, 1941; see also B. Lebenhaftowa to T. Frimer ["Write me, my only one. My sadness grows with each passing day," in Polish], Dec. 7, 1941, both in JHI. "Contents of the packages" in *Gazeta Żydowska* ["Jewish Newspaper"], a Jewish newspaper licensed by the Germans, Aug. 18, 1941, quoted in Engelking and Leociak, *Warsaw Ghetto*, 375; Bondy, "Miracle of the Loaves," 137.

52. War Organisation of the British Red Cross Society, Feb. 1941, and Margaret E. Jones to Rogers, Schauffler, and Kimber, Jan. 23, 1941, both in Schauffler, Yale. The Unitarian Committee sent 1,508 packages from Lisbon in the first six months of its program; see Statement of Marianne Pfeffer, July 16, 1941, Robert Dexter correspondence, 1941, bMS 16135, box 3, folder 22, USC Lisbon, Andover-Harvard; "figs" in "Elders of Jews in Terezin a/E Protectorate of Bohemia and Moravia," RG-48.015M, USHMM. Groups in Geneva and, to a lesser extent, Stockholm, Istanbul, and Ankara sent packages (Láníček, *Frischer and Jewish Politics*, 121); the state of Denmark did so as well (Fracapane, "'Wir erfuhren,'" 199).

53. Segev, *World Jewish Congress*, 143–46; Leshem, "Rescue Efforts," 239; and Katzki interviews, 58, JDC. On local communities and the WJC, see Minutes of JDC, New York, Apr. 21, 1941, AR3344_0013_00668.pdf, JDC. The WJC claimed to have sent 100,000 such packages eastward; see Gerhart Riegner, oral history (1991), RG-50.030*0189, 41, USHMM; see also *Guide to Ringelblum Archives, Warsaw*, 389, Geneva, Sept. 5, 1941, regarding parcels from Portugal, RG-17.079M, USHMM. For Terezin and Poland, see JDC New York Office Records, 1933–1945, Countries and Regions, Abyssinia–Philippines, Record Group 4.15: Czechoslovakia, Series 3: Czechoslovakia: Subject Matter; File 542: Relief Supplies, General, http://archives.jdc.org/our-collections/finding-aids/new-york-office/1933–1944/countries-and-regions-abyssinia-philippines. For further details, see Heinrich, Winterberg, and Kirkamm, *Lissabon*, 11; Milgram, *Portugal, Salazar, and the Jews*, 198–201, on letters and cards that came to the WJC; Helene Arnay (1995), #4265, seg. 22–23, Shoah, on individual families sending parcels to the Warsaw Ghetto; and Conard, memo, July 26, 1945, Committees and Organizations: American JDC to Cath. Mission, Foreign Service 1944, AFSC, 2002.296, USHMM.

54. "Buy food in Portugal" in report, 6 [early 1944], file 897 (2 of 2), JDC; "only to individuals" in Láníček, "Arnošt Frischer," 34. In 1944, the U.S. Treasury Department authorized JDC remittances of $12,000 per month for food parcels from Portugal to individuals in Poland; see JDC New York Office Records, 1933–1945, Countries and Regions, Poland–Venezuela, Record Group 4.47: Poland, Series 1: Poland: Administration, File 802: Poland: Administration, General, 1944, http://archives.jdc.org/our-collections/finding-aids/new-york-office/1933–1944/countries-and-regions-poland-venezuela; see also Relief and Reconstruction Excerpts, vol. 1, no. 11 (July 13, 1944), Schauffler, Yale.

55. "Publicity would be most undesirable" in JDC, Lisbon, to JDC, New York, general letter no. 395, Sept. 2, 1943 (on continued shipments), file #801, AR3344, JDC; "as late as 1944" in Katzki interviews, 68, JDC. Katzki left in December 1943 to join the U.S. Army. See also report, 6, [early 1944], file 897 (2 of 2), JDC; Milgram, *Portugal, Salazar, and the Jews*, 197–223; Y. Bauer, *American Jewry*.

56. Donald B. Hurwitz, JDC, New York, to JDC Lisbon, Feb. 13, 1945, regarding Moritz Schweitzer, Bergen-Belsen, Online JDC Archive. Even after the war, the JDC continued to support deliveries to Jews in liberated Poland; see also JDC New York Office Records, 1933–1945, Countries and Regions, Poland–Venezuela, Record Group 4.47: Poland, Series 1: Poland: Administration, File 801: Poland: Administration, General, 1942 (Sept.)–1943, and File 802: Poland, Administration, General, 1944.

57. "Never reached the addressees" in Láníček, *Frischer and Jewish Politics*, 121; see also Segev, *World Jewish Congress*, 145–46; Unitarians quoted in letter of May 15, 1944, [no names], Exec. Dir., USC, bMS 16007_Box 20_folder 11, RG-67.028, USHMM; German Red Cross [DRK] to Eichmann, report, Aug. 4, 1943, 1.1.0.2/82339788#1/ITS Digital Archive, USHMM. They listed 375 packages sent in April, 845 in May, and 1,803 in June.

58. "Packages went missing" in Katzki interviews, 68, JDC. For parcels from Lisbon to Terezin in October 1943, see also the Online JDC Archive. Other relevant letters on the JDC website are Moses Leavitt, JDC, New York, to JDC, Lisbon, Aug. 2, 1943, warning of confiscations (archival locator NY_AR3344_Poland_03_00622.pdf), and Katzki, JDC, Lisbon, to JDC, New York, Sept. 2, 1943, on limiting the monthly parcels to four tons, or about 8,000 small shipments (archival locator NY_AR3344_Poland_03_00603.pdf). The JDC states that it sent approx. 140,000 parcels during the period October 1943–August 1944. For returned packages from French camps, see

Unitarian Committee, *Living Church* 105 (Aug. 30, 1942), 9, file 896 (3 of 3), JDC.

59. Regarding attempts to stave off mass starvation, the Czech government-in-exile, for example, sent about 80,000 packages weighing less than a pound each to approximately 140,000 deportees. Thanks to Jan Láníček for these figures (email to the author, Jan. 13, 2017); see also Láníček, "Arnošt Frischer," 35.

60. Stanton, *Escape from the Inferno,* 158.

61. "Viable societies" in Parkin, "Mementoes," 304; "couldn't help running" in Koestler, *Arrival and Departure,* 11; "console one another" in Reston, "Lisbon's Refugees"; "filled with refugees" in F. Mann, *Drastic Turn of Destiny,* 156.

62. "Psychic hell" in Wriggins, *Picking Up the Pieces,* 58; "Polish ghettos" in Arendt, "We Refugees" (1994), 110; "members of the family" in Bitton, oral history, RG-50.030*0027, USHMM; "last escudo" in E. Mann, "In Lissabon gestrandet," 151; Koestler, *Arrival and Departure,* 7–8; Rosenwein quoted in Eustace et al., "AHR Conversation," 1516.

63. "Irreplaceable arenas" in Karády, *Jews of Europe,* 98; see also Wobick-Segev, "Buying, Selling, Being" and "German-Jewish Spatial Cultures"; "substitutes for" in Pinsker, *Literary Passports,* 37; for Warsaw, see Ury, *Barricades and Banners.*

64. "Coffee, cake, and conversation" in Mutschelknaus, *Kaffeeklatsch.* The term *Klatsch,* meaning "gossip," demeaned women's gatherings, ignoring the bonds they forged and the ideas, including women's emancipation, they discussed. "Café Loy" in Wobick-Segev, "German-Jewish Spatial Cultures," 53–56.

65. "Jewish space" in Pinsker, *Literary Passports,* 90–91; "Viennese spend" in Löw-Beer, "From Nowhere to Israel," 118; Zweig, *Tagebücher,* 374.

66. "Political activists" in Wobick-Segev, *Homes Away from Home,* 29–30; Sahl, *Memoiren,* 215.

67. "Jewish spaces" in Lässig and Rürup, "What Made a Space"; "acorns, dried peas" in Christine Morrow, *Abominable Epoch* (private pub. [1972]), 49, quoted in Gemie, Reid, and Humbert, *Outcast Europe,* 123; Seghers, *Transit,* 55 ("harbor gossip"), 35–36 ("All around me"); for more on Seghers and other artists, see also Jennings, *Escape from Vichy.*

68. *Aufbau,* Aug. 20, 1940, 2; "Ask directions" in F. Mann, *Drastic Turn of Destiny,* 91.

69. "Refugee telegraph" in Wriggins, *Picking Up the Pieces,* 58; Lenkway, 27–28, USHMM; see also Janina Lauterbach, #1138, seg. 36–41, Shoah; "little plots" in Bayles, "Lisbon," 77; Wakman's story in Walker interview.

70. "Similar losses" in Rudolf Graf, #508, seg. 47–49, Shoah; "sidewalk café tables" in Sevareid, "Escape Hatch," 94; "entire days" in Betty Harris (1996), #13459, seg. 49–51, Shoah. There is a video (1 min., 6 sec.) of refugees inside the Café Boccage, Caldas da Rainha, October 1943, at CriticalPast, critical-past.com/video/65675029919_Café-Boccage_refugee-town_Jewish-refugee_cattle-fair_improvised-Synagogue. "A place where" and "warm and cheap" in Stanton, *Escape from the Inferno*, 158; Sahl quoted in Skwara, "Hans Sahl," 97.

71. Karl Paetel remembered no connections between people in the cafés, but his memoir is the only one I have found expressing this view. Even he noted that "one met each other now and then by coincidence" (Paetel, *Reise*, 253). Elisabeth Bab, memoir, 216, LBI; E. Mann, "In Lissabon gestrandet," 158.

72. Leshem referred to twenty-one Jewish nationalities on a ship leaving Portugal for Palestine in January 1944 ("Rescue Efforts," 254). "Hungered for" in Pimentel, "Refugiados," 105, quoting Eva Lewinski; Tillinger cited in Pimentel and Heinrich, *Judeus*, 166; see also Farkas, "Lisboa," in *Farkas Endeckt Amerika;* "usually speaking" in F. Mann, *Drastic Turn of Destiny*, 173; "Waiters who might be spying" in Blaufuks, *Under Strange Skies;* "identify the individuals" in zur Mühlen, *Fluchtweg*, 158–59. The mass arrest happened in October 1940.

73. "Momentary rendezvous" in Nunes, *Ilse Losa*, 60; "did not assume" in Arnay, #4265, seg. 22–23, Shoah; Pekelis, *My Version*, 141–42; see also a video (2 min., 1 sec.) showing refugees boarding the *Serpa Pinto*, Oct. 1943, CriticalPast, criticalpast.com/video/65675029920_Portuguese-refugees _Port-of-Lisbon_Transport-ship-Serpa-Pinto_American-Export-Line-ship.

74. Marcu, *Ein Kopf*, 203. Marcu, a Romanian-Jewish publicist, wrote in German.

75. "Class remained a divide" in Lochery, who described Lisbon as an "enforced holiday camp" for wealthy refugees like Peggy Guggenheim and Max Ernst (*Lisbon*, 99–101); Tillinger, *Aufbau*, Sept. 6, 1940, 1; Kesten, *Dichter im Café*, 7, 12–13. Class and ethnic divides may have reemerged after refugees left Lisbon. One American social worker described a debarkation of Lisbon refugees in New York: "One did notice . . . that underneath some of the arguments and fights between the individual refugees, there was also the hostilities of the German-born groups to the Austrian and Polish-born refugees"; see Lotte Marcuse, "Arrival of Children on SS *Nyassa*, on April 23, 1941," YIVO, RG 249, folder 478.

76. "Consumed by waiting" in Seghers, *Transit*, 127; Losa, *Unter fremden Himmeln*, 19; Lustig, *Ein Rosenkranz*, 93.

77. Sevareid, "Escape Hatch," 94; Elizabeth Dexter to Edward Crocker, Feb. 14, 1944, Doc. 405, in Sutters, *Archives of the Holocaust,* 498; Parrish diaries, Oct. 24, 1943, 13–14, Refugee Services, Portugal, 1943, AFSC, Phila.; "fatal wounds" in Seghers, *Transit,* 20.

78. E. Mann, "In Lissabon gestrandet," 155.

79. "Separate from their spouses" and "Hunger and love" in Lustig, *Ein Rosen-kranz,* 91–93. This happened to other couples separated by war; see Vaizey, "Husbands and Wives," 394–95; "seemed to survive" in Wriggins, *Picking Up the Pieces,* 59.

80. Stanton, *Escape from the Inferno,* 143–44, 148, 158, 161, 166.

81. Ibid., 158, 167–68, 172, 178.

82. Ibid., 160.

83. Ibid., 148–49.

84. Ibid., 193.

85. "One for all" in Stanton, *Escape from the Inferno,* 194–95; JDC New York Office Records, 1933–1944, Subcollection 4: Countries and Regions, Record Group 4.47: Poland, Series 3: Poland: Subject Matter, File 884: Poland, Subject Matter, Polish Refugees in Jamaica, 1941–1942, http://archives.jdc.org/our-collections/finding-aids/new-york-office/1933–1944/countries-and-regions-poland-venezuela; see also Regev, "Exodus from Jamaica." Based on JDC files, Bartrop put the figure at five hundred sent to Jamaica ("From Lisbon to Jamaica," 48). Stanton cites 494, but JDC sources give a figure of about 180; see "JDC Arranges Emigration of Polish-Jewish Refugees from Lisbon to Jamaica," JTA, Jan. 12, 1942, jta.org/1942/01/12/archive/jdc-arranges-emigration-of-polish-jewish-refugees-from-lisbon-to-jamaica.

86. Bartrop, "From Lisbon to Jamaica"; for reasons why the British may have agreed to this plan, see 53–54.

7. Final Hurdles

Epigraph: Barbara Molinario, communication officer for the United Nations High Commissioner for Refugees in Italy, quoted in "Refugee Boat Found with 22 Dead Bodies off Libya Coast," *Al Jazeera,* July 21, 2016, aljazeera.com/news/2016/07/refugee-boat-22-dead-bodies-libya-coast-160721133439798.html.

1. "November 1939" in Klein, *Flüchtlingspolitik,* 284; "higher prices" in memo of conversation with Mr. Baerwald, Nov. 5, 1940, regarding the surge in Spanish ship costs, file 896 (1 of 3), JDC. Some French ships were still leaving in early 1941 (Klein, *Flüchtlingspolitik,* 288). Schnitzler, *Beziehungen.*

2. "Fervidly engaged" in H. Mann, *Ein Zeitalter*, 448, quoted in Voigt, *Heinrich Mann,* 54; Troper, JDC, Lisbon, to JDC, New York, Nov. 4, 1940, file 896 (1 of 3), JDC; Arendt to Adler-Rudel, Apr. 2, 1941, at hannaharendt.net/index.php/han/article/view/72/108; "whatever it costs" in 245.4, file no. XII-Portugal A-23, 1, HIAS-HICEM, YIVO.

3. "Half empty" in Conard, "Brief Report on the Lisbon Office of the AFSC, May to August '41," Aug. 23, 1941, 9, Schauffler, Yale; Hirsch, file 7192, AFSC, 2002.296, USHMM. The congressman was Thomas H. Eliot (D-Mass.). "Doctor" in Conard, Report on Work of AFSC, 1945 (notes for talks about AFSC, 1941–44), 6, Foreign Service, Portugal—Spain, AFSC, Phila.

4. Portuguese crews occasionally postponed departures; see letter from August Silberstein, June 26, 1941, AFSC, 2002.296, USHMM. "Said that they would never" in Conard, Report on Work of AFSC, 1945, 6, Foreign Service, Portugal—Spain, AFSC, Phila.

5. Blumberg, letters of Jan. 12, 1943, and June 10, 1946, file 2692, AFSC, 2002.296, USHMM. The new U.S. policy became effective in July 1941.

6. The Boeing 314 *Yankee Clipper* carried seventy-four day or thirty-six night passengers and eleven crew members. "Fleet of two" in Schauffler, Lisbon, to Mrs. A. Weddell, Mar. 28, 1941, Schauffler, Yale; "desperate need" in George Warren to Joseph Chamberlain, Feb. 1, 1940, Joseph Chamberlain papers, folder 69, YIVO.

7. S.S. *Quanza* video at facebook.com/holocaustmuseum/videos/the-ss-quanza/10155840631992677.

8. "Some ships" in minutes of meeting, July 18, 1940, in Administration Minute Books, May 1940–March 1941, DORSA file #35A, JDC; "keep prices down" in *Footnotes*, Dec. 1999, 2, 4, and Wriggins, *Picking Up the Pieces*, 12; "August 1941" in Wasserstein, *Ambiguity of Virtue*, 109–10; refugee estimates in zur Mühlen, *Fluchtweg*, 153. Most ships left for Shanghai from Trieste, but after Italy entered the war, some left from Lisbon and Marseille (Ristaino, *Port of Last Resort*, 101).

9. Zur Mühlen, *Fluchtweg*, 187; "picture our morale" in Charles Hahn file, AFSC, 2002.296, USHMM; "some Spanish ships" in Conard to his family, Jan. 3, 1942, AFSC, 2002.296, USHMM; "Gestapo" in Pimentel, "Refugiados," 104; "remained in operation" in War History Branch, A1–716, Box 29—Lisbon, 13, RG-59, NARA.

10. "Cook Travel Agency" and "One cannot understand" in *Aufbau*, Feb. 28, 1941, 7; "American Export Line" in Klein, *Flüchtlingspolitik*, 284, and Bayles, "Europe's Bottleneck," 77; Bayles, "Lisbon," 77; for the Eisingers, see Bazarov, "Racing at Death," 24.

11. Kracauer waited more than six weeks (Jansen and Schmidt, *In steter Freundschaft*, 118, 140). "Police" in Pimentel, "Refugiados," 104.

12. "Refugees in Lisbon," outtakes from "Portugal—Europe's Crossroads," a March of Time newsreel, RG 60.0788, USHMM, available at https://collections.ushmm.org/search/catalog/irn1000584.

13. Wyman, *Abandonment of the Jews*, 335–36.

14. DeBenedetti, "Between Fascism and Freedom," ch. 8, 4, accession 2004.57, USHMM.

15. "German refugees" comment by the journalist Hermann Budzislawski, quoted in zur Mühlen, *Fluchtweg*, 190, 200; Arendt to Adler-Rudel, Feb. 17 and Apr. 2, 1941, at hannaharendt.net/index.php/han/article/view/72/108.

16. "Being American" in Lolita Eschborn Goldstein, telephone interview by Laura Hobson Faure, Oct. 27, 2005; thank you to Laura Hobson Faure for sharing it. All other quoted material comes from an interview with Lolita Eschborn Goldstein by Olivia Mattis, Oct. 2014, posted on Vimeo by the Sousa Mendes Foundation, https://vimeo.com/155765492.

17. "Cost of this lifeline" in Pimentel, "Refugiados," 104, and Klein, *Flüchtlingspolitik*, 284; "sixty ticket agents" in Conard, "Brief Report on the Lisbon Office of the AFSC, May to August '41," Aug. 23, 1941, 9, Schauffler, Yale; "every little agent" in "Report of the HIAS-ICA Activities in Lisbon, July 1, 1940–Dec. 18, 1941," 2–3, 245.4, section I, files no. XII-Portugal A-2, HIAS-HICEM, YIVO; "windfall" in Goldstein interview by Mattis; "luxury liner" in Bodley, *Flight into Portugal*, 104; "$320" in Klein, *Flüchtlingspolitik*, 288.

18. Elisabeth Bab, memoir, 216–17, LBI; DeBenedetti, "Between Fascism and Freedom," ch. 8, 4, USHMM. The Allies oversaw operations of the *Nea Hellas* between 1939 and 1947. "Starting at $350" in David Kahane (1995), #1426, seg. 58, Shoah; "transporting troops" in Schauffler to Ambassador Weddell, memo, Mar. 22, 1941, regarding transportation from Lisbon, Schauffler, Yale; Rosenfeld, letter of June 13, 1942, file 6031, AFSC, 2002.296, USHMM; Dexter quoted in Klein, *Flüchtlingspolitik*, 288.

19. "Sense of compassion" in Bodley, *Flight into Portugal*, 104; Marcu, *Ein Kopf*, 203–4.

20. On the black market in tickets, see Israelitische Kultusgemeinde Vienna to Johanna Sara Bruchsteiner, Lisbon, Nov. 2, 1941, item #200, Lisbon Coll., MJH. Reported black-market prices varied widely: $500 (*Aufbau*, July–Aug. 2012, 28), $320–$340 (in 1940; Lisa Baer [1995], #6329, seg. 61, Shoah), $300 to as much as $2,500 from illegal vendors (Marcu, *Ein Kopf*, 205), $250 in

Lisbon or the United States (Wasserstein, *Ambiguity of Virtue*, 89), and $420 (Ryan, "Vichy and the Jews," 276).

21. "People at cafés" in Blaufuks, *Strange Skies;* Frank Furth, testimony, MJH, New York, 1990, videotape 3 of 5. He thought he could have bought a forged passport in a café. Marcu, *Ein Kopf,* 205; "children traveling alone" in Lotte Marcuse, "Arrival of Children on SS *Nyassa,* on April 23, 1941," YIVO, RG 249, folder 478; Frank Furth, testimony, MJH; "fake agencies" and "corrupt bureaucrats" in P. Turismo Portugal LDA [a private Portuguese travel agency] to Companhia Nacional de Navegação, Lisboa, May 6, 1941, Legião Portuguesa, Comando Geral, 2nd Repartição, Proc. 1566/15-B5, #150, Portuguese National Archive; "man who had provided" in Andersen, Ardoin, and Zilberman, *HIAS Stories,* 75.

22. "I am aware of " in *Aufbau,* Oct. 15, 1939, 3. The German Jewish Aid Committee in England seems to have required this, underlining the dangers that passengers could confront. "Illegal entry" in Klein, *Flüchtlingspolitik,* 286; Lax's story in James Barron, "The Mathematicians Who Ended the Kidnapping of an N.Y.U. Computer," *New York Times,* Dec. 6, 2015, nytimes.com/2015/12/07/nyregion/the-mathematicians-who-ended-the-kidnapping-of-an-nyu-computer.html?emc=eta1&_r=0; for U-boat attacks on the East Coast, see "U-Boat Attacks of World War II," New England Historical Society at newenglandhistoricalsociety.com/u-boat-attacks-of-world-war-ii–6-months-of-secret-terror-in-the-atlantic.

23. "German submarines" in Lenkway, 38–39, USHMM. The merchant ship, headed to Greenland, was the *Maria da Glória.*

24. The Marxes' story is in Angela Borgstedt, "Unrecht im Namen des Rechts," Nov. 14, 2007, at stafreiburg.de/pb/,Lde/1156483/?LISTPAGE=1156435.

25. *Times,* Oct. 15, 1940; the story of the *Dora* in memo, Aug. 16, 1940, file 896 (1 of 3), JDC; "JDC's assistance" in *Diário de Notícias,* July 29, 1940, Bitton Coll., 1990.205.01–15, USHMM.

26. Teller, "Bericht," 2, in DORSA, file 11A, JDC; "which was a mess" in Paul K., # T-3927 FVA; "no novelty" in "617 War Refugees Jam Small Ship," *New York Times,* July 14, 1941, 13. The *Nyassa,* built to hold 450 passengers, accepted 800 in mid-1941. It took the first shipload of refugees from Portugal and Spain to Palestine in January 1944; see *Informationsbericht zur Judenfrage,* Nr. 21, Feb. 1, 1944 (Der Chef der Sicherheitspolizei und des SD), 275, 1.2.7.1/82341987#1/ITS Digital Archive, USHMM; see also Bitton microfiche, RG-19.011*01, USHMM.

27. *Navemar* in Conard to AFSC, Phila., Sept. 16, 1941, Rottenstein, file 3612, AFSC, 2002.296, USHMM; see also Conard to his family, Aug. 12, 1941,

Conard Coll., AFSC, 2002.296, USHMM; Schwartz quoted in Klein, *Flüchtlingspolitik*, 288; *Aufbau* quoted in Pimentel and Heinrich, *Judeus*, 183; Weishaupt quoted in Andersen, Ardoin, and Zilberman, *HIAS Stories*, 75.

28. "Usual load" in Pimentel and Heinrich, *Judeus*, 182; Fittko, *Escape Through the Pyrenees*, 210; "crew members" in Klein, *Flüchtlingspolitik*, 288.

29. Margot Aal (1996), #10980, seg. 62–68, Shoah; *Aufbau*, Jan. 23, 1942, 3.

30. "Thirteenth boat" at https://www.ushmm.org/online/hsv/source_view. php?SourceId=31555; "Quakers had decided" in Klein, *Flüchtlingspolitik*, 286; leaving Spain, in "Report of activities for first 9 months of 1944," Dec. 10, 1944, 345.4, section I, file No. XII-Portugal A-19, HIAS-HICEM, YIVO.

31. Pekelis, *My Version*, 133–34; "as well as clearance" in JTA, "Singing, Dancing." The JDC financed other *Nyassa* voyages as well (file 377, JDC online catalog, 129). "Lisbon to Palestine" in zur Mühlen, *Fluchtweg*, 206–7.

32. "Ship of Destiny" in Dijn, *Das Schicksalsschiff*, 190; "JDC either financed" in JDC catalogue, item 132, file 387; "hopes grew" in *Aufbau*, Jan. 2, 1942, 1; "Betty Trapunski" in Les Perreaux, "Serpa Pinto: Voyages of Life and Death," *Toronto Globe and Mail*, Apr. 24, 2009, theglobeandmail.com/news/national/serpa-pinto-voyages-of-life-and-death/article1196753/?page=all; "perilous voyages" in Conard to AFSC, Phila., Sept. 16, 1942, Rottenstein, file 3612, AFSC, 2002.296, USHMM.

33. "Arrest and deportation" in Jacobson, *Embattled Selves*, 17; see also Bankier, *Germans and the Final Solution*, 101–16; Klemperer, *To the Bitter End*, 5, 21; "suicides rose" in M. Kaplan, *Dignity and Despair*, 180; "certainty among most Jews" in Kosmala, "Zwischen Ahnen."

34. "Mann" in "Listen, Germany," 76; "We didn't believe" in Schnabel, *Lisbon: Harbour of Hope;* "Hannah Arendt im Gespräch mit Günter Gaus," 37:16.

35. Wisla, memoirs/journal (n.d.), Digibaeck, 62.

36. "Zionist Federation" in Lichtheim, Geneva, to Schmulevitz, Lisbon, Mar. 20, 1942, Central Zionist Archives L22/14, RG68.127M, USHMM; "awful things" in Wriggins, *Picking Up the Pieces*, 41; Wriggins, journal entry, Aug. 7, 1942, box 1, folder 30, 1942, RG 67.008, USHMM. The roundups started on August 6 in the southern zone, so she had correct information, unless she was referring to the Vel' d'Hiv roundup in Paris in July.

37. "Transmitted through Lisbon" in Leshem, "Rescue Efforts," 239; "resist believing" in Segev, *World Jewish Congress*, 133; "Allied broadcast" in Milgram, *Portugal, Salazar, and the Jews*, 185; "pressure the U.S. government" in Feingold, *Politics of Rescue*, 172–79; Wriggins, *Picking Up the Pieces*, 41.

38. Lowrie, letter of Aug. 3, 1943, quoted in Subak, *Rescue and Flight*, 183; Herbert Katzki, interview, June 2, 1995, RG-50.030*0337, USHMM. In 1996, Wriggins of the Quakers and Katzki of the JDC met again. They discussed what they thought they knew in late 1942 (the deadliest year of the Holocaust) and early 1943, and concluded that they had not known about the annihilation of the Jews: "It came as a relief to . . . us . . . that we both had been ignorant of this. We both feared we had dismissed in disbelief what should then have been obvious to us both" (Wriggins, *Picking Up the Pieces*, 58).

39. F. Mann, *Drastic Turn of Destiny*, 163, 169, 171, 179, 185 (Vilna); Schwarz in James Mann Report, Aug. 30, 1944, 23, War Refugee Board, USHMM.

40. D'Esaguy disparaged the leader of the Luxembourger-Jewish community, Albert Nussbaum, as a collaborator for negotiating with the Germans to allow Luxembourger Jews to emigrate at the end of 1940 (Y. Bauer, *American Jewry*, 54–55). "Leave Paris" in James Mann Report, Aug. 30, 1944, 23, War Refugee Board, USHMM.

41. "Review of the Year 5704," *AJYB* 45, 239; Schauffler to Clarence Pickett, June 2, 1944, quoting Conard, Foreign Service 1944, Committees and Organizations (American JDC to Catholic Mission Board), AFSC, Phila.

42. "*Nea Hellas*" in Torberg, *Eine tolle*, 143; "They are trapped" in Sevareid, "Escape Hatch," 93.

43. *Mundo Gráfico*, Jan. 30, 1941, quoted in Ramalho, *Lisbon*, 37; Remarque, *Night in Lisbon*, 3.

44. "*Nyassa*" in Bitton, microfiche, RG-19.011*06, USHMM; "Refugees Board Ship in Lisbon," outtakes from "Portugal—Europe's Crossroads," a *March of Time* newsreel, RG 60.0790, USHMM, available at https://collections.ushmm.org/search/catalog/irn1000586.

45. "Rotten" RLB to Schauffler, Nov. 8, 1944, referring to David Nimiec, in Levy, file 8186, AFSC, 2002.296, USHMM; "Complain" in Abels, *Franz Werfel*, 126; Bitton interview (1990), RG 50.030*0027, USHMM; Marx, *Die Flucht*, 153; Farau quoted in Pfanner, *Exile in New York*, 136.

46. Marx, *Die Flucht*, 156.

47. Finger, #6981, Shoah; Kracauer quoted in Asper, "Man muss," 6; Walker interview.

48. Vishniac quoted in Kohn, "Naturally Berlin," 32; Sahl, *Das Exil*, 103–4; Marx, *Die Flucht*, 156; H. Mann, *Ein Zeitalter*, 448, quoted in Voigt, *Heinrich Mann*, 54. Mann wrote the memoir between 1943 and 1944. Tillinger quoted in Pimentel, "Salazar impediu," 22–23; Marcu, *Ein Kopf*, 205; see also Raskin, "Far from Where."

49. The figure 1,000 is in zur Mühlen, *Fluchtweg,* 163. The JDC also estimated 1,000, but excluded all those not receiving its help. The Lisbon Jewish community supported 390 of 426 refugees in August 1944. In July 1948, 116 refugees still being supported by the community left; see memo of Aug. 3, 1944 to JDC, New York, file 897 (2 of 2), JDC. For further information about Jewish refugees in Lisbon in 1948, see Report of July 1948 by Dr. Baruel, Lisbon, Code HMB/1584, Correspondência geral, Origin PO/Li, AII–12a/12, 1948, file 400281, Secção, CAHJP. For the situation in 1951, see Rosenfeld, file 6031, AFSC, 2002.296, USHMM.

Conclusion

Epigraph: Said, *Reflections on Exile,* 173.

1. Milgram, *Portugal, Salazar, and the Jews,* 116; See the review by M. Kaplan in *Shofar* 31, no. 1 (2012): 165–69.
2. "Thousands of people" in Ernest P., #T-1224, FVA; "hot, dusty" in W. Gallagher, "See You in Lisbon," 190–92; Remarque, *Night in Lisbon,* 4.
3. Gemie, Reid, and Humbert claim that rationality, too, motivated panicked postwar refugees (*Outcast Europe,* 252).
4. Eley, "Labor History." *Eigensinn,* which has been defined as a "creative reappropriation of the conditions of daily life," helps us see individual agency (Lüdtke, "Organizational Order").
5. *Manchester Guardian,* May 23, 1936, quoted in Sherman, *Island Refuge,* 112. For the number of Jews in Portugal, I am using a mix of data, which seem the most reasonable (Milgram, *Portugal, Salazar, and the Jews,* 289). "American Jewish Committee" in "Review of the Year 5701," *AJYB* 43, 203; "country again opened" in *AJYB* 45, 297; "Portugal's treatment" in Schauffler to AFSC staff, memo, Nov. 6, 1944, 6, Conard Coll., AFSC 2002.296, USHMM.
6. Text of the Hague Convention is available from the International Committee of the Red Cross, https://ihl-databases.icrc.org/ihl/INTRO/200, OpenDocument. Portugal outdid other neutral countries in the number of refugees it allowed to stay or pass through. For example, Switzerland allowed close to 30,000 Jews to pass through, although the country also turned away about 20,000 Jews. Sweden took in approximately 7,000 Danish Jews, and about 16,000 Jews passed through Turkey, which also accepted a few hundred Jewish academics in the early 1930s. During the first half of the war, some 20,000–30,000 Jews passed through Spain; see the USHMM and Yad Vashem

websites for statistics. "What Portugal did," comment by Fritz Adelsberger, quoted in Schnabel, *Lisbon: Harbour of Hope.*

7. Meissner, oral history (1992), RG-50.233*0087 (minutes 81–82), USHMM.

8. "All over the world" in Betty Harris (1996), #13459, seg. 49–51, Shoah; "visas to go anywhere" in Anny Coury (1996), #11780, seg. 47–57, Shoah.

9. Benthien, Fleig, and Kasten, *Emotionalität,* 10.

10. "No-man's-land" in Koestler, *Arrival and Departure,* 19.

11. "Refugee Convention" at "The 1951 Convention relating to the Status of Refugees and Its 1967 Protocol," Refugee Legal Aid Information for Lawyers Representing Refugees Globally, refugeelegalaidinformation. org/1951-convention; "Home," by Warsan Shire, available from Amnesty International, https://www.amnesty.ie/wp-content/uploads/2016/06/home-by-warsan-shire.pdf.

12. "65.3 million" at "Figures at a Glance," UNHCR: UK, unhcr.org/uk/figures-at-a-glance.html. As of Feb. 12, 2019, the figure had risen to 68.5 million.

13. Lipstadt, *Beyond Belief;* Press Association, "Calais: Hundreds of Migrants Remain a Year After Razing of Camp," *Guardian,* Oct. 22, 2017, https://www.theguardian.com/world/2017/oct/23/calais-refugees-year-after-razing-of-camp. On Turkey, see Ahmet İçduygu, "Syrian Refugees in Turkey: The Long Road Ahead," Apr. 2015, Migration Policy Institute, migrationpolicy.org/research/syrian-refugees-turkey-long-road-ahead. On Paris, see David Chazan, "Paris Migrant Tents Return Just Hours After Police Clear Influx from the Calais 'Jungle,'" *Telegraph,* Oct. 31, 2016, tele-graph.co.uk/news/2016/10/31/paris-authorities-begin-clearing-migrant-camps-after-influx-from. On Berlin, see Ben Knight, "Berlin to Stop Housing Refugees in Tempelhof Hangars—in Theory," DW, July 20, 2016, dw.com/en/berlin-to-stop-housing-refugees-in-tempelhof-hangars-in-theory/a-19415068.

14. Eleanor Acer, director of Human Rights First, quoted in *New York Times,* Mar. 21, 2015, A5.

15. David Crossland, "Arab Street in Berlin Brings Nostalgia for Syrian Refu-gees," Dec. 11, 2016, *National* (Abu Dhabi), thenational.ae/world/europe/arab-street-in-berlin-brings-nostalgia-for-syrian-refugees.

16. Emanuella Grinberg and Madison Park, "2nd Day of Protests over Trump's Immigration Policies," Jan. 30, 2017, CNN.com, cnn.com/2017/01/29/politics/us-immigration-protests.

17. "Nation's economic growth" in Patrick Young, "National Academy of Sciences: 'Immigration Integral to Growth,'" Long Island Wins, Sept. 21,

2016, https://longislandwins.com/news/national/national-academy-sciences-immigration-integral-growth; "outweighed sympathy" and "dangerous and different" in Nicholas Kristof, "Anne Frank Today Is a Syrian Girl," *New York Times,* Aug. 25, 2016, A19; Marion Kaplan, "Does Donald Trump Realize Jewish Refugees Were also Called 'Trojan Horses'?" *Forward,* Oct. 20, 2016, http://forward.com/opinion/352353/does-donald-trump-realize-jewish-refugees-were-also-called-trojan-horses/?attribution=author-article-listing–1-headline.

18. Paetel, *Reise,* 255.

Bibliography

Abels, Norbert. *Franz Werfel: Mit Selbstzeugnissen und Bilddokumenten*. Reinbek bei Hamburg, Germany: Rowohlt, 1990.

Adler, Eliyana, and Natalia Aleksiun. "Seeking Relative Safety: The Flight of Polish Jews to the East in the Autumn of 1939." *Yad Vashem Studies* 46:1 (2018): 41–71.

Adler, K. H., and Carrie Hamilton. *Homes and Homecomings: Gendered Histories of Domesticity and Return*. Oxford: Wiley-Blackwell, 2010.

Adorno, Theodor W. *Minima Moralia: Reflections from Damaged Life*. Translated by E. F. N. Jephcott. New York: Schocken, 1974.

Afonso, Rui, and António Pescada. *Um Homem Bom: Aristides de Sousa Mendes: O Wallenberg Português*. Lisbon: Caminho, 1995.

AJJDC [American Jewish Joint Distribution Committee]. *World Refugee Organizations: A Guide to Relief and Reconstruction Activities for Refugees from Germany*. Paris: AJJDC, 1937. Reprinted by Schoen, 2013.

AJYB [American Jewish Year Book] 42. New York: AJC, 1940–41.

AJYB [American Jewish Year Book] 43. New York: AJC, 1941–42.

AJYB [American Jewish Year Book] 44. New York: AJC, 1942–43.

AJYB [American Jewish Year Book] 45. New York: AJC, 1943–44.

Akbari, Suzanne Conklin, Tamar Herzog, Daniel Jütte, Carl Nightingale, William Rankin, and Keren Weitzberg. "AHR Conversation: Walls, Borders, and Boundaries in World History." *AHR* 122, no. 5 (Dec. 2017): 1501–53.

Alexander, Jack. "The Nazi Offensive in Lisbon." *Saturday Evening Post*, March 6, 1943.

Allen, John S. *Home: How Habitat Made Us Human*. New York: Basic Books, 2015.

Amato, Joseph Anthony. *Rethinking Home: A Case for Writing Local History*. Berkeley: University of California Press, 2002.

Améry, Jean. *At the Mind's Limits: Contemplations by a Survivor on Auschwitz and Its Realities.* Translated by Sidney Rosenfeld and Stella Rosenfeld. Bloomington: Indiana University Press, 1980.

Amipaz-Silber, Gitta. *Sephardi Jews in Occupied France: Under the Tyrant's Heel, 1940–1944.* Jerusalem: Rubin Mass, 1995.

Andersen, Kathleen, Morris Ardoin, and Margarita Zilberman, eds. *120 HIAS Stories.* New York: Hebrew Immigrant Aid Society, 2002.

Anderson, Benedict. *Imagined Communities: Reflections on the Origin and Spread of Nationalism.* London: Verso, 1983.

Anderson, Kay, and Susan J. Smith. "Editorial: Emotional Geographies." *Transactions of the Institute of British Geographers* 26, no. 1 (Mar. 2001): 7–10. https://doi.org/10.1111/1475-5661.00002.

Anthony, Elizabeth Paige. "Return Home: Holocaust Survivors Reestablishing Lives in Postwar Vienna." Ph.D. diss., Clark University, 2016.

Antunes, José Freire. *Judeus em Portugal: O Testemunho de 50 Homens e Mulheres.* Versailles, France: Edeline, 2002.

Applegate, Celia. "A Europe of Regions: Reflections on the Historiography of Sub-National Places in Modern Times." *AHR* 104, no. 4 (Oct. 1999): 1157–82.

Arendt, Hannah. Introduction to *Illumination: Essays and Reflections,* by Walter Benjamin, 1–58. New York: Schocken, 1969.

———. *The Origins of Totalitarianism.* Cleveland: Meridian, 1966.

———. "We Refugees." In *Altogether Elsewhere: Writers on Exile,* edited by Marc Robinson, 110–19. Boston: Faber and Faber, 1994. Available at www-leland.stanford.edu/dept/DLCL/files/pdf/hannah_arendt_we_refugees.pdf.

———. "We Refugees." In Arendt, *The Jewish Writings,* edited by Jerome Kohn and Ron H. Feldman, 264–74. New York: Schocken, 2007.

———. "What Remains? The Language Remains: A Conversation with Günter Gaus." In Arendt, *Essays in Understanding, 1930–1954: Formation, Exile, and Totalitarianism,* edited by Jerome Kohn, 1–23. New York: Schocken, 1994.

Asper, Helmut G. " 'Man muss eben struggeln, um oben zu bleiben': Eugen Schüfftan und Siegfried Kracauer im Amerikanischen Exil." In *Nachrichten aus Hollywood, New York und Anderswo: Der Briefwechsel Eugen und Marlise Schüfftans mit Siegfried und Lili Kracauer,* edited by Helmut G. Asper, 3–30. Trier, Germany: WVT Wissenschaftlicher Verlag Trier, 2003.

Auslander, Leora. "Coming Home? Jews in Postwar Paris." *Journal of Contemporary History* 40, no. 2 (Apr. 2005): 237–59.

———. "'Jewish Taste'? Jews and the Aesthetics of Everyday Life in Paris and Berlin, 1920–1942." In *Histories of Leisure,* edited by Rudy Koshar, 299–318. New York: Berg, 2002.

Auslander, Leora, and Tara Zahra, eds. *Objects of War: The Material Culture of Conflict and Displacement.* Ithaca, N.Y.: Cornell University Press, 2018.

Avni, Haim. *Spain, the Jews, and Franco.* Philadelphia: Jewish Publication Society of America, 1982.

———. "The Zionist Underground in Holland and France and the Escape to Spain." In *Rescue Attempts During the Holocaust,* edited by Yisrael Gutman and Efraim Zuroff, 561–90. Jerusalem: Yad Vashem, 1977.

Avrutin, Eugene. *Jews and the Imperial State: Identification Politics in Tsarist Russia.* Ithaca, N.Y.: Cornell University Press, 2010.

Baehr, Peter. *Caesarism, Charisma, and Fate: Historical Sources and Modern Resonances in the Work of Max Weber.* New Brunswick, N.J.: Transaction, 2011.

Baer, Alejandro. "Oma Clemens Reise nach Argentinien." *Münchner Beiträge zur Jüdischen Geschichte und Kultur* 5, no. 2 (2011): 112–21.

Bagger, Eugene S. *For the Heathen Are Wrong: An Impersonal Autobiography.* Boston: Little, Brown, 1941.

Baiôa, Manuel, Paulo Jorge Fernandes, and Filipe Ribeiro de Meneses. "The Political History of Twentieth-Century Portugal." *E-journal of Portuguese History* 1, no. 2 (Winter 2003). https://www.brown.edu/Departments/Portuguese_Brazilian_Studies/ejph/html/issue2/pdf/baioa.pdf.

Bajohr, Frank. *Unser Hotel ist Judenfrei: Bäder-Antisemitismus im 19. und 20. Jahrhundert.* Frankfurt am Main: Fischer Taschenbuch Verlag, 2003.

Bankier, David. *The Germans and the Final Solution: Public Opinion Under Nazism.* Oxford: Blackwell, 1992.

Barak, Yoram, and Henry Szor. "Lifelong Posttraumatic Stress Disorder: Evidence from Aging Holocaust Survivors." *Dialogues in Clinical Neuroscience* 2, no. 1 (2000). https://www.ncbi.nlm.nih.gov/pmc/articles/PMC3181591.

Barkai, Avraham. *From Boycott to Annihilation: The Economic Struggle of German Jews, 1933–1943.* Hanover, N.H.: University Press of New England, 1989.

Bartrop, Paul. "From Lisbon to Jamaica: A Study of British Refugee Rescue During the Second World War." *Immigrants and Minorities: Historical Studies in Ethnicity, Migration and Diaspora* 13, no. 1 (1994), 48–64.

Bauer, Maria. *Beyond the Chestnut Trees.* Woodstock, N.Y.: Overlook, 1984.

Bauer, Yehuda. *American Jewry and the Holocaust: The American Jewish Joint Distribution Committee, 1939–1945.* Detroit: Wayne State University Press, 1981.

Baumel, Judith. "Gender and Family Studies of the Holocaust." In *Teaching the Holocaust in a Changing World.* Vol. 2 of *Lessons and Legacies,* edited by Donald G. Schilling, 105–17. Evanston, Ill.: Northwestern University Press, 1998.

———. *Unfulfilled Promises: Rescue and Resettlement of Jewish Refugee Children in the United States.* Juneau, Alaska: Denali, 1990.

Bayles, William. "Lisbon: Europe's Bottleneck." *Life,* Apr. 28, 1941.

Bazarov, Valery. "HIAS and HICEM in the System of Jewish Relief Organizations in Europe, 1933–41." *East European Jewish Affairs* 39, no. 1 (Apr. 2009): 69–78.

———. "Racing with Death: HIAS (HICEM) Lisbon Files (1940–45)." *Avotaynu* 20, no. 4 (Winter 2004): 23–27.

Beauvoir, Simone de. *The Mandarins.* Translated by Leonard M. Friedman. New York: World, 1956.

Beevor, Antony. *The Second World War.* New York: Little, Brown, 2012.

Benarús, Adolfo. *O Antisemitismo.* Lisbon: Sociedade Nacional de Tipografia, 1937.

Ben-Dror, Graciela. *La Iglesia Católica Ante el Holocausto: España y América Latina 1933–1945.* Madrid: Alianza Editorial, 2003.

Benthien, Claudia, Anne Fleig, and Ingrid Kasten, eds. *Emotionalität: Zur Geschichte der Gefühle.* Cologne: Böhlau, 2000.

Benz, Wolfgang, ed. *Judenfeindschaft in Geschichte und Gegenwart, Länder und Regionen.* Vol. 1 of *Handbuch des Antisemitismus.* Munich: Saur, 2010.

Bergen, Doris L., Anna Hájková, and Andrea Löw, eds. *Alltag im Holocaust: Jüdisches Leben im Großdeutschen Reich, 1941–1945.* Berlin: De Gruyter Oldenbourg, 2013.

Berghahn, Marion. *German-Jewish Refugees in England: The Ambiguities of Assimilation.* New York: St. Martin's, 1984.

Berlant, Lauren. "Thinking About Feeling Historical." *Emotion, Space and Society* 1, no. 1 (2008): 4–9.

Biess, Frank. "Feelings in the Aftermath: Toward a History of Postwar Emotions." In *Histories of the Aftermath: The Legacies of the Second World War in Europe,* edited by Frank Biess and Robert G. Moeller, 30–48. New York: Berghahn, 2010.

Biess, Frank, Alon Confino, Ute Frevert, Uffa Jensen Lyndal Roper, and Daniela Saxer. "Forum: History of Emotions." *German History* 28, no. 1 (2010): 67–80.

Bitton, Isaac. *Letters to the Editor and Other Thoughts.* Woodstock, Ill.: Woodstock Printing and Publishing, 1999.

Blum, Matthias, and Claudia Rei. "Coming to America: Refugees from the Holocaust." Apr. 18, 2016. https://canvas.harvard.edu/files/2209056/download?download_frd=1&verifier=VrscoAsdWoVjP4jinTbmyDjOja L50WymToMRFC8b.

Blunt, Alison, and Robyn Dowling. *Home.* London: Routledge, 2006.

Boas, Jacob. "The Shrinking World of German Jewry, 1933–1938." *LBIYB* 31 (1986): 241–66.

Bodley, Ronald Victor Courtenay. *Flight into Portugal.* London: Jarrolds, 1941.

Bondi, Liz. "The Place of Emotions in Research." In *Emotional Geographies,* edited by Joyce Davidson, Liz Bondi, and Mick Smith, 231–46. Burlington, Vt.: Ashgate, 2005.

Bondy, Ruth. "The Miracle of the Loaves." In *Trapped: Essays on the History of the Czech Jews, 1939–1945.* Translated by Chaya Naor. Jerusalem: Yad Vashem, 2008.

Booth, Shirley, and Paul Buck. *Lisbon: A Cultural and Literary Companion.* New York: Interlink, 2002.

Borden, Louise. *The Journey That Saved Curious George: The True Wartime Escape of Margret and H. A. Rey.* Boston: Houghton Mifflin, 2005.

Borgstedt, Angela. "Unrecht im Namen des Rechts. Zum Gedenken an die 1933 bis 1935 aus dem badischen Justizdienst entlassenen jüdischen Richter." November 14, 2007. http://www.amtsgericht-loerrach.de/pb/,Lde/Startseite/Medien/Vortrag+Dr_+Borgstedt+ueber+Dr_+Emsheimer/?LISTPAGE=1156435.

Borut, Jacob. "Struggles for Spaces: Where Could Jews Spend Free Time in Nazi Germany?" *LBIYB* 56 (2011): 307–52.

Bourdieu, Pierre. *Distinction: A Social Critique of the Judgement of Taste.* Cambridge: Harvard University Press, 1984.

Bourke, Joanna. *Fear: A Cultural History.* Emeryville, Calif.: Shoemaker & Hoard, 2005.

Boym, Svetlana. *The Future of Nostalgia.* New York: Basic Books, 2001.

Brauch, Julia, Anna Lipphardt, and Alexandra Nocke. "Exploring Jewish Space: An Approach." In *Jewish Topographies,* edited by Brauch, Lipphardt, and Nocke, 1–26.

———, eds. *Jewish Topographies: Visions of Space, Traditions of Place.* Aldershot, U.K.: Ashgate, 2008.

Brecht, Bertolt. *Flüchtlingsgespräche.* Frankfurt am Main: Suhrkamp, 1961.

———. "Über die Bezeichnung Emigranten." http://exil.mako-home.de/brecht.htm.

Breitman, Richard, and Alan M. Kraut. *American Refugee Policy and European Jewry, 1933–1945.* Bloomington: Indiana University Press, 1987.

Breitman, Richard, and Allan J. Lichtman. *FDR and the Jews.* Cambridge, Mass.: Belknap, 2013.

Brenner, Arthur David. *Emil J. Gumbel: Weimar German Pacifist and Professor.* Boston: Humanities Press, 2001.

Brison, Susan J. *Aftermath: Violence and the Remaking of a Self.* Princeton: Princeton University Press, 2003.

Bromberger, Sylvain. "Memoirs of a 1940 Family Flight from Antwerp." *Portuguese Studies Review* 4, no. 1 (1995): 9–19.

Brown, Ryan Lenora. "Looking for Legal Status." *New York Times Magazine,* Aug. 5, 2016. https://www.nytimes.com/2016/08/07/magazine/looking-for-legal-status.html.

Bruneau, Thomas. "Church and State in Portugal: Crises of Cross and Sword." *Journal of Church and State* 18, no. 3 (1976): 463–90.

Buch, Esteban, Igor Contreras Zubillaga, and Manuel Deniz Silva, eds. *Composing for the State: Music in Twentieth-Century Dictatorships.* Abingdon, U.K.: Ashgate, 2016.

Caestecker, Frank, and Bob Moore, eds. *Refugees from Nazi Germany and the Liberal European States.* New York: Berghahn, 2010.

Caestecker, Frank, and Denis Scuto. "The Benelux and the Flight of Refugees from Nazi Germany: The Luxembourg Specificity." *Hémecht: Revue d'histoire Luxembourgeoise* 68, no. 4 (2016): 389–410.

Cancian, Sonia. *Families, Lovers, and their Letters: Italian Postwar Migration to Canada.* Manitoba: University of Manitoba Press, 2010.

Caplan, Jane, and John Torpey, eds. *Documenting Individual Identity: The Development of State Practices in the Modern World.* Princeton: Princeton University Press, 2001.

Caron, Vicki. *Uneasy Asylum: France and the Jewish Refugee Crisis, 1933–1942.* Stanford: Stanford University Press, 1999.

Cesarani, David. *Arthur Koestler: The Homeless Mind.* London: Heinemann, 1998.

Chantal, Suzanne. *Portugal: The Land and Its People.* Translated by Frank R. Holliday. Lisbon: Shell Portuguesa, 1944.

Cloke, Paul J., Phil Crang, and Mark Goodwin, eds. *Introducing Human Geographies.* London: Hodder Arnold, 2005.

Cohen, Richard. "A Jewish Leader in Vichy France: The Diary of Raymond-Raoul Lambert." *JSS* 43, nos. 3–4 (1981): 291–310.

Cole, Tim. *Holocaust Landscapes.* London: Bloomsbury, 2016.

Corkill, David, and José Carlos Pina Almeida. "Commemoration and Propaganda in Salazar's Portugal: The *Mundo Português* Exposition of 1940." *Journal of Contemporary History* 44, no. 3 (July 2009): 381–99.

Correa Martín-Arroyo, Pedro. "The Iberian Peninsula and the Jewish Refugee Crisis, 1933–44." Ph.D. diss., London School of Economics and Political Science, 2018.

Correia, Maria Assunção Pinto. "Abschied von Europa: Portugal als Exil-und Transitland." In *Alternative Lateinamerika: Das deutsche Exil in der Zeit des Nationalsozialismus,* edited by Karl Kohut and Patrik von zur Mühlen, 27–39. Frankfurt am Main: Vervuert, 1994.

Cova, Anne, and António Costa Pinto. "Women Under Salazar's Dictatorship." *Portuguese Journal of Social Science* 1, no. 2 (July 2002): 129–146. https://doi.org/10.1386/pjss.1.2.129.

Crossette, Barbara. "The Century of Refugees Ends. And Continues." *New York Times,* Dec. 31, 2000. https://www.nytimes.com/2000/12/31/weekinreview/the-world-the-century-of-refugees-ends-and-continues.html.

Dachs, Gisela, ed. *Grenzen Jüdischer Almanach.* Berlin: Jüdischer Verlag, 2015.

Darwin, Charles. *The Expression of the Emotions in Man and Animals.* 3rd ed. London: Harper Collins, 1998.

Da Silveira, Luís Espinha, Daniel Alves, Nuno Miguel Lima, Ana Alcântara, and Josep Puig. "Population and Railways in Portugal, 1801–1930." *Journal of Interdisciplinary History* 42, no. 1 (Summer 2011): 29–52.

Dauner, Eduardo Martín de Pozuelo. "Franco, Nazi Collaborator." *Volunteer,* June 20, 2013. albavolunteer.org/2013/06/franco-nazi-collaborator.

Davidson, Joyce, and Liz Bondi. "Spatialising Affect; Affecting Space: An Introduction." *Gender, Place and Culture* 11, no. 3 (Sept. 2004): 373–74.

Decker, William Merrill. *Epistolary Practices: Letter Writing in America Before Telecommunications.* Chapel Hill: University of North Carolina Press, 1998.

DeGooyer, Stephanie, Alastair Hunt, Lida Maxwell, and Samuel Moyn. *The Right to Have Rights.* London: Verso, 2018.

Dekker, Rudolf M. "Egodocumenten: A Virtual Conversation with Rudolf M. Dekker." Interview by Andreas Rutz, Stefan Elit, and Stephan Kraft. *Zeitenblicke* 1, no. 2 (2002). zeitenblicke.historicum.net/2002/02/dekker/index.html.

Dembitzer, Salamon. *Visas for America: The Story of an Escape.* Sydney: Villon, 1952.

Demos, John. *The Unredeemed Captive: A Family Story from Early America.* New York: Vintage, 1995.

D'Esaguy, Augusto. *Repaying a Debt Four Centuries Old.* Lisbon: Editorial Império, 1951. A speech delivered in Philadelphia, May 30, 1941.

Diamond, Hanna. *Fleeing Hitler: France, 1940.* Oxford: Oxford University Press, 2007.

DiFiglia, Ghanda. *Roots and Visions: The First Fifty Years of the Unitarian Universalist Service Committee.* Boston: Unitarian Universalist Service Committee, 1990.

Dijn, Rosine de. *Das Schicksalsschiff: Rio de Janeiro–Lissabon–New York, 1942.* Munich: Deutsche Verlags-Anstalt, 2009.

Döblin, Alfred. *Destiny's Journey.* Translated by Edna MacCown. New York: Paragon House, 1992.

Dodman, Thomas. "Before Trauma, Nostalgia, or the Melancholy of War." Lecture at the Library of Congress, Washington, D.C., 2015. https://stream-media.loc.gov/webcasts/captions/2015/150730klu1600.txt.

Dunker, Ulrich. *Der Reichsbund Jüdischer Frontsoldaten: 1919–1938.* Düsseldorf: Droste Verlag, 1977.

Dwork, Debórah, and Robert Jan van Pelt. *Flight from the Reich: Refugee Jews, 1933–1946.* New York: Norton, 2009.

Easthope, Hazel. "Fixed Identities in a Mobile World? The Relationship Between Mobility, Place, and Identity." *Identities: Global Studies in Culture and Power* 16, no. 1 (2009): 61–82.

Eiland, Howard, and Michael W. Jennings. *Walter Benjamin: A Critical Life.* Cambridge: Harvard University Press, 2014.

Eley, Geoff. "Labor History, Social History, *Alltagsgeschichte:* Experience, Culture, and the Politics of the Everyday—A New Direction for German Social History?" *Journal of Modern History* 61, no. 2 (1989): 297–343.

Ellis, Marc H. *Encountering the Jewish Future: With Elie Wiesel, Martin Buber, Abraham Joshua Heschel, Hannah Arendt, Emmanuel Levinas.* Minneapolis: Fortress, 2011.

Engelking, Barbara, and Jacek Leociak. *The Warsaw Ghetto: A Guide to the Perished City.* New Haven: Yale University Press, 2009.

Ephraim, Frank. *Escape to Manila: From Nazi Tyranny to Japanese Terror.* Urbana: University of Illinois Press, 2003.

Eschelbacher, Max. *Der Zehnte November 1938*. Essen, Germany: Klartext, 1998.

Estorick, Eric. "The Evian Conference and the Intergovernmental Committee." *Annals of the American Academy of Political and Social Science* 203, no. 1 (1939): 136–41.

Eustace, Nicole, Eugenia Lean, Julie Livingston, Jan Plumper, William M. Reddy, and Barbara H. Rosenwein. "AHR Conversation: The Historical Study of Emotions." *AHR* 117, no. 5 (Dec. 2012), 1487–531.

Fahrmeir, Andrea. "Governments and Forgers: Passports in Nineteenth-Century Europe." In Caplan and Torpey, *Documenting Individual Identity*, 218–34.

Fallaci, Oriana. "Italiani di Israele." *L'Europeo* 13 (1973).

Farkas, Karl. *Farkas Endeckt Amerika*. New York: Triton, 1941.

Feingold, Henry L. *Politics of Rescue: The Roosevelt Administration and the Holocaust, 1939–1945*. New York: Holocaust Publications, 1970.

Ferreira, Paula. "Home Bound: The Construct of Femininity in the *Estado Novo*." *Portuguese Studies* 12 (1996): 133–44.

Feuchtwanger, Lion. *The Devil in France: My Encounter with Him in the Summer of 1940*. Los Angeles and Berlin: Figueroa Press and Aufbau Verlag, 1997.

Feuchtwanger, Marta. "The Escape" and "An Émigré Life: Munich, Berlin, Sanary, Pacific Palisades." Interviews by Lawrence M. Weschler, Aug. and Sept. 1975. Vol. 3. UCLA Oral History Program and the Feuchtwanger Fund of the University of Southern California, 1976. Available from the Internet Archive, https://archive.org/details/emigrelifeoralhio4feuc.

Fittko, Lisa. *Escape Through the Pyrenees*. Evanston, Ill.: Northwestern University Press, 1991.

FitzGerald, David, and David Cook-Martín. *Culling the Masses: The Democratic Origins of Racist Immigration Policy in the Americas*. Cambridge: Harvard University Press, 2014.

Fracapane, Silvia. " 'Wir erfuhren, was es heisst hungrig zu sein': Aspekte des Alltagslebens dänischer Juden in Theresienstadt." In Bergen, Hájková, and Löw, *Alltag im Holocaust*, 199.

Fralon, José-Alain. *A Good Man in Evil Times: The Story of Aristides de Sousa Mendes*. New York: Carroll & Graf, 2000.

Frank, Tibor. "Budapest–Berlin–New York: Stepmigration from Hungary to the United States, 1919–1945." In *The Fruits of Exile: Central European Intellectual Immigration in America in the Age of Fascism*, edited by Richard Bodek and Simon Lewis, 197–221. Columbia: University of South Carolina Press, 2011.

Fraser, Howard, Mara Vishniac Kohn, and Aubrey Pomerance, eds. *Roman Vishniac's Berlin: An Exhibition at the Jewish Museum Berlin, November 4, 2005 to February 5, 2006*. Berlin: Nicolai, 2005.

Frevert, Ute. "Does Trust Have a History?" Lecture at the Max Weber Programme, European University Institute, Florence, 2009. http://cadmus.eui.eu/bitstream/handle/1814/11258/MWP_LS_2009_01.pdf?sequence=1.

———. "Forum: History of Emotions." *German History* 28, no. 1 (2010): 67–80.

———. "Honor, Gender and Power: The Politics of Satisfaction in Prewar Europe." In *An Improbable War? The Outbreak of World War I and European Political Culture Before 1914*, edited by Holger Afflerbach and David Stevenson, 233–55. New York: Berghahn, 2007.

———. "Trust as Work." In *Work in Modern Society: The German Historical Experience in Comparative Perspective*, edited by Jürgen Kocka, 93–108. New York: Berghahn, 2010.

———. "Was haben Gefühle in der Geschichte zu suchen?" *Geschichte und Gesellschaft* 35 (2009): 183–208.

———, ed. *Emotional Lexicons: Continuity and Change in the Vocabulary of Feeling, 1700–2000*. Oxford: Oxford University Press, 2014.

Fried, Marc. "Grieving for a Lost Home: Psychological Costs of Relocation." In *Urban Renewal: The Record and the Controversy*, edited by James Q. Wilson, 359–79. Cambridge: MIT Press, 1966.

Friedländer, Saul. *The Years of Extermination: Nazi Germany and the Jews, 1939–1945*. New York: HarperCollins, 2007.

Friman, Grete. "Von Wien nach Portugal." *Tranvía* 16 (1990).

Fritzsche, Peter. *Life and Death in the Third Reich*. Cambridge, Mass.: Belknap, 2008.

Frucht, Karl. *Verlustanzeige: Ein Überlebensbericht*. Vienna: Kremayr und Scheriau, 1992.

Fry, Varian. *Assignment: Rescue*. New York: Four Winds, 1968.

———. *Surrender on Demand*. New York: Random House, 1945.

———. "Our Consuls at Work." *Nation*, May 2, 1942.

Fuechtner, Veronika. *Berlin Psychoanalytic: Psychoanalysis and Culture in Weimar Republic Germany and Beyond*. Berkeley: University of California Press, 2011.

Gallagher, Tom. "Controlled Repression in Salazar's Portugal." *Journal of Contemporary History* 14, no. 3 (July 1979): 385–402.

———. *Portugal: A Twentieth-Century Interpretation*. Manchester, U.K.: Manchester University Press, 1983.

Gallagher, Wes. "See You in Lisbon." In *Reporting World War II: Part I— American Journalism, 1938–1944*, 190–95. New York: Library of America, 1995. Originally published in the *New York Times*, Sept. 3, 1941.

Gammerl, Benno. "Felt Distances." In Frevert, *Emotional Lexicons*, 177–200.

Garbarini, Alexandra. *Numbered Days: Diaries and the Holocaust*. New Haven: Yale University Press, 2006.

Garnier, Christine. *Salazar: An Intimate Portrait*. New York: Farrar, Straus and Young, 1954.

Gay, Peter. *The Bourgeois Experience: Victoria to Freud*. 5 vols. New York: Oxford University Press, 1984–98.

———. *My German Question: Growing Up in Nazi Berlin*. New Haven: Yale University Press, 1999.

Gemie, Sharif, Fiona Reid, and Laure Humbert. *Outcast Europe: Refugees and Relief Workers in an Era of Total War, 1936–48*. London: Continuum, 2012.

Gessen, Masha. "The Memory Keeper." *New Yorker*, Oct. 26, 2015. newyorker. com/magazine/2015/10/26/the-memory-keeper.

Gillick, Muriel R. *Once They Had a Country: Two Teenage Refugees in the Second World War*. Tuscaloosa: University of Alabama Press, 2010.

Goeschel, Christian. *Suicide in Nazi Germany*. New York: Oxford University Press, 2009.

Gold, Mary Jayne. *Crossroads Marseilles: 1940*. Garden City, N.Y.: Doubleday, 1980.

Gouveia, Helena Ferro de. "Lisbon: From Refuge to Home." *Deutsche Welle*, Nov. 29, 2012. dw.de/lisbon-from-refuge-to-home/a-16410819.

Grab, Hermann. *Hochzeit in Brooklyn: Sieben Erzählungen*. Vienna: Bergland, 1957.

Gramling, Oliver. *Free Men Are Fighting: The Story of World War II*. New York: Farrar and Rinehart, 1942.

Grewal, Daisy. "How Wealth Reduces Compassion." *Scientific American*, Apr. 10, 2012. scientificamerican.com/article/how-wealth-reduces-compassion.

Grossman, Lev. "10 Questions for E. L. Doctorow." *Time*, Mar. 6, 2006. http:// time.com/3967059/10-questions-el-doctorow-remembrance.

Gruner, Wolf. " 'The Germans Should Expel the Foreigner Hitler . . .' Open Protest and Other Forms of Jewish Defiance in Nazi Germany." *Yad Vashem Studies* 39, no. 2 (2011): 13–53.

Guggenheim, Peggy. *Out of This Century: The Informal Memoirs of Peggy Guggenheim*. New York: Dial, 1946.

Gumbel, Emil Julius. *Freie Wissenschaft: Ein Sammelbuch aus der Deutschen Emigration.* Strasbourg: Sebastian Brant Verlag, 1938.

Guttstadt, Corry. *Turkey, the Jews, and the Holocaust.* Cambridge: Cambridge University Press, 2013.

Guttstadt, Corry, et al., eds. *Bystanders, Rescuers or Perpetrators? The Neutral Countries and the Shoah.* Vol. 2 of *IHRA Series.* Berlin: Metropol Verlag & IHRA, 2016. https://www.holocaustremembrance.com/publications/bystanders-rescuers-or-perpetrators-neutral-countries-and-shoah?usergroup=3.

Hareven, Tamara K. "The Home and the Family in Historical Perspective." In Mack, *Home*, 227–60.

Harvey, David. *Spaces of Capital: Towards a Critical Geography.* New York: Routledge, 2001.

———. *Spaces of Hope.* Edinburgh: Edinburgh University Press, 2000.

Harwood, Edwin. "American Public Opinion and U.S. Immigration Policy." *Annals of the American Academy of Political Science* 487, no. 1 (Sept. 1986): 201–12.

Heinrich, Christa, Hans Winterberg, and Barb Kirkamm, eds., *Lissabon 1933–1945: Fluchtstation am Rande Europas.* Berlin: Akademie der Künste, Haus der Wannsee-Konferenz, 1995.

Hellman, Peter. *Avenue of the Righteous.* London: Dent, 1981.

Hess, Renate. " 'Denn unser Leben wäre ganz anders gewesen': Eine jüdische Emigrantin berichtet über ihr Leben." *Zeitschrift für Kulturaustausch* 44, no. 2 (1994). Hess interviewed Noemi Gelehrter Ricca Gonçalves (born 1919, Berlin) for this article.

———. " 'Was Portugal getan hat, hat kein anderes Land getan.' " In *Solidarität und Hilfe für Juden Während der NS-Zeit: Regionalstudien 3: Dänemark, Niederlande, Spanien, Portugal, Ungarn, Albanien, Weißrußland*, edited by Wolfgang Benz and Juliane Wetzel, 161–206. Berlin: Metropol, 1999.

Hilberg, Raul. *The Politics of Memory: The Journey of a Holocaust Historian.* Chicago: Dee, 1996.

Hobsbawm, Eric. "Exile: A Keynote Address: Introduction." In Mack, *Home*, 61–64.

Horváth, Ágnes, Bjørn Thomassen, and Harald Wydra. Introduction to *Breaking Boundaries: Varieties of Liminality*, edited by Horváth, Thomassen, and Wydra, 1–8. New York: Berghahn, 2015.

Hoskins, Janet. *Biographical Objects: How Things Tell the Stories of People's Lives.* New York: Routledge, 1998.

Hull, Cordell. *Memoirs of Cordell Hull.* Vol. 2. New York: Macmillan, 1948. Available through the Hathi Trust, https://babel.hathitrust.org/cgi/pt?id—dp.39015004963727;view=1up;seq=11.

Ikegami, Eiko. "Emotions." In *A Concise Companion to History,* edited by Ulinka Rublack, 333–54. Oxford: Oxford University Press, 2012.

Isenberg, Sheila. *A Hero of Our Own: The Story of Varian Fry.* New York: Random House, 2001.

Jacobs, Jack. *Ein Freund in Not: Das Jüdische Arbeiterkomitee in New York und die Flüchtlinge aus den deutschsprachigen Ländern, 1933–1945.* Bonn: Forschungsinstitut der Friedrich-Ebert-Stiftung, 1993.

Jacobs, Neil G. "Soirée bei Kohn: Jewish Elements in the Repertoire of Hermann Leopoldi." *Zutot* 2, no. 1 (2002): 200–208.

Jacobson, Kenneth. *Embattled Selves: An Investigation into the Nature of Identity Through Oral Histories of Holocaust Survivors.* New York: Atlantic Monthly Press, 1994.

Jäger, Gudrun. *Gertrud Kolmar: Publikations-und Rezeptionsgeschichte.* Frankfurt am Main: Campus, 1998.

Jansen, Peter-Erwin, and Christian Schmidt, eds. *In steter Freundschaft: Leo Löwenthal-Siegfried Kracauer Briefwechsel 1921–1966.* Springe, Germany: Zu Klampen, 2003.

Jason, Philip K., and Iris Posner, eds. *Don't Wave Goodbye: The Children's Flight from Nazi Persecution to American Freedom.* Westport, Conn.: Praeger, 2004.

Jennings, Eric. *Escape from Vichy: The Refugee Exodus to the French Caribbean.* Cambridge: Harvard University Press, 2018.

JTA. "Gestapo Gangs Reported Kidnapping Anti-Nazi Refugees in Lisbon." Nov. 4, 1941. jta.org/1941/11/04/archive/gestapo-gangs-reported-kidnapping-anti-nazi-refugees-in-lisbon.

———. "Portugal Protests as Brazil Bars Visas to Jews." June 5, 1941. jta.org/1941/06/05/archive/portugal-protests-as-brazil-bars-visas-to-jews.

———. "Singing, Dancing Marks Departure of Refugee Ship Bound from Lisbon to Palestine." Jan. 25, 1944. jta.org/1944/01/25/archive/singing-dancing-marks-departure-of-refugee-ship-bound-from-lisbon-to-palestine#ixzz33PWoVtcX.

Kalischer, Ben-Zwi. *Vom Konzentrationslager nach Palaestina: Flucht durch die halbe Welt.* Tel-Aviv: Olympia, 1945.

Kantorowicz, Alfred. *Exil in Frankreich: Merkwürdigkeiten und Denkwürdigkeiten.* Hamburg: Christians, 1983.

Kaplan, Marion A. " 'Based on Love': The Courtship of Hendele and Jochanan, 1803–1804." In *Jüdische Welten: Juden in Deutschland vom 18. Jahrhundert bis in die Gegenwart,* edited by Marion A. Kaplan and Beate Meyer, 86–107. Göttingen: Wallstein, 2005.

———. *Between Dignity and Despair: Jewish Life in Nazi Germany.* New York: Oxford University Press, 1998.

———. "Book Review: Portugal, Salazar, and the Jews." *Shofar* 31, no. 1 (2012): 165–69.

———. "Does Donald Trump Realize Jewish Refugees Were also Called 'Trojan Horses'?" *Forward,* Oct. 20, 2016. http://forward.com/opinion/352353/does-donald-trump-realize-jewish-refugees-were-also-called-trojan-horses/?attribution=author-article-listing–1-headline.

———. *Dominican Haven: The Jewish Refugee Settlement in Sosúa, 1940–1945.* New York: Museum of Jewish Heritage, 2008.

———. *The Making of the Jewish Middle Class: Women, Family, and Identity in Imperial Germany.* New York: Oxford University Press, 1991.

———. "Revealing and Concealing: Memoirs in German-Jewish History." In *Text and Context: Essays in Modern Jewish History and Historiography in Honor of Ismar Schorsch,* edited by Eli Lederhendler and Jack Wertheimer, 383–410. New York: Jewish Theological Seminary of America, 2005.

———, ed. *Jewish Daily Life in Germany, 1618–1945.* New York: Oxford University Press, 2005.

Karády, Viktor. *The Jews of Europe in the Modern Era: A Socio-Historical Outline.* Budapest: Central European University Press, 2004.

Karp, George A. *The Maquis Connection to Freedom.* Rev. ed. Edited by Susan Bernstein and Larry Bernstein. Glencoe, Ill.: Amber Mountain, 2016.

Katz, Jack. *How Emotions Work: From the Passions to the Emotions.* Chicago: University of Chicago Press, 1999.

Katznelson, Ira. "The Failure to Rescue." *New Republic,* July 1, 2013.

Kennan, George F. *Memoirs, 1925–1950.* Boston: Little, Brown, 1967.

———. "Problems of Diplomatic-Military Collaboration." Lecture at the National War College, Mar. 7, 1947. In *Measures Short of War: The George F. Kennan Lectures at the NWC, 1946–47,* edited by Miles D. Harlow and George C. Maerz, 130–55. Washington, D.C.: National Defense University Press, 1991.

Kessel, Martina. "Balance der Gefühle: Langeweile im 19. Jahrhundert." *Historische Anthropologie* 4 (1996): 234–55.

————. "Das Trauma der Affektkontrolle: Zur Sehnsucht nach Gefühlen im 19. Jahrhundert." In Benthien et al., *Emotionalität*, 156–77.

————. "Gefühle und Geschichtswissenschaft." In *Emotionen und Sozialtheorie*, edited by Rainer Schützeichel, 29–47. Frankfurt am Main: Campus, 2005.

————. "The 'Whole Man': The Longing for a Masculine World in 19th-Century Germany." *Gender and History* 15, no. 1 (April 2003): 1–31.

Kesten, Hermann. *Dichter im Café*. Munich: Desch, 1959.

Klein, Anne. *Flüchtlingspolitik und Flüchtlingshilfe, 1940–1942: Varian Fry und die Komitees zur Rettung politisch Verfolgter in New York und Marseille*. Berlin: Metropol, 2007.

Klemperer, Victor. *To the Bitter End: The Diaries of Victor Klemperer, 1942–1945*. London: BCA, 1999.

Klösch, Christian, and Regina Thumser. *"From Vienna": Exilkabarett in New York, 1938 bis 1950*. Vienna: Picus, 2002.

Klüger, Ruth. *Still Alive: A Holocaust Girlhood Remembered*. New York: Feminist Press at the City University, 2001.

Knowles, Anne Kelly, Tim Cole, and Alberto Giordano, eds. *Geographies of the Holocaust*. Bloomington: Indiana University Press, 2014.

Koch, Anna. "Home After Fascism? Italian and German Jews After the Holocaust, 1944–1952." Ph.D. diss., New York University, 2015.

Koestler, Arthur. *Arrival and Departure*. New York: Macmillan, 1943.

————. *The Invisible Writing*. New York: Macmillan, 1954.

————. *Scum of the Earth*. New York: Macmillan, 1941.

Kohn, Mara Vishniac. "Naturally Berlin! Remembering Roman Vishniac." In Fraser et al., *Roman Vishniac's Berlin*, 15–37.

Kohut, Karl, and Patrik von zur Mühlen, eds. *Alternative Lateinamerika: Das deutsche Exil in der Zeit des Nationalsozialismus*. Frankfurt am Main: Vervuert, 1994.

Kopytoff, Igor. "The Cultural Biography of Things: Commoditization as Process." In *The Social Life of Things: Commodities in Cultural Perspective*, edited by Arjun Appadurai, 64–94. Cambridge: Cambridge University Press, 1988.

Körte, Mona, and Toby Axelrod. "Bracelet, Hand Towel, Pocket Watch: Objects of the Last Moment in Memory and Narration." *Shofar* 23, no. 1 (Fall 2004): 109–20.

Kosmala, Beate. "Zwischen Ahnen und Wissen: Flucht vor der Deportation (1941–1943)." In *Die Deportationen der Juden aus Deutschland:*

Pläne-Praxis-Reaktionen, 1938–1945, edited by Birthe Kundrus and Beate Meyer, 135–59. Göttingen: Wallstein Verlag, 2004.

Krauss, Marita. *Heimkehr in ein fremdes Land: Geschichte der Remigration nach 1945*. Munich: Beck, 2001.

Krauss, Robert M., Yihsiu Chen, and Purnima Chawla. "Nonverbal Behavior and Nonverbal Communication: What Do Conversational Hand Gestures Tell Us?" 1996. Available at columbia.edu/~rmk7/PDF/Adv.pdf.

Kümin, Beate, and Cornelie Usborne. "At Home and in the Workplace: A Historical Introduction to the 'Spatial Turn.'" *History and Theory* 52, no. 3 (Oct. 2013): 305–18.

Kümper, Michal, ed. *Makom: Orte und Räume im Judentum: Real. Abstrakt. Imaginär: Essays*. Hildesheim, Germany: Olms, 2007.

LaCapra, Dominick. *History and Memory After Auschwitz*. Ithaca, N.Y.: Cornell University Press, 1998.

Laffer, Dennis Ross. "The Jewish Trail of Tears: The Evian Conference of July 1938." Master's thesis, University of South Florida, 2011. http://scholar-commons.usf.edu/etd/3195.

Lalli, Mario Tedeschini. "Descent from Paradise: Saul Steinberg's Italian Years (1933–1941)." *Quest: Issues in Contemporary Jewish History* 2 (2011). quest-cdecjournal.it/focus.php?id=221.

Lambert, Raymond-Raoul. *Diary of a Witness, 1940–1943*. Edited by Richard I. Cohen. Chicago: Ivan R. Dee, 2007.

Langer, Lawrence L. *Holocaust Testimonies: The Ruins of Memory*. New Haven: Yale University Press, 1991.

Láníček, Jan. *Arnošt Frischer and the Jewish Politics of Early 20th-Century Europe*. London: Bloomsbury, 2016.

———. "Arnošt Frischer und seine Hilfe für Juden im besetzten Europa (1941–1945)." *Theresienstädter Studien und Dokumente* 14 (2007): 11–91.

Laqueur, Walter. *The Terrible Secret: Suppression of the Truth About Hitler's Final Solution*. New York: Holt, 1980.

Laqueur, Walter, ed. *The Holocaust Encyclopedia*. New Haven: Yale University Press, 2001.

Lasch, Christopher. *Haven in a Heartless World: The Family Besieged*. New York: Norton, 1995.

Lässig, Simone, and Miriam Rürup. "Introduction: What Made a Space "Jewish"? Reconsidering a Category of Modern German History." In Lässig and Rürup, *Space and Spatiality*, 1–22.

Lässig, Simone, and Miriam Rürup, eds. *Space and Spatiality in Modern German-Jewish History*. New York: Berghahn, 2017.

Laughlin, Harry Hamilton. *The Codification and Analysis of the Immigration Control Law of Each of the Several Countries of Pan America*. Washington, D.C.: Carnegie Institution, 1936.

Lavsky, Hagit. *The Creation of the German-Jewish Diaspora: Interwar German-Jewish Immigration to Palestine, the USA, and England*. Oldenbourg, Germany: De Gruyter, 2017.

Le Goff, Jacques. *History and Memory*. Translated by Steven Rendall and Elizabeth Claman. New York: Columbia University Press, 1992.

Lehmann, Albrecht, and Klaus Schriewer. *Der Wald—Ein Deutscher Mythos? Perspektiven eines Kulturthemas*. Berlin: Reimer, 2000.

Lepore, Jill. "Historians Who Love Too Much: Reflections on Microhistory and Biography." *Journal of American History* 88, no. 1 (June 2001): 129–44.

Lerner, Jennifer S., et al. "Emotion and Decision Making." *Annual Review of Psychology* 66 (Jan. 2015): 799–823.

Leshem, Perez. "Rescue Efforts in the Iberian Peninsula." *LBIYB* 14 (1969).

Levi, Primo. *Survival in Auschwitz: The Nazi Assault on Humanity*. Translated by Stuart Joseph Woolf. New York: Touchstone, 1996. Originally published as *Se questo è un uomo*, 1947.

Liebersohn, Harry, and Dorothee Schneider, eds. *My Life in Germany Before and After January 30, 1933: A Guide to a Manuscript Collection at Houghton Library, Harvard University*. Philadelphia: American Philosophical Society, 2001.

Lindemann, Mary. "Sources in Social History." In *Encyclopedia of European Social History*, vol. 1, edited by Peter Stearns, 31–40. New York: Scribner, 2001.

Lipman, Jennifer. "Franco Made a Secret List of Jews for Nazis." *JC*, June 21, 2010. thejc.com/news/world-news/33264/franco-made-secret-list-jews-nazis.

Lipstadt, Deborah E. *Beyond Belief: The American Press and the Coming of the Holocaust, 1933–1945*. New York: Free Press, 1986.

Lochery, Neill. *Lisbon: War in the Shadows of the City of Light, 1939–1945*. New York: PublicAffairs, 2011.

Loewenberg, Peter. "The *Kristallnacht* as a Public Degradation Ritual." *LBIYB* 32 (1987).

Long, Breckinridge. *The War Diary of Breckinridge Long*. Edited by Fred Israel. Lincoln: University of Nebraska Press, 1966.

Longstreet, Stephen. *The Last Man Comes Home: American Travel Journals, 1941–1942*. New York: Random House, 1942.

López-Muñoz, Francisco, Ronaldo Ucha-Udabe, and Cecilio Alamo. "The History of Barbiturates a Century After their Clinical Introduction." *Neuropsychiatric Disease and Treatment* 1, no. 4 (Dec. 2005): 329–43. ncbi. nlm.nih.gov/pmc/articles/PMC2424120.

Losa, Ilse. *Unter fremden Himmeln: Roman.* Freiburg: Beck & Gluckler, 1991.

Lothar, Ernst. *Das Wunder des Überlebens: Erinnerungen und Ergebnisse.* Hamburg: Zsolnay, 1960.

Louçã, António. *Nazigold für Portugal: Hitler & Salazar.* Vienna: Holzhausen, 2002.

Louçã, António, and Ansgar Schäfer. "Portugal and the Nazi Gold: The 'Lisbon Connection.'" *Yad Vashem Studies* 27 (1999): 105–22.

Löw-Beer, Martin. "From Nowhere to Israel and Back: The Changing Self-Definition of Periodicals of German-Jewish Youth Since 1960." In *Jews, Germans, and Memory: Reconstructions of Jewish life in Germany,* edited by Y. Michal Bodemann, 101–30. Ann Arbor: University of Michigan Press, 1996.

Lowenstein, Steven M. *Frankfurt on the Hudson: The German-Jewish Community of Washington Heights, 1933–1983; Its Structure and Culture.* Detroit: Wayne State University Press, 1989.

———. "The Rural Community and the Urbanisation of German Jewry." *Central European History* 13, no. 3 (1980): 218–36.

Lucassen, Leo. "A Many-Headed Monster: The Evolution of the Passport System in the Netherlands and Germany in the Long Nineteenth Century." In Caplan and Torpey, *Documenting Individual Identity,* 235–55.

Lüdtke, Alf. "Organizational Order or *Eigensinn?* Workers' Privacy and Workers' Politics in Imperial Germany." In *Rites of Power: Symbolism, Ritual, and Politics Since the Middle Ages,* edited by Sean Wilentz, 303–34. Philadelphia: University of Pennsylvania Press, 1985.

Lühe, Irmela von der, Axel Schildt, and Stefanie Schüler-Springorum, eds. *"Auch in Deutschland waren wir nicht wirklich zu Hause": Jüdische Remigration nach 1945.* Göttingen: Wallstein Verlag, 2008.

Luhrmann, T. M. "How Places Let Us Feel the Past." *New York Times,* May 25, 2015.

Lustig, Jan. *Ein Rosenkranz von Glücksfällen: Protokoll einer Flucht.* Bonn: Weidle, 2001.

Lutz, Catherine, and Geoffrey White. "The Anthropology of Emotions." *Annual Review of Anthropology* 15 (1986): 405–36.

Mack, Arien, ed. *Home: A Place in the World.* New York: New York University Press, 1993.

Mahler-Werfel, Alma. "Alma & Lisbon." alma-mahler.at/archiv_lisboa/engl/ info_lisboa/almaundlisboa.html.

———. *And the Bridge Is Love*. New York: Harcourt, Brace, 1958.

Malkki, Liisa. "National Geographic: The Rooting of Peoples and the Territorialization of National Identity Among Scholars and Refugees." *Cultural Anthropology* 7, no. 1 (Feb. 1992): 24–44.

———. "Refugees and Exile: From 'Refugee Studies' to the National Order of Things." *Annual Review of Anthropology* 24 (Oct. 1995): 495–523.

Mann, Erika. "In Lissabon gestrandet." In *Im Fluchtgepäck die Sprache: Deutschsprachige Schriftstellerinnen im Exil*, edited by Claudia Schoppmann, 148–60. Berlin: Orlanda Frauenverlag, 1991.

Mann, Fred. *A Drastic Turn of Destiny*. Toronto: Azrieli Foundation, 2009.

Mann, Heinrich. *Ein Zeitalter wird besichtigt*. Berlin: Aufbau Verlag, 1982.

Mann, Klaus. *Briefe und Antworten. Band II: 1937–1949*. Edited by Martin Gregor-Dellin. Munich: Rowohlt, 1975.

Mann, Thomas. "Listen, Germany! Twenty-Five Radio Transmissions to the German People over BBC, 1940–1942." http://www.erichkuby.info/ListenGermany.pdf.

Manuel, Paul Christopher. "The Marian Apparitions in Fátima as Political Reality: Religion and Politics in Twentieth-Century Portugal." N.d. Working Paper 88, Center for European Studies, Harvard University. https://www.ciaonet.org/attachments/5377/uploads.

Marcu, Valeriu. *"Ein Kopf ist mehr als vierhundert Kehlkoepfe": Gesammelte Essays*. Edited by Erhard R. Wiehn. Konstanz, Germany: Hartung-Gorre Verlag, 2002.

Marcus, Claire Cooper. *House as a Mirror of Self: Exploring the Deeper Meaning of Home*. Berkeley, Calif.: Conari, 1995.

Marrus, Michael R. *The Unwanted: European Refugees from the First World War Through the Cold War*. Philadelphia: Temple University Press, 2002.

Marrus, Michael R., and Robert O. Paxton. *Vichy France and the Jews*. New York: Basic Books, 1981.

Marquina, Antonio. "The Spanish Neutrality During the Second World War." *American University International Law Review*, 14, no. 1 (1998): 171–84.

Martins, Jorge. *Judaísmo e Anti-semitismo no Século XX*. Vol. 3 of *Portugal e os Judeus*. Lisbon: Vega, 2006.

Marx, Hugo. *Die Flucht: Jüdisches Schicksal 1940*. Düsseldorf: Verlag Allgemeine Wochenzeitung der Juden in Deutschland, 1955.

Mason, Timothy W. *Social Policy in the Third Reich: The Working Class and the "National Community," 1918–1939*. Oxford: Berg, 1993.

Massey, Doreen. *Space, Place, and Gender*. Minneapolis: University of Minnesota Press, 1999.

Matos, Patrícia Ferraz de. *The Colours of the Empire: Racialized Representations During Portuguese Colonialism*. New York: Berghahn, 2013.

Matt, Susan J. "Current Emotion Research in History: Or, Doing History from the Inside Out." *Emotion Review* 3, no. 1 (Jan. 2011): 117–24.

Maurer, Trude. "From Everyday Life to a State of Emergency: Jews in Weimar and Nazi Germany." Translated by Allison Brown. In Kaplan, *Jewish Daily Life*, 271–374. New York: Oxford University Press, 2005.

McDonald, James G. *Advocate for the Doomed: The Diaries and Papers of James G. McDonald, 1932–1935*. Edited by Richard Breitman and Barbara McDonald Stewart. Bloomington: Indiana University Press, 2007.

———. *Refugees and Rescue: The Diaries and Papers of James G. McDonald, 1935–1945*. Edited by Richard Breitman, Barbara McDonald Stewart, and Severin Hochberg. Bloomington: Indiana University Press, 2009.

Meissner, Margit. *Margit's Story: An Autobiography*. Rockville, Md.: Schreiber, 2003.

Melammed, Renée Levine. *A Question of Identity: Iberian Conversos in Historical Perspective*. New York: Oxford University Press, 2004.

Meneses, Filipe Ribeiro de. *Salazar: A Political Biography*. New York: Enigma, 2009.

Meyer, Beate. *A Fatal Balancing Act: The Dilemma of the Reich Association of Jews in Germany, 1939–1945*. New York: Berghahn, 2013.

Milgram, Avraham. *Portugal, Salazar and the Jews*. Jerusalem: Yad Vashem, 2011.

———. "Portugal, the Consuls, and the Jewish Refugees." *Yad Vashem Studies* 27 (1999): 123–55.

Miller, Nancy K. "The Ethics of Betrayal: Diary of a Conundrum." In *Truth in Nonfiction: Essays*, edited by David Lazar, 42–57. Iowa City: University of Iowa Press, 2008.

Miller, Susan Gilson. "Passage to Casablanca: The Refugee Crisis in Morocco During World War II." Talk given at the University of California, Berkeley, Dec. 8, 2014. Posted to YouTube by UC Berkeley CMES, May 12, 2017, https://www.youtube.com/watch?v=Yvr1gij4M3c.

Miron, Guy. "The Home Experience of German Jews Under the Nazi Regime." *Past and Present*, Feb. 1, 2019, 1–39.

————. "'Lately, Almost Constantly, Everything Seems Small to Me': The Lived Space of German Jews Under the Nazi Regime." *Jewish Social Studies* 20, no. 1 (Fall 2013): 121–49.

Moltke, Johannes von. *No Place like Home: Locations of Heimat in German Cinema*. Berkeley: University of California Press, 2005.

Montaigne, Michel de. *The Essays: A Selection*. Edited by M. A. Screech. London: Penguin, 2004.

Morton, Andrew. *17 Carnations: The Royals, the Nazis, and the Biggest Cover-Up in History*. New York: Grand Central, 2015.

Murphy, Henry B. M. *Flight and Resettlement*. Paris: UNESCO, 1955.

Musil, Robert. *The Man Without Qualities*. Vol. 1. Translated by Eithne Wilkins and Ernst Kaiser. New York: Capricorn, 1965.

Mutschelknaus, Katja. *Kaffeeklatsch: Die Stunde der Frauen*. Berlin: Insel Verlag, 2014.

Neilson, William Allan. *We Escaped: Twelve Personal Narratives of the Flight to America*. New York: Macmillan, 1941.

Niederland, W. G. "Clinical Observations on the 'Survivor Syndrome.'" *International Journal of Psychoanalysis* 49 (1968): 313–15.

Ninhos, Cláudia. "What Was Known in the Neutral Countries About the On-Going Genocide of European Jews?" Presentation at the International Colloquium "Bystanders, Rescuers or Perpetrators? The Neutral Countries and the Shoah," Madrid, Nov. 24–26, 2014. In Guttstadt et al., *Bystanders, Rescuers or Perpetrators*, 125–38.

Norich, Anita. "The Family Singer and the Autobiographical Imagination." *Prooftexts* 10, no. 1 (Jan. 1990): 91–107.

Nunes, Adriana. *Ilse Losa, Schriftstellerin zwischen zwei Welten*. Berlin: Tranvía, 1999.

Nussbaum, Martha C. *Upheavals of Thought: The Intelligence of Emotions*. Cambridge: Cambridge University Press, 2003.

Nutkiewicz, Michael. "Shame, Guilt, and Anguish in Holocaust Survivor Testimony." *Oral History Review* 30, no. 1 (Jan. 2003): 1–22.

Ochs, Elinor, and Bambi Shieffelin. "Language Has a Heart." *Text* 9, no. 1 (1989): 7–26.

Ollila, Anne, ed. *Historical Perspectives on Memory*. Helsinki: Finnish Historical Society, 1999.

Orbach, Susie. "Work Is Where We Live: Emotional Literacy and the Psychological Dimensions of the Various Relationships There." *Emotion, Space and Society* 1, no. 1 (Oct. 2008): 14–17.

Packard, Reynolds, and Eleanor Packer. *Balcony Empire: Fascist Italy at War.* New York: Oxford University Press, 1942.

Paetel, Karl O. *Reise ohne Uhrzeit: Autobiographie.* Edited by Wolfgang D. Elfe and John M. Spalek. London: World of Books, 1982.

Papadopoulos, Renos K. "Refugees, Trauma and Adversity-Activated Development." *European Journal of Psychotherapy and Counselling* 9, no. 3 (2007) 301–12.

Parkin, David. "Mementoes as Transitional Objects in Human Displacement." *Journal of Material Culture* 4, no. 3 (1999): 303–20.

Parr, Hester. "Emotional Geographies." In *Introducing Human Geographies,* edited by Paul J. Cloke, Phil Crang, and Mark Goodwin, 746–60. London: Hodder Arnold, 2005.

Payne, Stanley G. *Franco and Hitler: Spain, Germany, and World War II.* New Haven: Yale University Press, 2009.

———. *A History of Spain and Portugal.* 2 vols. Madison: University of Wisconsin Press, 1973. Ch. 27, "Portugal Under the Salazar Regime," available at the Library of Iberian Resources Online, University of Central Arkansas, 1999. http://libro.uca.edu/payne2/payne27.htm.

Pekelis, Carla. *My Version of the Facts.* Translated by George Hochfield. Evanston, Ill.: Marlboro, 2004.

Pellew, Jill. "The Home Office and the Aliens Act, 1905." *Historical Journal* 32, no. 2 (1989): 369–85.

Petropoulos, Jonathan. "Co-Opting Nazi Germany: Neutrality in Europe During World War II." *Dimensions: A Journal of Holocaust Studies* 11, no. 1 (1997). https://www.adl.org/news/op-ed/neutrality-in-europe-world-war-ii.

Pfanner, Helmut F. *Exile in New York: German and Austrian Writers After 1933.* Detroit: Wayne State University Press, 1983.

Pfister, Tom, Peter Pfister, and Kathy Pfister, eds. *Eva and Otto: America's Vetting and Rescue of Political Refugees During World War II.* Los Angeles: Pfisters, 2017.

Philpot, Robert. "Was Franco the 'Good' Fascist?" *JC,* Nov. 23, 2015. thejc.com/comment-and-debate/comment/149674/was-franco-good-fascist.

Pimentel, Irene Flunser. *Espiões em Portugal durante a II Guerra Mundial.* 2nd ed. Lisbon: A Esfera dos Livros, 2014.

———. "Refugiados entre portugueses (1933–1945)." *Vértice* 69 (Nov.–Dec. 1995): 102–11.

———. "Salazar impediu os refugiados de contagiarem Portugal." *Público,* Mar. 18, 1995, 22–23.

Pimentel, Irene Flunser, and Christa Heinrich. *Judeus em Portugal durante a II Guerra Mundial: Em Fuga de Hitler e do Holocausto.* Lisbon: A Esfera dos Livros, 2006.

Pimentel, Irene Flunser, and Helena Pereira de Melo. *Mulheres Portuguesas.* Lisbon: Clube do Autor, 2015.

Pimentel, Irene Flunser, and Cláudia Ninhos. "Portugal, Jewish Refugees and the Holocaust." *Dapim: Studies on the Holocaust* 29, no. 2 (May 2015): 101–13.

———. *Salazar, Portugal e o Holocausto.* Lisbon: Temas e Debates, 2013.

Pinsker, Shachar. *Literary Passports: The Making of Modernist Hebrew Fiction in Europe.* Palo Alto: Stanford University Press, 2010.

Pinto, António Costa. *Modern Portugal.* Palo Alto: Society for the Promotion of Science and Scholarship, 1998.

Plamper, Jan. "The History of Emotions: An Interview with William Reddy, Barbara Rosenwein, and Peter Stearns." *History and Theory* 49, no. 2 (May 2010): 237–65.

———. *The History of Emotions: An Introduction.* Oxford: Oxford University Press, 2015.

Potworowski, Tomasz. "The Evacuation of Jewish Polish Citizens from Portugal to Jamaica, 1941–1943." *Polin* 19 (2007): 155–82.

Poznanski, Renée. *Jews in France During World War II.* Hanover, N.H.: University Press of New England, 2001.

Prutsch, Ursula, and Klaus Zeyringer, eds. *Leopold von Andrian (1875–1951): Korrespondenzen, Notizen, Essays, Berichte.* Vienna: Böhlau, 2003.

Querg, Thorsten. "Spionage und Terror das Amt VI des Reichssicherheitshauptamtes, 1939–1945." Ph.D. diss., Freie Universität Berlin, 1997.

Ramalho, Margarida de Magalhães. *Lisbon: A City During Wartime.* Lisbon: Imprensa Nacional–Casa da Moeda, 2012.

———. *Vilar Formoso: Frontier of Peace.* Almeida, Portugal: Almeida Council, 2014.

Raskin, Richard. "Far from Where? On the History and Meanings of a Classic Jewish Refugee Joke." *AJH* 85, no. 2 (June 1997): 143–50.

Reddy, William. "Historical Research on the Self and Emotions." *Emotion Review* 1, no. 4 (October 2009): 302–15.

———. *The Navigation of Feeling: A Framework for the History of Emotions.* Cambridge: Cambridge University Press, 2001.

Redford, Bruce. *The Converse of the Pen: Acts of Intimacy in the Eighteenth-Century Familiar Letter.* Chicago: University of Chicago, 1986.

Regev, David. "The Exodus from Jamaica." *Ynetnews,* Sept. 11, 2011. ynetnews. com/articles/0,7340,L–4113958,00.html.

Reginbogin, Herbert R. *Faces of Neutrality: A Comparative Analysis of the Neutrality of Switzerland and Other Neutral Nations During WW II.* Berlin: Lit Verlag, 2009.

Reichmann, Hans. *Deutscher Bürger und verfolgter Jude: Novemberpogrom und KZ Sachsenhausen 1937 bis 1939.* Edited by Michael Wildt. Munich: Oldenbourg, 1998.

Remarque, Erich Maria. *The Night in Lisbon.* New York: Harcourt, Brace & World, 1961.

Reston, James. "Lisbon's Refugees." *New York Times,* Dec. 15, 1940.

Ristaino, Marcia Reynders. *Port of Last Resort: The Diaspora Communities of Shanghai.* Stanford: Stanford University Press, 2003.

Robins, Jennet. *A Quest of Love.* London: Avon, 1997.

Robinson, Richard Alan Hodgson. *Contemporary Portugal: A History.* London: George Allen & Unwin, 1979.

Rony, George. *This, Too, Shall Pass Away.* New York: Creative Age, 1945.

Roosevelt, Franklin Delano. "May 26, 1940: Fireside Chat 15: On National Defense." http://millercenter.org/president/fdroosevelt/speeches/speech-3316.

Rosas, Fernando. "Portuguese Neutrality in the Second World War." In *European Neutrals and Non-Belligerents During the Second World War,* edited by Neville Wylie, 267–82. Cambridge: Cambridge University Press, 2002.

Rosen, Joseph. "New Neighbors in Sosúa." *Survey Graphic* 30 (Sept. 1941): 474–78.

Rosensaft, Menachem Z., ed. *The World Jewish Congress, 1936–2016.* New York: World Jewish Congress, 2017.

Rosenwein, Barbara. "Problems and Methods in the History of Emotions." *Passions in Context: International Journal for the History and Theory of Emotions* 1, no. 1 (2010): 1–32. https://www.passionsincontext.de/uploads/media/01_Rosenwein.pdf.

———. "Worrying About Emotions in History." *AHR* 107, no. 3 (June 2002): 821-45.

Rother, Bernd. "Franco als Retter der Juden? Zur Entstehung einer Legende." *Zeitschrift für Geschichtswissenschaft* 45, no. 2 (1997): 122–46.

———. "Franco und die Deutsche Judenverfolgung." *Vierteljahrshefte für Zeitgeschichte* 46, no. 2 (1998): 189–220.

————. *National-Spanien und die Juden 1938/39*. Vol. 5 of *Jahrbuch für Anti-semitismusforschung*. Frankfurt: Campus, 1996.

————. *Spanien und der Holocaust*. Tübingen: Niemeyer, 2001.

Rothstein, Mark A., Yu Cai, and Gary Marchant. "The Ghost in Our Genes: Legal and Ethical Implications of Epigenetics." *Health Matrix* 19, no. 1 (2009): 1–62. https://www.ncbi.nlm.nih.gov/pmc/articles/PMC3034450.

Rozenblit, Marsha L. *The Jews of Vienna, 1867–1914: Assimilation and Identity*. Albany: State University of New York Press, 1983.

————. *Reconstructing a National Identity: The Jews of Habsburg Austria During World War I*. New York: Oxford University Press, 2001.

Rünitz, Lone. *Danmark og de jødiske flygtninge, 1938–1945*. Copenhagen: Museum Tusculanum, 2000.

Ruppin, Artur. *Die Juden der Gegenwart*. Berlin: Calvary, 1904.

Rürup, Miriam. "Jüdische Studentenverbindungen im Kaiserreich: Organisationen zur Abwehr des Antisemitismus auf 'studentische Art.'" *Jahrbuch für Antisemitismusforschung* 10 (2000): 113–37.

————. "Lives in Limbo: Statelessness After Two World Wars." *Bulletin of the German Historical Institute* 49 (Fall 2011): 113–34.

Rutz, Andreas. "Ego-Dokument oder Ich-Konstruktion? Selbstzeugnisse als Quellen zur Erforschung des frühneuzeitlichen Menschen." *Zeitenblicke* 1, no. 2 (2002). zeitenblicke.de/2002/02/rutz/index.html.

Ryan, Donna F. *The Holocaust and the Jews of Marseille: The Enforcement of Anti-Semitic Policies in Vichy France*. Urbana: University of Illinois Press, 1996.

————. "Vichy and the Jews: The Example of Marseille, 1939–1944." Ph.D. diss., Georgetown University, 1984.

Saa, Mário. *A Invasão dos Judeus*. Lisbon: Imprensa Libanio Da Silva, 1925.

Sadlier, Darlene J. *The Question of How: Women Writers and New Portuguese Literature*. Westport, Conn.: Greenwood, 1989.

Sahl, Hans. *Das Exil im Exil*. Hamburg: Luchterhand-Literaturverl, 1994.

————. *Memoiren eines Moralisten*. Darmstadt: Luchterhand, 1991.

Said, Edward. *Reflections on Exile, and Other Essays*. Cambridge: Harvard University Press, 2000.

Saint-Exupéry, Antoine de. *Lettre à un Otage*. 1943. Available in Portuguese translation at *Alfobre de Letras* (blog), http://alfobre.blogspot.com/2011/03/saint-exupery-em–1940-fez-escala-em.html.

Santos, Gonçalo. "The Birth of Physical Anthropology in Late Imperial Portugal." *Current Anthropology* 53, no. S5 (Apr. 2012): S33–S45. jstor.org/stable/10.1086/662329.

Santos, Maria Ramalho de Sousa. "Women's Studies in Portugal." July 1995. Centro de Estudos Sociais, Colégio de São Jerónimo, Coimbra, Portugal. http://hdl.handle.net/10316/10954.

Sapega, Ellen W. *Consensus and Debate in Salazar's Portugal: Visual and Literary Negotiations of the National Text, 1933–1948.* University Park: Pennsylvania State University Press, 2008.

Sardinha, António. *O Valor da Raça: Introdução a uma Campanha Nacional.* Lisbon: Almeida, Miranda & Sousa, 1915.

Schama, Simon. "Homelands." In Mack, *Home,* 7–26.

———. *Landscape and Memory.* New York: Knopf, 1995.

Schellenberg, Walter. *The Labyrinth: Memoirs of Walter Schellenberg, Hitler's Chief of Counterintelligence.* Translated by Louis Hagen. Cambridge, Mass.: Da Capo, 2000.

———. *Memoiren.* Munich: Limes Verlag, 1985.

Schickert, Gerhart, and Thomas Denk. *Die Bartholomäus-Brüderschaft der Deutschen in Lissabon: Entstehung und Wirken vom späten Mittelalter bis zur Gegenwart.* Estoril, Portugal: Irmandade de São Bartolomeu dos Alemães, 2010.

Schlör, Joachim. "'Ach, Man Lässt mich Durch. Es ist Gelungen.' Die Überschreitung der deutschen Grenze in Emgrationsberichten." In *Jüdischer Almanach: Grenzen,* edited by Gisela Dachs, 95–105. Berlin: Jüdischer Verlag, 2015.

———. "'Menschen wie wir mit Koffern.' Neue kulturwissenschaftliche Zugänge zur Erforschung jüdischer Migrationen im 19. und 20. Jahrhundert." In *"Nach Amerika Nämlich!" Jüdische Migrationen in die Amerikas im 19. und 20. Jahrhundert,* edited by Ulla Kriebernegg, Gerald Lamprecht, Roberta Maierhofer, and Andrea Strutz. Göttingen: Wallstein, 2012.

Schnitzler, Arthur. *Beziehungen und Einsamkeiten: Aphorismen.* Edited by Clemens Eich. Frankfurt am Main: Fischer Taschenbuch, 1987.

Schrag, Otto, and Peter Schrag. *When Europe Was a Prison Camp: Father and Son Memoirs, 1940–1941.* Bloomington: Indiana University Press, 2015.

Scheiber, Ursula. *Politische Berge: Alpinismus und Alpenverein im Spannungsverhältnis mit der Politik.* Saarbrücken, Germany: Verlag Dr. Muller, 2008.

Schroth, Raymond A. *The American Journey of Eric Sevareid.* South Royalton, Vt.: Steerforth, 1995.

Schulze, Rainer. "The *Heimschaffungsaktion* of 1942–43: Turkey, Spain, and Portugal and Their Responses to the German Offer of Repatriation of

Their Jewish Citizens." *Holocaust Studies: A Journal of Culture and History* 18, nos. 2–3 (2012): 49–72.

Schulze, Winfried. *Ego-Dokumente: Annäherung an den Menschen in der Geschichte.* Berlin: Akademie, 1996.

Schwiefert, Peter. *The Bird Has No Wings: Letters of Peter Schwiefert.* Edited by Claude Lanzmann. Translated by Barbara Lucas. New York: St. Martin's, 1976.

Segev, Zohar. *The World Jewish Congress During the Holocaust: Between Activism and Restraint.* Berlin: de Gruyter Oldenbourg, 2014.

Seghers, Anna. *Transit.* Translated by Margot Dembo. New York: New York Review of Books, 2013.

Sevareid, Eric. "Lisbon, Escape Hatch of Europe." *Reader's Digest,* Jan. 1941, 91–95. Originally found in Legião Portuguesa, Comando Geral, 2nd Repartição, Proc. 1566/15-B5, #254–256, Portuguese National Archive.

———. *Not So Wild a Dream.* New York: Knopf, 1947.

Shadur, Joseph. *A Drive to Survival: Belgium, France, Spain, Portugal, 1940.* South Deerfield, Mass.: Schoen, 1999.

Sharp, Waitstill H., and Martha. *Journey to Freedom: The First Chapter of Unitarian Service.* Boston: Unitarian Service Committee, 1940.

Shenker, Noah. *Reframing Holocaust Testimony.* Bloomington: Indiana University Press, 2015.

Shepherd, Naomi. *Wilfred Israel: German Jewry's Secret Ambassador.* London: Weidenfeld and Nicolson, 1984.

Sherman, Ari Joshua. *Island Refuge: Britain and Refugees from the Third Reich, 1933–1939.* London: Paul Elek, 1973.

Shirer, William L. *Berlin Diary: The Journal of a Foreign Correspondent, 1934–1941.* New York: Knopf, 1941.

Shonkoff, J. P., W. T. Boyce, and B. S. McEwen. "Neuroscience, Molecular Biology, and the Childhood Roots of Health Disparities." *JAMA* 301, no. 21 (2009): 2252–59.

Sideri, Sandro. *Trade and Power: Informal Colonialism in Anglo-Portuguese Relations.* Rotterdam: Presses Universitaires, 1970.

Simons, Marlise. "Nazi Gold and Portugal's Murky Role." *New York Times,* Jan. 10, 1997. nytimes.com/1997/01/10/world/nazi-gold-and-portugal-s-murky-role.html?pagewanted=all&src=pm.

Skwara, Erich Wolfgang. "Hans Sahl: Leben und Werk." Ph.D. diss., State University of New York at Albany, 1985.

Smith, Mick. *Emotion, Place, and Culture.* Farnham, U.K.: Ashgate, 2009.

Smith-Rosenberg, Carroll. "The Female World of Love and Ritual: Relations Between Women in Nineteenth Century America." *Signs: Journal of Women in Culture and Society* 1, no. 1 (Autumn 1975): 1–29.

Soares, Mario. *Portugal: Rechtsdiktatur Zwischen Europa und Kolonialismus.* Reinbek bei Hamburg, Germany: Rowohlt, 1973.

Spared Lives: The Actions of Three Portuguese Diplomats in World War II: Documentary Exhibition and catalogue, Sept. 2000. Lisbon: Ministry of Foreign Affairs, 2000. raoulwallenberg.net/wp-content/files_mf/1349882040ebooksparedlifes.pdf.

Spitzer, Leo. *Hotel Bolivia: The Culture of Memory in a Refuge from Nazism.* New York: Hill and Wang, 1998.

Sprecher, Thomas, ed. *Thomas Mann und das "Herzasthma des Exils": (Über-) Lebensformen in der Fremde: die Davoser Literaturtage 2008.* Frankfurt am Main: Klostermann, 2010.

Stanislawski, Michael. *Autobiographical Jews: Essays in Jewish Self-Fashioning.* Seattle: University of Washington Press, 2004.

Stanton, Miriam M. *Escape from the Inferno of Europe.* London: Stanton, 1996.

Stearns, Carol Z., and Peter N. Stearns. *Anger: The Struggle for Emotional Control in America's History.* Chicago: University of Chicago Press, 1986.

Stearns, Peter N. *Jealousy: The Evolution of an Emotion in American History.* New York: New York University Press, 1989.

Stearns, Peter N., and Carol Z. Stearns. "Emotionology: Clarifying the History of Emotions and Emotional Standards." *AHR* 90, no. 4 (Oct. 1985): 813–36.

Steedman, Carolyn. *Dust: The Archive and Cultural History.* New Brunswick, N.J.: Rutgers University Press, 2002.

Stein, Sarah Abrevaya. *Extraterritorial Dreams: European Citizenship, Sephardi Jews, and the Ottoman Twentieth Century.* Chicago: University of Chicago Press, 2016.

Stellar, Jennifer E., Vida M. Manzo, Michael W. Kraus, and Dacher Keltner. "Class and Compassion: Socioeconomic Factors Predict Responses to Suffering." *Emotion* 12, no. 3 (2012): 449–59.

Stelmach, Anita. " 'We Can't Have Reds in Portugal': The Portuguese Response to the Spanish Civil War." *Flinders Journal of History and Politics* 30 (2014): 111–42. flinders.edu.au/sabs/sis-files/history/FJHP/Volume%2030/Anita%20Stelmach%20%20Vol%2030%202014.pdf.

Stern, Fritz R. *Five Germanys I Have Known.* New York: Farrar, Straus and Giroux, 2006.

Stone, Glyn. *The Oldest Ally: Britain and the Portuguese Connection, 1936–1941*. London: Royal Historical Society, 1994.

Stourton, Edward. *Cruel Crossing: Escaping Hitler over the Pyrenees*. London: Doubleday, 2013.

Strauss, Herbert. "Jewish Emigration from Germany: Nazi Policies and Jewish Responses, Part I." *LBIYB* 25 (1980): 313–61.

———. "Jewish Emigration from Germany: Nazi Policies and Jewish Responses, Part II." *LBIYB* 26 (1981): 343–409.

Stuczynski, Claude B. "Digging Portugal's Jewish Past: Samuel Schwarz (1880–1953)." Des Gens Intéressants, desgensinteressants.org/samuel-schwarz–4/claude_stuczynski_sur_samue.pdf.

Subak, Susan Elisabeth. *Rescue and Flight: American Relief Workers Who Defied the Nazis*. Lincoln: University of Nebraska Press, 2010.

Sutters, Jack, ed. *Archives of the Holocaust: An International Collection of Selected Documents*. Vol. 2. New York: Garland, 1990.

Tanzer, Frances. "Performing the Austrian-Jewish (Negative) Symbiosis: Stella Kadmon's Viennese Stage from Red Vienna to the Second Republic." *LBIYB* 63 (2018).

Tarso, Paulo de. *Crimes da Franco-maçonaria Judáica*. Guarda, Portugal: Empresa Veritas, 1924.

Taussig, Michael. "An Excerpt from *Walter Benjamin's Grave*." Chicago: University of Chicago Press, 2006. press.uchicago.edu/Misc/Chicago/790045.html.

Tec, Nechama. *Resilience and Courage: Women, Men, and the Holocaust*. New Haven: Yale University Press, 2003.

Teixeira, Christina Heine. " 'Warten auf das rettende Schiff'—Hannah Arendts Flucht über Lissabon." *Neuer Nachrichtenbrief der Gesellschaft für Exilforschung* 19 (June 2002): 15–16.

Thies, Jochen. *Hitler's Plans for World Domination: Nazi Architecture and Ultimate War Aims*. New York: Berghahn, 2012.

Thon, Jakob. *Die jüdischen Gemeinden und Vereine in Deutschland*. Berlin: Verlag des Bureaus für Statistik der Juden, 1906.

Torberg, Friedrich. *Eine tolle, tolle Zeit: Briefe und Dokumente aus den Jahren der Flucht, 1938–1941*. Vol. 18 of *Gesammelte Werke in Einzelausgaben*. Munich: Langen Müller, 1989.

Torga, Miguel. *La Création du monde*. Paris: Aubier, 1985.

Torpey, John. "The Great War and the Birth of the Modern Passport System." In Caplan and Torpey, *Documenting Individual Identity*, 256–70.

Traska, Georg, and Christoph Lind. *Hermann Leopoldi: The Life of a Viennese Piano Humorist*. Translated by Dennis McCort. Riverside, Calif.: Ariadne, 2013.

Treanor, Tom. "Lisbon Fiddles . . ." *Vogue*, Oct. 1, 1940.

Tuan, Yi-fu. *Space and Place: The Perspective of Experience*. Minneapolis: University of Minnesota Press, 1977.

Ury, Scott. *Barricades and Banners: The Revolution of 1905 and the Transformation of Warsaw Jewry*. Stanford: Stanford University Press, 2012.

Vaizey, Hester. "Husbands and Wives: Evaluation of the Emotional Impact of World War Two in Germany." *European History Quarterly* 40, no. 3 (2010): 389–411.

Vansant, Jacqueline. *Reclaiming Heimat: Trauma and Mourning in Memoirs by Jewish Austrian Reémigrés*. Detroit: Wayne State University Press, 2001.

Vigée, Claude. *Wintermond: Bericht, Journal, Essay*. Künzelsau, Germany: Swiridoff, 2003.

Voigt, Kai-Ingo. *Der Schriftsteller Heinrich Mann: Ein deutsches Leben*. Münster, Germany: Lit, 1998.

Wachstein, Sonia. *Too Deep Were Our Roots: A Viennese Jewish Memoir of the Years Between the Two World Wars*. New York: Harbor Electronic, 2001.

Wagenbach, Klaus. *Kafka's Prague: A Travel Reader*. Woodstock, N.Y.: Overlook, 1996.

Walker, David. "All Refugees in Portugal Are to Get Full Legal Status." *Christian Science Monitor*, Dec. 30, 1942.

Wallen, Jeffrey, and Aubrey Pomerance. "Circuitous Journeys: The Migration of Objects and the Trusteeship of Memory." In Auslander and Zahra, *Objects of War*, 251–69.

Wasserstein, Bernard. *The Ambiguity of Virtue: Gertrude van Tijn and the Fate of the Dutch Jews*. Cambridge: Harvard University Press, 2014.

Waxman, Zoë Vania. *Writing the Holocaust: Identity, Testimony, Representation*. Oxford: Oxford University Press, 2006.

Weber, Ronald. *The Lisbon Route: Entry and Escape in Nazi Europe*. Lanham, Md.: Ivan R. Dee, 2011.

Weil, Simone. *The Need for Roots: Prelude to a Declaration of Duties Towards Mankind*. Tranlsated by Arthur Wills. London: Routledge, 2003. Originally published as L'Enracinement: Prélude à une declaration des devoirs envers l'être humain, 1949.

Weiss, Hans, and Ronald Leopoldi, eds. *Hermann Leopoldi und Helly Möslein— "In einem kleinen Café in Hernals . . .": Eine Bildbiographie*. Vienna: Orac, 1992.

Welch, Susan. "American Opinion Toward Jews During the Nazi Era: Results from Quota Sample Polling During the 1930s and 1940s." *Social Science Quarterly* 95, no. 3 (2014): 615–35. https://www.researchgate.net/publication/260604054_American_Opinion_Toward_Jews_During_the_Nazi_Era_Results_from_Quota_Sample_Polling_During_the_1930s_and_1940s.

Wheeler, Douglas. "In the Service of Order: The Portuguese Political Police and the British, German and Spanish Intelligence, 1932–1945." *Journal of Contemporary History* 18, no. 1 (Jan. 1983): 1–25.

———. "The Price of Neutrality: Portugal and the Wolfram Question and World War II." *Luso-Brazilian Review* 23, no. 1 (Summer 1986): 107–27.

Widdowfield, Rebekah. "The Place of Emotions in Academic Research." *Area* 32, no. 2 (2000): 199–208.

Wilder-Okladek, F. *The Return Movement of Jews to Austria After the Second World War: With Special Consideration of the Return from Israel.* The Hague: Martinus Nijhoff, 1969.

Wildt, Michael. *Hitler's Volksgemeinschaft and the Dynamics of Racial Exclusion: Violence Against Jews in Provincial Germany, 1919–1939.* Translated by Bernard Heise. New York: Berghahn, 2012.

Wilhelmer, Lars. *Transit-Orte in der Literatur: Eisenbahn–Hotel–Hafen–Flughafen.* Bielefeld, Germany: Transcript, 2015.

Williams, Raymond. *The Country and the City.* London: Oxford University Press, 1973.

Wimmer, Adi, ed. *Strangers at Home and Abroad: Recollections of Austrian Jews who Escaped Hitler.* Jefferson, N.C.: McFarland, 2000.

Winkle, Ralph. *Der Dank des Vaterlandes: Eine Symbolgeschichte des Eisernen Kreuzes 1914 bis 1936.* Essen, Germany: Klartext, 2007.

Wischnitzer, Mark. *Visas to Freedom: The History of HIAS.* Cleveland: World, 1956.

Wise, J. Macgregor. "Home: Territory and Identity." *Cultural Studies* 14, no. 2 (2000): 295–310.

Wobick-Segev, Sarah. "Buying, Selling, Being, Drinking: Jewish Coffeehouse Consumption in the Long Nineteenth Century." In *The Economy in Jewish History: New Perspectives on the Interrelationship Between Ethnicity and Economic Life,* edited by Gideon Reuveni and Sarah Wobick-Segev, 115–34. New York: Berghahn, 2011.

———. "German-Jewish Spatial Cultures: Consuming and Refashioning Jewish Belonging in Berlin, 1890–1910." In *Longing, Belonging and the*

Making of Jewish Consumer Culture, edited by Gideon Reuveni and Nils H. Roemer, 39–60. Leiden: Brill, 2010.

———. *Homes away from Home: Jewish Belonging in Twentieth-Century Paris, Berlin, and St. Petersburg.* Stanford: Stanford University Press, 2018.

Wriggins, W. Howard. *Picking Up the Pieces from Portugal to Palestine: Quaker Refugee Relief in World War II: A Memoir.* Lanham, Md.: University Press of America, 2004.

Wylie, Neville, ed. *European Neutrals and Non-Belligerents During the Second World War.* Cambridge: Cambridge University Press, 2002.

Wyman, David S. *The Abandonment of the Jews: America and the Holocaust, 1941–1945.* New York: New Press, 1998.

———. *Paper Walls: America and the Refugee Crisis, 1938–1941.* Amherst: University of Massachusetts Press, 1968.

Zadoff, Mirjam. *Next Year in Marienbad: The Lost Worlds of Jewish Spa Culture.* Philadelphia: University of Pennsylvania Press, 2012.

Zahra, Tara. *The Lost Children: Reconstructing Europe's Families After World War II.* Cambridge, Mass.: Harvard University Press, 2011.

Zajonc, R. B., and Daniel McIntosh. "Emotions Research: Some Promising Questions and Some Questionable Promises." *Psychological Science* 3, no. 1 (Jan. 1992): 70–74.

Zalc, Claire, and Tal Bruttmann. "Introduction: Towards a Microhistory of the Holocaust." In Zalc and Bruttmann, *Microhistories,* 1–16.

———, eds. *Microhistories of the Holocaust.* New York: Berghahn, 2017.

Zim, Rivkah. *The Consolations of Writing: Literary Strategies of Resistance from Boethius to Primo Levi.* Princeton: Princeton University Press, 2014.

Zucker, Bat-Ami. *In Search of Refuge: Jews and U.S. Consuls in Nazi Germany, 1933–1941.* London: Vallentine Mitchell, 2001.

zur Mühlen, Patrik von. *Fluchtweg Spanien-Portugal: Die deutsche Emigration und der Exodus aus Europa 1933–1945.* Bonn: Dietz, 1992.

Zweig, Stefan. *Tagebücher.* Frankfurt am Main: Fischer, 1984.

———. *The World of Yesterday: An Autobiography.* Translated by Eden and Cedar Paul. New York: Viking, 1943.

Zweig, Stefan, and Paul Zech. *Briefe, 1910–1942.* Edited by Donald Daviau. Rudolstadt, Germany: Greifenverl, 1984.

Zwicker, Lisa Fetheringill, "Performing Masculinity: Jewish Students and the Honor Code at German Universities." In *Jewish Masculinities: German Jews, Gender, and History,* edited by Benjamin Maria Baader, Sharon Gillerman, and Paul Lerner, 114–37. Bloomington: Indiana University Press, 2012.

Filmography

Blaufuks, Daniel, dir. *Under Strange Skies*. Lisbon: LX Filmes, 2002. DVD.

CriticalPast. "Portuguese Refugees Embark the Transport Ship *Serpa Pinto* at Port of Lisbon, Portugal." criticalpast.com/video/65675029920_Portuguese-refugees_Port-of-Lisbon_Transport-ship-Serpa-Pinto_American-Export-Line-ship.

Curtiz, Michael, dir. *Casablanca*. 1942. Burbank, Calif.: Warner Home Video, 1999. DVD.

"Hannah Arendt im Gespräch mit Günter Gaus." Oct. 28, 1964. Posted to YouTube by ArendtKanal, July 24, 2013. https://www.youtube.com/watch?v=J9SyTEUi6Kw.

Kaplan, Richard, dir. *Varian and Putzi: A 20th Century Tale*. Lanham, Md.: National Film Network, 2004. DVD.

Mauas, David, dir. *Who Killed Walter Benjamin / Quién matóa Walter Benjamin*. Barcelona: Milagros Producciones, 2005. DVD.

Nir, Yonatan, dir. *The Essential Link: The Story of Wilfrid Israel*. Bnei Brak, Israel: Highlight Films, 2016.

Schnabel, Pavel, dir. *Lisbon: Harbour of Hope / Lissabon: Hafen der Hoffnung*. 1994. Lanham, Md.: National Film Network, 2010. DVD.

Sousa Mendes Foundation. "Lolita Goldstein Interview." Oct. 12, 2014. https://vimeo.com/155765492.

Interviews

Greenberg, Gabrielle (née Losser), New York City, Dec. 11, 2012

Hellman, Ruth, New York City, Mar. 24, 2014

Meissner, Margit, Washington, D.C., Nov. 19, 2014

Shomberg, Irene (née Westheimer), New York City, Dec. 6, 2013

Walker, Anita (née Wakman), Brooklyn, New York, Dec. 26, 2016

Index

Himmler, Heinrich, 75
Hirsch, Elisabeth, 61
Hirsch, Ella and Elizabeth, 212
Hirsch, Rudolf, 27
Hitler Youth, 116
Hobsbawm, Eric, 129
Holocaust, knowledge of, 86–88, 196–97, 211,
　223–26, 309n.38
Holocaust studies, of refugees, 4–5, 231
Home/homeland, loss of, 21, 127–34, 153,
　229
Housewives, in Portugal, 171–72; loss of
　occupation, 142
Housing: aid to refugees, 106; in fixed resi-
　dences, 21, 108, 170–71; Lisbon rentals, 69,
　155; pensions, 90, 92, 137, 155–56, 289n.5
Howard, Leslie, 114–15
How to Raise a State (Salazar), 71

Iberian Pact, 73
Immigration restriction policies, 10, 14–15, 45,
　77–78; Portuguese, 29, 67
Inquisition, Portuguese, 25, 27, 80
Intergovernmental Committee on Refugees, 15
International Socialist Combat League (ISK),
　47
Internment, in fixed residences, 21, 72, 108,
　124, 153, 155, 168–74, 177–80, 185, 216, 233,
　234
Internment camps: in France, 34–35; in U.S., 79
Israel, Kurt, xviii, 117, 163–68, 183
Israel, Wilfred, 114, 115
Italy, ports of departure, 14, 37

Jacob, Berthold, 122
Japanese Americans, internment of, 79
Jayne, Edith, 150
JDC (American Jewish Joint Distribution
　Committee), 3, 68, 114; cooperation with
　Quakers, 113–14; fear of German invasion,
　118; financial aid to refugees, 38, 106, 110;
　food parcels to Nazi-occupied Europe,
　200–201; knowledge of Holocaust, 225–26;
　letters sent care of, ix; Lisbon office of, 88,
　108, 160, 217, 225; rescue efforts of, 43, 48,
　53, 54, 55, 61, 110–11, 113; and ship trans-
　port to U.S., 213–14, 220, 222
Jewish Agency for Palestine, 110, 225

Jewish Children's Home, Newark, New
　Jersey, 191
Jewish community. *See* COMASSIS;
　Portugal, Jewish community
Jewish Joint Distribution Committee, Amer-
　ican. *See* JDC
Jewish Labor Committee, 48
Jewish refugees: countries of immigration,
　14–16; diplomatic assistance to, 79–82;
　flight from France, 31–39; immigration
　restriction policies and, 15; loss of social
　status, 13–14; mass emigration from
　Germany, 10–12; statelessness of, 12–13;
　unaccompanied children, 56–58. *See also*
　Border crossings; Children and teenagers;
　Portugal, refugees in
Joy, Charles, 77, 103

Kaffeeklatsch, 202
Kafka, Franz, 132, 163
Kalischer, Ben-Zwi. *See* Wisla, Heinz
Kantorowicz, Alfred, 35
Kaplan, Chaim, 154
Karp, George, 49
Karp, Giselle, 49
Katzenstein, Eduard, 115
Katzki, Herbert, 110, 225–26
Keepsake loss, 134
Kennan, George, 74
Kindertransport, 19, 59, 114, 151
Klemperer, Victor, 223
Kluger, Ruth, 59
Knitting circles, 172
Koestler, Arthur, 31, 67, 69, 143, 160, 202
Kolmar, Gertrud, 17
Kosher food, 156–57, 185; breaking Kosher
　laws, 157; matzot, 111, 157, 191, 209,
　277n.29
Kracauer, Siegfried, 137, 214–15, 229
Krüger, Chaim, Rabbi, 80

Ladino language, 25
Lambert, Raymond-Raul, 130
Language: English, 191; German, 133, 189,
　191; multilingual locations, 205; Portu-
　guese, 100, 166, 173, 217; "wrong one," 15
Lanzmann, Claude, 187
Law, rule of, 128–29

Trapunski, Betty, 223
Troper, Morris C., 60, 106, 141, 211
Tuan, Yi-Fu, 128
Turkey: Armenian genocide, 10; neutrality, 234; repatriation ultimatum, 87

Under Strange Skies (Losa), 139
Unitarian Service Committee (USC), 3, 35–36, 77, 103, 108–9, 113, 118, 144, 200
United States: aid to refugee children in, 109; antisemitism in, 77, 79; café culture recreated in, 132, 203; children's transports to, 59–61, 151–53, 184–85, 190; close family rule, 78, 213; entry visa, 52; expiration of visas, 212, 214, 218, 221; immigration restriction in, 10, 14–15, 45, 77–78; internment of Japanese Americans, 79; knowledge of Holocaust in, 225; Pearl Harbor attack on, 78–79, 114, 118, 180, 212, 214, 219, 223; and refugee crisis today, xi, 238; visa application process, 39, 78, 165–68, 179. *See also* Ship transport to U.S.
United States Committee for the Care of European Children (USCOM), 59–61
United States Legation, Lisbon, 159–60, 161
Uruguayan Embassy (Holland/Lisbon), Jewish refugees in, 163–64

Vasconcelos, Amadeu de, 82
Vichy France, 33–34, 41, 109
Vigée, Claude, 47–48
Villa de Madrid (ship), 221
Visas: application process, 159–68, 178; café rumors about, 203–4; for emigration, 39; exit, 33, 35, 41, 46, 50, 63; expiration (U.S.), 212, 214, 218, 221; forged, 45, 58; issued by Portuguese consuls, 79–80, 81; restrictive policies on, 14, 75; transit, 2, 41, 52, 62, 63, 67–68, 81, 121, 122, 129; waiting on lines, 21, 32, 35–36, 154–55, 159, 179
Visas for America (Dembitzer), 145
Vishniac, Mara, 229
A Voz (newspaper), 82, 83, 87

Waiting on lines, 21, 32, 35–36, 62, 154–55, 159–63, 179

Wakman, Anita, 229
Wakman, Glikla, 27
Wakman, Yitzchak, 204
Wannsee Conference, 119
War Refugee Board, 45, 108, 113
Warren, George, 213
Warsaw Ghetto, 194, 198–99, 206, 226
Weil, Simone, 129, 181
Weissmann, Isaac, 61, 85, 92, 113, 170
Weizmann, Chaim, 233
Werfel, Franz, 33, 35, 47, 51, 67, 138, 228
Westheimer, Friedrich, 26–27, 197, 299n.44
Westheimer, Irene, 148
Westheimer sisters, 100
Wieser, Stephanie, 137, 149
Windsor, Duke and Duchess of, 31
Winter, Kurt, 124
Wise, Stephen, 224
Wisla, Heinz (Ben-Zwi Kalischer), 95–96, 99, 123, 224, 249n.8
Wolfsohn, Heinz, 124
Women, Portuguese: gender restrictions on, 94–95; gender roles of, 93–96
Women, refugees: border guards' treatment of, 51; and café culture, 202; dress habits of, 96–97; emotional reactions of, 9, 18–20, 149–50; fear of sexual demands, 51; gender roles, 19, 171–72, 235; in prison, 124; and status loss, 141–42
Work of Mothers for National Education, 94
World Council of Churches, 108
World Jewish Congress, 43, 61, 88, 110, 170, 200, 225
World War I veterans, 130, 141
World Zionist Organization, 233
Wriggins, Howard, 122, 144, 153, 162, 207, 225, 226
Wyman, David, 216

Yankee Clipper, 213
Yollick, Liny, 149
Youth Aliyah, 54, 114

Zandmer, Pola, 135, 136
Zweig, Arnold, 143
Zweig, Stefan, 40, 132, 203